AI-READY DATA

ANDREW MADSON

WILEY

Published by John Wiley & Sons, Inc., Hoboken, New Jersey.

Library of Congress Cataloging-in-Publication Data has been applied for:

Paperback ISBN: 9781394371051
ePDF ISBN: 9781394371075
ePub ISBN: 9781394371068
Obook ISBN: 9781394421756

Cover Design: Wiley
Cover Image: Login/stock.adobe.com

Printed and bound by CPI Group (UK) Ltd, Croydon, CR0 4YY
C9781394371051_030926

AI-READY DATA

To Kaitlin, Luke, Finn, Nell, and Beau.

Contents

Author Bio

Andrew Madson is a member of the technical staff and head of developer relations and experience at Perplexity AI. His work sits at the intersection of data engineering, developer education, and AI adoption, with a practical emphasis on helping organizations turn existing data assets into systems that models, copilots, and agents can use safely.

He writes and speaks about data infrastructure, data quality, analytics engineering, and the shift from model-centered AI strategy to data-centered execution. In *AI-Ready Data*, he argues that the durable advantage in enterprise AI will come from data discipline: making information complete, retrievable, accurate, fresh, and traceable across the full pipeline from raw data to action.

Acknowledgments

This book reflects years of conversations with data engineers, analysts, architects, product builders, AI practitioners, and executives who were honest about what worked and what broke. Their practical experience shaped the central argument: AI value depends less on chasing the next model and more on making data complete, retrievable, accurate, fresh, and traceable.

I am grateful to the teams and communities that helped sharpen these ideas through review, debate, and implementation. I also want to thank the Wiley team for helping turn a working manuscript into a book that can reach the people responsible for building AI-ready data inside real organizations.

Most of all, thank you to the practitioners doing the hard operational work behind every credible AI system. The work is not always visible, but it is the difference between an impressive demo and a system people can trust.

Introduction

Every organization wants AI that works. They want copilots that answer accurately, agents that take action safely, analytics assistants that understand the business, and automation that compounds instead of creating new risk. Yet most AI programs stall in the same place. The model can produce language. The demo looks convincing. The pilot gives people a reason to be optimistic. Then the system meets enterprise data and starts to break.

The break is not random. It happens because the data was built for people, not for machines. A person can read around missing context, ask a coworker what a field means, recognize an outdated policy, or remember which dashboard definition the business uses this quarter. AI systems do not have that background unless the data layer gives it to them. They consume what is present, retrieve what is findable, act on what is specified, and guess when the system leaves gaps.

That gap is the subject of this book. AI-ready data is not a slogan. It is an operating requirement. Data must be complete enough to support the task, retrievable enough for the system to find, accurate enough to trust, fresh enough to reflect current reality, and traceable enough to audit. Those five dimensions make up the CRAFT standard. They provide a practical way to assess whether data is ready for AI use rather than merely available somewhere in the organization.

This book also argues that model selection is no longer the center of durable AI advantage. Models still matter. You need capable models, careful evaluation, and responsible deployment. But model capability is becoming broadly accessible. The organizations that win will be the ones that build the data systems, governance habits, semantic layers, context stores, action specifications, and feedback loops that make any competent model useful in their environment.

The chapters are organized around that shift. Early chapters explain why models are commoditizing and why the data-AI gap appears when human-optimized data meets machine consumption. The middle chapters define the four data levels that AI systems depend on: raw data, structured data, context data, and action data. Later chapters show how to evaluate, govern, improve, and scale those layers using CRAFT as the throughline.

The goal is practical. This is not a book about building foundation models. It is a book about making the data layer ready for the AI systems that most organizations are actually trying to deploy. That means the work is operational. It includes entity integrity, semantic clarity, source provenance, retrieval design, freshness monitoring, tool specifications, ownership, incentives, and the discipline to measure quality before systems fail in production.

The payoff is compounding. Better data does not serve one model once. It improves every AI use case that depends on that data. It reduces rework when models change. It makes governance easier because lineage and accountability are built into the system. It helps teams move faster because they stop rediscovering the same data problems in every pilot. Most important, it changes the question from *which model should we buy?* to *is our data ready for the work we expect AI to do?*

If you are a data leader, AI leader, architect, engineer, product owner, or executive trying to move AI from demos to dependable systems, this book is for you. The work is not glamorous. It is more durable than glamour. AI that works starts with data that is ready.

Chapter 1
Model Access Is Becoming a Commodity, and Data Is a Durable Advantage

Model releases attract intense attention. Buyers compare benchmarks, vendors emphasize new capabilities, and teams revisit architecture choices. That attention can create an incomplete assumption: that selecting the best model is the primary determinant of enterprise AI value.

For many organizations, that assumption is incomplete.

Models are necessary, but enterprise outcomes depend on more than the model. Data, evaluation, application design, workflow integration, governance, human oversight, security, and operations also shape results. When teams treat model choice as the entire strategy, they can underinvest in the rest of the system.

Access to capable AI models is becoming cheaper and more interchangeable for many enterprise use cases. Performance gaps have narrowed on some benchmarks, but meaningful differences remain across tasks and deployment contexts. OpenAI listed the March 2023 GPT-4 API at $30 per million prompt tokens and $60 per million completion tokens. In August 2024, it listed gpt-4o-2024-08-06 at $2.50 per million input tokens and $10 per million output tokens. Across those named endpoints, the listed input price fell 91.7% and the listed output price fell 83.3% (OpenAI, 2023; Pokrass, 2024). The comparison covers one provider and two model generations; it is not an industry price index. Model choice still matters,

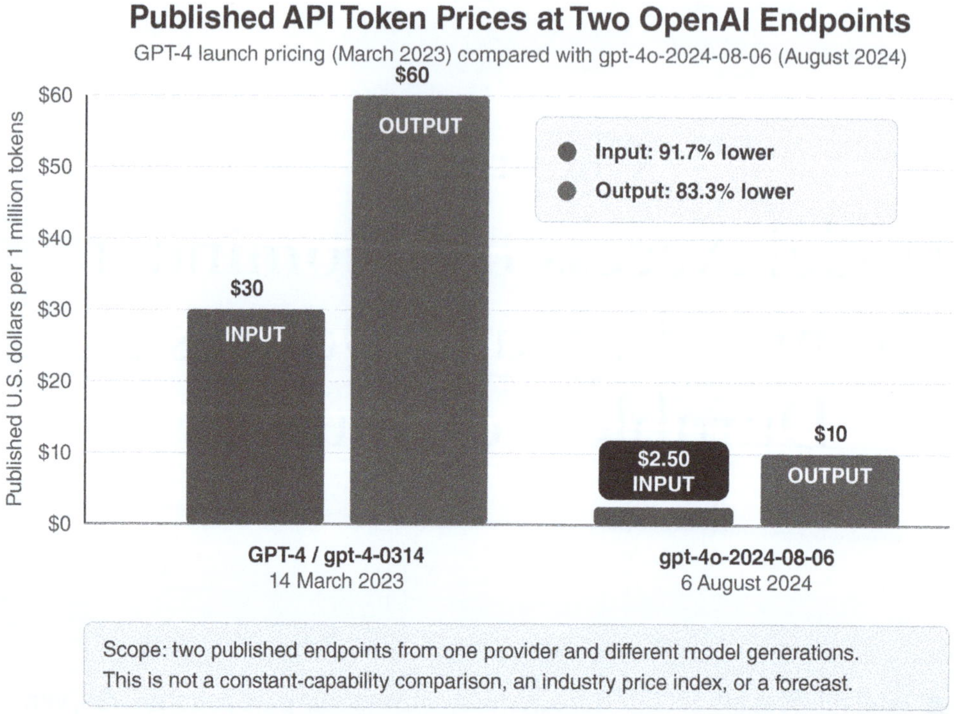

Figure 1.1 Two OpenAI API price endpoints.
SOURCE: OpenAI (2023) for GPT-4 launch pricing and Pokrass (2024) for gpt-4o-2024-08-06 pricing.

while proprietary data, domain knowledge, evaluation, integration, governance, and operating discipline can be harder for competitors to reproduce. See Figure 1.1.

The strategic question is not whether models or data matter more in every case. It is whether the organization can combine a suitable model with trusted data, rigorous evaluation, and a workflow people can operate.

The Great Convergence

Model vendors emphasize differentiation, while widely watched benchmarks also show closer competition on some measures. Those measures are useful signals, but they do not establish that models are equivalent across tasks.

The Stanford 2025 AI Index reported that the relative Chatbot Arena score gap between the first- and tenth-ranked models narrowed from 11.9% in the prior report to 5.4% by early 2025. It also reported that the gap between the leading closed-weight and open-weight models narrowed from 8.04% in January 2024 to 1.70% by February 2025 (Stanford HAI, 2025). These snapshots show a more competitive frontier, not universal interchangeability. Model suitability still depends on the task, reliability, latency, safety controls, deployment constraints, and cost.

By 2024, several leading models could support many of the same enterprise tasks. Their differences still mattered, but teams also had to weigh reliability, latency, safety controls, deployment options, and cost.

When many organizations can access capable models through low-cost APIs, the decision shifts from access alone to fit. Teams still have to compare task performance, reliability, latency, safety controls, deployment options, and cost.

For many enterprise use cases, model access became more interchangeable. The model remained important, but it was no longer the whole strategy.

An open data infrastructure can reduce switching costs by using portable formats, documented interfaces, and modular components. It cannot guarantee future compatibility, and a model change may still require new evaluation, prompting, retrieval, security, and application work.

The Inflection Point: From Model-centric to Data-centric

For decades, the AI research community operated under a simple assumption: if you want better AI, build better models. That made sense when models were the limiting factor. AlexNet crushed traditional computer vision. ResNets proved extremely deep networks could train effectively. Transformers revolutionized NLP. Each innovation opened new possibilities. Model improvements drove real, measurable progress.

The incentive structures reinforced this focus. Academic conferences rewarded novel architectures. Research labs competed on benchmark leaderboards. The path to recognition ran through model innovation, and the improvements were genuinely delivering breakthroughs.

A capable model may be sufficient for a bounded task, but suitability depends on the task, risk level, data, evaluation results, and operating constraints.

GPT-3 showed that scaling a transformer with more data and compute could improve few-shot performance across the tasks evaluated in the paper (Brown et al., 2020). The result was not a model-versus-data verdict; architecture, data, compute, training, and evaluation worked together.

By 2023, transformer architectures and training techniques were widely documented, and several organizations had built capable foundation models. The remaining differences were not reducible to one secret. Model design, compute, training data, curation, evaluation, and product execution all mattered.

Training-data details for frontier models are often only partially disclosed. Proprietary datasets, filtering rules, and mixing choices can create know-how that competitors cannot copy directly, but public evidence does not support attributing competitive performance to data alone.

The shift was not from algorithms to data. It was from a model-only view to a system view in which data discipline became a first-class engineering capability.

The Meaning of Data-centric AI

Data-centric AI changes the iteration loop. Teams treat data as an engineered component that can be measured and improved, while continuing to evaluate the model, application, workflow, and operating environment.

Models still matter. Once a model clears a task's capability threshold, data improvement can be the highest-payoff next step when evaluation points to coverage, labeling, retrieval, or freshness failures.

Capable pretrained models lower the starting cost for many applications. The ceiling still depends on model architecture, data, evaluation, and system design.

In data-centric work, domain experts and engineers can improve performance by finding errors, gaps, and inconsistent definitions. The work can start with a bounded dataset, but maintaining quality at scale still demands tooling, governance, and specialized skill. Table 1.1 compares the two improvement lenses.

Andrew Ng, the Stanford adjunct professor who co-founded Google Brain, has been a prominent advocate for data-centric AI. He described the potential shift this way: "In the last decade, the biggest shift in AI was a shift to deep learning. I think it's quite possible that in this decade the biggest shift will be to data-centric AI" (Strickland, 2022).

Ng organized the Data-Centric AI Competition in 2021 specifically to test whether this approach worked in practice. The rules were deliberately constraining. Participants got a fixed model (ResNet-50, a standard convolutional neural network) and could only modify the dataset. No architecture changes. No hyperparameter tuning. Just data work.

In the competition's reported Roman-numeral recognition results, the baseline model achieved 64.4% accuracy and the winning submission achieved 85.8% after participants changed the data while the model remained fixed (Data-Centric AI Competition, 2021). In a separate talk, Ng reported an industrial example in

Table 1.1 Complementary Model-Centric and Data-Centric Improvement Lenses

Model-Centric Improvement Lens	Data-Centric Improvement Lens
Improve performance by changing model architecture or configuration	Improve performance by changing data coverage or quality
Focus on models, training, prompting, and inference	Focus on collection, labeling, retrieval, freshness, and lineage
Evaluate model and system behavior	Evaluate data fitness and system behavior
Potential advantage from model capability or intellectual property	Potential advantage from proprietary data or domain context
Iterate on hyperparameters and training techniques	Iterate on data collection, cleaning, and curation
Treat data as an input to the model workflow	Treat data as a continuously managed product
Vendor-specific stack optimized around a chosen model	Portable data layer built on open formats and documented interfaces

which accuracy improved from 76% to more than 90% after the team held the model fixed and improved the data (Ng, 2021). These are bounded examples of data work improving a fixed-model result; they do not show that data is always the limiting factor.

The Cultural Reality

For enterprises, a model-centric mindset can lead to heavy spending on model evaluation, licensing, fine-tuning, and prompt optimization while data work is treated as a preliminary task. A balanced portfolio tests whether that allocation matches the use case's actual constraints.

In some organizations, data teams receive less visibility than model or application teams, and data engineering is treated as support work. Academic and industry incentives can reinforce that imbalance by rewarding visible model innovation more readily than ongoing data maintenance. The result can be underinvestment in the work that makes AI systems reliable.

A data-centric mindset rebalances these priorities. Leaders fund data infrastructure, quality processes, governance, and data engineering alongside model evaluation and application development. They select models that meet defined requirements, then direct effort to whichever part of the system evaluation shows is limiting performance. Data work becomes a first-class part of AI delivery, not a preliminary chore.

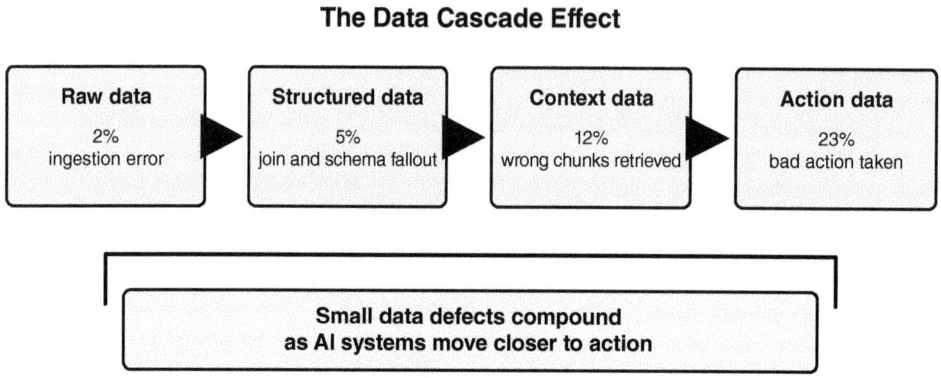

Figure 1.2 The data cascade effect.

A qualitative study of 53 AI practitioners working in high-stakes domains found that 92% reported experiencing at least one data cascade (Sambasivan et al., 2021). The authors described data work as frequently undervalued and conducted under deadline and resource pressure. Data cascades begin with upstream data problems and create compounding downstream effects; in the study, some remained latent for two to three years. Figure 1.2 uses an illustrative example to show how small errors can compound through a pipeline. Its 2%, 5%, 12%, and 23% values are examples, not empirical measurements.

Proprietary data can be a durable source of advantage when it reflects unique operations, domain knowledge, feedback, and history. It is not the only one. Evaluation methods, integration, governance, workflow design, and operating discipline can also be difficult to reproduce.

Falling model-access costs can increase the relative importance of data, integration, evaluation, and workflow execution. Organizations still pay for capability, reliability, latency, security, and support.

The Golden Goals of Dataset Engineering

When evaluation identifies data as a limiting factor, what does fit-for-purpose data look like? Balance three interconnected goals:

- Quantity
- Quality
- Diversity

Quantity: The Limits of Scale

Large training corpora can matter, but volume is not an independent performance lever. Scaling studies show that dataset size, model size, and compute interact, so adding data alone is not a guarantee of improvement (Kaplan et al., 2020; Hoffmann et al., 2022).

But the relationship between data quantity and model performance follows a pattern that should concern anyone planning to compete purely on volume. Kaplan et al. mapped power-law relationships among model performance, model size, dataset size, and compute (Kaplan et al., 2020). Hoffmann et al. then showed that model size and training tokens should scale together for compute-optimal training (Hoffmann et al., 2022). These power laws aren't straight lines. Each further increase in data produces progressively smaller gains when the other factors remain constrained.

For most enterprises, matching frontier-lab pretraining scale is neither feasible nor necessary. Enterprise teams usually adapt existing models to bounded domains and tasks. In those settings, additional volume helps only when it improves coverage or reduces a measured error; low-quality additions can add cost without improving the use case.

Quality: Where the Returns Compound

Well-governed data can retain value and improve through reuse, correction, and feedback. Its value can also decay when definitions, populations, processes, or conditions change.

Quality has several dimensions. For labels and annotations, definitions and application should be accurate and consistent. Across 10 widely used benchmark test sets, Northcutt et al. estimated an average label-error rate of at least 3.3%, with dataset estimates ranging from well under 1% to roughly 10%, including about 6% for ImageNet's validation set (Northcutt et al., 2021). Enterprise data often receives less public scrutiny. Comparable or higher error rates are plausible, but that is an inference rather than a finding from the study. Label errors can distort training and evaluation.

Consistency matters. Training data should follow documented conventions. Mixed representations for missing values or unevenly applied annotation rules can introduce noise and contradictory signals. The effect depends on the model, task, frequency, and evaluation design.

Relevance to the target task also matters. Data that does not represent production conditions creates distribution mismatch. A customer-service assistant trained only on another industry or an outdated operating model may perform poorly on current queries. Teams should measure coverage against the intended production population and conditions.

Formatting cleanliness is another control. Residual HTML, encoding errors, inconsistent delimiters, and invisible control characters can introduce spurious patterns or break downstream processing. Their impact should be tested rather than assumed.

Models can learn from limited examples when the task, model capacity, and data quality line up. They can also fail when the data is too narrow or the model lacks the required capability. A 2022 MIT Sloan article noted that in domains such as manufacturing and healthcare, large datasets are not always available and smaller amounts of high-quality data may be sufficient (Brown, 2022).

Diversity: The Generalization Factor

The third pillar is diversity. Models learn to generalize by encountering varied examples. A language model that only saw formal business writing would struggle with casual conversation. A vision model trained only on professional photography would fail on smartphone snapshots.

Diversity operates across multiple dimensions: domain diversity (different subject areas and contexts), task diversity (different types of problems and output structures), and demographic/perspective diversity (different voices and viewpoints). But diversity has practical limits. Once you've covered the core concepts and major edge cases relevant to your use case, adding unrelated or random content doesn't necessarily help. It may actually distract the model.

The aim is intentional coverage: include the domains, tasks, populations, conditions, and edge cases the use case must handle, while preserving accuracy and relevance.

When Data Quality Is the Limiting Factor: The Evidence

Quality can deliver higher returns than adding volume when errors, duplication, weak coverage, or inconsistent labels are the limiting problem. What do the studies show?

The studies below show that results vary in specific settings. They do not establish a universal rule that smaller datasets are better.

The LIMA Experiment

The 2023 LIMA study fine-tuned a 65-billion-parameter LLaMA model on 1,000 curated prompts and responses, without reinforcement learning or human-preference modeling in that fine-tuning stage (Zhou et al., 2023). The experiment tested alignment of an already capable base model; it was not pretraining and does not establish that 1,000 examples are enough for every task.

In the authors' controlled comparison, evaluators rated LIMA's response equivalent to or better than GPT-4's in 43% of cases. GPT-4 was preferred in the remaining comparisons (Zhou et al., 2023). The result shows that careful curation can be effective for a bounded alignment task when the base model already contains substantial capability.

One thousand examples is small enough to inspect deliberately, but producing and reviewing high-quality examples still takes domain expertise and time.

The LIMA authors called their explanation the "superficial alignment hypothesis": much of a model's knowledge and capability is learned during pretraining, while supervised alignment teaches preferred response formats and styles. Under that hypothesis, a strong base model may need a relatively small, carefully designed alignment set. The paper presents this as a hypothesis supported by its experiments, not a rule for every model or task.

Massive datasets are not automatically better. The right quantity depends on task complexity, coverage, error rate, model capacity, evaluation design, and the cost of collecting and reviewing examples.

The Phi Trajectory: Quality-focused Training at Scale

Microsoft's Phi series provides another case study in quality-focused training. Phi-1 targeted code generation and used a filtered code corpus plus synthetic "textbook-quality" material generated with GPT-3.5. The reported pretraining corpus contained just under 7 billion tokens (Gunasekar et al., 2023). This is a task-specific publisher-reported result, not evidence that one recipe generalizes to every domain.

The Phi-1 paper reported a 50.6% pass@1 result on HumanEval and stronger HumanEval and MBPP results than almost all of the named open-source comparators in that evaluation, with GPT-4 and WizardCoder identified as HumanEval exceptions (Gunasekar et al., 2023). The comparison is specific to the reported code-generation benchmarks.

Phi-2 and Phi-3 extended the series with small language models trained using curated and synthetic data, together with model, training, and post-training choices (Javaheripi and Bubeck, 2023; Abdin et al., 2024a). Microsoft reported that the 2.7-billion-parameter Phi-2 matched or outperformed larger named models across several benchmark groups, while also cautioning that public benchmarks may be contaminated and that use-case testing remains necessary (Javaheripi and Bubeck, 2023).

Microsoft reported that Phi-4, a 14-billion-parameter model, surpassed its GPT-4 teacher on the report's STEM-focused question-answering evaluations. The authors attributed the result to improved data, training curriculum, and post-training methods, not to data quality alone (Abdin et al., 2024b).

Why Did It Work?

The Phi-1 study argued that broad code corpora contain material that is not equally useful for teaching clear reasoning and coding practices. Its filtering and synthetic data strategy sought to increase the share of task-relevant examples. The reported result reflects the complete experimental recipe and does not isolate data as the sole cause (Gunasekar et al., 2023).

The practical target is not minimum or maximum volume. It is enough representative, accurate, current, and well-governed data to meet the use case's evaluation threshold.

For many organizations, improving existing data is more realistic than matching a frontier lab's scale. That does not make it the only viable strategy.

Research on Deduplication and Annotation Quality

Sometimes improving data quality means removing data instead of adding it. Research on training-data deduplication has shown that removing duplicate or near-duplicate examples can improve model performance. One study found that deduplication reduced memorized output and required fewer training steps to achieve the same or better accuracy (Lee et al., 2021). The model learned more effectively from a smaller set of unique examples than from a larger set contaminated with repetition.

The mechanism makes intuitive sense. When training data contains duplicates, the model sees those examples multiple times. It effectively over-weights them relative to unique examples. This can encourage memorization of duplicated patterns while rarer but important variations receive less weight. In one controlled study, repeating 0.1% of the data 100 times degraded an 800-million-parameter model to the performance level of a 400-million-parameter model (Hernandez et al., 2022).

Annotation quality provides another lens on the quantity-quality trade-off. Training labels should follow a clear definition and be applied consistently. Contradictory labels weaken the training signal and make evaluation harder to interpret.

In practice, teams should treat annotation consistency as a design requirement. Clear guidelines, trained annotators, and measured inter-annotator agreement can make a smaller dataset more useful than a larger dataset whose labels contradict one another.

The Northcutt analysis also tested how mislabeled examples can affect benchmark ordering. In its controlled ImageNet sensitivity analysis, increasing the prevalence of originally mislabeled test examples by about six percentage points caused ResNet-18 to rank above ResNet-50 (Northcutt et al., 2021). This conditional result shows ranking sensitivity; it does not establish that benchmark rankings are universally wrong.

That doesn't prove enterprise data is worse. It does show how much error can survive even in benchmark datasets under intense scrutiny, which is reason enough to audit enterprise labels rather than assume they're correct.

The Strategic Implication: Data-driven ROI

The evidence supports a conditional conclusion: when data defects or coverage gaps are the limiting factor, targeted quality work can outperform undirected data accumulation.

Hyperscalers can draw on data and compute at a scale most enterprises will not reproduce. Enterprises can still compete in bounded domains by using proprietary context, rigorous evaluation, and focused workflows.

Research does not establish one universal data quantity. The required scale depends on the task, model, risk, coverage, and evaluation threshold.

A bounded, carefully curated dataset can be the right starting point for some organizations and tasks. It is not a universal prescription.

Make the scale explicit and illustrative: a team might curate hundreds of representative support logs, map its highest-impact business rules, and build a dedicated edge-case set. The numbers should come from the use case, not a generic prescription.

Investment should follow the use case and evaluation evidence. Teams may need model access, compute, application engineering, subject matter expertise, curated datasets, human review, lineage, and quality monitoring. The mix depends on which constraint is limiting the system.

A data lake and a curated evaluation dataset solve different problems. The lake preserves broad, reusable source data. The curated set makes a bounded AI behavior testable. Many programs benefit from both: a governed foundation and smaller, purpose-built data products.

The goal is to connect a governed data foundation to curated, use-case-specific data products.

Building a Durable AI Data Capability

AI investment has often emphasized visible model advances. Enterprise value, however, depends on a complete system: model capability, data, evaluation, application design, workflow integration, governance, human oversight, security, and operations.

Model access may be table stakes in some markets, but model capability, data, evaluation, workflow fit, governance, and execution can all affect the outcome.

Open formats, documented interfaces, and modular components can reduce switching risk. They do not guarantee that any model can use the data without adaptation.

Changing models can still require new evaluation, prompting, retrieval, security, and application work, even when the data layer is portable.

Do not debate models in the abstract. Define the task, evidence, risk, and operating constraints, then evaluate the complete system.

This book introduces the CRAFT assessment framework for evaluating whether required data is complete, retrievable, accurate, fresh enough, and traceable for a defined use case (see Figure 1.3). CRAFT assesses the data layer. It does not replace model evaluation, security, privacy, fairness testing, human oversight, application design, or legal review (NIST, 2023).

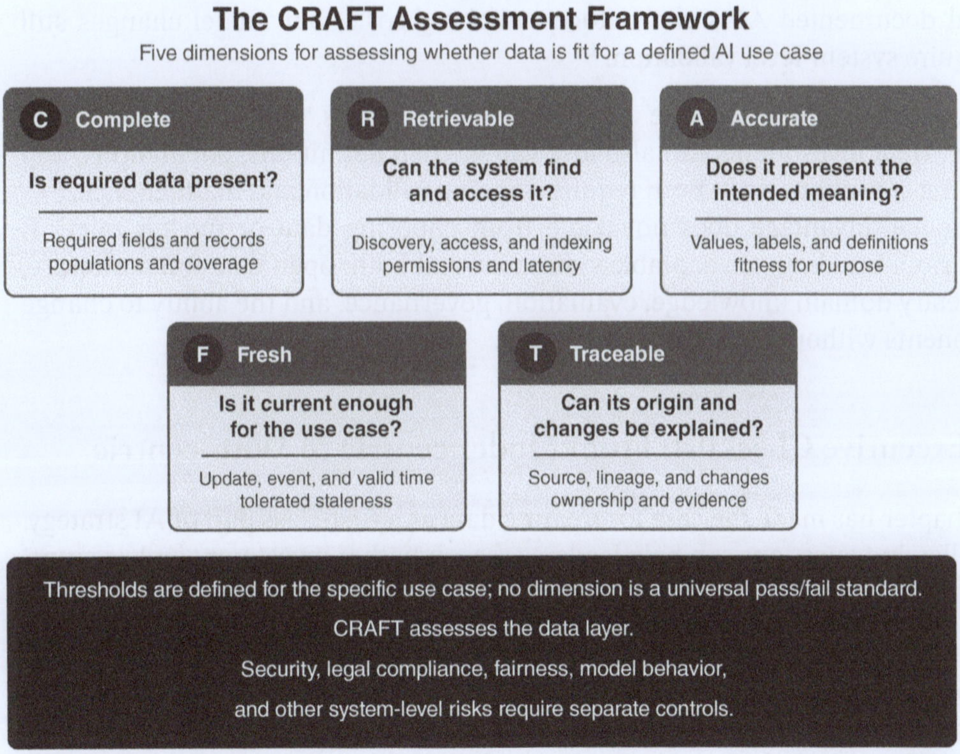

Figure 1.3 The CRAFT assessment framework.

The leadership question is how to balance model, data, application, governance, and operating capabilities for each use case.

Investing in Reusable Data Capabilities

These ideas affect capital allocation. Consider two complementary investment categories:

- **Model and application investment:** You spend on model access, evaluation, fine-tuning, application engineering, and compute. These investments can be necessary for a defined use case, and they must be reevaluated as capabilities, vendors, requirements, and risks change.
- **Data-layer investment:** You spend on data engineering, semantic layers, retrieval, governance, and curation. These investments can support multiple use cases when definitions, interfaces, and controls are reusable. Open formats

and documented APIs can reduce switching costs, but model changes still require system-level validation.

Model investments can lose value when requirements, vendors, or capabilities change. Data investments can also lose value when definitions, populations, and operating conditions drift. Both require ongoing validation and maintenance.

Durable advantage does not come from choosing data or models once. It comes from building an adaptable system around both: open data infrastructure, proprietary domain knowledge, evaluation, governance, and the ability to change components without rebuilding everything.

Executive Checklist: From Model-centric to Data-centric

This chapter has made the case for treating data as a first-class part of AI strategy. The following questions can help leaders assess whether investment and accountability are balanced across the system:

- ☐ **Audit your AI investment allocation**
  How is the budget allocated across model access, data engineering, evaluation, application development, security, governance, and operations? Does that allocation match the use case's measured constraints and risks?
- ☐ **Identify your highest-value use case**
  Where does evaluation show that better data would have the most impact? Which failures involve coverage, quality, retrieval, freshness, or traceability? Start with a bounded use case and a measurable gap.
- ☐ **Assess your current data quality baseline**
  What would prevent the complete system from performing reliably? Assess the relevant CRAFT dimensions, then test model behavior, security, privacy, fairness, application logic, workflow fit, human oversight, and operational controls.
- ☐ **Understand your competitive context**
  Which competitors have distinctive data, model, workflow, distribution, or operating advantages? Which capabilities should you build, buy, partner for, or differentiate from?
- ☐ **Build internal data curation capacity**
  You can hire outside specialists, but you cannot outsource accountability for domain data, definitions, quality, access, and use.

- ☐ **Start with fit for purpose**
  When you build training or fine-tuning datasets, start with a representative set that can test the required behavior and edge cases. Expand it deliberately when evaluation shows a coverage or reliability gap.
- ☐ **Plan for continuous data improvement**
  Model selection and data quality both require ongoing review as tasks, risks, sources, and capabilities change.
- ☐ **Measure AI value through system evidence**
  When an AI project fails, diagnose the observed failure across data, model, application, workflow, and operational layers. Keep a record of root causes so investment follows evidence rather than assumption.

Looking Ahead

Chapter 4 introduces the CRAFT assessment framework. Chapters 7 through 14 apply it to the data AI systems consume. Chapters 15 through 19 turn that assessment into an operating plan for teams, governance, economics, and a 90-day execution path. Models and data will change; a disciplined, adaptable foundation helps the organization respond.

References

Abdin, Marah, et al. "Phi-3 Technical Report: A Highly Capable Language Model Locally on Your Phone." arXiv, 2024a, https://arxiv.org/abs/2404.14219.

Abdin, Marah, et al. "Phi-4 Technical Report." Microsoft Research Technical Report MSR-TR-2024-57, Dec. 2024, https://www.microsoft.com/en-us/research/publication/phi-4-technical-report/.

Brown, Sara. "Why It's Time for 'Data-Centric Artificial Intelligence.'" MIT Sloan, 7 June 2022, https://mitsloan.mit.edu/ideas-made-to-matter/why-its-time-data-centric-artificial-intelligence.

Brown, Tom, et al. "Language Models Are Few-Shot Learners." Advances in Neural Information Processing Systems, vol. 33, 2020, pp. 1877–1901, https://arxiv.org/abs/2005.14165.

Data-Centric AI Competition. "Data-Centric AI Competition 2021." DeepLearning.AI and Landing AI, 2021, https://https-deeplearning-ai.github.io/data-centric-comp/.

Gunasekar, Suriya, et al. "Textbooks Are All You Need." arXiv, 2023, https://arxiv.org/abs/2306.11644.

Hernandez, Danny, et al. "Scaling Laws and Interpretability of Learning from Repeated Data." arXiv, 2022, https://arxiv.org/abs/2205.10487.

Hoffmann, Jordan, et al. "Training Compute-Optimal Large Language Models." arXiv, 2022, https://arxiv.org/abs/2203.15556.

Javaheripi, Mojan, and Sébastien Bubeck. "Phi-2: The Surprising Power of Small Language Models." Microsoft Research Blog, 12 Dec. 2023, https://www.microsoft.com/en-us/research/blog/phi-2-the-surprising-power-of-small-language-models/.

Kaplan, Jared, et al. "Scaling Laws for Neural Language Models." arXiv, 2020, https://arxiv.org/abs/2001.08361.

Lee, Katherine, et al. "Deduplicating Training Data Makes Language Models Better." arXiv, 2021, https://arxiv.org/abs/2107.06499.

National Institute of Standards and Technology. Artificial Intelligence Risk Management Framework (AI RMF 1.0). NIST AI 100-1, 26 Jan. 2023, https://doi.org/10.6028/NIST.AI.100-1.

Ng, Andrew. "The Data-Centric AI Approach With Andrew Ng." Scale TransformX, 6 Oct. 2021, https://learn.scale.com/public/videos/the-data-centric-ai-approach-with-andrew-ng. Accessed 23 July 2026.

Northcutt, Curtis G., et al. "Pervasive Label Errors in Test Sets Destabilize Machine Learning Benchmarks." arXiv, 2021, https://arxiv.org/abs/2103.14749.

OpenAI. "GPT-4." OpenAI, 14 Mar. 2023, https://openai.com/index/gpt-4-research/.

Pokrass, Michelle. "Introducing Structured Outputs in the API." OpenAI, 6 Aug. 2024, https://openai.com/index/introducing-structured-outputs-in-the-api/.

Sambasivan, Nithya, et al. "'Everyone Wants to Do the Model Work, Not the Data Work': Data Cascades in High-Stakes AI." CHI 2021, https://doi.org/10.1145/3411764.3445518.

Stanford HAI. "Technical Performance." AI Index Report 2025, Stanford Institute for Human-Centered Artificial Intelligence, 2025, https://hai.stanford.edu/ai-index/2025-ai-index-report/technical-performance. Chapter 2 of the 2025 edition. Accessed 27 July 2026.

Strickland, Eliza. "Andrew Ng: Unbiggen AI." IEEE Spectrum, 9 Feb. 2022, https://spectrum.ieee.org/andrew-ng-data-centric-ai.

Zhou, Chunting, et al. "LIMA: Less Is More for Alignment." Advances in Neural Information Processing Systems, 2023, https://proceedings.neurips.cc/paper_files/paper/2023/file/ac662d74829e4407ce1d126477f4a03a-Paper-Conference.pdf.

Chapter 2
The Data-AI Gap

AI teams can fail even when they choose a capable model. A common barrier is organizational data designed for human workflows rather than reliable machine use. This mismatch is the data-AI gap: the distance between having data and making it usable, understandable, governable, and auditable for AI systems.

"AI-ready data" means data can reliably be discovered, understood, acted upon by AI systems, and audited. Chapter 4 defines the specific criteria through the CRAFT framework.

Why AI Projects Fail: The Evidence

RAND Corporation's 2024 exploratory report cites estimates that more than 80% of AI projects fail, about twice the failure rate of non-AI corporate IT projects (Ryseff et al., 2024). In 50 industry interviews drawn from a larger 65-interview study, leadership misunderstanding or miscommunication was the most common reported root cause, followed by limitations in the quality and utility of training data (Ryseff et al., 2024).

Data Built for Humans, Not for Machines

For decades, enterprise data systems were designed around one primary user: a person. Data warehouses organized information for analyst queries. Dashboards visualized metrics for executive review. Reports formatted information for human reading. Quality programs measured what mattered for human interpretation.

Table 2.1 Why Data Built for Humans Fails for AI

Human Data Consumption	AI Data Consumption
Interprets visual presentation	Processes literal text and numbers
Brings background knowledge	Draws on supplied context, learned patterns, and available tools
Asks clarifying questions	Asks follow-up questions only when the workflow supports it
Tolerates ambiguity	May propagate unresolved ambiguity unless the system detects or surfaces it
Aggregates mentally	Depends on retrieval, interfaces, permissions, and appropriate granularity

That stack did its job. It helped humans make decisions with data.

AI systems consume data through APIs, retrieval pipelines, context windows, and tool calls. Data designed mainly for human interpretation can fail in those interfaces when key meaning is visual, implicit, or undocumented. The risk is not simply model capability. It is whether the system receives data in a form it can use reliably.

People often fill gaps by drawing on context and institutional knowledge. They may infer which revenue definition a dashboard uses and notice duplicated records or missing fields. A model may also infer, but that inference can be wrong when definitions and data-quality issues are implicit. Table 2.1 compares common human and AI data-consumption patterns.

This difference in how data is consumed explains why so many AI initiatives feel like they "almost work." The model demo looks great because it uses test data. The proof of concept answers a few questions correctly. Everyone gets excited. Then you plug it into real enterprise data and hit one of these failures: generic answers because retrieval fails, confident answers that are subtly wrong because context is missing, plausible answers with no source grounding, or the inability to take action even when the action is easy for a human.

The Perception Gap

AvePoint's 2024 report drew on a survey of 762 managers and executives with responsibility for AI implementation across 16 countries, fielded in November and December 2023. It found that 80% believed their data was ready for AI, while 52% reported internal data-quality and categorization challenges during implementation (AvePoint, 2024). In the same vendor-produced survey, 95% reported at least one data challenge during AI implementation. Figure 2.1 places those self-reported findings beside two other readiness signals.

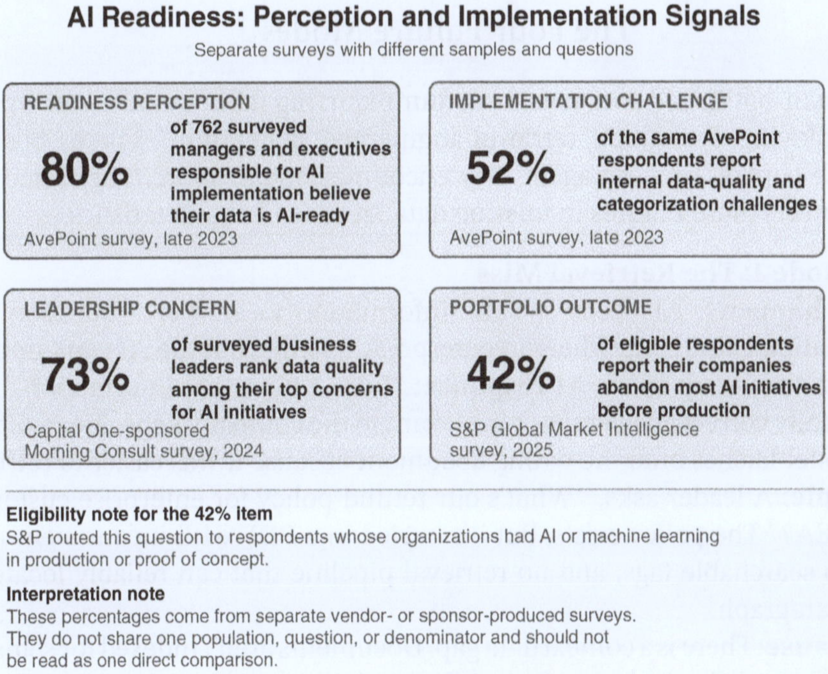

Figure 2.1 AI readiness: perception and implementation signals.

SOURCE: AvePoint (2024) for the 80% and 52% figures; Capital One (2024) for 73%; S&P Global Market Intelligence (2025) for 42%. The S&P item was limited to respondents whose organizations had AI or machine learning in production or proof of concept.

This overconfidence stems from different standards. Data that passes traditional quality checks for reporting can still be unusable for AI. The criteria are simply different.

In a qualitative CHI 2021 study of 53 practitioners working on high-stakes AI, 92% of participants recruited through purposive and snowball sampling reported at least one data cascade (Sambasivan et al., 2021). The authors define these cascades as compounding downstream effects from data problems. They found that cascades could remain opaque until deployment; the most severe cases sometimes took two to three years to appear. These findings describe the study sample, not a population estimate for all AI practitioners.

The interviews also exposed a cultural bias. Practitioners described data work as time-consuming and hard to make visible, often performed under pressure from deadlines and margins. Model work carried more prestige. The authors linked that imbalance to poor data practices and the cascades they observed (Sambasivan et al., 2021).

The Four Failure Modes

When human-optimized data meets AI, four recurring failure modes can emerge. Teams deploying a chatbot, retrieval-augmented generation system, business intelligence copilot, or early agent may encounter one or more. The framework below connects those failures to missing data layers and characteristics.

Failure Mode 1: The Retrieval Miss

What happens: AI needs specific information to answer a question. The information exists somewhere in enterprise systems, but the AI can't find it.

How it shows up in an AI response: "I don't have that information." Or a technically correct answer that's irrelevant to the company's specific reality. Or the model latches onto the wrong document because it was easier to retrieve.

Example: A leader asks, "What's our refund policy for enterprise customers in EMEA?" The policy exists, but it's buried in a PDF with inconsistent naming, no searchable tags, and no retrieval pipeline that can reliably locate the right paragraph.

Root cause: There is a context data gap. Documents aren't indexed for semantic search, knowledge isn't chunked well, or metadata is missing or inconsistent.

What teams often do instead: Blame the model, do more prompt engineering, or add more documents without improving retrieval quality.

What actually fixes it: Build a real context data layer that makes content retrievable by meaning. Treat retrieval quality as a product requirement rather than an engineering detail.

Failure Mode 2: The Context Void

What happens: AI retrieves data, but it lacks the context to interpret it correctly. The model sees a field or a value, but it doesn't know what it means, what rules apply, or how the business uses it.

How it shows up in an AI response: There is a wrong interpretation of a metric, incorrect business logic is applied to status fields, confusion occurs between similar entities, or answers are provided that are internally consistent but semantically wrong.

Example: A model retrieves a row with `status_code = 3` and says the order is "shipped" because that's a common mapping in other systems. In your system, `3` means "held for compliance review." The model inferred a familiar mapping without enough system-specific context. You gave it a code without meaning.

Root cause: There is a structured data gap. Your tables and schemas may be clean for analytics, but they rely on tribal knowledge: undocumented business rules, abbreviations only insiders understand, hidden joins needed to interpret a record, and inconsistent definitions across domains.

What teams often do instead: Add longer prompts with ad hoc explanations, hardcode mappings in application logic, or rely on a few subject matter experts to "teach the model" informally.

What actually fixes it: Treat semantic clarity as part of the data product. Make definitions explicit and machine-usable. Document business rules where the AI pipeline can access them.

Failure Mode 3: The Grounding Failure

What happens: AI generates answers that sound plausible but aren't grounded in verified enterprise facts. Sometimes the answer is flat wrong. Sometimes it's almost right, which is worse because it's harder to detect.

How it shows up: There are confident answers with no source references, contradictions across repeated questions, citations that don't actually support the claim, or "policy style" responses that feel generic, like the model is making it up.

Example: A user asks, "What are the top three drivers of churn for mid-market customers this quarter?" The AI produces a well-written answer that reads like a management consultant wrote it. But it isn't tied to any actual churn analysis, data pull, or documented finding.

Root cause: There are context and structured data gaps. Context data may not be grounded to authoritative sources with clear provenance. Structured data may not be accessible in a way that supports factual verification and consistent definitions.

What teams often do instead: Tighten the prompt with "don't hallucinate" instructions, add more guardrails at the UI layer, or accept "good enough" because the answer sounds reasonable.

What actually fixes it: Design for grounding as a core requirement. Require citations to authoritative sources where possible. Connect answers to specific structured facts, not unsupported inference. Log and audit model outputs so you can learn where grounding breaks.

Failure Mode 4: The Action Gap

What happens: AI is asked to take action but doesn't know what actions are possible or how to execute them safely.

How it shows up in an AI response: "I can't do that." The assistant suggests steps but won't actually do them. The agent calls the wrong tool or formats the parameters incorrectly. The system refuses action because safety constraints are undefined.

Example: A user says, "Reset this customer's MFA and open a ticket with the security team." The organization can do this in minutes through existing systems. But the AI can't because it doesn't know which tools exist, doesn't know how to call them, doesn't know what constraints apply, and doesn't know what success looks like.

Root cause: There are action data gaps. Enterprises have plenty of process documentation, runbooks, and API docs. But they're rarely packaged as executable specifications that an agent can reliably use.

What teams often do instead: Build brittle, one-off integrations, hardcode tool instructions in prompts, or avoid agentic use cases entirely because they feel risky.

What actually fixes it: Define the action data as a first-class layer. Create tool specifications, constraints, and workflows in machine-usable forms. Make actions discoverable by intent. Instrument actions so the system can be audited and monitored.

The Pattern: Failure Modes and Data Gaps

Table 2.2 previews the four failure modes against the CRAFT dimensions and data layers that the rest of the book defines in detail. CRAFT is introduced fully in Chapter 4, and the data layers become the operating model for the chapters that follow. This mapping matters because it stops the usual blame game. If you treat these as model problems alone, you can spend time switching models and revising prompts without fixing the underlying data path. If you treat them as data layer problems, you can fix them systematically.

Table 2.2 The Pattern: Failure Modes and Data Gaps

Failure Mode	Primary CRAFT Dimension to Assess	Missing Data Layer
Retrieval miss	Retrievable	Context data
Context void	Accurate	Structured data
Grounding failure	Traceable	Context + structured data
Action gap	Complete	Action data

These failure modes also stack. A retrieval miss often turns into a grounding failure because the model fills the gap with generated content. A context void can become a grounding failure because the model invents meaning when definitions are ambiguous. An action gap can create safety failures if the agent tries to act without complete constraints.

Once you see the pattern, you start diagnosing faster.

The Financial Impact

A 2024 Morning Consult survey conducted for Capital One included nearly 4,000 business leaders and technical practitioners at organizations with more than 500 employees. Among business leaders, 73% ranked data quality as a top concern for AI initiatives, second to data security at 76% (Capital One, 2024). Those are operational risks that model selection alone doesn't address.

Among respondents whose organizations had AI or machine learning in production or proof of concept, 42% reported that their organizations abandoned most AI initiatives before production, compared with 17% in the prior-year survey. The 2025 online survey included 1,006 midlevel and senior IT and line-of-business professionals in North America and Europe overall, but S&P does not disclose the routed sample size for this item. Eligible respondents also reported that their organizations scrapped an average of 46% of proof-of-concept projects before production (Johnston, 2025).

The Deloitte AI Institute's third-quarter 2024 survey of 2,770 AI-experienced leaders across 14 countries found that 55% of organizations avoided certain generative AI use cases because of data-related issues (Deloitte AI Institute, 2024). The finding shows that data constraints narrowed which use cases organizations pursued; it doesn't establish how much value the deferred use cases would have produced.

The Opportunity: Competitive Advantage Through Data Readiness

The data-AI gap is the conversion opportunity. It's the work of turning existing assets into something AI can reliably use.

Most organizations are sitting on valuable data and valuable processes. The problem is that those assets are locked in forms designed for humans.

The opportunity is to close the gap systematically, not by replacing everything you've built, but by adding the layers that make existing assets AI-ready.

The data-AI gap isn't just a quality problem, though. It's also an infrastructure problem. Proprietary formats and vendor-specific interfaces can make access, portability, and integration harder even when the underlying data is well curated. Closing the gap requires both quality criteria, which the CRAFT framework (Figure 2.2) provides, and the Open Data Infrastructure (ODI) principle introduced in Chapter 1: building your data layer on open standards so it supports data ownership, interoperability with other tools, flexibility to evolve, and freedom from vendor lock-in. This isn't about avoiding commercial software. Tools that move data through open, nonproprietary formats and avoid locking it inside one vendor's storage layer fit this principle well. That includes ingestion tools that write to open table formats such as Iceberg or Delta Lake, and transformation tools whose logic runs as portable, version-controlled code instead of proprietary black-box pipelines. The principle is about making sure your data investment compounds rather than depreciates as your AI needs change.

Do it well and you get compounding advantage: better AI experiences with the same models your competitors use, faster deployment because your data foundation

CRAFT Framework Grid: five dimensions across four data levels

	Raw	Structured	Context	Action
Complete	●	●	●	●
Retrievable	●	●	●	●
Accurate	●	●	●	●
Fresh	●	●	●	●
Traceable	●	●	●	●

Figure 2.2 CRAFT Framework Grid: five dimensions across four data levels.

SOURCE: Author's analysis — Figure 2.2 is the authors' own preview of the CRAFT framework introduced fully in Chapter 4; no external source line is needed.

is reusable across use cases, lower risk because you can trace and govern what AI is doing, and less rework because improvements persist across model upgrades.

BCG's 2025 global study of 1,250 CxOs and senior executives who were AI decision-makers classified 5% of companies as "future-built." Those respondents expected twice the revenue increase and 1.4 times the cost reductions by 2028 compared with laggards in areas where they applied AI (Apotheker et al., 2025). Separate Capital IQ data showed that future-built companies had 3.6 times the three-year total shareholder return of the combined stagnating and emerging groups. BCG cautions that company performance has multiple drivers beyond AI, so these comparisons don't show that AI maturity caused the financial results.

A reusable data foundation can make later projects easier, although each use case still needs its own data, controls, evaluation, and adoption work. Reuse creates value when teams maintain shared components and measure whether they improve delivery.

Competitors may be able to license many of the same foundation models. They cannot quickly replicate context-specific institutional knowledge that has been curated into a reliable knowledge base, semantic layer, and set of tool specifications. Those assets take time to build and maintain, which can create a durable lead.

Existing Assets Awaiting Transformation

Many enterprises already have valuable starting assets. The remaining gap is often their form, accessibility, semantics, governance, or control.

Documents containing institutional knowledge need *retrievability*. The policies, procedures, technical manuals, and domain expertise exist. They're sitting in SharePoint folders, Confluence wikis, and shared drives. The content is valuable. It just isn't indexed, chunked, and embedded in ways that AI can search semantically.

Databases with business facts need *accuracy* through semantic clarity. The numbers are there. The transactions are recorded. What's missing is the explicit documentation of what fields mean, how metrics are calculated, and what business rules apply. That semantic layer makes the difference between AI that misinterprets your data and AI that understands it.

Processes that could be automated need *completeness* in specifications. The workflows exist. The tools exist. The APIs exist. What's missing is the machine-readable specification that tells AI what actions are available, what parameters they require, what constraints apply, and what success looks like.

Many organizations face both model and packaging problems. Even a capable model can underperform when knowledge, facts, and tools are not prepared in forms the system can use reliably. Those assets can also be difficult to repackage when they are trapped in formats and systems designed for a previous generation of tools, locked inside infrastructure that wasn't built to evolve.

A Learnable Discipline

Closing the gap isn't luck and it isn't heroics. It's a capability you build.

Chapter 4 contains the book's canonical CRAFT-by-data-form matrix and explains how the five CRAFT dimensions apply across raw, structured, context, and action data.

This is good news. If AI data readiness were a matter of genius or special circumstances, most organizations would be locked out. Instead, it's a matter of systematic investment in defined capabilities. Organizations can build this capability through systematic investment, although priorities, resources, and constraints will differ.

Organizations that recognize this early can build reusable advantages. While competitors debate model choice alone, they invest in data infrastructure that can improve compatible systems across use cases. Those capabilities create value when teams maintain them, reuse them, and measure the result.

Build the Data Foundation First

The remainder of this book provides the framework and practical guidance to close the data-AI gap. The next chapters map four AI capability types, perception, analytical, generative, and agentic, to the four data levels they require: raw, structured, context, and action.

The CRAFT framework gives you the quality criteria. You'll know exactly what makes data complete, retrievable, accurate, fresh, and traceable at each level.

The remaining chapters cover the systems, the organizational design, the governance, and the financial case for making the investment.

The bottom line is this: AI that works starts with data that's ready.

Practical Starting Points

Here is how to get started closing the data-AI gap. Begin with one high-value use case where failure is obvious and measurable. Support tickets, policy Q&A, internal engineering knowledge, or sales enablement are common candidates. Don't try to boil the ocean.

Build the minimum context data layer that can answer those questions with citations. If you can't ground answers, don't scale. Grounding failures destroy trust. Trust is hard to rebuild.

Don't pretend that your structured data is "already fine." If your definitions are inconsistent, you'll just automate inconsistency faster. The semantic layer investment pays dividends across every AI use case that touches your structured data.

Treat the action data like a product. Tool specs, constraints, and workflow definitions need versioning, testing, and ownership. They're not documentation that sits in a wiki. They're executable artifacts that AI depends on.

Measure outcomes users care about: answer usefulness, citation correctness, action success rate, and time saved. These metrics tell you whether you're actually closing the gap or just moving boxes around.

The Gap as Opportunity

The data-AI gap exists because enterprise data was built for a different consumer. Data infrastructure built over decades for human analysts doesn't automatically transfer to AI systems. The formats are wrong, the semantics are implicit, the retrieval mechanisms don't match, and the action specifications don't exist.

This isn't a criticism of the traditional data infrastructure. It did what it was designed to do. The gap exists because AI is a new kind of consumer with different requirements.

The opportunity is to close that gap systematically. Add layers that make existing assets AI-ready. Context data that makes knowledge retrievable. Semantic layers that make structured data accurate. Action data that makes automation possible.

Organizations that build these capabilities remove major barriers to production AI. They still need a sound use case, a capable model, secure integration, evaluation, governance, and adoption. Teams that skip the data foundation will keep rediscovering the same failures in their pilots.

Looking Ahead

Closing the data-AI gap starts with matching the system you want to build to the data it actually needs. Chapter 3 maps four AI capabilities to four data levels so you can invest in the right foundation before you build.

References

Apotheker, Jessica, et al. "The Widening AI Value Gap: Build for the Future 2025." Boston Consulting Group, Sept. 2025, https://media-publications.bcg.com/The-Widening-AI-Value-Gap-October-2025.pdf.

AvePoint. "AI & Information Management Report: The Data Problem That's Stalling AI Success." AvePoint, 2024, https://cdn.avepoint.com/pdfs/en/shifthappens/AI-IM-Whitepaper-v4.pdf.

Capital One. "AI Readiness Survey: Are Companies Ready for AI Adoption?" Capital One Tech, 21 Nov. 2024, https://www.capitalone.com/tech/ai/ai-readiness-survey/.

Deloitte AI Institute. "Despite Increased Investment and Early Enthusiasm, Data and Risk Remain Key Challenges to Scaling Generative AI, Reveals New Deloitte Survey." Deloitte, 20 Aug. 2024, https://www.deloitte.com/us/en/about/press-room/state-of-generative-ai-Q3.html.

Johnston, Alex. "Generative AI Shows Rapid Growth but Yields Mixed Results." S&P Global Market Intelligence, 27 Oct. 2025, https://www.spglobal.com/market-intelligence/en/news-insights/research/2025/10/generative-ai-shows-rapid-growth-but-yields-mixed-results. The figures cited in the text are from this 2025 edition; its body text requires S&P Global Market Intelligence registration. Accessed 27 July 2026.

Ryseff, James, Brandon De Bruhl, and Sydne J. Newberry. "The Root Causes of Failure for Artificial Intelligence Projects and How They Can Succeed: Avoiding the Anti-Patterns of AI." RAND Corporation, 2024, https://www.rand.org/content/dam/rand/pubs/research_reports/RRA2600/RRA2680-1/RAND_RRA2680-1.pdf.

Sambasivan, Nithya, et al. "'Everyone Wants to Do the Model Work, Not the Data Work': Data Cascades in High-Stakes AI." CHI Conference on Human Factors in Computing Systems, 2021, https://doi.org/10.1145/3411764.3445518.

Chapter 3
Mapping Your Data for AI

A manufacturing company pours resources into cleaning their enterprise resource planning (ERP) databases. They create pristine tables of inventory levels and supplier information. Great work for analytical forecasting. But their actual project is a computer vision system for detecting defects on the assembly line. That system needs high-resolution images of products under various lighting conditions. Not cleaner spreadsheets. The structured data investment doesn't address what they're actually building.

The reverse happens just as often. A financial services firm collects millions of documents, scans contracts, and builds elaborate document processing pipelines. This is solid preparation for document understanding. But their immediate need is a fraud detection model that runs on structured transaction records. The document infrastructure sits unused while data scientists struggle with transaction data that nobody prioritized.

These aren't hypothetical. They're the lived reality of enterprise AI programs that treat "data for AI" as one undifferentiated bucket.

In a Cloudera-sponsored *Harvard Business Review* Analytic Services survey of 231 *Harvard Business Review* audience members involved in organizational data decisions, 7% said their organization's data was completely ready for AI adoption, while 73% said processing and preparing data for AI was challenging (Harvard Business Review Analytic Services, 2026). The survey documents a perceived readiness and preparation gap. It does not identify a single cause or constitute an objective audit of enterprise data.

Understanding AI capabilities comes before understanding AI data requirements. If you know what kind of AI you're building, you can map it to the right data level and apply the right quality standard.

Why Capability Matters for Data

When an organization says "we need more data for AI" without being specific about which AI, the result is predictable waste. Perception AI extracts structure from raw signals. Analytical AI finds patterns in organized facts. Generative AI synthesizes content from learned knowledge and supplied context. Agentic AI executes actions through tools and workflows. Each use case has a primary data dependency and may also need supporting forms based on its architecture, evidence, risk, governance, and control needs. This chapter defines four complementary data forms, then maps them to common starting points for each capability.

Get the mapping wrong and you waste resources on infrastructure that doesn't serve your goals. Executives approve budgets for "AI data infrastructure" without specifying which AI capabilities they're targeting. Teams clean databases obsessively when their actual use case needs embedded documents. Others collect millions of images when what they really need is structured transaction records. The mismatch between data investment and AI capability is one of the most expensive mistakes in enterprise technology right now.

The Four Data Levels

Data for AI appears in four complementary forms, each serving a different purpose. The book calls them levels as a taxonomy, not as a universal maturity ranking or mandatory sequence. Table 3.1 introduces the four forms and their typical primary consumers.

The four forms can build on one another, but they aren't a mandatory conversion pipeline. Raw signals can become structured facts. Structured facts can be enriched with context. Context and system specifications can support action. Each step adds meaning or control when that transformation serves the use case.

Dependency fit matters because each required form must meet the quality criteria for the selected system and workflow. Chapter 4 introduces CRAFT, a five-dimension assessment framework for those requirements. The primary form has to match the task, and any supporting dependencies have to match the use case.

Table 3.1 The Four Data Levels for AI

Level	What It Is	Common Forms	Primary Consumer
Raw	Unprocessed signals from reality	Images, audio, sensor data, documents	Perception AI
Structured	Organized facts with explicit schemas	Databases, warehouses, APIs	Analytical AI
Context	Meaning-enriched knowledge for reasoning	Vector embeddings, knowledge graphs, semantic layers	Generative AI
Action	Executable specifications for action	Tool schemas, workflow specs, constraints	Agentic AI

The problem isn't that organizations lack data. Their data often doesn't fit the system they want to deploy. A particular analytical task may require facts extracted from raw documents. A grounded assistant may require retrievable evidence and business context. Other use cases may start elsewhere.

Raw Data: Reality Captured

Raw data is the closest digital representation of reality. It is unprocessed or minimally processed signals from the world, captured before any significant structuring or interpretation. Common forms include documents like contracts, PDF reports, emails, policy manuals, and technical specifications. Images such as photographs, scanned paperwork, screenshots, and architectural drawings. Audio including customer service calls, meeting recordings, voicemails, and dictated notes. Video with security footage, training recordings, product demonstrations, and webinars. Sensor data from IoT telemetry, server logs, network traffic, and manufacturing equipment readings.

All of these contain valuable information, but that information is implicit. A camera image of a production line implicitly contains objects, defects, and text, but only as pixels. A customer service call implicitly contains sentiment, intent, and resolution, but only as audio waveforms.

Raw data quality needs complete capture. Record information in full fidelity. Scan documents at resolution sufficient to read fine print. Record calls without dropouts. Capture sensor data at frequencies that preserve meaningful variation. Raw data needs to be stored and indexed so that AI systems can find it. Many organizations have years of valuable recordings and documents scattered across file shares and forgotten archives. A data lake with proper cataloging beats terabytes of inaccessible content. It must be accurate. Audio recordings without compression artifacts that distort speech. Images without blur that obscures details. Documents without missing pages or corrupted sections. It needs to be timely and relevant. Sensor data about yesterday's conditions may be worthless for today's decisions. And you need traceable provenance. Which device captured this image? Under what conditions? When?

Structured Data: Organized Facts

Structured data is made up of clean, well-defined tables with consistent schemas, resolved entities, and documented relationships. The meaning that was implicit in raw data becomes explicit through labeled fields and records.

Common forms include relational databases with customer tables, transaction records, and inventory levels. Data warehouses containing historical sales, aggregated metrics, and dimensional models. CRM systems with account records, opportunity pipelines, and contact information. Spreadsheets with financial models, planning templates, and tracked metrics. API outputs delivering JSON or XML responses with defined schemas.

This is familiar territory for most organizations. Decades of enterprise software have produced vast stores of structured data. The challenge isn't having it. The challenge is making it AI-ready. Structured data optimized for human analysts often fails when AI is the consumer. Field names are cryptic. Business rules are implicit. Definitions vary across systems.

Structured data needs to be complete. You want all relevant fields, records, and relationships present. It must be accessible via queries or APIs, accurate enough for AI workloads, current enough to reflect reality, and traceable from source to consumption.

Context Data: The Semantic Knowledge Layer

Context data is knowledge represented in forms the model can retrieve and reason over. It captures semantics, the latent connections and concepts that give data its full meaning.

Common forms include vector embeddings (numerical representations of text, images, or other content that encode meaning in ways machines can compare and search), knowledge graphs (networks of entities and relationships that represent facts and their interconnections), semantic layers (centralized definitions of metrics, dimensions, and business concepts), and annotated knowledge bases (source content enriched with metadata, tags, and cross-references).

Context data enables generative AI to work with enterprise information. Retrieval-Augmented Generation (RAG) explicitly pairs language models with context data. The model first pulls relevant knowledge from a database or document store, then uses that retrieved context to generate the answer (Lewis et al., 2020).

The impact on hallucination can be substantial, but not magical. A 2024 Stanford RegLab study found that legal research tools still hallucinated at meaningful rates even with retrieval, with rates ranging from 17% to 33% across tools such as Lexis+ AI (Magesh et al., 2024). A separate JMIR Cancer study found that adding curated external knowledge reduced unsupported claims in cancer-information chatbots (Nishisako et al., 2025).

Context data needs complete coverage. The knowledge layer needs to span the domains and scenarios AI will encounter. Gaps become blind spots. It must be retrievable by meaning. That's the entire point of context data. It should be searchable via semantic queries, not just keyword matching. Semantic representation must be accurate. If embeddings distort meaning or knowledge graphs encode wrong relationships, AI reasoning goes off the rails. Content must be current. Knowledge bases become obsolete as policies change, products evolve, and procedures update. And every piece of knowledge needs to link back to primary evidence.

Action Data: Executable Knowledge

Action data includes specifications of what tools exist, how to use them, what constraints apply, and what workflows govern multi-step processes. It's the instruction manual and toolset for autonomous agents.

Components of action data include tool definitions (what tools exist and how to invoke them), parameter specifications (what inputs each tool requires), behavior descriptions (what each tool does and returns), constraint specifications (what the agent can and can't do), workflow definitions (how multi-step processes work), and observability configuration (how actions are logged and monitored). Most enterprises have elements of action data scattered across existing systems. API documentation describes tool interfaces. Process documentation explains workflows. Policy documents encode constraints. The challenge is consolidating and formalizing these into specifications AI agents can reliably use.

Action data needs complete specifications. The agent must have a full picture of its capabilities and constraints. It must be discoverable. Agents need to find the right tools for their goals. Specifications must be accurate and precise. There's no room for ambiguity. You need to keep specifications synchronized with current system state. And every action must be logged and auditable.

The Four AI System Types

The four AI system types work because each one transforms data in a different way: perception turns signals into structure, analytical systems turn structure into predictions, generative systems turn context into responses, and agentic systems turn specifications into action.

Perception AI: Seeing and Hearing

Perception AI gives machines the ability to sense the world, closing what Chapter 2 called the *perception gap*. These systems take raw signals like images, audio, video, or sensor readings and convert them into structured, actionable information.

In practical terms, Perception AI bridges analog reality and digital understanding. A computer vision model takes pixels from a camera and outputs "defective part" or "acceptable product." A speech recognition model takes an audio waveform and produces a transcript. A document understanding system takes a scanned invoice and extracts the vendor name, line items, and total amount.

In steel manufacturing, Aboulhosn et al. evaluated U-Net and Feature Pyramid Network semantic-segmentation approaches for detecting and localizing surface defects (Aboulhosn et al., 2024). That matters because perception AI works only when the raw signal captures the thing the model is supposed to detect.

For perception tasks that interpret images, audio, sensor streams, or other signals, raw data is usually the primary form. The work is to capture reality at enough fidelity for the task, preserve the signal, and label it well enough for the model to learn the pattern. The broader workflow may also require structured state, business context, or action controls.

Analytical AI: Understanding Patterns and Predicting

Analytical AI addresses the *reasoning gap*, enabling organizations to move from data to insight. It finds patterns in organized information and uses them to make predictions or informed decisions. This is classic machine learning on structured data: forecasting, classification, anomaly detection, and optimization.

The U.S. Department of the Treasury reported that its combined fraud-detection processes, including risk-based screening, transaction prioritization, and machine learning, prevented and recovered more than $4 billion in fraud and improper payments in fiscal year 2024, more than six times the $652.7 million recovered and prevented in fiscal year 2023 the previous year (U.S. Department of the Treasury, 2024). Treasury attributed $1 billion of that total to machine learning used to detect check fraud. That is the part of the result that came from applying existing analytical techniques to structured transaction data.

For analytical tasks built on defined features, entities, and relationships, structured data is usually the primary form. The work includes consistent schemas, resolved entities, documented relationships, and clear definitions. Raw-source fidelity matters when those features are derived from raw signals, but not every analytical workflow consumes raw data directly.

Generative AI: Creating and Conversing

Generative AI tackles the *knowledge gap*, where organizations have expertise trapped in documents and heads. It produces new content based on learned patterns and provided context. Large language models, image generators, and code assistants all fall into this category. These systems don't simply retrieve existing information. They synthesize something new that resembles what they've learned but addresses the specific situation at hand.

In McKinsey's 2024 Global Survey, 65% of respondents said their organizations regularly used generative AI in at least one function, nearly double the share in the firm's survey ten months earlier. The online survey included 1,363 participants across regions, industries, and organization sizes and weighted results by respondents' nations' shares of global GDP (McKinsey, 2024).

Among respondents whose organizations had AI or machine learning in production or proof of concept, 42% reported that their companies abandoned most AI initiatives before production, versus 17% in the prior-year survey. The 2025 report drew on an overall survey of 1,006 midlevel and senior IT and line-of-business professionals in North America and Europe, but routing limited the base for this item (S&P Global Market Intelligence, 2025). The survey did not establish that data problems caused the abandonment. Separately, hallucination remains a practical risk because generative models can produce plausible but nonfactual content.

RAG addresses this risk by retrieving external information at runtime and using it to ground the model's response.

Grounded enterprise generative AI often uses context data as its primary form when output must reflect current, organization-specific knowledge. The system must retrieve the right evidence at the right time and preserve enough provenance to ground the answer. Structured facts, raw inputs, or action specifications are supporting dependencies only when the use case requires them. Without a usable context layer, the model relies on its parameters and whatever information the application supplies at runtime.

Agentic AI: Acting and Automating

Agentic AI closes Chapter 2's *action gap*, enabling AI to execute rather than just recommend. These systems don't just answer questions. They actually do things: call APIs, execute workflows, and interact with systems.

Agentic AI is moving from demo to infrastructure. Anthropic released Claude Computer Use in October 2024, the first frontier AI model to offer computer use in a public beta (Anthropic, 2024a). OpenAI followed with Operator in January 2025, a computer-using agent that can navigate websites and execute tasks (OpenAI, 2025). Anthropic also introduced the Model Context Protocol (MCP), a standard way to expose tools and context to models (Anthropic, 2024b).

Agentic workflows commonly use action data as their primary form: specifications of available tools, parameters, permissions, constraints, and multi-step workflows. The Model Context Protocol (MCP) makes part of this concrete through a small set of standard primitives (Anthropic, 2024b). An agent may also need operational state, business context, structured facts, or raw signals when the selected workflow consumes them. The capability-specific point is controlled execution.

The governance challenge matters. The Cloud Security Alliance and Google Cloud found that governance maturity is the strongest predictor of AI readiness, with organizations that have comprehensive policies reporting higher early agentic AI adoption (Cloud Security Alliance and Google Cloud, 2025). Action data isn't only tool access. It's also the boundaries that tell an autonomous system what it can and can't do.

The Data-AI Map

Each AI capability has a primary data form that most directly supports the function described here. The mapping isn't exclusive, and a real workflow may require additional forms. Table 3.2 shows the common starting points.

For a vision, speech, or sensor task, raw signals are primary because the system extracts meaning from those signals. The surrounding application may also use structured context or action controls.

For forecasting, scoring, or classification over defined features, structured facts are primary. Consistent schemas and stable definitions matter. Raw data

Table 3.2 Primary Data Required for Each AI System Type

AI Capability	Primary Data Type	What's Happening
Perception AI	Raw data	Extracts structure from signals
Analytical AI	Structured data	Learns patterns from organized facts
Generative AI	Context data	Reasons over semantic knowledge
Agentic AI	Action data	Executes specified capabilities

is a supporting dependency only when those features are derived from raw sources.

Enterprise generative AI often needs context data when its output must reflect current, organization-specific knowledge. Without a usable context layer, the model relies on its parameters and whatever information the application supplies at runtime.

For a tool-using workflow, action specifications are primary because the system must know which tools exist, how to invoke them, what parameters to pass, and which constraints apply. Operational state and business context may also be required.

As workflow autonomy increases, integration and control needs often increase, but the dependency set remains use-case-specific. Agentic AI may combine action specifications, operational state, business context, and raw perception when the selected workflow requires them. Figure 3.1 marks typical starting points, not universal requirements.

If you already know your strategic priority, Table 3.3 tells you which capability to target and which data level to invest in first. The remaining chapters in this book are designed to be read sequentially, but this map lets you prioritize based on where your organization will see the fastest return.

Mapping the Dependencies Your Use Case Actually Needs

The four data forms often connect, but they don't form a mandatory chain. Raw signals can feed structured facts. Structured facts can support context. Context can inform action. The exact path depends on the use case, and teams may build required forms in parallel. A missing dependency that the selected system actually needs creates risk.

Organizations under pressure often skip a dependency their selected workflow actually needs. A grounded assistant can fail when evidence and business context are incomplete. An agent can be unsafe when tool specifications, permissions,

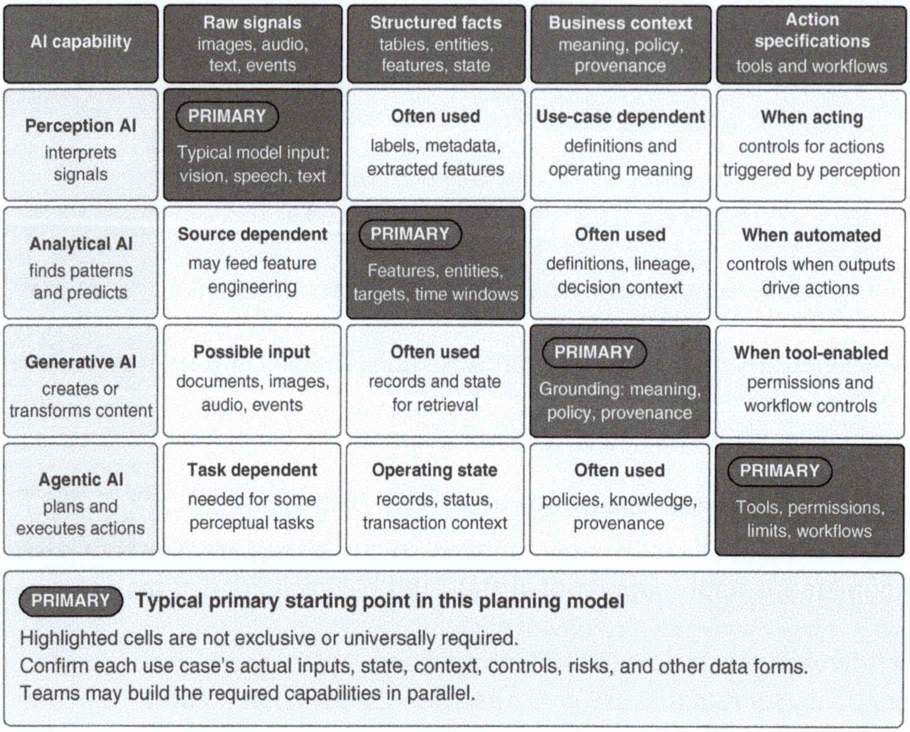

Figure 3.1 AI capability and data dependency planning map.

Table 3.3 Starting from Business Outcomes

Business Priority	Start With	Primary Data Level	Entry Chapters
Quality control, safety, defect detection	Perception AI	Raw data	Chapter 7
Customer intelligence, operational efficiency, forecasting	Analytical AI	Structured data	Chapter 9
Knowledge work productivity, content, customer support	Generative AI	Context data	Chapter 11
Process automation at scale, autonomous workflows	Agentic AI	Action data	Chapter 13

constraints, or stop conditions are missing. These are missing-dependency failures, not proof that every system needs one universal sequence.

RAND Corporation's 2024 exploratory report cites estimates that more than 80% of AI projects fail, about twice the failure rate of non-AI corporate IT projects

(Ryseff et al., 2024). In 50 industry interviews drawn from a larger 65-interview study, leadership misunderstanding or miscommunication was the most common reported root cause, followed by limitations in the quality and utility of training data (Ryseff et al., 2024). The report is exploratory and does not establish a universal failure rate.

In a Capital One-sponsored Morning Consult survey of nearly 4,000 business leaders and technical practitioners at organizations with more than 500 employees, 76% of the business-leader sample ranked data security as its top concern for AI initiatives, followed by data quality at 73% and data management at 65% (Capital One, 2024).

In the 53-practitioner study introduced in Chapter 2, 92% of participants reported at least one data cascade (Sambasivan et al., 2021). Those findings describe the study sample, not all AI practitioners. The most severe cascades sometimes took two to three years to manifest. The longest-running cases involved real-world hardware and environmental drift and emerged almost always in production. By then you've invested enormous resources in a system built on a bad foundation.

Quality problems propagate when one artifact is actually derived from another. OCR errors can flow into structured facts. Sensor drift can corrupt extracted features. Inconsistent entity definitions can weaken a context layer built from those records. An agent can act on false premises when the state or context it consumes is wrong. Figure 3.2 shows common dependency paths, while teams may build the forms their use case needs in parallel.

A common example is a grounded enterprise assistant launched without a usable context layer. The organization has documents and databases, connects a language model to a repository with basic search, and launches before confirming retrieval quality, coverage, provenance, and freshness.

The assistant may give confident answers that are subtly wrong, retrieve irrelevant material, or cite outdated policies. The model may not be the only problem. Poor chunking can separate evidence from essential context. Weak embedding choices can degrade retrieval. Missing deduplication and version controls can surface obsolete material.

In this example, source documents and structured records existed, but a required context dependency wasn't ready. Figure 3.3 summarizes data-related signals to investigate. The patterns don't prove one cause, so teams should also check the model, application, evaluation, workflow, security, and governance.

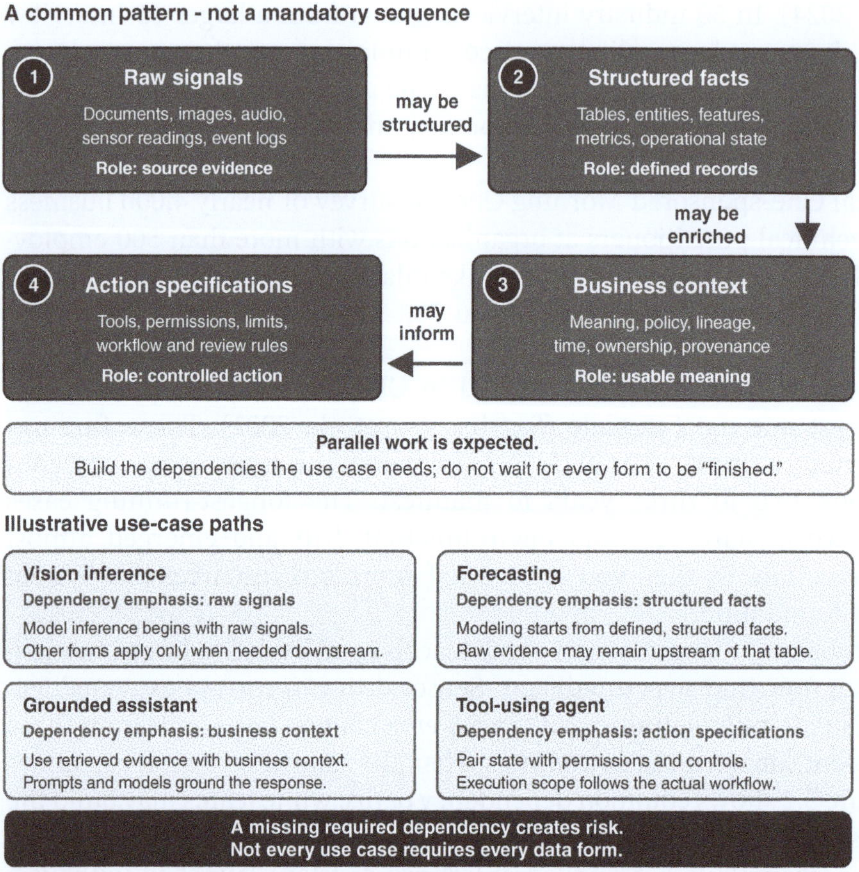

Figure 3.2 Common data dependency paths by AI use case.

For each capability type, start with the primary dependency and add only the supporting dependencies the use case requires:

- **Perception AI:**
  1. Confirm the raw signals required by the task.
  2. Add the labels, context, state, or controls the workflow requires, then evaluate the model.

- **Analytical AI:**
  1. Define the structured facts, entities, and target variables.
  2. Confirm raw-source fidelity only when those facts are derived from raw signals.
  3. Add required context or action controls, then evaluate the model.

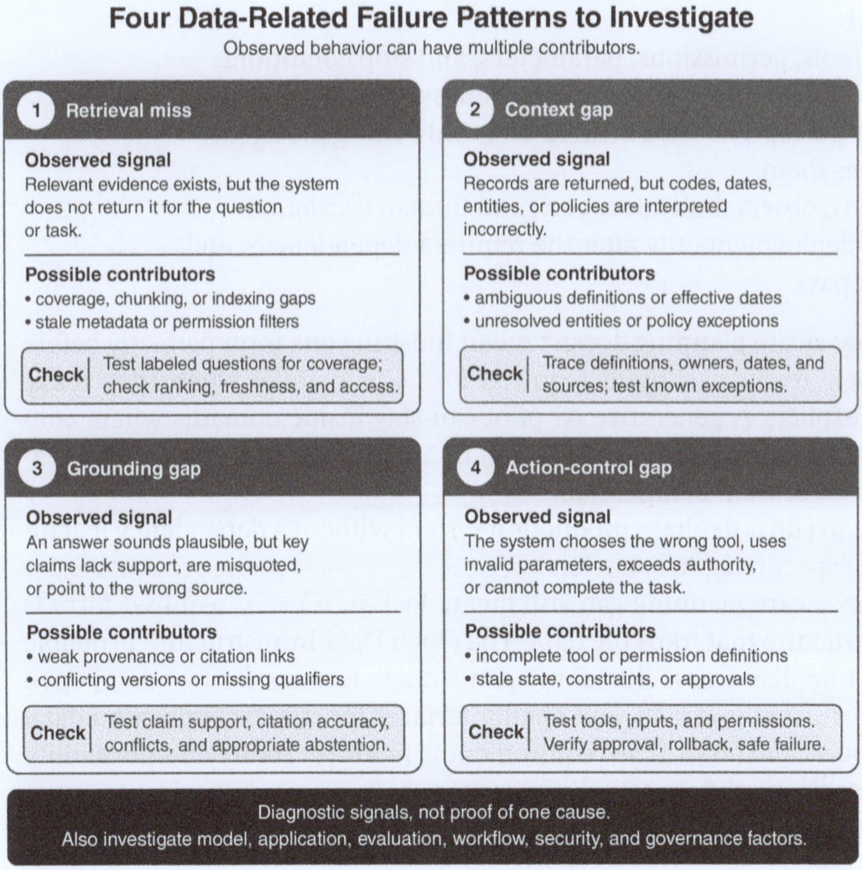

Figure 3.3 Four data-related failure patterns to investigate.

- **Generative AI:**
  1. Define the knowledge and evidence the application must use.
  2. Build or connect the context layer needed for grounded responses.
  3. Add structured facts, raw inputs, or action specifications only when the workflow requires them.
  4. Evaluate grounding, coverage, freshness, and refusal behavior before broader deployment.

  A grounded assistant fails when a dependency it actually needs is missing; that doesn't prove every generative AI system needs the same sequence.

- **Agentic AI:**
  1. Specify tools, permissions, parameters, and stop conditions.
  2. Connect the operational state and business context the workflow requires.
  3. Add raw perception or structured facts only when the agent consumes them.
  4. Test safety, observability, recovery, and human escalation.
  5. Expand deployment only after the required dependencies and controls pass.

Dependency-aware planning doesn't mean finishing one form perfectly before starting another. Teams can build required forms in parallel when they make dependencies explicit. A generative AI pilot can stay inside domains where context coverage is strong. An agent can remain in a sandbox while action specifications and controls are still being tested.

What you can't do is deploy a production system without a dependency it actually needs and expect reliable behavior.

Dependency-aware planning can still create lock-in if every required form is built on infrastructure that traps the data. The Open Data Infrastructure principle from Chapter 1 applies across the map: open storage formats for raw data, open table formats for structured data, and open interfaces for context and action data. Commercial tools can still fit. The requirement is interoperability and portability across the forms the workflow actually uses.

Before launching an AI initiative, ask yourself:

1. What capability and workflow am I targeting? Identify the primary data form it consumes.
2. Is that primary form ready for AI? Ask whether the system can use it reliably, not merely whether the organization has it.
3. Which supporting dependencies does this workflow actually require, and is each one ready?

If the answer to any of these questions is no, you have two choices. Build the foundations first, or proceed with a clear view of the limitations and the technical debt you're taking on. Most organizations pick a third option: proceed without honest assessment, blame the model when things fail, switch models, fail again, and eventually write off the initiative as an AI failure.

High-failure estimates aren't inevitable, and no single framework explains them all. Mapping the dependencies a use case actually needs helps teams avoid a predictable class of mistakes.

Table 3.4 AI Capabilities, Primary Data, and Illustrative CRAFT Priorities

Capability	Core Function	Primary Data	Illustrative CRAFT Priorities
Perception AI	Signal to structure	Raw data	Accurate (fidelity), complete (representativeness)
Analytical AI	Structure to insight	Structured data	Complete (entity integrity), accurate (semantic clarity)
Generative AI	Context to content	Context data	Retrievable, traceable (groundability)
Agentic AI	Intent to action	Action data	Complete (specifications), fresh (currency), traceable (safety)

Know What You're Building

The four AI system types often begin with different primary data forms, as shown in Table 3.4. Supporting forms and CRAFT priorities vary by use case.

The mapping in Table 3.4 matters because it stops the blame game that derails so many AI initiatives. When a computer vision system fails, the instinct is often to try a different model. But if the failure comes from non-representative training images, a different model won't help. When a chatbot hallucinates, the instinct is to fine-tune more aggressively. But if the context data is incomplete or stale, fine-tuning won't fix it.

Know what you're building. Know what it eats. Everything else follows.

Looking Ahead

A map identifies the primary and supporting data dependencies for an AI use case. It doesn't tell you whether those inputs are ready to carry the load. That's the next question.

Chapter 4 introduces CRAFT: complete, retrievable, accurate, fresh, and traceable. Those five dimensions turn the data-AI map into an assessment you can use to decide whether each required data form is ready for production.

References

Aboulhosn, Zeina, et al. "Detection of Manufacturing Defects in Steel Using Deep Learning with Explainable Artificial Intelligence." *IEEE Access*, vol. 12, 2024, pp. 99240–99257, https://doi.org/10.1109/ACCESS.2024.3430113.

Anthropic. "Introducing computer use, a new Claude 3.5 Sonnet, and Claude 3.5 Haiku." *Anthropic*, 22 October 2024a, https://www.anthropic.com/news/3-5-models-and-computer-use.

Anthropic. "Introducing the Model Context Protocol." *Anthropic*, 25 November 2024b, https://www.anthropic.com/news/model-context-protocol.

Capital One. "AI Readiness Survey: Are Companies Ready for AI Adoption?" *Capital One*, 21 November 2024, https://www.capitalone.com/tech/ai/ai-readiness-survey/.

Cloud Security Alliance and Google Cloud. "The State of AI Security and Governance." CSA, December 2025, https://cloudsecurityalliance.org/artifacts/the-state-of-ai-security-and-governance.

Harvard Business Review Analytic Services. "Taming the Complexity of AI Data Readiness." Pulse Survey, sponsored by Cloudera, March 2026, https://www.cloudera.com/content/dam/www/marketing/resources/whitepapers/taming-the-complexity-of-ai-data-readiness.pdf?daqp=true.

Lewis, Patrick, et al. "Retrieval-Augmented Generation for Knowledge-Intensive NLP Tasks" *NeurIPS*, 2020, https://proceedings.neurips.cc/paper/2020/hash/6b493230205f780e1bc26945df7481e5-Abstract.html.

Magesh, Varun, et al. "Hallucination-Free? Assessing the Reliability of Leading AI Legal Research Tools." Regulation, Evaluation, and Governance Lab, Stanford University, 2024, https://reglab.stanford.edu/publications/hallucination-free-assessing-the-reliability-of-leading-ai-legal-research-tools/.

McKinsey & Company. "The state of AI in early 2024: Gen AI adoption spikes and starts to generate value." *McKinsey*, 2024, https://www.mckinsey.com/capabilities/quantumblack/our-insights/the-state-of-ai-2024.

Nishisako, Sota, Takahiro Higashi, and Fumihiko Wakao. "Reducing Hallucinations and Trade-Offs in Responses in Generative AI Chatbots for Cancer Information: Development and Evaluation Study." *JMIR Cancer*, vol. 11, 2025, https://doi.org/10.2196/70176.

OpenAI. "Introducing Operator." *OpenAI*, 23 January 2025, https://openai.com/index/introducing-operator/.

Ryseff, James, et al. "The Root Causes of Failure for Artificial Intelligence Projects and How They Can Succeed." *RAND Corporation*, 13 August 2024, https://www.rand.org/pubs/research_reports/RRA2680-1.html.

Sambasivan, Nithya, et al. "'Everyone Wants to Do the Model Work, Not the Data Work': Data Cascades in High-Stakes AI." CHI, 2021, https://doi.org/10.1145/3411764.3445518.

S&P Global Market Intelligence. "Generative AI Experiences Rapid Adoption, but with Mixed Outcomes: Highlights from VotE: AI & Machine Learning." Voice of the Enterprise: AI & Machine Learning, Use Cases 2025, https://www.spglobal.com/market-intelligence/en/news-insights/research/ai-experiences-rapid-adoption-but-with-mixed-outcomes-highlights-from-vote-ai-machine-learning.

U.S. Department of the Treasury. "Treasury Announces Enhanced Fraud Detection Processes, Including Machine Learning AI, Prevented and Recovered Over $4 Billion in Fiscal Year 2024." Press Release, 17 October 2024, https://home.treasury.gov/news/press-releases/jy2650.

Chapter 4
The CRAFT Assessment Framework

You need a consistent way to test whether data is fit for a defined AI use case. CRAFT evaluates five dimensions: complete, retrievable, accurate, fresh, and traceable. Each dimension exposes a different class of data risk.

CRAFT is an author-developed assessment framework. It helps teams evaluate whether data is fit for a defined AI use case. It isn't a legal standard, a certification scheme, or a complete AI risk-management system. Security, privacy, fairness, model behavior, human oversight, application design, and regulatory obligations still require their own controls.

Throughout this book, evaluate all five dimensions for the data forms a use case depends on, then set thresholds that match the system's purpose, impact, and risk.

Enterprise AI outcomes depend on model capability, data quality, application design, workflow integration, governance, human oversight, security, and operations. CRAFT provides a disciplined way to assess the data component. NIST's AI Risk Management Framework likewise treats trustworthy AI as a socio-technical, lifecycle concern rather than the result of any single control (NIST, 2023).

Why CRAFT Exists

Data quality isn't a new idea. A foundational contribution is Wang and Strong's 1996 study of what data quality means to data consumers (Wang and Strong, 1996). The authors surveyed data consumers and organized 15 dimensions into four categories: intrinsic quality, contextual quality, representational quality, and accessibility. Their framework remains an important reference point for data-quality practice.

The DAMA UK Working Group condensed practical data quality into six core dimensions: accuracy, completeness, consistency, timeliness, uniqueness, and validity (DAMA UK Working Group, 2013). ISO/IEC 25012:2008, the software quality data model, formalized characteristics assessed from a system-dependent point of view, including trace-ability and recoverability (ISO, 2008).

These frameworks solved real problems, but they weren't written for today's AI consumption patterns. Wang and Strong (1996) defined data quality from the perspective of data consumers and the tasks they perform. ISO/IEC 25012:2008 defines a general data-quality model for structured data retained in computer systems, including inherent and system-dependent characteristics. Neither source addresses modern retrieval-augmented generation, foundation-model training, or tool-using AI. CRAFT adapts earlier data-quality work to those AI-specific consumption patterns.

AI systems don't work that way.

AI systems can consume data in ways that earlier quality frameworks did not specifically address. During training, models may encode statistical patterns across large datasets. At inference time, retrieval-augmented systems may query vector indexes, while tool-using systems may parse schemas and execute authorized API calls when the application is designed to permit them. These patterns create AI-specific quality questions:

- **Retrievability for AI consumption**
  Traditional "accessibility" means a database is available and a user has permissions. AI retrievability means the right information surfaces through semantic search, vector similarity, or structured tool calls at inference time. A RAG system can have perfect access to a knowledge base and still fail because its chunking strategy buries the answer in the wrong passage. Databricks found that fine-tuning embedding models on domain-specific data improved retrieval and downstream RAG accuracy on some datasets, while gains were limited

when retrieval was not the bottleneck (Portes et al., 2025). Retrieval quality has to be measured on the data and tasks the system will actually face.

- **Temporal validity for model freshness**
  Traditional "timeliness" means data is current when a human looks at it. AI freshness means training data hasn't drifted from the deployment distribution, knowledge bases reflect the current state of the world, and tool schemas match current API behavior. Knowledge cutoffs vary by model and vendor, which can leave a model unaware of recent events. This is a structural source of wrong answers. Kalai et al. argue that common training and evaluation practices reward guessing over acknowledging uncertainty (Kalai et al., 2025). Current, grounded information can reduce errors caused by stale knowledge, but teams still need to measure the effect for each model and task.
- **Traceability for AI governance**
  Traditional frameworks include data provenance, but AI governance often needs more detailed records. For high-risk AI systems within scope, Article 10 of Regulation (EU) 2024/1689 establishes data and data-governance requirements, and Article 12 requires systems to permit automatic event logging (European Parliament and Council of the European Union, 2024). These records can help reconstruct the data path and investigate an output. They do not, by themselves, explain why a model generated a particular response or satisfy every regulatory obligation.

As discussed earlier, among respondents whose organizations had AI or machine learning in production or proof of concept, 42% reported that their companies abandoned most AI initiatives before production. The report also said that the average organization scrapped 46% of proofs of concept before production (S&P Global Market Intelligence, 2025). The overall survey included 1,006 midlevel and senior IT and line-of-business professionals in North America and Europe, but routing limited the base for these items. S&P Global identified cost, privacy, security as major barriers; the survey did not establish that data failures caused the abandoned projects or that a CRAFT assessment would have prevented them. CRAFT addresses one diagnosable part of a broader production-readiness problem.

CRAFT emerged from recurring patterns I observed in practitioner and consulting work with organizations pursuing data and AI strategies. Teams with strong traditional data-quality programs still struggled to make AI reliable. Others had invested heavily in infrastructure yet couldn't explain why models failed.

Leaders often sensed that data was part of the problem but lacked a framework specific enough to diagnose it. CRAFT is my response to the question behind those conversations: What, exactly, does data need to be for a defined AI use case?

The Five CRAFT Dimensions

CRAFT defines five dimensions for assessing whether data is fit for a defined AI use case, as shown in Table 4.1. Each dimension asks a different data-layer question. Teams define measurable thresholds for those questions in the context of the use case.

The word "craft" is deliberate. Craftsmanship implies intentionality, skill, and care. Data doesn't become AI-ready by accident. You build it on purpose, with discipline, applying standards that match what AI systems actually need.

CRAFT evaluates all five dimensions for the data forms a defined use case depends on. A team should not omit a dimension without an explicit rationale, but readiness thresholds are use-case specific. Raw signals, structured facts, business context, and action specifications may require different controls for training and inference. The checks and minimum acceptable scores should reflect the system's purpose, impact, and risk.

Weakness in any dimension can create a distinct failure mode. Complete, accurate, fresh, and traceable data that can't be retrieved remains unavailable to the system. Complete, retrievable, fresh, and traceable data that carries the wrong meaning can produce confident errors. Figure 4.1 keeps the framework in view.

Table 4.1 The Five CRAFT Dimensions

CRAFT Dimension	Definition	Assessment Question
Complete	Required data is present for the defined use case.	Is required data present?
Retrievable	The system can find and access the required data.	Can the system find and access it?
Accurate	The data represents the intended meaning.	Does it represent the intended meaning?
Fresh	The data is current enough for the use case.	Is it current enough for the use case?
Traceable	The data's origin and changes can be explained.	Can its origin and changes be explained?

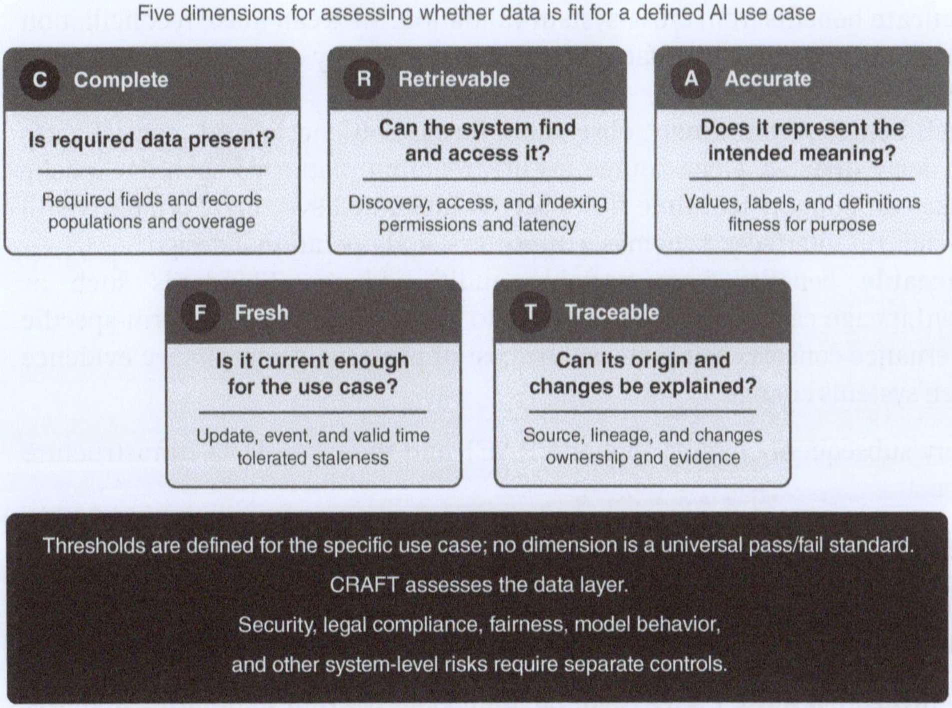

Figure 4.1 The CRAFT assessment framework.

Why CRAFT Needs Open Infrastructure

CRAFT defines what data should be able to do for a defined use case. Open data infrastructure can help teams preserve those qualities as systems evolve by reducing dependence on proprietary formats and interfaces. It does not by itself show that the defined CRAFT thresholds are met, because architecture, governance, operations, and implementation still determine outcomes. The connection is easiest to see dimension by dimension:

- **Complete** benefits from data that can move across systems. Proprietary formats can fragment metadata and schema information. Open formats can support cross-system measurement and maintenance.
- **Retrievable** benefits from documented discovery interfaces. Vendor-specific languages and APIs can limit access. Open APIs and interoperable metadata platforms such as OpenMetadata can make data discoverable through compatible tools and AI systems.

- **Accurate** benefits from cross-system validation. Silos can make reconciliation harder. Interoperable interfaces can support accuracy checks across compatible systems.
- **Fresh** benefits from timely, observable flows. Bottlenecks and manual gates can delay updates. Open-source event-streaming platforms such as Apache Kafka can support real-time flows across integrated systems. Portability still depends on interfaces, schemas, connectors, and operational design.
- **Traceable** benefits from portable audit evidence. Standards such as OpenLineage can make lineage easier to move and reuse. Platform-specific governance consoles can increase the cost of preserving compliance evidence when systems change.

Every subsequent chapter applies CRAFT and the Open Data Infrastructure together.

CRAFT Applied to Inference and Training

CRAFT's true power is that it's one framework applied twice:

- **For inference data**, CRAFT can be applied across four data forms: raw signals, structured facts, business context, and action specifications. Table 4.2 lists representative assessment focuses. Teams select measures and thresholds for the forms their use case actually depends on.
- **For training data**, CRAFT applies the same five dimensions to how models learn. Evidence shows that careful curation can matter as much as, and sometimes more than, raw volume on defined tasks.

The evidence presented in Chapter 1 tells the story: LIMA produced results preferred or equal to GPT-4's in 43% of comparisons in a human study with just 1,000 carefully curated examples (Zhou et al., 2023). Phi-2 matched or outperformed models up to 25 times its size on selected benchmarks after training on curated textbook-quality and web data (Javaheripi and Bubeck, 2023). These examples show what disciplined data curation can accomplish. They trace back to the same CRAFT dimensions that apply to inference data.

The same pattern appears in pre-training. FineWeb contains 15 trillion tokens drawn from 96 Common Crawl snapshots, while FineWeb-Edu is a 1.3-trillion-token collection selected from FineWeb for educational value. In the study's reported comparisons, models trained on FineWeb-Edu performed better on

Table 4.2 Applying the CRAFT Dimensions Across Four Data Forms

CRAFT Dimension	Raw Signals	Structured Facts	Business Context	Action Specifications
Complete	Expected sources, modalities, populations, and coverage are present for the use case.	Required entities, fields, relationships, and populations are present.	Required definitions, policies, ownership, and known exceptions are documented.	Required tools, parameters, constraints, approvals, and recovery paths are specified.
Retrievable	Signals are discoverable and accessible under the intended permissions and latency.	Records are queryable or indexed through stable identifiers and usable access paths.	Definitions, policies, provenance, and ownership can be retrieved with the relevant data.	Approved tools and workflows can be found and invoked through documented interfaces.
Accurate	Signal fidelity, labels, capture metadata, and units represent the intended observation.	Values, entities, relationships, units, and definitions match the source and intended meaning.	Definitions, policies, owners, exceptions, and effective dates are correct and reconciled.	Tool schemas, parameters, constraints, and outcome definitions reflect actual behavior.
Fresh	Capture and update times meet the use case's tolerance.	Event time, valid time, synchronization, and processing latency meet the use case's tolerance.	Policies, definitions, ownership, and exceptions reflect the effective version.	Permissions, tool state, constraints, and workflow rules are current at execution time.
Traceable	Source, capture time, collection conditions, and transformations are recorded.	Lineage, versions, transformations, and evidence connect records to their sources.	Authority, provenance, ownership, effective dates, and changes are documented.	Inputs, decisions, approvals, tool calls, outcomes, and recovery events are auditable.

knowledge- and reasoning-intensive benchmarks such as MMLU and ARC than models trained on several other open datasets (Penedo et al., 2024). The result supports the value of task-relevant curation; it doesn't establish that smaller datasets are generally better.

In TinyStories experiments with small language models, Sajith and Kathala found that 25% duplication produced a 0.87% accuracy increase, while 100% duplication produced a 40% accuracy drop (Sajith and Kathala, 2024). The result shows that duplication level affected performance in that experimental setup. It does not establish a universal duplication threshold or show that quality is the only factor separating outcomes.

The training-data questions parallel the inference questions: Is the data complete, retrievable, accurate, fresh, and traceable for the defined task? The answers help teams assess risks in what a model may learn or memorize; they do not determine model behavior on their own. CRAFT can be applied when curating data for pre-training, fine-tuning, reinforcement learning from human feedback, and synthetic-data generation, with checks tailored to each method.

Applying CRAFT Across Four Data Forms

Table 4.2 applies the five CRAFT dimensions across four data forms. It lists assessment focuses, not universal requirements. Teams should select the checks their use case needs and define measurable thresholds for those checks. CRAFT assesses the data layer; it does not by itself certify security, legal compliance, fairness, model behavior, or the complete AI system.

Each cell in Table 4.2 identifies an assessment focus that may matter to a use case. The examples below illustrate how a material gap can contribute to failure; they do not establish that one gap is always the sole cause:

- A raw-signal freshness gap can misalign streams that the use case needs to correlate. In a manufacturing example, a three-second offset between video and temperature readings could lead a model to learn or infer the wrong association unless synchronization and tolerance checks catch it.
- A structured-fact completeness gap can leave unresolved entities or duplicate records. If a customer model counts duplicate profiles as separate entities, forecasts and personalization can be distorted until entity-resolution controls reconcile them.
- A business-context coverage gap can leave a grounded assistant without current product definitions or policies. Depending on the system's fallback

Table 4.3 CRAFT Dimensions for Training Data

CRAFT Dimension	Training Data Characteristics
Complete	Task coverage, representativeness, deduplication
Retrievable	Pipeline accessibility, versioning, iterability
Accurate	Behavioral alignment, annotation consistency, factual correctness, contamination control
Fresh	Temporal validity, behavioral currency, refresh cadence
Traceable	Provenance, compliance verification, curation documentation

behavior, it may decline to answer, return incomplete guidance, or generate an unsupported response.

- An action-specification freshness gap can leave an agent with a stale tool schema. If an endpoint changes from `customer_id` to `account_id`, validation may reject the call; weak validation could allow a malformed request to reach downstream systems.

The lesson is straightforward: not meeting one or more defined CRAFT thresholds leaves residual data risk. Teams should assess every dimension relevant to the use case and investigate material gaps at each required data form.

Applying CRAFT to Training Data

Table 4.3 applies the same dimensions to representative training-data characteristics. The checks and thresholds still depend on the model, task, evaluation design, impact, and risk.

Each row in Table 4.3 identifies an assessment focus. A material gap can contribute to failure, but its effect depends on the training objective, data distribution, model, and evaluation design.

The same five dimensions can be applied to inference and training data, while the specific checks vary by data form, consumption pattern, and use case.

The Dimensions in Detail

This section unpacks each CRAFT dimension in practical terms. The goal is to show how different data gaps can contribute to different failure modes across training and inference. A CRAFT score is diagnostic evidence, not proof that one missing dimension caused an entire system outcome.

Complete: Is Required Data Present?

Completeness asks whether the data required for the defined use case is present at the needed coverage. It is not a claim that a dataset can contain every condition a system may encounter. For inference, teams define the sources, populations, topics, entities, and edge cases the use case depends on, then measure material gaps. For training, teams define task-coverage and representation targets and test whether missing groups, classes, conditions, or edge cases could distort learning or evaluation.

Historical training data can carry representation gaps into model behavior. Amazon developed a machine-learning recruiting tool using patterns learned from resumes submitted over a 10-year period (Dastin, 2018). Because most of those resumes came from men, the system learned patterns that disadvantaged women, including penalizing resumes containing the word "women's" and downgrading graduates of two all-women's colleges. Reuters reported that Amazon abandoned the project by early 2017 after attempts to make the system gender-neutral did not resolve the underlying risk. The case illustrates a representation problem in historical training data; it does not show that missing coverage was the only design failure.

Joy Buolamwini and Timnit Gebru's Gender Shades study evaluated commercial gender-classification systems on the more balanced Pilot Parliaments Benchmark (PPB) and reported error rates of up to 34.7% for darker-skinned women and up to 0.8% for lighter-skinned men (Buolamwini and Gebru, 2018). The study separately documented representation gaps in established facial-analysis benchmarks: darker-skinned women accounted for 4.4% of IJB-A and lighter-skinned men for 59.4%. PPB was designed to be more balanced, with 21.3% darker-skinned women and 30.3% lighter-skinned men. The performance results and benchmark-composition findings are related evidence about subgroup evaluation, but they come from different datasets.

ProPublica's investigation of the COMPAS recidivism algorithm found false-positive rates of 44.9% for Black defendants and 23.5% for white defendants (Angwin et al., 2016). The disparity shows why teams must test consequential models across relevant groups instead of relying on aggregate accuracy.

These cases illustrate different ways that missing or unrepresentative data can contribute to failure; they do not establish data incompleteness as the sole cause. In generative AI, large language models can generate plausible but false answers when retrieved evidence does not cover a query. Kalai et al. argue that common training and evaluation practices reward guessing over acknowledging uncertainty (Kalai et al., 2025). In experiments on four question-answering datasets, Sen et al. found that augmenting language-model prompts with facts retrieved from a knowledge graph improved performance over a language model alone by an average of 83% (Sen et al., 2023). That result supports evaluating retrieval coverage and structured knowledge for the defined task; it is not evidence that data coverage alone eliminates hallucinations.

For training data, completeness includes task coverage (does the data cover the material scenarios, populations, and conditions defined for the intended use?), representativeness (are relevant demographic groups, edge cases, and minority classes adequately represented?), and deduplication (has redundant data been identified and managed so repeated examples do not receive unintended weight?).

For inference data, completeness varies by data form. Raw signals need the sources, modalities, populations, and coverage defined for the use case. Structured facts need required entities, fields, relationships, and populations. Business context needs the required definitions, policies, ownership, and known exceptions. Action specifications need the required tools, parameters, constraints, approvals, and recovery paths.

Retrievable: Can the System Find and Access It?

The best data in the world creates zero value if AI systems can't find it. This sounds obvious. It isn't.

A Splunk global survey of more than 1,300 business and IT leaders found that 55% of enterprise data was "dark," meaning untapped, hidden, or unknown to the organization (Splunk, 2019). Among organizations McKinsey identified as AI high performers, 70% reported data-related difficulties involving governance, integration, or insufficient training data (McKinsey & Company, 2024).

Think about what that means for your AI deployment. When your AI is built on top of a data lake where the majority of content is undiscovered and unindexed, the AI's effective knowledge base is a fraction of what the organization actually knows. The AI isn't dumb. It's blind.

Barnett et al. (2024) catalogued seven failure points in RAG systems. Several are retrieval failures, including cases where relevant content exists but is missing from the retrieved context, ranks too low, or is obscured by noise. The lesson is practical: teams need to diagnose retrieval, context, generation, and answer-quality failures separately instead of assuming a larger model will solve them.

For training data, retrievability means the data is organized, versioned, and accessible to training infrastructure in ways that support iteration. Training is often iterative: teams run experiments, adjust the data mix, add examples for topics where the model underperforms, remove examples that introduce unwanted behaviors, then retrain and evaluate. The number of cycles varies by project. If training data lives in unversioned spreadsheets and ad hoc file dumps, each iteration becomes harder to reproduce. Versioning code, data, and models together helps teams trace which inputs and configurations produced a result.

For inference data, retrievability varies by data form. Raw signals need discoverable, permissioned access within the use case's latency tolerance. Structured facts need stable identifiers and usable query or index paths. Business context must be retrievable with the relevant data. Approved tools and workflows need documented interfaces through which they can be found and invoked.

Accurate: Does It Represent the Intended Meaning?

Accuracy goes beyond factual correctness. It encompasses whether data faithfully conveys its intended meaning to an AI system, including the semantic precision and structural coherence that AI needs to interpret it properly.

One underappreciated accuracy problem is semantic ambiguity. A field named "Revenue" might mean gross revenue in one system, net revenue in another, and recognized revenue in a third. A human analyst may know which definition applies from context. Without sufficient metadata or context, an AI system may treat those fields as equivalent and produce a numerically plausible but semantically wrong result.

Even how you prepare data for AI consumption affects accuracy. Parent-child chunking changes what context a retriever can surface, so teams should benchmark it against flat chunking on their own corpus. If chunks split semantic units at the wrong boundaries, the AI receives fragments that don't represent the original meaning, no matter how accurate the source document was. Figure 4.2 shows where retrieval and accuracy failures enter a RAG pipeline.

Drawing on research by Experian and two data-quality consultants, Thomas Redman estimated that bad data costs most companies 15% to 25% of revenue (Redman, 2017). Much of that cost appears downstream, when decisions rely on data that looks correct but carries the wrong meaning.

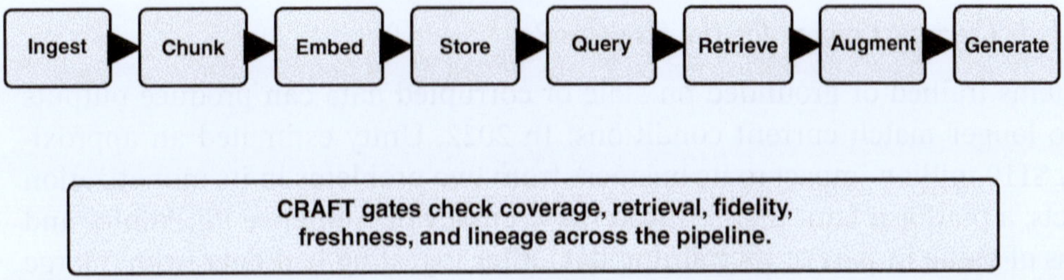

Figure 4.2 RAG architecture pipeline.

For training data, accuracy has multiple facets. Behavioral accuracy means the examples correctly demonstrate the behaviors you want the model to learn. Annotation consistency means multiple annotators would produce the same labels for the same examples. A medical-image segmentation study showed how annotator variability introduces noise that can affect AI performance and proposed metrics for measuring agreement (Yang et al., 2023). A separate review of 591 NLP dataset publications found that about 70% used good or excellent quality management, while roughly 30% were rated subpar (Klie et al., 2024). Unresolved disagreement can become label noise, thereby weakening both model training and benchmark reliability.

Factual correctness means the facts in training examples are verified and current. Algan and Ulusoy's survey explains that deep neural networks can memorize random noise and reviews methods for reducing its effects. Label noise is often measured as a percentage (%), but its effect depends on how labels are corrupted and how the model is trained. The survey first circulated as a 2019 preprint, and the peer-reviewed Knowledge-Based Systems article was published in 2021 (Algan and Ulusoy, 2021). Label errors can come from random mistakes or systematic annotation bias, and both distort what a model learns.

Data contamination is another critical accuracy threat. When benchmark evaluation data leaks into training sets, performance metrics become unreliable. The compilation (CONDA Shared Task, 2024) included 566 reported entries covering 91 contaminated sources from 23 contributors. A model that scores well on leaked benchmarks may be reproducing material it already encountered instead of showing that it can generalize.

Fresh: Is It Current Enough for the Use Case?

AI systems trained or grounded on stale or corrupted data can produce outputs that no longer match current conditions. In 2022, Unity estimated an approximately $110 million impact to its business from two problems in its monetization products: a platform fault that reduced the accuracy of Audience PinPointer and the loss of value in part of its training data after ingesting bad data from a large customer (Unity Software Inc., 2022). Unity's prepared remarks attribute the estimate to the two issues together, not to bad data alone. The case illustrates how product and data failures can interact; it is not a general estimate of the cost of stale data.

In a 2021 Fivetran-commissioned survey conducted by Wakefield Research among 300 vice president-level or higher data and analytics leaders familiar with their organizations' data strategy and use, at companies with at least 100 employees and $100 million in annual revenue in the United States, United Kingdom, Germany, and France, 71% said end users made decisions with old or error-prone data at least some of the time. Among the 213 respondents who reported such decisions, 85% said those decisions had cost their company money (Fivetran and Wakefield Research, 2021).

An early systematic analysis of machine-learning model aging observed temporal degradation in 91% of 128 model-dataset pairs (Vela et al., 2022). Models that worked when deployed became less reliable over time. In that experiment, decay was the observed default.

Generative AI has its own freshness problem. Knowledge cutoffs vary by model and vendor, and a model may present outdated information with the same confidence as a current fact. Grounding gives the model access to current sources, but teams still need to test whether those sources improve accuracy for the task at hand.

For training data, freshness has two components. Temporal validity asks whether the data reflects the conditions or behavior the system needs to handle now rather than six months ago. Behavioral currency asks whether examples rely on deprecated APIs or outdated procedures. If fine-tuning examples reflect last year's customer-service protocol after that protocol changes, the model may reproduce outdated steps unless evaluation and controls catch the mismatch.

For inference data, freshness varies by data form. Raw-signal capture and update times must meet the use case's tolerance. Structured facts require appropriate event time, valid time, synchronization, and processing latency. Business context must reflect effective policies, definitions, ownership, and exceptions. Action specifications must reflect current permissions, tool state, constraints, and workflow rules.

Traceable: Can Its Origin and Changes Be Explained?

Traceability is where data quality meets governance, compliance, and trust. For high-risk AI systems within scope, Article 10 of Regulation (EU) 2024/1689 establishes requirements for training, validation, and testing data and related governance; Article 12 requires automatic event-logging capability; and Article 17 requires providers to maintain a quality-management system. Regulation (EU) 2026/1744 was published on 24 July 2026, and Article 4 provides that it enters into force on the third day following publication. Article 1(40) sets the application dates for Chapter III, Sections 1, 2, and 3, except Article 6(5), at 2 December 2027 for systems classified as high-risk under Article 6(2) and Annex III, and 2 August 2028 for systems classified as high-risk under Article 6(1) and Annex I (European Parliament and Council of the European Union, 2024; 2026). Classification, exceptions, transitional provisions, later amendments, and other applicable law can affect a particular system. This summary is not legal advice.

Without traceability, teams have less evidence for verifying an output, reconstructing the data path, or investigating a failure. Traceability can improve verification and incident response; it does not by itself prevent hallucinations.

Dahl et al. executed more than 800,000 legal queries, more than 200,000 per model, and found hallucination rates ranging from 58% to 88% (Dahl et al., 2024). Purpose-built legal AI tools didn't eliminate the problem. Westlaw's AI-Assisted Research hallucinated in one-third of its responses (Magesh et al., 2025). In an adversarial clinical study, models repeated or elaborated on planted false details in 64.1% of longer case summaries under the default prompt (Omar et al., 2025).

These numbers should worry anyone deploying AI in regulated industries. Grounding AI outputs in traceable, citable sources makes claims easier to verify. It doesn't guarantee correctness, and its effect on hallucination rates has to be measured for each model and task. A fivefold reduction shouldn't be generalized across models without task-specific evidence.

Data lineage, the documented record of where data came from, how it was transformed, and where it flows, is an operational foundation for traceability. It can shorten incident response by showing investigators where to start and which transformations to inspect. Without adequate lineage, teams may have to reconstruct the data path manually; with it, they can follow the recorded path and verify where evidence is complete or missing.

For training data, traceability means documented provenance (do you know where each example came from?), compliance verification (has the data been reviewed for PII, copyright issues, and policy compliance?), and curation documentation (can you trace how the dataset was curated?). For synthetic data, this includes documenting the generation process itself: which model generated the data, what prompts were used, and what filtering criteria were applied.

For inference data, traceability varies by data form. Raw signals need recorded source, capture time, collection conditions, and transformations. Structured facts need lineage, versions, transformations, and evidence that connect records to their sources. Business context needs documented authority, provenance, ownership, effective dates, and changes. Action specifications need auditable inputs, decisions, approvals, tool calls, outcomes, and recovery events.

CRAFT and Open Infrastructure

CRAFT describes the data qualities to manage. Infrastructure choices affect how costly those qualities are to maintain. Proprietary formats or interfaces can make metadata exchange, cross-system validation, timely movement, and portable audit evidence harder. Open formats, APIs, and lineage standards can reduce those frictions when they are implemented consistently. They don't remove the need for governance, testing, monitoring, or vendor-specific integration.

This is why the open data infrastructure introduced in Chapter 1 matters for CRAFT. Open standards and interfaces can reduce switching costs and make controls easier to reuse across compatible systems. Their value depends on implementation quality, ecosystem support, and operational discipline. The rest of this book applies the CRAFT framework to each data form and shows where open infrastructure can help.

CRAFT as a Diagnostic Tool

Knowing the framework and applying it are different things. CRAFT works as a diagnostic tool when you score each dimension for a specific data asset. Table 4.4 presents the five questions to ask.

Table 4.4 Diagnostic Questions for Each CRAFT Dimension

CRAFT Dimension	Diagnostic Question
Complete	Is required data present?
Retrievable	Can the system find and access it?
Accurate	Does it represent the intended meaning?
Fresh	Is it current enough for the use case?
Traceable	Can its origin and changes be explained?

A simple 1-to-5 scale can start the assessment, but each score should be tied to defined criteria and documented evidence. Higher-impact uses may require more formal measurement, independent review, or continuous monitoring.

Consider the example of assessing a customer database that will power a Generative AI assistant for your sales team. The scoring of each dimension could result in the following:

Complete: 3/5. Entity resolution is incomplete. In this hypothetical assessment, duplicate customer records across CRM and billing systems mean the AI may see two profiles for the same company. Assume that parent-subsidiary links are missing for about 40% of accounts. The number is illustrative, but the diagnosis is real: incomplete relationship data weakens entity resolution.

Retrievable: 4/5. The data is queryable via SQL and your BI tools can access it. A semantic layer is partially implemented, covering the top 20 metrics, but many fields still require tribal knowledge to interpret. An AI system could find the data, but it might misunderstand what it found.

Accurate: 3/5. Several critical fields use cryptic abbreviations that made sense to the team that created them 10 years ago. Business rules about what counts as an "active" customer versus a "churned" one live in someone's head, not in the data. An AI system may infer a definition from the available context, and that interpretation may not match the organization's intended rule.

Fresh: 2/5. There's no point-in-time query capability, so the AI can't answer "what did this customer's profile look like last month?" Temporal integrity is weak. Records get updated in place with no history. Data from integrated systems arrives on different schedules, so the CRM might show a deal as open while billing already recorded the payment.

Traceable: 4/5. Good news here. Field-level documentation exists. Data lineage is tracked through your transformation layer. You can trace most fields back to their source system.

The CRAFT profile for this database is 3-4-3-2-4, which suggests that freshness is the weakest dimension. Before deploying a use case that depends on timely state, investigate point-in-time capability and synchronization across source systems. Then address completeness through entity resolution and relationship enrichment, followed by accuracy through explicit semantic definitions.

This is how CRAFT turns a vague sense that data is not ready into a specific action plan. Instead of launching a generic data-quality initiative, teams can identify which dimension is weakest, for which data form and use case. That specificity helps direct effort toward the gap most likely to block deployment.

Reassess on a cadence tied to risk and change rate, and trigger a review after material changes to models, data sources, schemas, or workflows. A quarterly review may suit some critical assets, but it isn't a universal minimum. The Unity example shows why monitoring, validation, and recovery controls should detect both platform faults and training-data problems before their effects compound.

Key Principles

Three principles guide use of the CRAFT assessment framework:

- **Assess all five dimensions for each defined use case:** Evaluate all five dimensions for the data forms the use case depends on. A weak score in one dimension can create a distinct failure mode, even when the other scores are strong. Treat every material gap as a risk to investigate, then set thresholds and controls in proportion to the use case.
- **A production release remains a binary decision:** CRAFT scores are diagnostic and remain matters of degree. The release decision is still yes or no. Before production, every material dimension must meet the minimum threshold defined for the use case, or the system should not ship.
- **CRAFT supports governance; it does not replace it:** Meeting the defined CRAFT thresholds makes the data foundation easier to assess and audit. But auditable data that violates copyright law still isn't usable. Documented data that contains unmasked PII still isn't deployable. CRAFT creates the foundation. Legal review, compliance certification, and policy enforcement are separate organizational functions that operate on top of that foundation.

Looking Ahead

You now have an assessment method: evaluate complete, retrievable, accurate, fresh, and traceable data for the forms a defined use case depends on, then set use-case-specific thresholds. Meeting those thresholds describes the state of the data layer. It does not certify legal compliance or the trustworthiness of the broader AI system.

CRAFT differs from earlier data-quality frameworks because it is organized around how AI systems encode patterns, retrieve context, learn behaviors, and act through software. Human judgment still matters in design, evaluation, governance, and oversight. The framework focuses the data questions on what the system consumes and what people must be able to verify.

The rest of this book is organized around building data that meets defined CRAFT thresholds. Parts on inference data examine each of the four data forms and the CRAFT characteristics, systems, architectures, and engineering practices associated with them. The examples are implementation guidance, not universal requirements.

AI-ready data is built deliberately. Teams define the use case, assess all five CRAFT dimensions for the relevant data forms, set thresholds in proportion to impact and risk, and preserve evidence that others can review. This discipline strengthens the data layer of trustworthy AI. It does not by itself establish that the model, application, workflow, or organization is trustworthy.

References

Algan, Görkem, and Ilkay Ulusoy. "Image Classification with Deep Learning in the Presence of Noisy Labels: A Survey." *Knowledge-Based Systems*, vol. 215, 2021, article 106771. Originally circulated as arXiv:1912.05170 in 2019.

Angwin, Julia, Jeff Larson, Surya Mattu, and Lauren Kirchner. "Machine Bias." *ProPublica*, 23 May 2016.

Barnett, Scott, et al. "Seven Failure Points When Engineering a Retrieval Augmented Generation System." arXiv, 2024, arXiv:2401.05856, https://doi.org/10.48550/arXiv.2401.05856.

Buolamwini, Joy, and Timnit Gebru. "Gender Shades: Intersectional Accuracy Disparities in Commercial Gender Classification." *Proceedings of Machine Learning Research*, vol. 81, 2018, pp. 77–91. https://proceedings.mlr.press/v81/buolamwini18a.html.

CONDA Shared Task. "Data Contamination Report from the 2024 CONDA Shared Task." By Oscar Sainz et al. *Proceedings of the 1st Workshop on Data Contamination*, ACL, 2024, pp. 41–56.

Dahl, Matthew, Varun Magesh, Mirac Suzgun, and Daniel E. Ho. "Large Legal Fictions: Profiling Legal Hallucinations in Large Language Models." *Journal of Legal Analysis*, vol. 16, no. 1, 2024, pp. 64–93.

DAMA UK Working Group. "The Six Primary Dimensions for Data Quality Assessment: Defining Data Quality Dimensions." DAMA UK, Oct. 2013, https://www.dama-uk.org/resources/the-six-primary-dimensions-for-data-quality-assessment.

Dastin, Jeffrey. "Insight: Amazon Scraps Secret AI Recruiting Tool That Showed Bias Against Women." *Reuters*, 10 Oct. 2018.

European Parliament and Council of the European Union. "Regulation (EU) 2024/1689 of 13 June 2024 Laying Down Harmonised Rules on Artificial Intelligence." Official Journal of the European Union, 12 July 2024, https://eur-lex.europa.eu/eli/reg/2024/1689/oj/eng.

European Parliament and Council of the European Union. 2026. "Regulation (EU) 2026/1744 of the European Parliament and of the Council of 8 July 2026 amending Regulations (EU) 2024/1689, (EU) 2018/1139 and (EU) 2023/1230 as regards the simplification of the implementation of harmonised rules on artificial intelligence (Digital Omnibus on AI)." Official Journal of the European Union, 24 July 2026, https://eur-lex.europa.eu/eli/reg/2026/1744/oj/eng.

Fivetran and Wakefield Research. "Wakefield Research Analysis of Results for Fivetran." Research report, 2021, https://get.fivetran.com/rs/353-UTB-444/images/2021-CDL-Wakefield-Research.pdf.

ISO. ISO/IEC 25012: 2008: Software engineering — Software product Quality Requirements and Evaluation (SQuaRE) — Data quality model. International Organization for Standardization, 2008. https://www.iso.org/standard/35736.html.

Javaheripi, Mojan, and Sébastien Bubeck. "Phi-2: The Surprising Power of Small Language Models." *Microsoft Research*, 12 Dec. 2023.

Kalai, Adam Tauman, Ofir Nachum, Santosh S. Vempala, and Edwin Zhang. "Why Language Models Hallucinate." *arXiv*, 2025, arXiv:2509.04664.

Klie, Jan-Christoph, Richard Eckart de Castilho, and Iryna Gurevych. "Analyzing Dataset Annotation Quality Management in the Wild." *Computational Linguistics*, vol. 50, no. 3, 2024, pp. 817–866.

Magesh, Varun, Faiz Surani, Matthew Dahl, Mirac Suzgun, Christopher D. Manning, and Daniel E. Ho. "Hallucination-Free? Assessing the Reliability of Leading AI Legal Research Tools." *Journal of Empirical Legal Studies*, vol. 22, no. 2, 2025, pp. 216–242. https://doi.org/10.1111/jels.12413.

McKinsey & Company. "The State of AI in Early 2024: Gen AI Adoption Spikes and Starts to Generate Value." *McKinsey*, 2024. https://www.mckinsey.com/capabilities/quantumblack/our-insights/the-state-of-ai-2024.

National Institute of Standards and Technology. Artificial Intelligence Risk Management Framework (AI RMF 1.0). NIST AI 100-1, 26 Jan. 2023, https://doi.org/10.6028/NIST.AI.100-1.

Omar, Mahmud, et al. "Multi-Model Assurance Analysis Showing Large Language Models Are Highly Vulnerable to Adversarial Hallucination Attacks During Clinical Decision Support." *Communications Medicine*, vol. 5, 2025, article 330.

Penedo, Guilherme, et al. "The FineWeb Datasets: Decanting the Web for the Finest Text Data at Scale." arXiv, 2024, arXiv:2406.17557, https://doi.org/10.48550/arXiv.2406.17557.

Portes, Jacob, et al. "Improving Retrieval and RAG with Embedding Model Finetuning." *Databricks Blog*, 20 Feb. 2025, https://www.databricks.com/blog/improving-retrieval-and-rag-embedding-model-finetuning.

Redman, Thomas C. "Seizing Opportunity in Data Quality." *MIT Sloan Management Review*, 2017. https://sloanreview.mit.edu/article/seizing-opportunity-in-data-quality/.

S&P Global Market Intelligence. "Generative AI Experiences Rapid Adoption, but with Mixed Outcomes – Highlights from VotE: AI & Machine Learning." 30 May 2025, https://www.spglobal.com/market-intelligence/en/news-insights/research/ai-experiences-rapid-adoption-but-with-mixed-outcomes-highlights-from-vote-ai-machine-learning.

Sajith, Aryan, and Krishna Chaitanya Rao Kathala. "Is Training Data Quality or Quantity More Impactful to Small Language Model Performance?" *arXiv*, 2024, arXiv:2411.15821.

Sen, Priyanka, et al. "Knowledge Graph-Augmented Language Models for Complex Question Answering." *Amazon Science*, 2023.

Splunk. "The State of Dark Data." 2019.

Unity Software Inc. "1Q22 Prepared Remarks." 10 May 2022, pp. 1–2. https://s205.q4cdn.com/200788659/files/doc_events/2022/05/Q1-2022-Prepared-Remarks.pdf. See also "Unity Announces First Quarter 2022 Financial Results," 10 May 2022. https://investors.unity.com/news/news-details/2022/Unity-Announces-First-Quarter-2022-Financial-Results/default.aspx; and 2022 Annual Report (Form 10-K), U.S. Securities and Exchange Commission, 27 Feb. 2023, https://www.sec.gov/Archives/edgar/data/1810806/000181080623000016/unity-20221231.htm.

Vela, Daniel, et al. "Temporal Quality Degradation in AI Models." *Scientific Reports*, vol. 12, 2022, article 11654.

Wang, Richard Y., and Diane M. Strong. "Beyond Accuracy: What Data Quality Means to Data Consumers." *Journal of Management Information Systems*, vol. 12, no. 4, 1996, pp. 5–33. https://doi.org/10.1080/07421222.1996.11518099.

Yang, Feng, et al. "Assessing Inter-Annotator Agreement for Medical Image Segmentation." *IEEE Access*, vol. 11, 2023, pp. 21300–21312.

Zhou, Chunting, et al. "LIMA: Less Is More for Alignment." arXiv, 2023. arXiv:2305.11206. https://arxiv.org/abs/2305.11206.

Chapter 5
CRAFT, Ethics, Privacy, and Compliance

By now you understand the framework's technical spine. CRAFT provides five questions for assessing the data layer. Open data infrastructure provides patterns for moving and governing data. Ethics, privacy, security, and legal compliance are separate operating constraints:

- Ethics
- Privacy
- Compliance

An AI system built on strong data and open infrastructure can still be unsafe, unfair, unlawful, or unacceptable to the people it affects. Ethics, privacy, security, and legal compliance aren't CRAFT dimensions. They are operating constraints that shape how the framework is applied.

You'll see how CRAFT can reduce specific data-related risks, how completeness supports some fairness problems, how traceability and governed retrieval support privacy work, and where ethics review, security engineering, legal counsel, and regulatory processes must take over.

Risk as a Scaling Constraint

Consider a common scenario: an organization selects a promising AI use case, the technical team builds a laboratory prototype, and leadership gets excited. Then legal raises questions about training-data provenance, compliance asks how the system will be audited, and the CISO asks who can access which data. The project can enter "pilot purgatory" and stall before production.

In a vendor retrospective, ModelOp described an AI production gap in 2024, reporting a 42% shortfall between anticipated and actual AI deployments (ModelOp, 2024). BCG's 2024 survey of 1,000 C-suite and senior executives across more than 20 sectors and 59 countries found that 74% of companies had yet to show tangible value from AI and 4% had developed cutting-edge capabilities and were consistently generating significant value (BCG, 2024). These sources use different samples and measures and do not establish a single cause.

AI initiatives stall for many reasons, including unclear business value, weak data, integration cost, model limitations, security, privacy, governance, and organizational design. The cited studies don't isolate one universal cause. Teams that can't answer basic governance questions create avoidable delays and risk.

KPMG and the University of Melbourne surveyed more than 48,000 people across 47 countries between November 2024 and mid-January 2025 and found that 46% were willing to trust AI systems (KPMG and University of Melbourne, 2025). The result describes attitudes in that study; it is not a measure of deployment success. In a Google-commissioned Cloud Security Alliance online survey of 300 IT and security professionals in summer 2025, 46% of respondents from organizations with comprehensive AI-governance policies reported early Agentic AI adoption, compared with 25% among those with partial guidelines (Cloud Security Alliance and Google Cloud, 2025). The association does not establish that governance caused faster adoption.

Governance can slow a release when evidence and controls are assembled late. Built into the work, it can make responsible scaling faster.

CRAFT addresses the data evidence behind some of those concerns (see Table 5.1). It doesn't resolve the full risk.

Figure 5.1 distinguishes selected CRAFT data evidence from the broader controls each risk requires.

Table 5.1 How CRAFT Can Support Broader Risk Controls

Scaling Risk	What Happens	How CRAFT Can Contribute
Compliance uncertainty	Legal and regulatory review may delay deployment	Traceability can organize provenance and audit evidence. Accuracy checks can support reviews; neither establishes compliance.
Bias concerns	Fairness review may delay launch	Completeness checks can expose representation gaps. Separate fairness assessment and mitigation remain necessary.
Trust deficit	Users or stakeholders may decline adoption	Traceability can support source verification when the system records usable provenance. It does not establish trust or truth.
Security concerns	Security review may restrict data access	Retrieval and traceability evidence can support access-control design. Security engineering and testing remain separate.
Training data liability	Potential legal exposure from training data	Traceability can document provenance and licenses. Counsel determines lawful use.

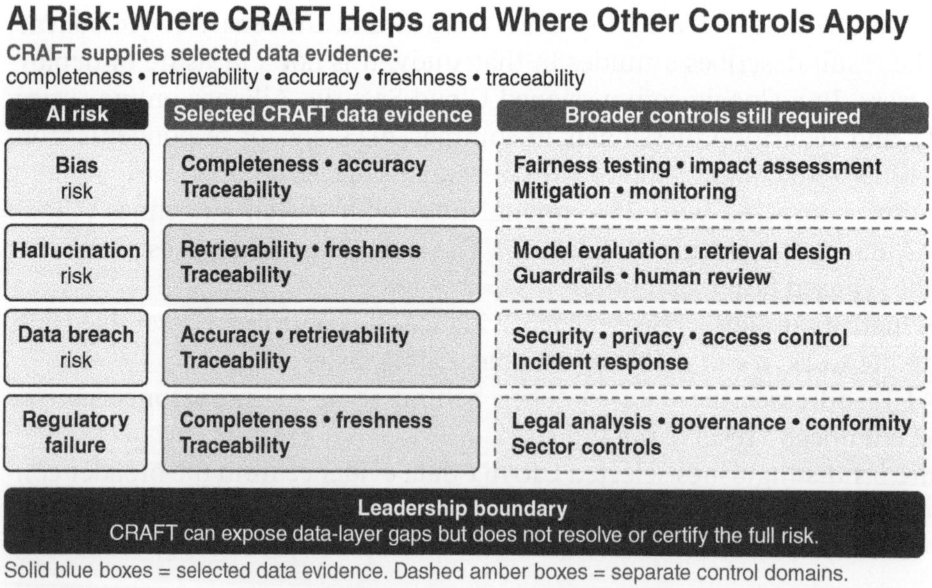

Figure 5.1 CRAFT data evidence and broader controls for selected AI risks.

Copyright and licensing questions are separate from provenance. Lineage can document where training data came from, but it does not determine whether a particular use is licensed or qualifies for a defense such as fair use. That assessment depends on the works, source, purpose, output controls, and other circumstances (U.S. Copyright Office, 2025). Counsel must evaluate authorization and applicable law.

Arion Research, an advisory firm, argues that organizations with governance infrastructure can "plug the agents into the existing governance stack and go live in days," while those without it may wait three to six months for a manual audit of each agent (Arion Research, 2026). This is a vendor perspective, not an independently measured benchmark, but the operational point is useful: governance built in advance can remove avoidable deployment friction.

CRAFT and AI Fairness

AI bias can enter through historical inequity, representation, selection, measurement, labeling, optimization, deployment, and feedback loops. Incomplete or unrepresentative data is one major source.

A 2026 review by Ahmad, Vallès, and Idaghdour identifies bias origins in four families: historical and representational, selection and measurement, algorithmic and optimization, and feedback and emergent (Ahmad et al., 2026). The authors note that "biases in training data are among the most thoroughly documented sources of algorithmic unfairness."

These cases illustrate distinct bias mechanisms rather than one shared cause. Amazon's recruiting tool learned from resumes submitted over a decade, most from men, and Reuters reported that it penalized terms associated with women (Reuters, 2018). Gender Shades found that darker-skinned women were the most misclassified group across three commercial gender classifiers, with error rates as high as 34.7%, while the maximum for lighter-skinned men was 0.8% (Buolamwini and Gebru, 2018). ProPublica reported unequal COMPAS error rates in Broward County, including a false-positive rate for Black defendants nearly twice that for white defendants (Angwin et al., 2016).

Obermeyer et al. (2019) found substantial racial bias in a widely used health-management algorithm because healthcare cost was used as a proxy for health need. In a counterfactual analysis that equalized marginal health across the program threshold, the share of Black patients selected rose from 17.7% to 46.5%. A separate predictor trained on chronic-condition counts placed 26.7% of patients in the highest-risk group as Black, versus 14.1% under the original cost-based predictor. These are distinct analyses, not a general guarantee that a proxy change will improve outcomes.

Across five commercial speech-recognition systems and the study's speech sample, Koenecke et al. (2020) observed average word error rates of 35% for Black speakers and 19% for white speakers. In a resume-ranking simulation using massive text-embedding models, Wilson and Caliskan (2024) reported statistically significant preference for white-associated names in 85.1% of cases.

When representation or measurement is the mechanism, better data can reduce disparities (see Table 5.2). It won't fix every fairness problem, and each intervention has to be evaluated on the affected groups and outcomes. IBM released Diversity in Faces, a one-million-image dataset annotated to support research on fairer and more accurate face-recognition systems (Merler et al., 2019). Marchesi et al. (2025) found that augmenting an underrepresented Black patient cohort with synthetic data narrowed the between-ethnicity performance gap in a sepsis blood-lactate prediction task from delta AUC 0.083 to 0.025, reported as 8% to 2% ($p = 0.0236$). These examples show how data interventions can address specific representation-related mechanisms; they do not establish fairness by themselves.

Many documented bias cases involve completeness failures, but others arise from measurement choices, optimization objectives, or unequal error distributions.

Table 5.2 Data-Layer Contributions to Fairness Review

CRAFT Characteristic	Contribution to Fairness
Representativeness (raw data)	Can reveal missing representation when demographic coverage is relevant
Entity integrity (structured data)	Can reduce duplicate or fragmented records that distort group-level analysis
Coverage (context data)	Can expose missing contextual coverage about relevant groups and topics
Task coverage (training data)	Can reveal whether training examples cover relevant scenarios
Distribution match (training data)	Can reveal over- or under-representation relative to a defined target distribution

Improving representativeness can reduce disparities when representation is the mechanism, but it is not a universal remedy.

For covered high-risk systems, Article 10 requires training, validation, and test data to be relevant, sufficiently representative, and, to the best extent possible, free of errors and complete in view of the intended purpose. The requirement is binding when the relevant high-risk-system provisions apply (Regulation (EU) 2024/1689, Article 10; Regulation (EU) 2026/1744).

CRAFT and Data Privacy

Privacy and data quality aren't enemies. They're complementary constraints. For AI privacy work, traceability and retrievability can support provenance and access evidence; governed access remains a separate control.

Traceability

GDPR Article 17 provides a right to erasure in specified circumstances and subject to exceptions. Under the CCPA, covered businesses generally must respond to verified deletion requests within 45 calendar days and may extend by another 45 days with notice (California Department of Justice, n.d.). AI systems can complicate discovery because relevant personal data may appear in training sets, vector stores, logs, and other processing records. Traceability can support location and scoping, but identity resolution, legal review, exceptions, model-unlearning decisions, and response delivery remain separate.

Financial institutions deploying AI copilots face this directly. BNY reported $52.1 trillion in assets under custody and administration in its fourth-quarter 2024 fact sheet (BNY, 2024). Solidatus, BNY's lineage-tooling vendor, separately reported that BNY built complete end-to-end lineage for three regulatory reports in under four weeks (Solidatus, 2025). The first figure comes from BNY; the lineage outcome is a vendor-reported case study.

Lineage can make deletion work more systematic, but it does not make a request simple or complete.

Retrievability

Retrievability also has to preserve access controls. FINOS states that a source's "original access control permissions, restrictions, and entitlements ... must be understood, preserved, and effectively enforced." It also warns that enforcing access controls "by merely instructing an LLM via its system prompt ... is highly unreliable, inefficient, and proven to be easily bypassable through adversarial prompting" (FINOS, 2025, MI-16).

Retrievability designed with privacy in mind means that the AI can find what it needs while respecting who should see it. That's not a limitation on retrieval quality. It's a requirement for deployable retrieval.

Data Subject Access Requests

Traceability can support data subject access requests by documenting provenance, transformation history, and some usage records. It doesn't create a complete response process by itself. Identity resolution, legal scoping, exemptions, retention rules, search coverage, secure delivery, and review still matter.

In December 2024, the Italian Garante imposed a €15 million fine on OpenAI, citing an inadequate legal basis for training-data processing, transparency failures, an unnotified data breach, and insufficient age-verification measures. In March 2026, the Court of Rome upheld OpenAI's appeal in judgment 4153/2026, and the Garante temporarily removed the underlying decision from its website (Garante per la Protezione dei Dati Personali, 2024). Separately, the Dutch Data Protection Authority fined Clearview AI €30.5 million in 2024 for unlawfully processing biometric data in a facial-recognition database built from more than 30 billion photos scraped from the internet without consent (Autoriteit Persoonsgegevens, 2024). These matters show that governance can fail even when the underlying technology works.

Privacy's Role in CRAFT

Privacy isn't a CRAFT dimension. It is a separate constraint on collection, access, documentation, use, retention, and deletion. CRAFT evidence can support those decisions, but the framework does not determine legal basis, retention periods, or permissible use.

Privacy-enhancing technologies can reduce some exposures, but their fit depends on the threat model, data, and purpose. They should not be described as satisfying privacy requirements by themselves or as CRAFT dimensions.

Well-governed data evidence can make some privacy work easier, but privacy can also require collecting less, restricting retrieval, or deleting data. Treat the objectives as coordinated, not interchangeable.

CRAFT and Regulatory Compliance

Regulation (EU) 2024/1689 entered into force on 1 August 2024, and some provisions already apply. Regulation (EU) 2026/1744 was published on 24 July 2026 and enters into force on 27 July 2026. It sets 2 December 2027 as the application date for Chapter III, Sections 1 to 3, for Article 6(2) and Annex III high-risk systems, and 2 August 2028 for Article 6(1) and Annex I high-risk systems; other provisions follow different dates. Colorado's SB 26-189, signed 14 May 2026, requires specified technical documentation, records, notices, correction rights, and meaningful human review for covered automated decision-making technology from 1 January 2027 (Colorado General Assembly, 2026). California's SB 53, approved 29 September 2025, created transparency, safety-framework, incident-reporting, and whistleblower requirements for large frontier-model developers (California State Legislature, 2025). New York City Local Law 144 continues to require annual bias audits for covered automated employment decision tools (New York City Department of Consumer and Worker Protection, n.d.).

Enforcement is not theoretical. The OpenAI and Clearview matters illustrate the legal and evidentiary questions authorities may examine, while the OpenAI appeal shows that enforcement outcomes can change through judicial review. Organizations need records and controls matched to the laws that apply.

The EU AI Act creates demanding obligations for systems within its scope, but it isn't a universal substitute for other jurisdictions. Requirements can differ on privacy, discrimination, consumer protection, sector regulation, employment, biometric data, records, and enforcement. Use the EU framework as one input, then map every deployment to the laws that actually apply.

Vendor-neutral lineage and log formats can reduce migration friction and help teams reuse evidence across platforms. Portability does not make evidence complete, satisfy a statute, or eliminate platform-specific controls.

When it comes to regulatory compliance, CRAFT provides the following:

- **Audit trails for AI systems:** For covered high-risk systems when Article 12 applies, the AI Act requires technical capability for automatic recording of events over the system's lifetime. Articles 19 and 26(6) separately require providers and deployers to retain logs under their control for a period appropriate to the intended purpose and at least six months, unless other law provides otherwise. The Regulation does not require a log of every input and output or use the term "tamper-evident." CRAFT traceability can organize selected logging evidence; it does not define statutory logging design.
- **Data lineage for assessments:** Colorado SB 26-189 does not require the impact-assessment cadence in the repealed framework. Beginning January 1, 2027, it requires developers of covered automated decision-making technology to provide technical documentation, and it requires developers and deployers to keep compliance records for at least three years. It also establishes notices, correction rights, and meaningful human review after specified adverse consequential decisions (Colorado General Assembly, 2026). Separately, Article 27 of Regulation (EU) 2024/1689 requires certain deployers to describe intended use, affected people, risks of harm, human oversight, and response measures in a fundamental-rights impact assessment. Data representativeness remains an Article 10 issue.
- **Provenance for training-content disclosure:** Article 53(1)(d) requires providers of general-purpose AI models to make public a sufficiently detailed summary of the content used for training. CRAFT traceability can help organize provenance evidence, but the statutory summary, copyright policy, and lawful-basis analysis are separate requirements.
- **Documentation supporting transparency requirements:** Stanford's Foundation Model Transparency Index found that the average developer score rose from 37 out of 100 in October 2023 to 58 out of 100 in May 2024, with several developers publishing model cards for flagship models for the first time (Stanford Center for Research on Foundation Models, 2024). CRAFT can structure selected documentation questions; it does not establish transparency compliance.

There are, however, boundaries to CRAFT:

- **Legal-basis determination:** CRAFT can document where data came from and how it was collected. It can't determine whether you have the legal right to use it. That analysis requires counsel who understands applicable lawful bases, purpose limitation, copyright, contract, and sector rules.

- **Policy enforcement:** CRAFT can ask whether authorized users can retrieve needed data, but role-based access controls, consent management, policy enforcement, and adversarial testing are separate security and privacy work.
- **Privacy engineering implementation:** CRAFT does not implement de-identification, pseudonymization, encryption, or differential privacy. When a HIPAA covered entity or business associate uses an AI tool to create, receive, maintain, or transmit electronic protected health information, the Security Rule applies to that ePHI and requires appropriate administrative, physical, and technical safeguards and a risk analysis (U.S. Department of Health and Human Services, n.d.). The Rule is technology-neutral and does not prescribe an AI-specific engineering review by name.
- **Compliance certification:** CRAFT can organize selected data evidence. ISO/IEC 42001 certification, EU AI Act conformity assessments, SOC 2 Type II examinations, and FDA reviews for regulated medical devices have their own scopes, criteria, and procedures. None is satisfied by CRAFT.

CRAFT can support compliance evidence. It doesn't guarantee compliance.

In a Fivetran-commissioned survey conducted by Redpoint Content in the first quarter of 2025 among 401 data leaders and professionals, 59% named regulatory compliance as a top challenge in managing data for AI (Fivetran, 2025).

Data quality is one part of compliance. It cannot establish compliance, and poor data can undermine it.

EU AI Act: A CRAFT Lens

If you provide, deploy, import, or distribute an AI system within the Act's scope, first determine the system category, actor role, territorial reach, and applicable date. This section examines three provisions for covered high-risk systems through a CRAFT lens:

- Article 10: Training Data Requirements
- Article 12: Automatic Logging
- Article 17: Quality Management System

Figure 5.2 shows partial overlaps, not a compliance mapping. Under Article 99, administrative fines can reach up to EUR 15 million or 3% of worldwide annual turnover for specified operator obligations, and up to EUR 35 million or 7% for

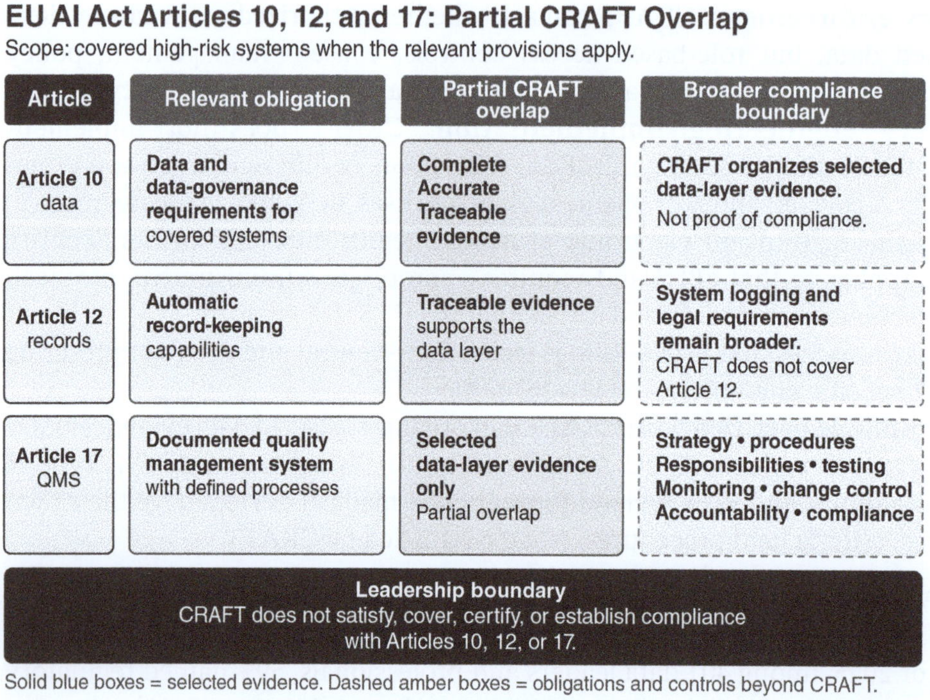

Figure 5.2 Partial overlap between selected EU AI Act obligations and CRAFT data evidence.

prohibited AI practices, subject to the Regulation's scope, infringement, and proportionality rules (Regulation (EU) 2024/1689).

Article 10: Training Data Requirements

For covered high-risk systems when Article 10 applies, paragraph 3 requires training, validation, and test datasets to be relevant, sufficiently representative, and, to the best extent possible, free of errors and complete in view of the intended purpose.

Article 10 overlaps with CRAFT questions about completeness and accuracy, but its data-governance requirements are broader. It also addresses data preparation, assumptions, availability, suitability, bias examination, gaps, and context. CRAFT does not satisfy Article 10.

Article 10 does not establish a violation for any fixed geographic split. It requires data to be sufficiently representative and to reflect the geographic, contextual, behavioral, and functional setting of the intended use (Regulation (EU) 2024/1689, Article 10(3) to (4)). An 80/20 Western Europe and rest-of-world split may be inadequate for a global deployment, but the answer depends on where the system is used and whom it serves.

Article 12: Automatic Logging

Article 12 requires high-risk AI systems to technically allow automatic recording of events over the system's lifetime. It does not set a retention period. Articles 19 and 26(6) separately require providers and deployers to retain logs under their control for a period appropriate to the intended purpose and at least six months, unless other law provides otherwise (Regulation (EU) 2024/1689).

Article 12 overlaps with traceability but is not equivalent to CRAFT. It does not require a record of every input and output or use the terms "tamper-proof" or "tamper-evident." Logging design must match the system's intended purpose and applicable legal requirements.

The Act links logging to traceability appropriate to the intended purpose and to post-market monitoring. Logging can support investigations, but it does not by itself reproduce a model decision or establish compliance.

Article 17: Quality Management System

For providers of covered high-risk systems when Article 17 applies, it requires a documented quality management system designed to ensure compliance with the Regulation. Its written policies, procedures, and instructions span activities that include regulatory strategy, design and development, testing, data management, risk management, post-market monitoring, incident reporting, communication, record management, resources, and accountability.

Article 17 overlaps with several CRAFT concerns, including data management, documentation, testing, monitoring, and change control. Its quality management system is broader than CRAFT and includes responsibilities the framework doesn't cover.

If you are deploying in Europe, CRAFT can supply part of the evidence needed for regulatory compliance. It does not replace the full quality management system, risk management, conformity assessment, human oversight, or legal analysis required by the regulation.

CRAFT Guidance: European Deployments

Most readers won't be operating only in Europe. That's fine. The legal obligations differ in the United States, but the readiness logic still holds: know what data you use, document how the system behaves, and keep evidence you can hand to counsel, compliance, and privacy teams.

If you're targeting European markets or have European users, the following sections show how selected CRAFT evidence can support regulatory preparation. They organize the work into three moments: before deployment, during deployment, and after deployment.

Pre-deployment Planning

Begin the CRAFT assessment early enough to resolve material data gaps before deployment. This is practical guidance, not a statutory deadline. Assess training and inference data separately. For training data, start with completeness. Does it represent the diversity of the target population? Are relevant geographic regions, minority classes, and operating conditions covered? Document material gaps and the rationale for accepting or remediating them.

Document traceability thoroughly. Can you identify each material source, its license or terms, and the transformations applied? Lineage can surface unlicensed scraping, unclear dataset terms, or restricted sources. It cannot establish the legal right to use data; counsel must assess copyright, data protection, contracts, exceptions, and sector rules.

Validate accuracy across relevant groups and operating conditions. Article 10 requires representative data in view of the intended purpose, but it does not establish a 5% disparity threshold or a universal audit pass mark. Any numeric threshold is an internal control choice that has to fit the system, population, and risk.

At Deployment

Implement automatic event logging before the system goes live. The level of detail should be sufficient for the system's purpose, risk, and legal obligations. Retention volume depends on what is captured and can become substantial at scale. The six-month floor, where applicable, comes from Articles 19 and 26(6), not Article 12. This is operational guidance, not a statutory countdown.

Establish lineage from source data through preparation, training, retrieval, and inference inputs. Lineage can show which datasets, transformations, model versions, prompts, retrieved records, and tools were involved. It usually can't prove which training example caused one model decision. Use separate explainability, evaluation, logging, and human-review controls when the decision requires that level of evidence.

Document retrievability controls. How are you ensuring that access to the AI's data and outputs respects GDPR and local privacy requirements? If the AI can be queried for information about individuals, how do you prevent unauthorized access? These are operational security questions that go beyond CRAFT but build on it.

Post-deployment

Monitor data and policy dependencies after deployment. Laws, guidance, population characteristics, source systems, and operating context can change. Freshness checks can identify stale inputs, while legal change management determines whether the system's design or use must change.

Set a fairness-review cadence based on impact, deployment context, population change, data drift, and legal requirements. Measure performance across relevant groups before deployment and while the system operates. Quarterly review may fit some systems, while high-impact or fast-changing systems may need more frequent monitoring and event-triggered review.

Track regulatory changes actively. The European Commission continues to publish AI Act guidance and implementation material (European Commission, 2026). Verify the official legal text and current guidance before each deployment decision; a prior review is not a continuing legal conclusion.

Organizations can reduce rework by building data evidence and controls before legal review becomes a release gate. CRAFT-conforming data can support that work, but regulatory compliance never becomes a documentation exercise alone. Legal basis, risk management, human oversight, security, conformity assessment, and sector-specific obligations still apply.

CRAFT's Boundaries

CRAFT is powerful. It's also not a magic solution. Understanding its boundaries is important. These boundaries include ethical trade-offs, legal reviews, bias elimination, and privacy by default. Let's look at each of these.

Ethical Trade-offs

A model can use CRAFT-conforming data and still make unfair, unsafe, unethical, or unlawful decisions. A credit model may have complete, accurate, fresh, retrievable, and traceable data while a proxy variable, objective function, threshold, or deployment policy creates harmful disparities.

CRAFT can help identify representation and provenance gaps, but it cannot define a fair outcome or decide whether a disparity is justified. Those decisions require explicit fairness criteria, affected-stakeholder input, domain expertise, legal review, testing, mitigation, and accountable governance.

Legal Review

Lineage can support compliance evidence but is not sufficient and may not be required in the same form for every obligation. It can document provenance; it cannot determine lawful basis, license scope, or copyright. Those questions require legal analysis.

The Italian Data Protection Authority's 2024 OpenAI decision was temporarily removed from the authority's website after a Court of Rome judgment upheld the appeal against it; the judgment was published on 18 March 2026 (Garante per la Protezione dei Dati Personali, 2024). The sequence is a reminder that regulatory findings may be contested and that data documentation does not replace legal analysis.

Bias Elimination

CRAFT can expose documented representation and provenance gaps. It can't guarantee that a team detects every bias or prove fairness to a regulator. Fairness testing, impact assessment, mitigation, and monitoring remain separate work. NIST AI RMF 1.0 likewise treats fairness-related harms within a broader voluntary risk-management process; it is guidance, not a legal standard (NIST, 2023).

CRAFT supports fairness work. It doesn't define fairness, and it isn't sufficient to establish it.

Privacy by Default

You still need privacy engineering. Depending on the use case, that may include encryption, access control, data minimization, de-identification, differential privacy, federated approaches, retention controls, and secure deletion. Each technique has limits. Federated learning can reduce centralized data movement, but model updates and metadata can still create privacy risk. De-identification can reduce identifiability, but it doesn't guarantee anonymity or preserve utility in every case.

Where an AI system carries out large-scale profiling or automated decisions with legal or similarly significant effects, GDPR Article 35 may require a Data Protection Impact Assessment before processing begins. CRAFT can help structure the data and traceability analysis, but it is an internal framework, not a legal instrument.

CRAFT can support AI governance. It is not sufficient, and it is not a legal requirement or a substitute for another governance system.

Teams can use CRAFT for data-quality and provenance questions while retaining separate ethics, legal, privacy, security, and policy controls. This division of responsibilities can make reviews clearer without promising faster approval or deployment.

CRAFT and the Bottleneck Problem

Teams can often build a working AI prototype faster than they can assemble the governance evidence needed for production. Legal wants data documentation, compliance wants audit trails, privacy wants proof of access controls, and the model can sit idle while teams reconstruct evidence.

That is the governance bottleneck: teams reconstruct provenance, audit trails, and access-control evidence after the fact. Earlier governance work can reduce that rework, but there is no defensible universal deployment-speed benchmark.

Building CRAFT-conforming data early can reduce the evidence reconstruction that creates governance bottlenecks. It doesn't guarantee that documentation, lineage, access controls, or legal approvals are complete. Those controls must be designed, tested, and maintained.

That difference can determine whether a useful system ships on schedule or waits while teams reconstruct evidence.

Looking Ahead

You now have the full picture of how CRAFT intersects with concerns that shape whether AI initiatives reach production. CRAFT can surface selected data-layer risks and organize evidence. Completeness can support some representation-related fairness work. Traceability and governed retrieval can support privacy and compliance processes. None of the five dimensions establishes fairness, privacy, security, legality, or trust.

Organizations that build this evidence early can make reviews faster and more predictable. The result depends on the system, the controls, and the obligations that apply.

You'll give legal, privacy, security, ethics, and governance teams better evidence for their decisions. Some initiatives will still need to change, narrow their scope, or stop.

The goal isn't automatic trust. It's evidence strong enough to decide where trust is warranted.

References

Ahmad, Amar, Yvonne Vallès, and Youssef Idaghdour. "Bias in AI Systems: Integrating Formal and Socio-technical Approaches." Frontiers in Big Data, vol. 8, 2025, article 1686452. https://doi.org/10.3389/fdata.2025.1686452.

Angwin, Julia, Jeff Larson, Surya Mattu, and Lauren Kirchner. "Machine Bias." ProPublica, 23 May 2016. https://www.propublica.org/article/machine-bias-risk-assessments-in-criminal-sentencing.

Arion Research. "Governance as a Competitive Advantage: Why the Safest Companies Will Be the Fastest." Arion Research Blog, March 2026. https://arionresearch.com/blog/governance-as-a-competitive-advantage-why-the-safest-companies-will-be-the-fastest.

Autoriteit Persoonsgegevens. "Dutch DPA Imposes a Fine on Clearview Because of Illegal Data Collection for Facial Recognition." 3 September 2024. https://www.autoriteitpersoonsgegevens.nl/en/current/dutch-dpa-imposes-a-fine-on-clearview-because-of-illegal-data-collection-for-facial-recognition.

BNY. "At a Glance: 4Q24 Corporate Fact Sheet." BNY, 2024. https://www.bny.com/assets/corporate/documents/pdf/newsroom/at-a-glance-corporate-fact-sheet-4Q24.pdf.

Boston Consulting Group. "AI Adoption in 2024: 74% of Companies Struggle to Achieve and Scale Value." BCG, 24 October 2024. https://www.bcg.com/press/24october2024-ai-adoption-in-2024-74-of-companies-struggle-to-achieve-and-scale-value.

Buolamwini, Joy, and Timnit Gebru. "Gender Shades: Intersectional Accuracy Disparities in Commercial Gender Classification." Proceedings of Machine Learning Research, vol. 81, 2018, pp. 77–91. https://proceedings.mlr.press/v81/buolamwini18a.html.

California Department of Justice. "California Consumer Privacy Act (CCPA)." Office of the Attorney General, n.d. https://oag.ca.gov/privacy/ccpa.

California State Legislature. "SB-53 Artificial Intelligence Models: Large Developers." Chapter 138, approved 29 September 2025. https://leginfo.legislature.ca.gov/faces/billNavClient.xhtml?bill_id=202520260SB53.

Cloud Security Alliance and Google Cloud. "The State of AI Security and Governance." CSA, December 2025. https://cloudsecurityalliance.org/artifacts/the-state-of-ai-security-and-governance.

Colorado General Assembly. "SB26-189 Automated Decision-Making Technology." Signed 14 May 2026. https://www.leg.colorado.gov/bills/SB26-189.

European Commission. "AI Act." Shaping Europe's Digital Future, updated 11 May 2026. https://digital-strategy.ec.europa.eu/en/policies/regulatory-framework-ai. Unversioned rolling page. Accessed 27 July 2026.

European Union. "Regulation (EU) 2024/1689 of the European Parliament and of the Council of 13 June 2024 Laying Down Harmonised Rules on Artificial Intelligence." Official Journal of the European Union, 12 July 2024. https://eur-lex.europa.eu/legal-content/EN/TXT/?uri=CELEX:32024R1689.

European Parliament and Council of the European Union. 2026. "Regulation (EU) 2026/1744 of the European Parliament and of the Council of 8 July 2026 amending Regulations (EU) 2024/1689, (EU) 2018/1139 and (EU) 2023/1230 as regards the simplification of the implementation of harmonised rules on artificial intelligence (Digital Omnibus on AI)." Official Journal of the European Union, 24 July 2026. https://eur-lex.europa.eu/eli/reg/2026/1744/oj/eng.

FINOS. "Preserving Source Data Access Controls in AI Systems (MI-16)." AI Governance Framework, version 1, June 2025. https://air-governance-framework.finos.org/mitigations/mi-16_preserving-source-data-access-controls-in-ai-systems.html. Version 1 (June 2025) is the edition cited; the framework now labels this mitigation AIR-DET-016. Accessed 27 July 2026.

Fivetran. "Fivetran Report Finds Nearly Half of Enterprise AI Projects Fail Due to Poor Data Readiness." 13 May 2025. https://www.fivetran.com/press/fivetran-report-finds-nearly-half-of-enterprise-ai-projects-fail-due-to-poor-data-readiness.

Garante per la Protezione dei Dati Personali. 2024. "Provvedimento del 2 novembre 2024 [10085455]." Status notice reports Court of Rome judgment No. 4153/2026, published 18 March 2026. https://garanteprivacy.it/web/guest/home/docweb/-/docweb-display/docweb/10085455. Accessed 25 July 2026.

Koenecke, Allison, et al. "Racial Disparities in Automated Speech Recognition." Proceedings of the National Academy of Sciences, vol. 117, no. 14, 2020, pp. 7684–7689. https://doi.org/10.1073/pnas.1915768117.

KPMG and University of Melbourne. "Trust, Attitudes and Use of Artificial Intelligence: A Global Study 2025." KPMG, May 2025. https://kpmg.com/xx/en/our-insights/ai-and-technology/trust-attitudes-and-use-of-ai.html.

Marchesi, Raffaele, et al. "Generative AI Mitigates Representation Bias and Improves Model Fairness through Synthetic Health Data." PLOS Computational Biology, 2025. https://doi.org/10.1371/journal.pcbi.1013080.

Merler, Michele, et al. "Diversity in Faces." arXiv, 29 January 2019, arXiv:1901.10436. https://arxiv.org/abs/1901.10436.

ModelOp. "AI Governance Unwrapped: Insights from 2024 and Goals for 2025." ModelOp, 2024. https://modelop.com/good-decisions-series/ai-governance-unwrapped-insights-from-2024-and-goals-for-2025.

National Institute of Standards and Technology. Artificial Intelligence Risk Management Framework (AI RMF 1.0). NIST AI 100-1, 26 January 2023. https://doi.org/10.6028/NIST.AI.100-1.

New York City Department of Consumer and Worker Protection. "Automated Employment Decision Tools." n.d. https://www.nyc.gov/site/dca/about/automated-employment-decision-tools.page.

Obermeyer, Ziad, et al. "Dissecting Racial Bias in an Algorithm Used to Manage the Health of Populations." Science, vol. 366, no. 6464, 2019, pp. 447–453. https://doi.org/10.1126/science.aax2342.

Reuters. "Amazon Scraps Secret AI Recruiting Tool That Showed Bias Against Women." 10 October 2018. https://www.reuters.com/article/world/insight-amazon-scraps-secret-ai-recruiting-tool-that-showed-bias-against-women-idUSKCN1MK0AG/.

Solidatus. "Why Data Lineage Is Essential for AI: 7 Governance Challenges Solved by AI-Ready Lineage." Solidatus, 2025. https://www.solidatus.com/blog/why-data-lineage-is-essential-for-ai-7-governance-challenges-solved-by-ai-ready-lineage/.

Stanford Center for Research on Foundation Models. "The Foundation Model Transparency Index after 6 months." 21 May 2024. https://crfm.stanford.edu/2024/05/21/fmti-may-2024.html.

U.S. Copyright Office. 2025. Copyright and Artificial Intelligence, Part 3: Generative AI Training. Pre-Publication Version, May 2025. https://www.copyright.gov/ai/Copyright-and-Artificial-Intelligence-Part-3-Generative-AI-Training-Report-Pre-Publication-Version.pdf. Accessed 25 July 2026.

U.S. Department of Health and Human Services. "The Security Rule." HHS, n.d. https://www.hhs.gov/hipaa/for-professionals/security/index.html.

Wilson, Kyra, and Aylin Caliskan. "Gender, Race, and Intersectional Bias in Resume Screening via Language Model Retrieval." AAAI/ACM Conference on AI, Ethics, and Society, 2024. https://arxiv.org/abs/2407.20371.

Chapter 6
Framework Summary

This chapter is a reference map for the framework introduced so far and the data-level concepts developed in Chapters 7 through 14. It brings together the four AI capability categories, the four formal data levels, and CRAFT's five assessment dimensions. Ethics, privacy, legal obligations, security, fairness, and model validation remain separate requirements that shape which checks and thresholds a use case needs. CRAFT doesn't certify compliance or end-to-end system readiness.

What follows is a reference you can use when diagnosing an AI problem, planning an initiative, or explaining to leadership how data readiness and model fit affect the decision. Use it as a map, then follow the chapter references for implementation detail.

These summary tables consolidate concepts from across the book, including terms defined in detail in Chapters 7 through 14. If you're reading sequentially, bookmark this chapter and return to it as you work through the data-level chapters. If you're looking up a specific concept, the tables will point you to the right chapter.

The Complete Framework at a Glance

Table 6.1 summarizes the book's four AI capability categories and their usual primary data dependency. The primary dependency is the data level most directly consumed by the use case. Supporting dependencies vary with the workflow, architecture, risk, evidence, governance, and control needs. Better data can improve system performance, but it doesn't eliminate the need to choose and evaluate a model that fits the use case.

Table 6.2 summarizes CRAFT's five assessment dimensions. Teams apply the dimensions to the data levels, inference inputs, and training data relevant to a defined use case, then set measurable thresholds for the checks they select. A missed requirement creates risk when the use case depends on it. CRAFT itself isn't a pass/fail certification.

Table 6.3 separates two ways systems use data. Inference uses data at runtime, while training uses data to train, fine-tune, or align models. The book organizes these uses through a 26-characteristic inference matrix and a 16-characteristic

Table 6.1 The Data-AI Map

Capability	Perception AI	Analytical AI	Generative AI	Agentic AI
Primary data	Raw data	Structured data	Context data	Action data
Core function	Signal → structure	Structure → insight	Context → content	Intent → action

Table 6.2 The CRAFT Assessment Dimensions

Dimension	The Question It Answers	What Happens Without It
Complete	Is everything present?	Blind spots, bias, partial capability
Retrievable	Can AI find and use it?	Wasted assets, the AI can't access what it needs
Accurate	Does it represent truth?	Wrong outputs, compounded errors
Fresh	Is it current?	Stale answers, outdated actions, temporal confusion
Traceable	Can we trust and oversee it?	Weak oversight, unsupported outputs, or missing recovery evidence

Table 6.3 CRAFT Assessment Scope

Use	What It Covers	CRAFT Application
Inference	Data consumed at runtime (raw, structured, context, action)	26 inference characteristics across the four formal data levels
Training	Data used to train, fine-tune, or align models	16 training-data characteristics across five CRAFT dimensions

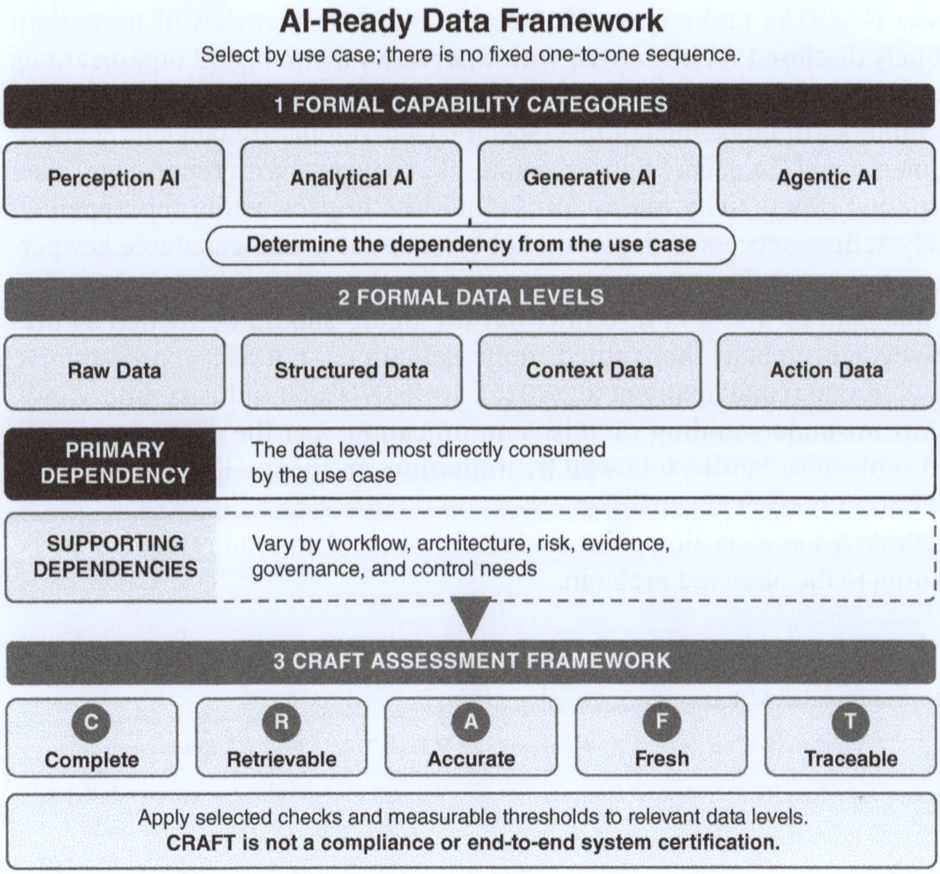

Figure 6.1 The AI-ready data framework and selective dependency model.

training matrix. These matrices are assessment aids, not claims that they exhaust every way an AI system can consume data.

Figure 6.1 summarizes the framework and its use-case-specific dependency model in one view.

Diagnostic Reference: How to Fix Your Bottleneck

When an AI system underperforms, teams may reach first for visible changes such as swapping models, rewriting prompts, or adjusting hyperparameters. Those changes can help, but teams should also test whether the data supporting the use case meets the required thresholds.

Project NANDA's preliminary 2025 report combined a review of more than 300 publicly disclosed AI initiatives with interviews involving 52 organizations and responses from 153 senior leaders. In its directional, interview-based deployment exhibit, 5% of embedded or task-specific GenAI tools are labeled "successfully implemented." A page-7 note associates that category with reported marked and sustained productivity and/or profit-and-loss impact, while the appendix separately defines success as deployment beyond pilot with measurable key performance indicators. The report doesn't reconcile those definitions. It describes the complement as a 95% failure rate, but the figure should be treated as preliminary evidence about the studied implementations, not as a representative market-wide rate (Challapally et al., 2025). In RAND's 50 industry interviews, leadership misunderstanding or miscommunication was the most frequently reported root-cause family, followed by limitations in the quality and utility of training data (Ryseff et al., 2024).

Use Table 6.4 as a starting point for testing which data requirements may be contributing to the observed problem.

Table 6.4 Common CRAFT Diagnostic Signals and Responses to Test

If You See	Possible Gap	At This Level	Check This	A Response to Test
"I don't have information about that"	Retrievability gap	Context	Embeddings, chunking, semantic layer	Improve embedding quality and retrieval strategy
Confidently wrong answers	Accuracy gap	Structured	Field definitions, business rules	Document semantic clarity explicitly
Outdated information	Freshness gap	Context or action	Refresh pipelines, tool schemas	Build continuous update infrastructure
Plausible hallucinations	Traceability gap	Context or structured	Source attribution, provenance	Ground outputs in citable sources
Works on common cases, fails on others	Completeness gap	Raw or context	Coverage audits, representation	Make sure all scenarios are represented
Model underperforms in production	Multiple gaps (training)	Training data	Task coverage, annotations, provenance	Assess the CRAFT dimensions and training-data checks the use case requires

Table 6.4 is a diagnostic aid, not a causal test. Start with the observed symptom, then examine the CRAFT dimension and data level most relevant to the use case. Also test model fit, prompts, orchestration, infrastructure, and operating conditions when the evidence points there.

The Four Failure Modes

Chapter 2 introduced four recurring production failure patterns. Table 6.5 maps each pattern to one CRAFT-related hypothesis and a data area to examine. The mapping doesn't prove a single cause or prescribe a universal remedy.

The failure modes in Table 6.5 can overlap. A team may find more than one gap, but the relationships aren't automatic. Traceability and accuracy problems can occur together, and action data completeness can depend on context data coverage when the use case consumes that context. Treat each connection as a hypothesis to test.

Table 6.5 Failure Diagnostics

Failure Mode	What You See	CRAFT Gap	Data Layer	What to Test
Retrieval miss	"I don't have information about that"	Retrievable	Context	Embedding quality, chunking strategy, semantic layer coverage
Context void	AI misunderstands what data means	Accurate	Structured	Semantic clarity, field definitions, business rule documentation
Grounding failure	Plausible-sounding hallucinations	Traceable	Context + structured	Source attribution, provenance tracking, groundability
Action gap	"I can't do that" for automatable tasks	Complete	Action	Tool specifications, parameter definitions, workflow coverage

Use Table 6.5 to form a testable diagnosis. Identify the observed failure pattern, assess the relevant CRAFT dimensions and data levels, and compare the evidence with other plausible causes, including model fit, prompts, orchestration, infrastructure, and operating conditions. The response should target the requirement that falls below a use-case-specific threshold, not assume that changing either the model or the data will always solve the problem.

The 26-characteristic Matrix for Inference

Table 6.6 organizes 26 inference characteristics across five CRAFT dimensions and four formal data levels. These 26 characteristics are specific assessment checks. They don't replace the five dimensions or the 20 dimension-by-level cells.

Each cell in Table 6.6 identifies a place where a use case may need a defined requirement and threshold. A missed requirement can contribute to failure when the system depends on it. The matrix doesn't establish that every cell is relevant to every implementation.

Table 6.6 The 26 Inference Characteristics

CRAFT Dimension	Raw Data	Structured Data	Context Data	Action Data
Complete	Consistency, representativeness	Entity integrity, relational completeness	Coverage	Completeness
Retrievable	Accessibility	Computational accessibility	Retrievability, dual accessibility	Discoverability
Accurate	Fidelity	Semantic clarity	Semantic fidelity, coherence	Precision
Fresh	Temporal alignment	Temporal integrity	Freshness	Currency
Traceable	Provenance	Documentation	Groundability	Safety, observability, recoverability

The 16-characteristic Matrix for Training Data

Training data uses the same five CRAFT dimensions, expressed through 16 training-data characteristics. Table 6.7 summarizes those characteristics. They are a separate assessment view from the 26 inference characteristics, not additions to the four formal data levels or the 20 dimension-by-level cells.

The Selective Data Dependency Map

AI capabilities have a usual primary data dependency, but supporting dependencies are use-case specific. They depend on the workflow, architecture, risk, evidence, governance, and control needs. Teams can build required levels in parallel, and a missing level creates risk only when the selected use case consumes or relies on it. Table 6.8 gives examples to test, not a mandatory sequence.

Table 6.7 CRAFT Training Data Characteristics

CRAFT Dimension	Training Data Characteristics
Complete	Task coverage, representativeness, deduplication
Retrievable	Pipeline accessibility, versioning, iterability
Accurate	Behavioral alignment, annotation consistency, factual correctness, contamination control
Fresh	Temporal validity, behavioral currency, refresh cadence
Traceable	Provenance, policy and rights evidence, curation documentation

Table 6.8 Illustrative Primary and Supporting Data Dependencies

Capability	Primary Data	Illustrative Supporting Dependencies
Perception AI	Raw data	Use-case specific; no additional dependency is assumed
Analytical AI	Structured data	May include raw data for features or context data for governed meaning
Generative AI	Context data	May include structured data for grounding or raw data for multimodal inputs
Agentic AI	Action data	May include context data, structured data, operational state, or raw data

Primary dependency identifies the data level most directly consumed by the use case. Supporting dependencies identify other data levels, state, evidence, or controls that the selected design actually needs.

Building Blocks Checklist

Use this checklist before an AI launch or major release decision. For each item, record the accountable owner, evidence, threshold, trade-off, and measure of readiness. The aim is to test whether the selected data and controls can support the capability, not to force every initiative through the same sequence.

- ☐ **Capability decision:** Which formal capability category is primary for this use case: perception AI, analytical AI, generative AI, or agentic AI?
- ☐ **Primary data assessment:** Has the team selected the required CRAFT checks, defined measurable thresholds, and evaluated the primary data level against them?
- ☐ **Supporting dependencies:** Which additional data levels, operational state, evidence, permissions, or controls does this use case actually require, and do they meet the selected thresholds?
- ☐ **Governance foundation:** Do we have audit trails, lineage tracking, and access controls documented?
- ☐ **Privacy architecture:** Are privacy requirements incorporated into retrievability and traceability?
- ☐ **Fairness assessment:** Have we audited completeness for representativeness across relevant demographics?
- ☐ **Infrastructure portability:** Have we defined the formats, interfaces, ownership, interoperability, and migration evidence needed to limit proprietary coupling? Open Data Infrastructure doesn't eliminate adapters, semantic compatibility work, security, or migration cost.

Looking Ahead

This chapter has assembled the book's reference map: four formal data levels, five CRAFT dimensions, the 20 dimension-by-level assessment cells, 26 inference characteristics, and 16 training-data characteristics. The six-characteristic raw data and structured data profiles are level-specific views introduced in their own chapters; they don't change those book-wide counts. Apply the framework only to the data levels and checks the selected use case needs. Ethics, privacy, legal obligations, security, fairness, and model validation remain separate requirements. CRAFT can organize relevant data evidence, but it doesn't certify compliance or end-to-end system readiness.

The coming chapters take this from theory to practice. They focus on one data level at a time and follow the same structure:

- **Raw data** focuses on source signals used by perception AI and other workloads. The chapter explains completeness for image capture, retrievability for large unstructured collections, and fidelity for sensor data.
- **Structured data** focuses on typed entities, attributes, measures, events, and relationships used by analytical AI and other workloads. The chapter covers entity integrity, semantic clarity, temporal integrity, and documentation.
- **Context data** focuses on governed meaning and retrieved evidence used by generative AI and other capabilities. The chapter covers vector embeddings, knowledge graphs, semantic layers, chunking, and indexing.
- **Action data** focuses on tool, policy, and workflow specifications used by agentic AI and other systems that act. The chapter covers tool definitions, parameter schemas, constraints, permissions, approvals, recovery paths, and orchestration.

Each data-level chapter follows a common rhythm: define the level, identify the CRAFT checks relevant to it, and show implementation patterns for meeting use-case-specific thresholds.

The 26-characteristic inference matrix is one roadmap for the data-level chapters. Each characteristic receives implementation context, but a given project uses only the characteristics its selected use case and risk profile require.

The practical question is now narrower: which data levels and CRAFT checks does this use case require, what thresholds will leadership approve, and what evidence will show that the release criteria are met? Apply the framework to inference, training, or both as the design requires. Don't assume that every capability uses every level.

How do you build it?

That's where we're headed.

References

Challapally, Aditya, Chris Pease, Ramesh Raskar, and Pradyumna Chari. "The GenAI Divide: State of AI in Business 2025." Preliminary findings, Project NANDA, July 2025. Archived official-origin report, https://web.archive.org/web/20250818145714id_/https://nanda.media.mit.edu/ai_report_2025.pdf. Current Project NANDA overview, https://www.media.mit.edu/groups/nanda/overview/.

Ryseff, James, Brandon F. De Bruhl, and Sydne J. Newberry. "The Root Causes of Failure for Artificial Intelligence Projects and How They Can Succeed: Avoiding the Anti-Patterns of AI." RAND Corporation, 13 August 2024, https://www.rand.org/content/dam/rand/pubs/research_reports/RRA2600/RRA2680-1/RAND_RRA2680-1.pdf.

Chapter 7
Raw Data and CRAFT

The line was running at full speed, 20 m/s of hot-rolled steel coil gliding under a bank of cameras. The AI vision system had been performing well for months, catching surface defects that human inspectors routinely missed. Then the plant changed around it, and the model's confidence stopped matching reality.

Then the numbers started to shift.

It wasn't dramatic. Nobody sounded an alarm. What happened was subtler and, ultimately, more damaging. The overhead lighting in one section of the inspection zone had been replaced during a weekend maintenance window. The new fixtures were brighter and cooler in color temperature. To the human eye, the steel looked the same. To the neural network analyzing 16,000 pixels per line of coil surface, it was a different world.

False rejects began rising. Not enough to halt production, but enough to create a rework backlog. Then came the false accepts: coils with hairline cracks and pitting that the system scored as clean. These slipped downstream to customers. By the time the pattern was traced back to the lighting change, three weeks of production had passed through the compromised inspection zone.

This story is an illustrative composite, but the pattern it describes isn't unusual. Tensorleap describes the same failure cascade in AI visual quality control: "Lighting angles shift after maintenance. Lenses haze. Fixtures wear. Vibration changes alignment. Operators adjust placement. Suppliers change surface texture or finish..." (Tensorleap, 2026). The article describes a pattern of gradual, quiet erosion in inspection performance that rarely trips an alarm until defects have already reached customers.

The pattern repeats across the industry. Public reporting has surfaced similar cases at major electronics and automotive manufacturers, where AI inspection systems have missed subtle assembly defects, failed to catch paint imperfections after lighting or environmental shifts, or overlooked micro-defects later linked to recalls and rework.

The root cause wasn't the algorithm. It was the data feeding the algorithm. Blurry images. Inconsistent lighting. Sensor drift. Conditions at inference time that didn't match conditions at training time. The AI didn't fail because it was stupid. It failed because the raw data it depended on had quietly degraded, and nobody noticed until the damage was done.

The cost of poor quality in manufacturing is enormous. Intel's AI vision inspection system saves up to $2 million each year in scrap avoidance alone (Intel, 2023). The gap between those numbers, the losses from bad data and the savings from good data, is the territory this chapter maps.

That failure is raw data quality in practice. It isn't a theoretical concern, and it isn't a nice-to-have. Raw data is the foundation that every downstream model rests on. When that foundation shifts without warning, the system built on top of it goes silent instead of sounding the alarm.

The lesson travels beyond manufacturing. Any AI system that learns from images, audio, video, sensor streams, or documents starts with raw data. If the raw signal is incomplete, inaccessible, distorted, stale, or undocumented, the model inherits that weakness.

What Raw Data Is

Raw data is what the world looks like before humans organize it. It's the image captured by a camera sensor, pixel by pixel. The audio waveform recorded by a microphone, sample by sample. The stream of temperature readings from an IoT sensor, timestamp by timestamp. The scanned document waiting for a machine to read it.

Enterprise raw data falls into five signal types:

- Images (photographs, medical scans, satellite imagery, product inspection photos)
- Audio (call center recordings, voice commands, machinery sounds)

- Video (surveillance feeds, manufacturing inspection streams, dashcam footage)
- Sensor and IoT streams (temperature, pressure, vibration, acceleration, LiDAR – Light Detection and Ranging – point clouds)
- Documents (PDFs, scanned forms, invoices, contracts)

The scale is staggering. The vast majority of enterprise data, estimated at 80–90%, is unstructured. Images alone represent the largest segment. IoT data is the fastest-growing segment, with organizations generating exponentially more sensor data each year as connected devices proliferate across industries.

A single Waymo autonomous vehicle can potentially generate over 1,100 gigabytes per hour of driving. A single Toyota assembly robot generates enough data daily to fill entire storage systems. And most of it goes to waste. Industry practitioners report that less than 1% of the data generated by autonomous vehicles while driving is considered useful for model training. Most of it is never stored. This is the raw data paradox: we're drowning in signals but starving for usable data.

The irony is that this waste rests on a wrong assumption. Many organizations assume that preprocessing data before AI consumes it is helpful. It isn't. Neural networks discover their own features directly from raw signals. A convolutional neural network learns feature representations directly from raw pixels. A transformer-based speech model learns acoustic features from raw waveforms. The features a neural network discovers are often ones that no human engineer would have thought to extract. Preprocessing that seems helpful to human intuition can destroy exactly the patterns the network relies on.

Deepgram documented the pattern: applying noise reduction algorithms before feeding audio to modern speech-to-text systems often decreases transcription accuracy (Maldonis, 2026). Noise reduction makes audio sound cleaner to human ears. But modern end-to-end ASR models are trained to handle noisy audio natively. The noise reduction strips acoustic cues that the neural network uses for phonetic distinctions.

The most consequential form of preprocessing is lossy compression. Once you compress an image to JPEG, you can't get the original pixels back. Once you compress audio to MP3, the spectral information is gone forever. Empirical studies of how compression affects downstream models have shown large relative accuracy drops on tasks such as image segmentation, music source separation, and image classification under heavy compression settings, even when the compressed media still looks or sounds acceptable to humans.

This distinction between raw and processed data isn't academic. It's the difference between preserving optionality and foreclosing it. In a database or spreadsheet, quality usually means clean schemas, valid keys, consistent formats, and correct values. For raw data, quality starts earlier. Did the camera capture enough resolution? Was the sensor calibrated? Was the audio sampled at the right rate? Were the collection conditions documented? Did compression destroy information the model will need later? Every lossy compression decision is a permanent reduction in the information ceiling for every AI system that will ever touch that data.

The Information Ceiling

All five CRAFT dimensions converge on a single principle: raw data quality sets an information ceiling that no algorithm can overcome. You can build a more sophisticated model. You can add more training compute. You can engineer clever data augmentation strategies. But you can't recover information that was never captured, lost to compression, corrupted by sensor drift, or rendered invisible by poor metadata.

The accuracy ceiling for any AI system is determined at data capture time, not at model training time. Engineers who discard raw data, compress it carelessly, or fail to document its provenance are making permanent decisions about the performance ceiling for every AI application that will ever touch that data, including applications that don't exist yet.

This is why raw data quality isn't just a data engineering concern. It's a strategic one. And it's why preserving raw data in its original fidelity isn't an expense. It's an investment with compounding returns.

Why Preservation Matters

If raw data quality sets the ceiling, then preserving raw data is how you keep that ceiling as high as possible, not just for today's AI systems, but for every system that will ever exist. Raw data becomes more valuable over time as algorithms improve. Researchers at the University of Bologna fed 60-year-old CORONA satellite images into an AI system (Pistola et al., 2025). Four previously unknown archaeological sites were discovered, sites that had since been destroyed or damaged by decades of agriculture, canal-digging, and urban encroachment. The AI achieved roughly 90% accuracy on features that had not been picked up by earlier ground-based archaeological surveys.

The same principle applies to medical imaging. Retrospective AI analyses of mammograms originally read as benign have identified early cancer signs in a substantial share of those prior scans.

Roughly one-third of newly detected early breast cancers are retrospectively locatable in the patient's earlier images. If those images had been compressed, downsampled, or deleted, those retrospective detections would be impossible.

The economics of storage have made preservation remarkably cheap. In 1980, a gigabyte of storage cost roughly $193,000 (Komorowski, 2009). Since then, storage costs have fallen by orders of magnitude, and cloud archive tiers have made long-term retention cheap enough that preservation is usually a governance decision before it's a storage-budget decision.

Regulations increasingly mandate preservation. The EU AI Act is the most significant. Article 10 requires providers of high-risk AI systems to document data collection processes and origins, all data preparation operations, assessments of dataset availability and suitability, examinations for possible biases, and identifications of data gaps. Under the July 2026 amending regulation (Regulation (EU) 2026/1744), compliance deadlines for high-risk AI systems begin December 2, 2027. And the Act has extraterritorial effect: if your AI system serves EU users, these rules apply regardless of where you're based.

Healthcare adds another layer. HIPAA compliance documentation must be retained for six years from creation or last effective date, and some states require permanent retention of certain records. Financial services pile on too. SEC Exchange Act Rules 17a-3 and 17a-4 require broker-dealers to preserve records so they can be reproduced or reconstructed, either through WORM storage or through a timestamped audit trail sufficient to re-create the originals. FDA 21 CFR Part 11 requires electronic records to be trustworthy, reliable, and equivalent to paper records, with controls for accurate and ready retrieval throughout the retention period.

The regulatory direction is unambiguous. Across industries and jurisdictions, the requirement is to preserve data in its original form, document everything done to it, and be able to prove it all on demand. Organizations that mistake comprehensive data documentation for full compliance are accumulating compliance risk that compounds over time.

Preservation alone isn't enough. Raw data that's preserved but ungoverned is a data swamp, not a data lake. A data lake stores raw data in its native format with strong governance: clear metadata, documented lineage, access controls, and quality profiling. A data swamp is what that lake becomes when governance is absent.

For raw data, the governance requirements are specific. Every file needs metadata capturing its source system, collection conditions, sensor parameters, and temporal context. Every transformation that produces a derived dataset from raw inputs must be documented. The raw data itself should sit in an immutable tier: write-once storage where originals can never be overwritten, only read.

The Human Cost of Getting This Wrong

According to preliminary findings from MIT's Project NANDA, roughly 95% of surveyed organizations report zero measurable ROI on Generative AI initiatives, despite an estimated $30 to $40 billion in enterprise investment (MIT NANDA, 2025). Many enterprises also report persistent AI job failures, with data quality and completeness showing up as a recurring barrier to production value.

Successful AI deployments typically consume 60–80% of project resources on data preparation. That's not a bug. That's the work. Organizations that treat raw data as a commodity to be collected and compressed will spend those resources fighting data quality problems that could have been prevented at capture time. Organizations that treat raw data as a strategic asset, preserving it at full fidelity with strong governance, will spend those resources building AI systems that actually work.

The information ceiling is real. And it's set long before anyone writes a line of model code.

CRAFT for Raw Data: Six Characteristics

The previous sections established what raw data is, why it matters, and why preserving it is nonnegotiable. This section gets specific about what CRAFT compliance means for raw data.

Raw data CRAFT compliance has six characteristics across the five CRAFT dimensions:

- **Complete** covers consistency and representativeness.
- **Retrievable** covers accessibility.
- **Accurate** covers signal fidelity.

- **Fresh** covers temporal alignment.
- **Traceable** covers documented provenance.

Each characteristic represents a real failure mode. Real failures have cost organizations money, patient outcomes, and user trust.

Complete: Consistency and Representativeness

Completeness for raw data has two sides. First, the data must be captured under consistent, controlled conditions so that variation in the data reflects variation in the real world, not variation in how you collected it. Second, the data must represent the full range of conditions that the AI system will face in production.

Consistency: When Capture Conditions Drift

In industrial computer vision, inconsistent capture conditions are the primary cause of AI model failure. Not inadequate algorithms. Not insufficient compute. Lighting.

Tensorleap's engineering team documented four triggers for silent drift in factory quality control systems: optics degrade as haze builds on camera lenses, supplier lot changes introduce subtle texture variations, fixture wear shifts camera alignment, and shift-to-shift lighting variation between day and night crews introduces distribution shift.

The financial stakes are enormous. For an automotive plant producing 250,000 cars annually, a single percentage point increase in defect rate can cost millions. Intel's Intelligent Wafer Vision Inspection system, designed around controlled capture conditions, saves the company up to $2 million each year in scrap avoidance alone, and the paper describes a rollout across multiple facilities globally (Intel, 2023).

Medical imaging tells the same story at higher stakes. Systematic reviews of deep learning algorithms for radiologic diagnosis have consistently found that most show decreased accuracy on external datasets, with some experiencing substantial performance drops. In neuro-oncology, models built for glioma classification on data from a single institution or vendor have been shown to generalize poorly to multicenter datasets, one reason such models struggle to progress through regulatory review.

Assessment Questions for Consistency

- Are capture conditions (lighting, temperature, sensor settings) documented and controlled at the point of collection?
- Do you have monthly calibration checks and baseline defect samples to verify system behavior?

Representativeness: Coverage Gaps Create Blind Spots

Consistency keeps noise out of your data. Representativeness makes sure signal gets in.

A Stanford study published in PNAS tested five major commercial speech recognition systems against audio from Black and white speakers matched for age and gender (Koenecke et al., 2020). The average word error rate was 35% for Black speakers compared to 19% for white speakers, nearly twice as high. For Black men specifically, error rates exceeded 40 errors per 100 words. The likely cause was insufficient audio data from Black speakers in the training corpora. The models simply hadn't heard enough diverse speech to recognize it.

Follow-up research on newer speech-recognition models, including Whisper, has continued to find that minority dialects perform substantially worse than the majority-dialect baseline. Other work has found especially poor performance for speakers with severe speech impairments. These aren't edge cases. They're entire populations excluded from AI-powered services.

Dermatology AI has an even starker coverage gap. A systematic review of 232 AI studies for skin cancer detection found that only 3.2% of training images represented darker skin tones (Fitzpatrick types IV through VI). The performance consequences are dramatic: one field evaluation on darker-skinned patients reported top-1 diagnostic accuracy of just 17%, compared with about 70% originally reported by the developers on lighter-skinned training data, a gap of more than 50 percentage points on materially different populations.

But the fix works. When researchers expanded training to include diverse skin tones, specificity improved from 0.91 to 0.98. The gap isn't inherent. It's caused by what's missing from the data.

The canonical example for completeness is Joy Buolamwini and Timnit Gebru's Gender Shades study from 2018 (Buolamwini and Gebru, 2018). They tested three commercial facial analysis systems and found error rates of just 0.8% for lighter-skinned males, but up to 34.7% for darker-skinned females, a 43-fold gap. The cause was straightforward: the benchmark datasets commonly used to evaluate such systems were overwhelmingly composed of lighter-skinned subjects, 79.6% in one dataset and 86.2% in another.

In dermatology, the ISIC dataset, one of the most widely used benchmarks for skin cancer detection AI, contains over 70% light skin images while dark skin represents fewer than 8%. Studies document that AI melanoma detection accuracy drops from 71% for lighter skin types to 42% for darker ones.

Completeness also means covering the full distribution of operating conditions. A manufacturing vision system trained only on day shift images will fail on the night shift, when ambient light, thermal conditions, and equipment calibration create a different data distribution. By the same token, an autonomous driving model trained mostly in clear weather degrades significantly in rain, fog, or glare.

Assessment Questions for Representativeness

- Do you have coverage audits comparing your training distribution to production conditions?
- Have you performed bias testing using tools like IBM's AI Fairness 360 or Google's Slice Finder across relevant demographic and condition dimensions?

Retrievable: Accessibility

Having data and being able to use it are two very different things. If 55% of enterprise data is dark, then more than half the raw material for AI is effectively invisible to the teams that need it (Splunk, 2019). Dark data is data an organization stores but can't find, access, understand, or connect to a working pipeline. The problem isn't that the data was deleted. It's that it exists in a place and form the team can't use.

The practical consequence is severe. Data scientists spend roughly 60% of their time cleaning and organizing data rather than building models (CrowdFlower,

2016). And storage infrastructure itself matters. Stability AI found that eliminating storage bottlenecks reduced average training epoch times by three weeks and pushed GPU utilization to 93%.

The problem is worse for raw data than for structured data. A JPEG file contains basic EXIF metadata, but nothing about its subject, quality, provenance, or AI-readiness. Audio files lack transcripts. Video lacks scene descriptions. Sensor readings lack context about calibration status. Raw data doesn't describe itself.

Cataloging raw data requires active metadata enrichment. Someone, or something, has to add the descriptions, quality scores, and contextual tags that make raw assets findable. Without that work, your data lake is just a data landfill.

Organizations that solve this problem see dramatic results. Discover Financial Services deployed an enterprise data catalog covering more than one million datasets, cutting discovery time from days to minutes and saving more than 200,000 hours of search and preparation time. NTT DOCOMO achieved a 10× productivity boost after cataloging its data assets, specifically strengthening the foundation for its Generative AI initiatives. The ODI principle matters here too. Raw data stored in open formats like Parquet and on open object storage APIs (S3-compatible stores) is retrievable by any tool in the stack, now and in the future. Raw data stored in proprietary formats becomes a liability when you change platforms.

Assessment Questions for Accessibility

- Can your AI pipelines discover raw assets by content, quality, and provenance through semantic search, not just by filename matching?
- Do you have programmatic API access (REST, streaming) with appropriate authentication between the "data exists" and the "AI pipeline can consume it"?

Accurate: Signal Fidelity

Accuracy for raw data isn't about whether a label is correct or a number adds up. It's about signal fidelity. Does the captured signal preserve enough information for AI to make correct decisions?

Every decision about how to capture, compress, and store raw data either preserves or destroys the information AI needs. And those decisions are irreversible.

Resolution: The Nonnegotiable Baseline

An empirical study measuring how image resolution affects deep neural network classification found that even a barely perceptible drop in resolution (scale factor of 2, which looks nearly identical to the human eye) caused a 2–4 percentage point accuracy drop across AlexNet, VGGNet, and ResNet architectures. At severe downscaling (scale factor of 8), accuracy dropped by 27–30 percentage points, a catastrophic loss for any production system.

What looks fine to you doesn't look fine to the model.

For document processing, the threshold is clearer. Higher-resolution scans produce dramatically better OCR accuracy, while low-resolution scans can render OCR nearly useless. OCR errors don't stay contained. A 2025 study found that using raw OCR outputs in a RAG system substantially increased downstream error rates. One misread character cascades into a wrong word, wrong retrieval, and wrong AI response.

Compression: The Silent Destroyer

Lossy compression is irreversible by mathematical definition. This isn't a technology limitation that better hardware will solve. Discarded information can't be reconstructed from what remains.

Compression can still leave traces that models detect even when people don't. In digital pathology, models have been shown to distinguish compressed from uncompressed image tiles even when human reviewers see no visible difference. The models aren't learning the medical content. They're learning the compression artifacts.

Audio tells the same story. Pollák and Behuňek (CTU) observed approximately a 50% reduction in recognition accuracy in noisy conditions when comparing uncompressed PCM with 24 kbps MP3 for MFCC-based connected-digit ASR. Clean recordings tolerate moderate compression. But background noise combined with lossy compression creates catastrophic degradation. Deepgram's research found that benchmark-to-production accuracy degradation ranges from 2.8 to 5.7 times because benchmarks use 16 kHz clean speech while contact centers use 8 kHz spontaneous speech.

Sensor Calibration: When Instruments Lie

A 2025 ECG study provides one of the most striking demonstrations. At high sensor quality (Class 1 and 2), over 99% of signal segments produced accurate readings. At the lowest quality (Class 4), only 1.0% did. This is a 99× degradation. When those sensors moved from clinical settings to at-home use, unusable data jumped from 2.57% to 16.51%.

For predictive maintenance, poor sensor data quality is the primary reason AI initiatives fail. Sensor drift introduces gradually wrong readings that the model accepts as normal. Miscalibration produces plausible-but-incorrect values. Insufficient sampling rates miss diagnostic frequencies entirely.

Label Accuracy: When Ground Truth Is Wrong

A landmark 2021 study by researchers at MIT systematically identified label errors across 10 major benchmark datasets and found an average error rate of at least 3.3% (Northcutt et al., 2021). ImageNet's validation set alone contained an estimated 6% label errors, with the true rate potentially closer to 20%. Even MNIST, widely considered error-free, had 15 confirmed mislabeled examples. These errors distort model evaluation: the study showed that on corrected labels, a smaller ResNet-18 can outperform a larger ResNet-50, reversing the published performance rankings.

When your data doesn't faithfully represent reality, whether because of signal degradation or labeling mistakes, your AI learns the wrong lessons. Upgrading a perception model to the next generation typically improves accuracy by single-digit percentages. Fixing raw data quality problems, filling representativeness gaps, correcting label errors, and calibrating sensors, routinely delivers 20–40% accuracy improvements on the same model. The payoff is in the data.

Assessment Questions for Accuracy

- What is your minimum signal quality threshold (resolution for images, sampling rate for audio, calibration intervals for sensors)?
- Are you using lossless formats for AI training and monitoring for label accuracy across your datasets?

Fresh: Temporal Alignment

The most comprehensive study of ML model degradation examined 128 model-dataset pairs across four industries and found temporal degradation in 91% of cases (Vela et al., 2022). That's not an occasional risk. It's the default.

For AI systems that combine multiple raw signal streams, freshness has a unique dimension: multi-sensor synchronization. An autonomous vehicle's cameras capture at 30 frames per second, its LiDAR (Light Detection and Ranging) scans at 10 Hz, and its inertial sensors measure hundreds of times per second. If these streams aren't precisely aligned in time, the fusion system creates a distorted view of reality, placing obstacles where they aren't or missing them where they are.

When sensor streams fall out of sync, the consequences are severe. Even small delays in LiDAR or camera data can cause catastrophic drops in 3D object detection and tracking accuracy. These aren't subtle degradations. A major accuracy drop means the car essentially can't see.

For audio-video alignment, the thresholds are tighter than most teams realize. The ITU-R detectability thresholds are roughly 45 ms of early audio or about 125 ms of late audio, and even sub-threshold misalignment can make content feel less trustworthy.

In manufacturing, concept drift is the silent killer. Lighting changes after maintenance. Lenses haze over months. Suppliers change surface textures. Each of these shifts the data distribution away from what the model learned, and the degradation is gradual enough that it doesn't trip any alarms until quality escapes have already reached customers.

In distributed sensor networks, every device has its own clock, and those clocks drift. Temperature, electromagnetic interference, aging, and manufacturing inconsistencies all cause oscillators to deviate. Standard NTP typically achieves on the order of 1–50 ms accuracy on a LAN, but this can degrade to tens of milliseconds or more over cellular connections. GPS-disciplined clocks can reach tens of nanoseconds of accuracy, while IEEE 1588 PTP with hardware timestamping routinely delivers sub-microsecond precision.

For AI systems trained on time-synchronized sensor data, temporal misalignment directly affects what correlations the model learns. As offsets grow from tens to hundreds of milliseconds, the model increasingly "sees" events in the wrong order or as overlapping when they are not, which can degrade performance on tasks that depend on fine-grained timing (e.g., multimodal perception, sensor fusion, or high-frequency control). Rather than relying on a single universal threshold, practitioners should derive acceptable timing error bands empirically for each application and treat them as part of the data quality specification. If your sensors are routinely misaligned by hundreds of milliseconds in a domain that depends on precise timing, your training data is effectively teaching the AI spurious or reversed causal relationships.

Assessment Questions for Temporal Alignment

- For multi-sensor systems, do you have hardware-level synchronization (IEEE 1588 PTP) with sub-microsecond precision?
- Are you monitoring clock drift continuously with automated alerting when synchronization exceeds application-specific thresholds?

Traceable: Documented Provenance

Traceability has moved from a best practice to a legal obligation. The EU AI Act, with compliance deadlines for high-risk AI systems beginning December 2, 2027, explicitly requires documentation of data collection processes, origins, and all preparation operations including annotation, labeling, cleaning, and enrichment. Article 10 mandates that training datasets be "relevant, sufficiently representative, and to the best extent possible, free of errors and complete."

Beyond the EU AI Act, HIPAA requires audit trails for medical imaging AI, SEC and FINRA rules require preserved records that can be reproduced or reconstructed, and FDA 21 CFR Part 11 requires trustworthy, reliable electronic records with accurate and ready retrieval throughout the retention period.

For raw data, traceability means knowing which camera or sensor produced each data point, what the environmental conditions were at capture time, what processing was applied, and who annotated it.

When a model fails, you need to trace back to the specific data that shaped the problematic behavior. Without that trail, you're debugging in the dark.

The practical stakes are high. Getty Images alleged that Stability AI used over 12 million Getty-owned images from the LAION-5B dataset to train Stable

Diffusion without authorization. The critical provenance failure: Stability AI couldn't demonstrate where its training data came from with enough granularity to defend against specific infringement claims.

In healthcare, documented HIPAA violations include an organization that shared an ML model trained on identifiable patient data without de-identification. Blue Shield of California's misconfigured analytics code led to data sharing potentially affecting 4.7 million members. Without provenance tracking showing how de-identification was performed on raw data, demonstrating HIPAA compliance is structurally impossible.

There's a newer provenance problem growing fast. Detected deepfake cases have surged more than tenfold in recent years. For any AI system that trains on web-collected media, this creates a fundamental question: How do you know your training data is what it claims to be?

The C2PA standard (Coalition for Content Provenance and Authenticity), now being fast-tracked to become ISO standard 22144, provides cryptographically signed manifests embedded in media files documenting how content was created and what modifications were made. U.S. and allied government cybersecurity agencies have recommended C2PA-style content-provenance adoption to help defend against synthetic-media threats. For AI training data, C2PA metadata enables automated compliance verification. Open lineage standards like OpenLineage make provenance portable across tools, so your audit trails aren't locked inside a single vendor's governance console.

Assessment Questions for Provenance

- Can you document the capture device, operator/system, timestamp, location, and calibration state for every raw asset at time of capture?
- Do you maintain the original lossless files as ground truth and track the complete chain of custody through every processing step?

Six Questions for Assessing Raw Data Readiness

Each characteristic in Table 7.1 represents a real failure mode. Not theoretical. Real failures have cost organizations money, patients, and users' trust.

Table 7.1 The CRAFT Profile for Raw Data

CRAFT Dimension	Raw Data Characteristic	Critical Question
Complete	Consistency	Are capture conditions controlled and documented with regular calibration checks?
Complete	Representativeness	Does your training distribution match production conditions across all relevant dimensions?
Retrievable	Accessibility	Can AI pipelines discover and programmatically access raw data without manual intervention?
Accurate	Fidelity	Do you preserve signal quality through resolution, lossless formats, and sensor calibration?
Fresh	Temporal Alignment	For multi-sensor systems, are streams synchronized to sub-millisecond or better precision?
Traceable	Provenance	Can you document origins, transformations, and chain of custody for every asset?

When you're assessing whether your raw data is AI-ready, Table 7.1 condenses the diagnostic questions into one operating question for each raw-data characteristic. The specifics of how to measure and operationalize each one become the subject of the systems chapters that follow.

For organizations fine-tuning AI models on raw signals, the CRAFT requirements in the previous sections apply with greater force to training data. A training dataset with representativeness gaps doesn't just produce errors on edge cases. It encodes those blind spots into model weights. The bias examples in this chapter, speech recognition, dermatology AI, and facial analysis, are all training data failures.

Raw data is your foundation layer. If it's locked into proprietary formats or vendor-specific storage, every system built on top of it inherits that dependency. The Open Data Infrastructure principle applies here with particular force: store raw data in open, lossless formats accessible through standard interfaces. When you need to switch tools, retrain a model, or adopt a new AI capability, your raw data should be portable without a migration project.

Raw data is the foundation. Get it right, and every AI system built on top of it has a chance at success. Get it wrong, and no amount of algorithmic sophistication will compensate for the information that was never captured, lost to compression, or rendered invisible by poor governance.

The information ceiling is set at data capture time, not at model training time. Engineers who discard raw data, compress it carelessly, or fail to document its provenance are making permanent decisions about the performance ceiling for every AI application that will ever touch that data, including applications that don't yet exist.

This is why raw data quality isn't just a data engineering concern. It's a strategic one. And it's why preserving raw data in its original fidelity isn't an expense. It's an investment with compounding returns.

Organizations that get raw data right set an information ceiling their competitors can't reach. Those that don't are building AI on a foundation that guarantees failure.

References

Buolamwini, Joy, and Timnit Gebru. "Gender Shades: Intersectional Accuracy Disparities in Commercial Gender Classification." *Proceedings of Machine Learning Research*, vol. 81, 2018, pp. 1–15.

CrowdFlower. "2016 Data Scientist Report." *CrowdFlower*, 2016.

Intel IT. "Optimizing Manufacturing with AI at the Edge: Intel Uses AI to Reduce Costly False Positives and Improve Quality with Inline Wafer Inspection." Intel Corporation, Dec. 2023, www.intel.com/content/dam/www/central-libraries/us/en/documents/2023-11/intel-it-smart-manu-using-ai-inline-paper.pdf.

Koenecke, Allison, et al. "Racial Disparities in Automated Speech Recognition." *Proceedings of the National Academy of Sciences*, vol. 117, no. 14, 7 Apr. 2020, pp. 7684–7689, https://doi.org/10.1073/pnas.1915768117.

Komorowski, Matt. "A History of Storage Cost." *mkomo.com*, 2009, mkomo.com/cost-per-gigabyte.

Maldonis, Jason. "The Noise Reduction Paradox: Why It May Hurt Speech-to-Text Accuracy." Deepgram, 27 Apr. 2026, deepgram.com/learn/the-noise-reduction-paradox-why-it-may-hurt-speech-to-text-accuracy.

MIT NANDA. "The GenAI Divide: State of AI in Business 2025." MIT Project NANDA, July 2025, nanda.media.mit.edu.

Northcutt, Curtis G., et al. "Pervasive Label Errors in Test Sets Destabilize Machine Learning Benchmarks." *arXiv*, 2021, arxiv.org/abs/2103.14749.

Pistola, Alessandro, et al. "AI-ming Backwards: Vanishing Archaeological Landscapes in Mesopotamia and Automatic Detection of Sites on CORONA Imagery." *PLoS One*, vol. 20, no. 8, 18 Aug. 2025, p. e0330419, dx.plos.org/10.1371/journal.pone.0330419.

Pollák, P., and Behuňek, M. (2011). Accuracy of MP3 speech recognition under real-world conditions. In *Proceedings of the International Conference on Signal Processing and Multimedia Applications (SIGMAP 2011)*. SciTePress.

Splunk. "The State of Dark Data." *Splunk*, 2019.

Tensorleap. "AI-Based Visual Quality Control Fails Quietly, Until It Forces Recalls and Manual Re-Inspection." *Tensorleap*, 2026.

Vela, Daniel, et al. "Temporal Quality Degradation in AI Models." Scientific Reports, vol. 12, article 11654, 2022, https://doi.org/10.1038/s41598-022-15245-z.

Chapter 8
Systems for Raw Data

Knowing what good raw data looks like is one problem. Building infrastructure that produces it is a different one. A lot of organizations get stuck in that gap. They can articulate exactly what AI-ready raw data should look like. They just can't build the pipelines, platforms, and processes to make it happen at scale. That's where this chapter comes in.

One principle guides all the system recommendations here: The Open Data Infrastructure principle. Raw data is your foundation layer, and foundations shouldn't have single points of vendor failure. The tools covered in this chapter (Great Expectations, Apache NiFi, lakeFS, S3-compatible object storage, Apache Ranger, and OpenLineage) follow open standards and open APIs. That's deliberate. When your raw data sits in open formats and flows through open pipelines, any compute engine, any AI system, and any future tool can access it without a migration project. Lock your raw data into a proprietary ingestion platform, and every downstream system inherits that dependency.

The payoff for getting raw data infrastructure right extends far beyond a single AI project. Every AI capability you build, at every data level, inherits the quality of your raw data foundation. Organizations that invest here once unlock every use case above it: analytics, Generative AI, and autonomous agents all draw from the same well. The infrastructure in this chapter is the highest-payoff investment in the book.

System Requirements by CRAFT Dimension

Table 8.1 contains the full system requirements by CRAFT dimension. Each row represents a distinct infrastructure layer. Some organizations have pieces of this already, usually built for BI or compliance rather than AI. That's a starting point, not a finish line. The systems that serve traditional analytics often fall short when AI is the consumer. A refresh schedule that works for weekly dashboards won't work for a real-time perception model. The rest of this chapter digs into the details of these system requirements by looking at each CRAFT dimension.

Completeness: Capture Governance

Completeness for raw data means every signal you need is actually being captured, at the right frequency, from the right sources, and without gaps. The system that delivers this is capture governance: a combination of protocols, monitoring, and quality gates that makes sure nothing falls through the cracks.

Before you evaluate any platform, define the capture contract. It should specify the signals you need, source systems, required frequency, allowed latency, ownership, validation rules, and the response when capture fails. Good capture governance is less about one vendor's service and more about making those decisions explicit, enforceable, and observable.

Capture Protocol Definitions and Enforcement

Start with the protocols themselves. For IoT and sensor data, AWS IoT SiteWise lets you create digital models of physical assets, production lines, robots, and factory equipment that define exactly what data should be collected and at what frequency. Its edge gateways collect data locally via OPC-UA (Open Platform

Table 8.1 The Full System Requirements by CRAFT Dimension

CRAFT Dimension	System Requirement	Key Capabilities
Complete	Capture governance	Protocols, coverage monitoring, gap detection
Retrievable	Catalog and access	Discovery, organization, retrieval APIs
Accurate	Capture infrastructure	Quality controls, format standards, validation
Fresh	Synchronization	Time services, alignment validation, drift correction
Traceable	Provenance tracking	Metadata capture, lineage, audit trails

Communications Unified Architecture) and sync to the cloud, so capture continues even when connectivity drops. AWS Lookout for Equipment documentation uses a 14-day minimum date range for historical datasets, which is a practical reminder that anomaly detection needs enough history to learn normal operating patterns (Amazon Web Services, 2026a).

Azure IoT Hub takes a different approach through device twins, which are JSON documents that store both desired and reported device state. The cloud sets desired properties, such as telemetry intervals and temperature thresholds, and devices report back their actual configuration. This creates a governance pattern: you can query across your entire fleet to find devices that haven't applied the latest settings, are disconnected, or have low battery.

For document capture, Intelligent Document Capture platforms enforce structured workflows: preparation, scanning at settings appropriate to the source material and OCR requirements, image enhancement, OCR processing, quality assurance, classification, indexing, and archival storage. Every step is governed. Every output is validated.

Coverage Monitoring

Knowing that your protocols are defined isn't enough. You need to know they're working. The most sophisticated approach operates at the entity level, not just the table level. You maintain a canonical registry of every entity that should have data: every sensor, every camera, and every document source. Then you compute observed entities at each pipeline layer (raw ingestion, transformation, and final output) and classify any gaps by root cause. Is it an ingestion failure? An ID mapping problem? A join that silently drops records? Each root cause routes to a different team for resolution.

In autonomous driving, the same pattern shows up differently. Training datasets can overrepresent clear-weather conditions and underrepresent difficult operating conditions such as adverse weather, night driving, unusual vehicle types, or rare road hazards. The coverage gap doesn't show up as a row count anomaly. It shows up as a model that works great in sunny California and fails in a snowstorm in Michigan.

Quality Gates for Ingestion

The last line of defense for completeness is the quality gate: a system that validates data before it enters production. The gold standard is the Write-Audit-Publish (WAP) pattern. Data lands in a staging area. Automated checks validate it against expectations. Only data that passes reaches production. If it fails, it goes to a dead letter queue for investigation. Bad data never reaches your models.

Choose the ingestion-control pattern by risk. If bad data can reach production models, use a Write-Audit-Publish flow. If the risk is operational, streaming validation plus quarantine may be enough. If every change needs review against production-scale data, branch-based versioning fits better.

Great Expectations is a widely adopted open-source validation framework with a supported core gallery of expectations and a broader community ecosystem. You define expectation suites (like "this column can't be null" or "values must fall between X and Y"), attach them to checkpoints, and run them against staged data before publishing. The framework generates human-readable Data Docs so your team can see exactly what passed and what failed.

Apache NiFi adds complementary capabilities: schema validation at ingestion, duplicate detection, data provenance tracking for every file that flows through the system, and guaranteed delivery through a persistent write-ahead log. For regulated industries, that provenance capability is especially valuable.

lakeFS takes a version-control approach. Every data change happens on a branch, isolated from production. Pre-merge hooks run quality checks before anything can be merged to main. If checks fail, the merge is blocked. Bad data never reaches production, and zero-copy branching means you're testing against production-scale data without duplicating it.

The principle across all of these is to validate at the point of capture. That's the cheapest place to catch problems. Every downstream consumer benefits. And the cost math is stark. A long-standing rule of thumb in quality management holds that the cost of an error grows roughly tenfold at each stage it goes uncaught. A data quality issue that costs 1x to fix at ingestion can cost 10x to fix mid-pipeline and 100x once it reaches end users.

Retrievability: Catalog and Access

The best raw data in the world creates zero value if nobody can find it. A 2019 Splunk-commissioned survey of more than 1,300 business and IT decision-makers found that 55% of enterprise data is dark, meaning untapped, hidden, or unknown (Splunk, 2019). IBM estimated in 2015 that up to 90% of data generated by connected devices and sensors is never analyzed or acted on (IBM, 2015). Data scientists report spending 60% of their time cleaning and organizing data, with another 19% just collecting datasets (CrowdFlower, 2016).

Think about what that means for AI. Your organization has petabytes of raw data: images, audio, video, sensor streams, scanned documents, and more. Most of it is invisible to the systems that could use it. Retrievability requires two subsystems: a catalog for discovery and an access layer for consumption.

Making Raw Data Findable

A data catalog is where raw data becomes findable. Historically, catalogs were built for structured databases. The leading platforms are now evolving quickly to handle unstructured data too.

For raw data, the catalog has to do more than list table names. It needs to index file formats, locations, ownership, access rules, retention policies, lineage, and content-derived metadata such as OCR text, image labels, audio transcripts, or embedding IDs. The right catalog is the one your teams can search, govern, and connect to pipelines without trapping metadata inside one vendor.

Databricks Unity Catalog is one of the most feature-rich platforms for cataloging unstructured data alongside structured data. Its Volumes feature provides first-class storage objects for images, PDFs, audio, and video. You can run LLM queries directly against image files to auto-generate descriptions and classifications. File-level access control and auto-classification of sensitive data come built in.

DataHub, originally built at LinkedIn and now used by thousands of organizations, provides an event-driven architecture backed by Kafka, Elasticsearch, and GraphQL (DataHub, 2026). It supports full-text search with popularity-based ranking and end-to-end lineage, including column-level granularity. It's open source and extensible.

The metadata that makes raw data findable comes in three layers:

- **Technical metadata** (file size, format, resolution, duration, EXIF data) gets extracted automatically at ingestion.
- **Content-derived metadata** (objects in images, speech transcriptions, text extracted via OCR) comes from AI models applied during or after ingestion.
- **Business metadata** (project name, department, compliance classification) requires human curation or auto-classification rules.

All three layers need to be present and searchable for raw data to be truly retrievable.

Vector databases store *embeddings*, which are numeric representations of content that support semantic similarity searches. Instead of relying on keyword-based metadata, embedding models like CLIP, which connects images and text in the same embedding space, or BERT, a language model used for text representations, transform raw data into high-dimensional vectors. A user searching for "sunset over mountains" can find relevant images even if nobody ever tagged them with those words. For organizations with massive archives of untagged raw data, this is transformative.

Access Infrastructure

Discovery is half the problem. The other half is getting the data into AI pipelines efficiently, reproducibly, and securely.

Select access infrastructure by access pattern. Start with how often the data will be read, how fast it must return, who can see it, whether reads need to be reproducible, and how long the original object must be retained. Cost optimization comes after those requirements, not before.

Tiered storage keeps costs manageable. For example, AWS offers graduated S3 tiers: S3 Standard at $0.023 per GB per month for frequently accessed data, down to S3 Glacier Deep Archive at roughly $0.001 per GB per month for long-term retention (Amazon Web Services, 2026b). S3 Intelligent-Tiering and Azure's Smart Tier automate the lifecycle, monitoring access patterns and moving objects between tiers. Other major object stores follow the same hot, cool, and archive tier pattern, with different prices, retrieval speeds, and retrieval fees. For raw data with unpredictable access patterns, auto-tiering is the right default.

Data versioning makes access reproducible. Data Version Control (DVC) extends Git to track large files and datasets, storing metadata pointers in Git while the actual data lives in cloud storage. lakeFS provides Git-like branching and merging for entire data lakes with zero-copy clones. When an AI pipeline needs to reproduce a training run from six months ago, versioned data makes that possible.

Access control must be fine-grained. Role-Based Access Control (RBAC) is the baseline, but it suffers from "role explosion" as organizations grow. Attribute-Based Access Control (ABAC) makes decisions based on multiple factors: role, location, data sensitivity, and time. Apache Ranger provides centralized security administration with file, folder, database, table, and column-level controls, plus integration with Apache Atlas for tag-based policies.

And every access event needs to be logged. Immutable, append-only audit logs with cryptographic integrity checks. Role and permission state recorded at the time of access. SIEM integration for real-time anomaly detection. This isn't just good practice. Under the EU AI Act, it's increasingly the law.

Accuracy: Capture Infrastructure

Accuracy for raw data means the captured signal faithfully represents reality. A blurry image, a clipped audio recording, or an incorrectly calibrated sensor all produce data that looks like raw data but doesn't carry the information AI needs to learn from it.

The system that delivers accuracy is capture infrastructure: the devices, settings, validation tools, and format standards that make sure every captured signal preserves the information it's supposed to carry.

Capture Devices and Calibration

Accurate data capture starts with the devices themselves. ISO 9001 requires that measuring equipment be calibrated or verified against measurement standards traceable to international or national measurement standards when traceability is necessary. ISO 17025 mandates that calibration results include calculated uncertainty. In regulated industries like medical devices (ISO 13485), aerospace (AS9100), and pharmaceuticals (FDA GMP), the standards require organizations to set calibration intervals through risk-based assessment. In practice, many companies choose cycles ranging from quarterly to annually depending on equipment criticality.

For digital imaging, ISO 12233 defines how to measure camera resolution, with test charts providing spatial frequency response data. Enterprise document scanners use platforms like Kofax VRS, which automatically evaluates images during scanning and rejects those that fail brightness, contrast, color confidence, crop, deskew, or orientation checks. The rejected images are flagged for correction, not silently passed through.

Quality Validation at Capture Time

Beyond calibration, you need automated quality checks at the moment data is captured. For images, BRISQUE (Blind/Referenceless Image Spatial Quality Evaluator) is a no-reference quality metric available in OpenCV and MATLAB.

MathWorks documents that its BRISQUE implementation usually returns scores in the 0 to 100 range, where lower scores mean better perceived quality (MathWorks, 2026). You set a threshold and reject anything above it.

For blur specifically, the Laplacian variance method is simpler and faster. Sharp images have many edges, meaning high variance in Laplacian values. Blurry images don't. It's a few lines of OpenCV code. The threshold depends on your optics and scene content, but it's a reliable first-pass filter.

For documents, scan mode can determine whether OCR works at all. A U.S. Government Publishing Office study found that bitonal scanning of older documents produced only 77% OCR accuracy, while grayscale and color scanning reached over 98% because they preserved the shading information needed to read faded or yellowed text (U.S. Government Publishing Office, 2006). The difference between those two numbers is the difference between a usable document and a liability. Upscaling or enhancement can't restore missing optical information. If detail is insufficient at capture, re-scanning is usually the only fix.

For audio, a 16 kHz sampling rate is standard practice for many speech recognition systems, and heavier compression can measurably degrade transcription accuracy at low bitrates.

Preservation with Format Standards

Format choice determines your information ceiling. Lossless formats (TIFF, WAV, FLAC, PNG, and RAW camera formats) preserve every captured bit. Lossy formats (JPEG, MP3, and AAC) permanently discard data to reduce file size. The discarded data can't be recovered. Ever.

The impact on AI is measurable. JPEG quality levels are encoder settings, usually expressed from 0 to 100, where higher values keep more visual detail and create larger files. A study testing nine object-detection models found that JPEG compression below quality level 40 causes accelerating performance degradation. At quality levels in the 25 to 30 range, visible artifacts remain human-readable but model performance declines substantially (Gandor and Nalepa, 2022). Small objects suffered the most: average precision for small objects declined at a steeper rate than for medium or large objects, which the authors attribute to compression's suppression of high-frequency detail. The authors describe the pattern as "first gradually, then suddenly": performance declines roughly linearly down to quality level 40, then degrades faster in a knee-shaped curve, with the steepest decline near quality 15.

For AI purposes, the recommendation is clear: capture and archive in lossless formats. Use lossy formats only for delivery and display, never as your canonical source.

Preserve Your Original Raw Data

The most important architectural principle is simple. Preserve your originals, including all raw data. Traditional BI-oriented pipelines were built with a specific assumption: raw data is transformed into structured form, and the originals are discarded or archived to cold storage where nobody looks at them again. This worked fine when the only consumer was a dashboard. But AI changes the equation. AI models can learn from raw signals directly. Future models may extract value from details that current models ignore. And once the raw data is transformed and the originals are gone, the information loss is permanent and irreversible.

The AI-oriented pipeline preserves both: raw data stays available in its original form, with transformed derivatives created from it. This ensures that raw data preserved in archive remains available for future AI training, reprocessing, and new use cases.

The cost argument overwhelmingly favors preservation. Storage costs have fallen from $193,000 per gigabyte for a January 1980 Morrow Designs drive to roughly $0.01 per gigabyte today (Komorowski, n.d.). At archive tier pricing, storing 1 TB of raw data can cost roughly $1 to $4 per month, depending on the storage class and retrieval pattern (Amazon Web Services, 2026b). Backblaze found that hard-drive cost per gigabyte fell roughly 9% per year on average from 2017 to 2022, though the decline has since flattened (Backblaze, 2022). Meanwhile, 85% of organizations experienced data loss in 2024, and large-scale data loss involving 100 million or more records can cost between $5 million and $15.6 million (DataNumen, 2024).

Storage bills continue for as long as you retain the data, but the unit cost keeps declining. Information loss is permanent and compounding. Every byte of preserved raw data is an option on future analytical capability. The storage bill can be managed. The lost signal can't be recovered.

Select storage systems by retention horizon, expected access frequency, retrieval latency, durability guarantees, lifecycle automation, encryption, geographic residency, and compatibility with open object-storage APIs. Archive tiers are cheap only when slow retrieval and retrieval fees fit the use case.

Freshness and Traceability Infrastructure

The final two CRAFT dimensions, freshness and traceability, share enough infrastructure that it makes sense to cover them together. Both depend on metadata captured at the moment data enters your system, and both rely on tracking what happens to that data over its lifetime.

For freshness and traceability, start with the shared operating model. Every source needs a clock policy, timestamp standard, ingestion metadata, lineage event model, and audit policy before you pick monitoring or lineage tools.

Synchronization Infrastructure (Freshness)

Freshness for raw data means temporal alignment: every data point carries an accurate, trustworthy timestamp, and data from multiple sources can be reliably synchronized in time.

This matters because clocks lie. Unsynchronized computer clocks can drift by several seconds per day. Over extended periods without resynchronization, systems can differ by minutes. In a banking scenario, that drift means a credit appears to happen before its corresponding debit. In autonomous driving, delays or misalignment between LiDAR and camera data streams can significantly degrade detection and tracking accuracy.

Even time offsets in the hundreds of milliseconds can produce considerable ML performance degradation in multi-sensor systems.

The synchronization stack has layers. NTP (Network Time Protocol) is the baseline, providing roughly sub-millisecond-to-1 millisecond accuracy on well-configured local networks and tens of milliseconds over the public internet. For applications that need better precision, PTP (Precision Time Protocol, IEEE 1588) delivers sub-microsecond synchronization and is the standard in industrial automation, financial trading, and telecom. For demanding scenarios like autonomous vehicle sensor fusion, gPTP (IEEE 802.1AS) with hardware timestamping can support sub-microsecond synchronization across time-sensitive networks, with actual accuracy depending on the implementation and network design.

For your ingestion pipelines, the practical guidance is straightforward. Store all timestamps in UTC. Use epoch integers across raw data layers, applying time zone conversions only in presentation layers. Add an ingestion timestamp as a secondary time dimension. And never adjust timestamps during raw data ingestion. The raw layer should accurately represent the original sources.

Drift detection closes the loop. Monte Carlo offers freshness monitors that track "time since last update" and "time since last row count change," using both ML-based thresholds and manual thresholds for business-specific SLAs. Without continuous drift monitoring, clock skew accumulates silently until it corrupts your model's temporal reasoning.

Cross-source alignment is the hardest freshness problem. Cameras, LiDARs, radars, IMUs, and microphones each have their own clocks and capture frequencies. Hardware-based synchronization, such as a shared trigger or hardware timestamping, gives each sensor stream a common timing basis. Software-only synchronization depends on each sensor's drifting clock and can let timing error accumulate silently. For AI systems that fuse multiple raw signals, the goal isn't just lower latency. It's trustworthy temporal alignment.

Provenance Infrastructure (Traceability)

Traceability means knowing where every piece of raw data came from, how it was captured, what's happened to it since, and being able to prove all of this when asked.

The regulatory pressure around traceability is real and growing. The EU AI Act's transparency requirements for general-purpose AI models went live in August 2025, requiring providers to publish sufficiently detailed summaries of training data. Full transparency rules, including content labeling and provenance requirements, take effect in August 2026. Penalties reach up to 15 million euros or 3% of worldwide annual turnover (European Parliament and Council of the European Union, 2024).

Metadata capture at ingestion is the foundation. When raw data enters your system, you should automatically extract and store: EXIF data for images (camera, GPS, settings, dimensions), codec and frame rate information for video, sample rate and bit depth for audio, device ID and firmware version for IoT sensors, and author and modification history for documents. The C2PA (Coalition for Content Provenance and Authenticity) standard provides provenance records that function like a "nutrition label for digital content" (C2PA, 2023). Those credentials can include information about who created the content, when it was created, which tools were used, and what edits were made along the way.

Lineage tracking extends provenance through the data lifecycle. OpenLineage provides an open, vendor-neutral standard for capturing lineage events, with integrations for Apache Airflow, Spark, and dbt. This is ODI in practice: your lineage data isn't locked inside one vendor's observability console. When a model produces unexpected outputs, you trace backward through every transformation layer to the original source, using whatever tools you choose.

Audit logging ties it all together. Best practice calls for immutable, WORM (Write Once, Read Many) storage providing tamper-proof records of every data access and model execution. Real-time compliance dashboards should display policy violations, data residency status, and key risk indicators. Data governance is also a risk-control discipline, not just a cataloging exercise: IBM notes that the global average cost of a data breach reached USD 4.4 million in 2025 (Jonker, 2025).

Raw Data CRAFT Checklist

The systems in this chapter share a design philosophy: open interfaces, open formats, and no single vendor dependency. That's intentional. Raw data infrastructure outlives individual tools. The catalog you choose today may not be the catalog you use in three years, but if your data sits in open formats behind standard APIs, the switch is a migration, not a rebuild. That's the Open Data Infrastructure principle in practice.

The systems in this chapter aren't infrastructure for infrastructure's sake. They're the difference between an AI investment that compounds with every successful deployment and one that depreciates with every model update.

Score yourself honestly. Any unchecked box is a potential failure mode for your AI systems. These checklists aren't aspirational. They're operational requirements for AI systems that can be trusted to work reliably in production.

Use the following checklist to assess your current state. It's not exhaustive, but it covers the essentials:

Complete

- ☐ Capture protocols documented for all raw data sources
- ☐ Entity-level coverage monitoring in place, with gap classification by root cause
- ☐ Quality gates (WAP pattern or equivalent) validate data before production

Retrievable

- ☐ Central catalog exists with support for unstructured data types
- ☐ Raw data is findable through metadata search, including content-derived metadata

- ☐ Tiered storage with lifecycle policies manages cost and access appropriately
- ☐ Programmatic access with versioning supports reproducible AI pipelines

Accurate

- ☐ Capture devices calibrated per applicable standards (ISO 9001, 17025, etc.)
- ☐ Automated quality validation runs at capture time (resolution, blur, noise checks)
- ☐ Raw originals preserved in lossless formats alongside any transformed derivatives

Fresh

- ☐ All systems synchronized via NTP at minimum, PTP/gPTP for precision applications
- ☐ Timestamps stored in UTC with ingestion timestamps added as secondary dimension
- ☐ Multi-source data temporally aligned with drift detection and alerting

Traceable

- ☐ Provenance metadata (source, device, capture conditions) captured at ingestion
- ☐ Lineage tracked from raw data through all transformations to derived outputs
- ☐ Immutable audit logs record all access events with role and permission state
- ☐ Privacy and compliance metadata captured to support regulatory requirements

References

Amazon Web Services. "Amazon Lookout for Equipment: Formatting Your Data." Amazon Web Services, 2026a, docs.aws.amazon.com/lookout-for-equipment/latest/ug/formatting-data.html.

Amazon Web Services. "Amazon S3 Pricing." Amazon Web Services, 2026b, aws.amazon.com/s3/pricing/.

Backblaze. "The Cost Per Gigabyte of Hard Drives Over Time." Backblaze, 2022, www.backblaze.com/blog/hard-drive-cost-per-gigabyte/.

Coalition for Content Provenance and Authenticity (C2PA). "Introducing Official Content Credentials Icon." C2PA, 2023, c2pa.org/introducing-official-content-credentials-icon/.

CrowdFlower. "2016 Data Scientist Report." CrowdFlower, 2016, visit.figure-eight.com/rs/416-ZBE-142/images/CrowdFlower_DataScienceReport_2016.pdf.

DataHub. "datahub-project/datahub." GitHub, 2026, github.com/datahub-project/datahub.

DataNumen. "Data Loss Statistics Report 2024: 85% of Organizations Affected." DataNumen, 2024, www.datanumen.com/reports/data-loss-statistics-2024/.

European Parliament and Council of the European Union. "Regulation (EU) 2024/1689 of the European Parliament and of the Council of 13 June 2024 Laying Down Harmonised Rules on Artificial Intelligence (Artificial Intelligence Act)." Official Journal of the European Union, 12 July 2024, eur-lex.europa.eu/legal-content/EN/TXT/?uri=CELEX:32024R1689.

Gandor, Tomasz, and Jakub Nalepa. "First Gradually, Then Suddenly: Understanding the Impact of Image Compression on Object Detection Using Deep Learning." Sensors, vol. 22, no. 3, 2022, p. 1104. MDPI, doi.org/10.3390/s22031104.

IBM. "IBM Connects 'Internet of Things' to the Enterprise." CNW, 31 Mar. 2015, www.newswire.ca/news-releases/ibm-connects-internet-of-things-to-the-enterprise-517411821.html.

Jonker, Alexandra. "What Is AI-Ready Data?" IBM Think, 11 Nov. 2025, ibm.com/think/topics/ai-ready-data. Accessed 31 Mar. 2026.

Komorowski, Matt. "A History of Storage Cost." mkomo.com, n.d., mkomo.com/cost-per-gigabyte. Accessed 3 July 2026.

MathWorks. "brisque." MathWorks, 2026, www.mathworks.com/help/images/ref/brisque.html.

Splunk. "The State of Dark Data." Splunk, 2019, www.splunk.com/en_us/form/the-state-of-dark-data.html.

U.S. Government Publishing Office. "A Study of Scan Mode, File Enhancement, and Software Products." GPO, Rev. June 2006, www.govinfo.gov/media/WhitePaper-OptimizingOCRAccuracy.pdf.

Chapter 9
Structured Data and CRAFT

"This concept of fusing structured information and Generative AI will repeat itself in one industry after another. Structured data is the foundation of trustworthy AI." (Huang, 2026). When the CEO of the company at the center of the AI infrastructure buildout says structured data is the foundation of trustworthy AI, it is worth taking seriously.

Structured data is the oldest, most managed, and most trusted form of enterprise data. It powers your ERP, your CRM, your financial systems, and the analytics platforms your leadership team checks every morning. It lives in tables with rows and columns, enforced by schemas that define exactly what goes where. And it's the foundation for *Analytical AI*, the machine learning systems that find patterns, make predictions, and optimize decisions across every industry built on numbers.

Most enterprise structured data was designed for a specific consumer: a human analyst writing SQL queries and building dashboards. It was optimized for Business Intelligence (BI). And "good for BI" isn't the same as "good for AI." The gap between those two standards is where most Analytical AI projects go to die.

If your business outcome depends on pattern recognition, forecasting, or decision support, you need Analytical AI. And Analytical AI runs on structured data.

Structured data doesn't exist in isolation. It's built from the raw data foundation covered in Chapters 7 and 8. If your raw data isn't CRAFT-compliant, your structured data inherits those problems.

The Nature of Structured Data

Structured data is information organized into rows and columns, with explicit schemas defining data types, constraints, and relationships. A transaction table has columns for *transaction_id*, *amount*, *timestamp*, and *customer_id*. A customer table has columns for *customer_id*, *name*, *address*, and *account_status*. The relationships between these tables are explicit: *customer_id* appears in both, creating a join path that links transactions to customers.

It's the oldest type of data in enterprise systems, and in many ways the most understood. Decades of database systems, query languages, and data warehousing have optimized how we store, retrieve, and query structured data. SQL remains the *lingua franca* across nearly every organization. It's been standardized, optimized, and deeply embedded in enterprise practice.

It's also the type of data that ML and AI systems depend on most, despite the recent fixation on raw unstructured data. The most business-critical AI applications (credit scoring, fraud detection, churn prediction, demand forecasting, supply chain optimization, financial planning) run on structured data. Generative AI has captured headlines, but the ML systems creating measurable business value, especially at enterprise scale, still run on structured tables queried with SQL.

Structured data comes in three layers:

- **Operational data:** Live databases supporting core business processes. Customer order history, inventory levels, account balances, production schedules. This data changes constantly. It's optimized for transactional consistency (ACID properties) and fast single-row access (point queries). It's designed for operational systems to work correctly, not for AI systems to learn from.
- **Data warehouse:** Historical, aggregated data organized for analytical queries. Customer lifetime value, monthly revenue by region, cohort behavior, product performance trends. This data changes periodically (nightly or weekly) and is optimized for full-table scans and aggregations. It's the layer most organizations think of as "data for analytics." And for BI, it's quite good.
- **Feature stores and serving systems:** Precomputed features designed specifically for ML inference. A customer profile table with features like "days since last purchase," "average order value," "number of support tickets in the last 30 days." This layer is built specifically to serve ML models, both for training and for production inference. It's the most specialized layer and the newest architecturally.

Most organizations have the first two. Many have nothing resembling the third. That's a critical gap, because the third layer is where structured data becomes fully AI-ready.

A Brief Evolution

The history of structured data is, in many ways, the history of enterprise computing. It starts with accounting ledgers, the original structured data. It includes rows of transactions, columns of accounts, and explicit rules for how debits and credits balance. When mainframe computers arrived in the 1950s, those same structures went digital. IBM's RAMAC introduced the world's first hard disk drive, and with it, the first machine-readable structured data stores.

In the 1960s, database choices were slim: hierarchical or network models, both tightly coupled to physical storage. Retrieving a record meant navigating a tree of pointers from root to leaves. If you wanted to ask a different question, you needed a different navigation path.

Then in 1970, Edgar F. Codd published an 11-page paper that changed everything. "A Relational Model of Data for Large Shared Data Banks" proposed organizing data into relations (tables) based on set theory and predicate logic. The key insight was data independence: separating the logical structure of data from how it was physically stored. You could ask any question you wanted without knowing where the bytes lived on disk.

SQL emerged in the early 1970s and was standardized by ANSI in 1986. By the 1990s, the relational model had effectively replaced older approaches.

The data warehouse revolution came next. Bill Inmon published *Building the Data Warehouse* in 1992, proposing a centralized, normalized repository as the single source of truth. Ralph Kimball countered in 1996 with *The Data Warehouse Toolkit,* introducing star schemas and dimensional modeling optimized for analytical queries. Kimball's approach, with its fact tables of measurements surrounded by dimension tables of descriptive context, became the standard for BI environments.

Star schemas were explicitly designed for human analysts. The denormalized structure simplified query writing. Star joins enabled efficient queries on the hardware of the 1990s. Memory was expensive, so separating data into smaller individual tables made it cheaper to store and easier to understand. This is an important point. The schemas that power most enterprise analytics today were designed in an era when the only consumer was a person writing a SQL query.

Today, the landscape has expanded. Data lakehouses combine the low-cost storage and open formats of data lakes with the management features of data warehouses, including ACID transactions, schema evolution, and fine-grained governance. Open table formats like Apache Iceberg, Delta Lake, and Apache Hudi bring these capabilities to cloud object storage. This is the ODI pattern for structured data: open formats separate storage from compute, so you aren't locked to a single query engine. Your data stays in open formats on open storage, and any compute engine, including Spark, Trino, Dremio, and DuckDB, can read it. Feature stores serve precomputed, ML-ready features for both batch training and real-time inference. Real-time streaming is no longer bolted on. It's embedded.

The infrastructure has evolved dramatically. But much of the data inside still carries the design assumptions of the BI era. That's the gap this chapter closes.

Complete: Entity Integrity

Completeness for structured data means the fundamental building blocks are correct: entities (customers, products, transactions) are captured completely, with no missing records, and relationships between entities are intact.

The Entity Problem

Entity integrity means that every real-world entity your business cares about is represented by exactly one record in your data systems. Not zero. Not three. One.

This sounds like a solved problem. It isn't.

The fragmentation problem runs deeper than most organizations realize. Validity's 2024 State of CRM Data Management report found that 53% of organizations cite duplicate records among their top CRM data struggles (Validity, 2024). Applied to a database of 50,000 contacts, even a modest duplicate rate means thousands of records can describe the same customers, prospects, and accounts.

How does this happen? It's not negligence. It's architecture.

The average enterprise runs 991 applications, yet only 28% are integrated (MuleSoft, 2024). A customer's data lives in CRM, ERP, billing, support ticketing, and loyalty systems with no shared key. Each system creates its own record. The same person becomes a billing account in one system, a support contact in another, and a marketing lead somewhere else. The model does not know those are the same customer unless the entity layer tells it.

The problem isn't that someone did something wrong. The problem is structural. Enterprises evolved organically, department by department, system by system, and nobody designed for a unified entity layer.

Why Analytical AI Needs Entity Integrity

Entity fragmentation causes more than operational annoyance. It corrupts machine learning at the foundational level. When entity resolution has not been applied before model training, the model treats one real-world person as three different data records, or merges two distinct people into one. These false positives and false negatives propagate as corrupted labels in training data. A Harvard Business School study of an AI scheduling system across 6,200 retail stores found that managers manually overrode 84% of 99 million algorithm-generated shifts, though only about 8% of those overrides were attributed to inaccurate input data. Most reflected managers adding local information the system did not have. The lesson is narrower and more useful: bad entity data matters, but AI also fails when structured data does not capture the operational context people use to make decisions (HBS Working Knowledge, 2025).

The cost can be staggering. Unity Technologies provides the most expensive single example. In 2022, a single erroneous data stream from a major client corrupted the datasets used to train Unity's advertising ML models (Yackel, 2022). The result was roughly $110 million in lost revenue and a 37% stock drop on the earnings announcement. One bad data entity, merged with the main dataset without proper disambiguation, destroyed nine figures of value.

The Fairness Connection

Entity integrity is an accuracy problem and a fairness problem. Neural entity matching models produce significantly higher false discovery rates for African American names compared to Caucasian names in security matching contexts (Shahbazi et al., 2023). Names from certain linguistic backgrounds, such as Chinese names in English transliteration, see both higher false-positive and higher false-negative rates in neural entity matching because within-group similarity in transliterated names makes models more sensitive to minor character-level differences. Standard string-matching algorithms can also produce demographic disparities in record linkage, with elevated error rates for Hispanic and Black names relative to non-Hispanic white names.

These aren't obscure academic findings. They describe what happens in your systems right now. If your entity resolution systematically under-links records for certain demographic groups, every ML model downstream of that data inherits a distorted view of those populations. The model doesn't see complete profiles. It sees fragments. And it makes worse predictions for the people whose records are most fragmented.

Diagnostic Question

Can you name the single canonical entity identifier that resolves a customer across your CRM, billing, support, and operational systems? If you hesitated, you have an entity integrity problem.

AI-ready Standard for Entity Integrity

For entity integrity to be AI-ready, the controls need to be concrete and testable:

- Every business entity has a single, canonical identifier that resolves across all source systems.
- Duplicate detection runs continuously, not as a quarterly cleanup project.
- Entity resolution accuracy is measured and reported by demographic group, not just in aggregate.
- False positive and false negative rates are tracked and fall within defined thresholds.
- The entity resolution process is auditable and its methodology documented.

Relational Completeness

Entity integrity gets each record right. Relational completeness gets the connections between records right. A customer record in isolation tells you their name, address, and account tier. What makes that record valuable for Analytical AI is its relationships: the orders they've placed, the support tickets they've filed, the products they've used, and the payments they've made. Those relationships live in foreign keys, join paths, and hierarchical structures across tables. When those connections are broken, incomplete, or inaccessible, the AI loses the relational signal that often matters more than any individual attribute.

Why Analytical AI Needs Relational Completeness

The evidence for relational completeness is striking. RelBench, developed by researchers at Stanford University and Kumo.AI with Max Planck contributors, compared Relational Deep Learning (which treats a relational database as a graph and applies graph neural networks) against manually engineered features for traditional models like XGBoost, a gradient-boosted tree model (Robinson et al., 2024). On entity classification tasks, the graph-based approach achieved 75.83 AUROC, a classification metric for ranking positive examples above negative ones, versus 63.66 for the manual approach, roughly a 20% relative gain. On recommendation tasks, the gap was even wider: 277 to 297% higher MAP@K scores, which measure whether relevant recommendations appear near the top of a ranked list.

The key insight from RelBench is that traditional models only matched graph-based approaches on tasks when the target table had extremely rich features on its own. The moment predictive signal was distributed across related tables, the approach that could traverse relationships won by large margins. Well-crafted relational features derived from joins, aggregations, or graph structure can materially improve model accuracy, which is exactly why benchmarks like RelBench test whether models can use relationships instead of flat target tables alone.

With only 28% of enterprise applications integrated, the vast majority of the relational graph (the customer-order-product-support interaction network) is siloed and unavailable to ML models. A machine learning model trained on a single CRM extract has no access to billing history, support ticket sentiment, or product usage telemetry unless proper integration and entity resolution are applied first. The relational signal is there. It is just locked behind integration gaps.

Diagnostic Question

When you train an ML model on your customer data, how many related entities can the model access without manual feature engineering: orders, support tickets, product usage, payment history, communications? If you can't immediately answer, your relational graph is fragmented.

AI-ready Standard for Relational Completeness

Relational completeness is AI-ready only when the relationships are explicit, tested, and available to ML pipelines:

- Foreign key relationships are maintained and enforced across integrated datasets.
- Cross-system entity linkage preserves the full relationship graph for each business entity.
- Join paths between related tables are documented, tested, and accessible to ML pipelines.
- Orphaned records (transactions without customers and line items without orders) are identified and resolved.
- Hierarchical relationships (parent-subsidiary and product-category) are explicitly modeled, not implicit.

Retrievable: Computational Accessibility

Retrievability for structured data is about whether AI systems can actually find the data they need and consume it efficiently enough to be useful. There are two areas where you need to consider accessibility:

- **Training accessibility:** An ML system training a model needs access to the full raw training data, not summary statistics. It needs to scan every row. It needs to engineer features by joining tables and computing aggregations. It needs scan throughput in the hundreds of MB/s to make iteration practical. It needs to iterate repeatedly on feature definitions, so the data needs to be stored in a format that supports fast full-table scans, not just point queries.
  Spark DataFrames, pandas, and DuckDB all provide this capability. So do columnar databases like Snowflake and BigQuery. What doesn't work is querying your production OLTP database, where point-query latency optimization makes full-table scans extremely slow.
- **Serving accessibility:** An ML system in production needs something completely different: the ability to retrieve precomputed features for a specific entity in milliseconds so a production model can score a request in real time.

These aren't the same architecture. Feature stores exist precisely to bridge this gap, serving as dual-database systems with a columnar offline store for training and a key-value online store for serving. Without this infrastructure, teams end up rebuilding features differently for training and production, which is one of the primary causes of training-serving skew.

Computational accessibility means data is reachable through interfaces that AI teams can actually use, with enough performance to support feature engineering, training, and production serving. It also includes discoverability. According to CrowdFlower's 2016 Data Scientist Report, respondents spent 60% of their time cleaning and organizing data and another 19% collecting datasets, together about 79% of a typical workweek (CrowdFlower, 2016). Anaconda's 2023 State of Data Science survey of 2,414 respondents ranked data preparation and cleaning as the most time-consuming tasks, ahead of model training and selection (Anaconda, 2023). Andrew Ng framed the priority this way: "If 80 percent of our work is data preparation, then ensuring data quality is the important work of a machine learning team" (Ng, 2021).

Part of that preparation burden is just finding the right data. The precise percentage varies by survey and role, but the operational pattern is consistent: teams spend large parts of their week discovering, cleaning, and interpreting data before they can model anything. This is not a minor inconvenience. It is operational waste at scale.

Why Analytical AI Needs Computational Accessibility

The cost of inaccessible structured data compounds at scale. Databricks reported that organizations put 11 times more AI models into production in 2024 compared to 2023 (Databricks, 2024). That 11-fold increase represents a corresponding explosion in demand for feature stores, semantic layers (shared definitions for metrics, dimensions, relationships, and business rules), and data access infrastructure. At that scale, manual feature engineering and undocumented schemas don't just slow you down. They become operationally unsustainable.

Training-serving skew, where features calculated during training differ from features calculated at inference time, is a well-documented failure mode in production ML systems and one of many hidden sources of technical debt identified in the ML-systems engineering literature (Sculley et al., 2015). Google's TFX data-validation system caught a real-world skew case at Google Play: several features were always missing from live serving logs but always present in training data. Once the skew was fixed, an online A/B test showed a 2% improvement in the app-install rate on the Play Store's landing page (Breck et al., 2019). That sounds small until you consider Google Play's scale.

Diagnostic Question

If a data scientist asks, "Do we have a feature that represents customer support sentiment in the last 30 days?", can you point them to it in under five minutes, or do they need to hunt across documentation, ask colleagues, and likely rebuild it themselves?

AI-ready Standard for Computational Accessibility

Computational accessibility is AI-ready only when teams can find the data, reach it through standard interfaces, and run the workloads AI systems require:

- Training data is accessible via SQL or DataFrame APIs with scan throughput sufficient for full-dataset feature engineering.
- Online serving delivers precomputed features with sub-50 ms latency for production inference.
- Feature definitions are computed once and shared across training and serving to prevent training-serving skew.
- Data assets are cataloged with descriptions, owners, and usage metadata so data scientists can find what exists.
- Access controls enforce who can query what, without creating friction that pushes teams to create shadow copies.

Accurate: Semantic Clarity

Accuracy for structured data is primarily a problem of meaning, not numbers. The most common accuracy failure in enterprise data isn't that a value is wrong. It's that the value is right in one context and wrong in another, and nobody documented which context applies.

The Ambiguity Problem

A field named *revenue* might mean gross revenue in one system, net revenue in another, and recognized revenue in a third. A column called *customer_id* in CRM is *cust_num* in billing and *client_reference* in operations. When AI systems attempt to answer questions in this environment, they lack the semantic bridges that experienced analysts maintain mentally: the shared understanding that these different labels point to the same concept, or that the same label points to different concepts.

The consequences are measurable. Three teams asking AI the same question, "Show me the total customer value for Project X in Q3," receive three different answers: Finance sees $100 K, Marketing sees $200 K, Sales sees $40 K. The AI isn't hallucinating. It's pulling from conflicting logic because each team's ecosystem has its own definition of "customer value." Each answer is technically correct within its own context. None of them is useful for cross-functional decision-making.

Microsoft's Fabric documentation illustrates this concretely: a user asks, "What were our sales last quarter?" and the system contains Total Revenue, Gross Sales, Net Sales, and Sales After Returns. Without explicit semantic configuration, the AI returns Gross Sales when the team typically uses Net Sales (Microsoft Learn, n.d.). Metric definitions frequently drift across departments even within the same company. Sales might define an "active customer" as someone who purchased in the last 90 days while Finance uses a 60-day window. A model training on data that mixes these definitions learns an incoherent signal.

When you scale this to real enterprise schemas, the problem gets exponentially worse. GPT-4, using zero-shot prompting directly against enterprise SQL databases, achieved just 16.7% accuracy (Sequeda et al., 2023). That's not a typo. On enterprise data with real-world complexity, the most capable AI model in the world got it right less than one time in five. For the hardest questions involving high schema complexity, accuracy dropped to 0%.

The fix isn't a better model. It's better semantic context. When the same enterprise data was represented through a knowledge graph with explicit semantic definitions, accuracy jumped to 54.2%, a three-fold improvement (Sequeda et al., 2023). Organizations that implement full semantic layers, with codified metric definitions, relationship mappings, and business rules, achieve 80–90% accuracy on complex analytical queries. Those relying solely on better models remain stuck at 40–50%.

In AtScale's own benchmark testing of its semantic-layer product with TPC-DS, LLMs were incorrect over 80% of the time when working directly with raw data models. With semantic layers providing context, accuracy improved to 92 to 100% (AtScale, 2024).

The pattern is consistent across every study: semantic context matters more than model capability for enterprise data queries. You could upgrade from one frontier model to the next and see smaller improvements than you'd get from defining what your fields actually mean.

The market agrees. Mordor Intelligence estimates that the semantic layer and knowledge graph market for agentic AI will reach $1.73 billion in 2025 and grow to $4.93 billion by 2030 (Mordor Intelligence, 2025). Enterprise adoption remains limited today but is expected to grow substantially over the next several years. One caveat: a semantic layer locked inside a proprietary BI tool defeats the purpose. If only that tool's AI can access your metric definitions, you have not solved the problem. Semantic layers built on open standards, like dbt's MetricFlow under Apache 2.0, mean your business definitions are portable across tools and AI systems.

Diagnostic Question

If three different people in your organization run the same SQL query for "customer revenue," will they get the same answer? If you're not sure, you don't have semantic clarity.

AI-ready Standard for Semantic Clarity

Semantic clarity is AI-ready only when business meaning is encoded where both people and AI systems can use it:

- Every metric has a single, codified definition accessible to both humans and AI systems.
- Business terms map explicitly to physical schema elements (tables, columns, joins).
- Aggregation rules, filters, and calculation logic are defined in a semantic layer, not in individual reports or dashboards.
- Ambiguous field names are resolved through a governed data dictionary, not tribal knowledge.

- AI systems query through the semantic layer rather than directly against raw schemas.

Fresh: Temporal Integrity

Freshness for structured data goes well beyond "is the data current?" It encompasses a set of temporal problems that are unique to machine learning and that traditional data quality frameworks never anticipated. Three distinct failure modes threaten Analytical AI when temporal integrity breaks down. They show up as training-serving skew, label leakage, and point-in-time violations.

Training-serving Skew

Training-serving skew is a difference between how data behaves during model training and how it behaves during production serving (Sato and Iyer, 2021). Google's "Data Validation for Machine Learning" paper identifies a pattern they call "time travel," where a feature like click count appears higher in training data than in serving data because training data is generated after the serving event, incorporating clicks that occurred between serving and dataset creation. The model learns from a distribution of click rates that does not match what it sees in production. Breck et al. describe this as biasing the model against a different distribution of click rates than the one observed at serving time (Breck et al., 2019).

Without ongoing monitoring, production data drifts away from training data. Google Cloud's Vertex AI guidance focuses on comparing training and serving distributions because the failure can be invisible from aggregate model metrics until predictions begin to degrade. The control is straightforward: monitor skew continuously, alert when distributions diverge, and make feature definitions shared between training and serving rather than duplicated in separate pipelines (Sato and Iyer, 2021).

Label Leakage

Label leakage occurs when information that would not be available at prediction time is inadvertently incorporated into model training. Princeton researchers compiled evidence of a reproducibility crisis in ML-based science, finding 41 papers across 30 scientific fields where data leakage was discovered, collectively affecting 648 papers and "in some cases leading to wildly overoptimistic conclusions" (Kapoor and Narayanan, 2024). In a particularly telling case from political science, all papers claiming that complex ML models vastly outperformed logistic regression for predicting civil wars failed to reproduce once data leakage was corrected.

In healthcare, a 2025 JAMA Network Open study found that 37 of 92 published AI models (40.2%) built to predict same-admission clinical outcomes from MIMIC hospital data used diagnostic codes as features, even though those codes are not finalized until after patient discharge (Ramadan et al., 2025). Models trained on these codes to predict in-hospital mortality achieved areas under the ROC curve of 0.971 to 0.976, performance that collapses in real-time clinical deployment where those codes simply do not yet exist.

In fraud detection, the pattern shows up as a "time travel" production failure. A daily batch-computed feature like "user chargeback count in the last 30 days" joins to transactions with a value that includes chargebacks reported after the transaction occurred. Training recall is high because the model sees confirmed fraud signals. Production recall collapses because at actual transaction time, those signals don't yet exist.

Point-in-time Violations

Point-in-time violations happen when current feature values are used for historical events. Joining a customer's current credit score to a loan application from 18 months ago injects future knowledge into the model. The mechanism for preventing this is the *as-of join*, which retrieves the most recent feature value that existed at or before each event's timestamp. Databricks' Feature Store documentation states: "This is important to prevent data leakage, which occurs when you use feature values for model training that were not available at the time the label was recorded. This type of error can be hard to detect and can negatively affect the model's performance."

Why Analytical AI Needs Temporal Integrity

A Scientific Reports study of ML model aging tested four model types across 32 datasets (128 model-dataset pairs) and observed temporal degradation in 91% of cases (Vela et al., 2022). The point is not that these were obviously unstable environments. The study found degradation even when datasets had no abrupt changes in the target variable. The paper identified multiple degradation patterns, including gradual degradation, explosive failure (abrupt accuracy collapse after a long stable period), increasing unpredictability, chaotic behavior, and evolving feature bias. The authors concluded: "AI models do not remain static, even if they achieve high accuracy when initially deployed, and even when their data comes from seemingly stable processes."

Zillow's iBuying collapse is the highest-profile real-world example. Zillow shut down its algorithmic home-buying business in November 2021, ultimately reporting $881 million in iBuying losses for full-year 2021, laying off roughly 2,000 employees, and seeing its stock fall roughly 25% on the announcement (Zillow Group, 2022; CNBC, 2021). Independent analyses of Zillow's inventory at the time found the pricing algorithm had overpaid on roughly two-thirds of the homes it purchased, 64% in one 963-home sample and 66% in a KeyBanc analysis of 650 Zillow-owned homes (Business Insider, 2021; Wolf Street, 2021). The program was shut down entirely.

Diagnostic Question

When you rebuild a training dataset for model retraining, can you reconstruct the exact data state that existed at the time each historical label was observed, or are you pulling current values and joining them to historical events?

AI-ready Standard for Temporal Integrity

Temporal integrity is AI-ready only when training data can be reconstructed exactly as it existed at prediction time:

- Feature stores or equivalent infrastructure enforce point-in-time correctness through as-of joins for all training dataset construction.
- Training and serving pipelines compute features identically, with automated skew detection comparing distributions between the two.
- Slowly changing dimensions (SCD Type 2) or temporal tables preserve historical attribute values, not just current state.
- Model performance is monitored continuously for drift, with automated alerts when metrics degrade beyond defined thresholds.

- Data platforms support time travel queries (Delta Lake's *TIMESTAMP AS OF* and Iceberg's *FOR SYSTEM_TIME AS OF*) for reproducible training runs and audit trails.

Traceable: Documentation

Traceability for structured data comes down to one thing: *data lineage*. Can you explain what the data means, where it came from, how it got here, and what rules govern its use? If the answer is "ask Sarah, she's been here since 2014," that's not traceability. That's organizational fragility.

The Documentation Gap Is Severe and Expensive

Only 3% of companies' data meets basic quality standards when measured by whether the data is fit for purpose (Nagle, Redman, and Sammon, 2017). Monte Carlo Data's 2022 survey found that data teams spend 40% of their time handling data quality issues and that those issues affect 26% of company revenue (Monte Carlo Data, 2022).

The downstream effects are severe. Monte Carlo Data's 2023 survey found that data downtime nearly doubled year over year, with monthly incidents rising from 59 to 67 and average time to resolution increasing 166% to 15 hours per incident (Monte Carlo Data, 2023). Without documentation, every incident is a detective story. With it, you follow the map.

Data lineage, the documented record of where data came from and how it was transformed, cuts incident resolution from days to minutes by providing a debugging roadmap from broken output back through transformations to source. Without lineage, engineers waste time checking log files across platforms and interviewing teammates about recent changes. With lineage, they trace the issue upstream in minutes.

The impact of documentation goes beyond debugging. A 2025 survey by Precisely and Drexel University's LeBow College of Business found that organizations investing in data governance report improved analytics quality (58%), improved data quality (58%), increased cross-team collaboration (57%), increased regulatory compliance (50%), and faster access to relevant data (36%) (Precisely and Drexel LeBow, 2025). Discover Financial Services cataloged more than one million datasets with Alation and reports saving more than 200,000 hours, cutting data-discovery time from up to two days to as little as 15 minutes (Alation, n.d.).

The Regulatory Imperative Is Now Operational Necessity

The EU AI Act's Article 10 requires that high-risk AI systems document data governance and management practices for all training, validation, and testing datasets, including data collection processes, preparation operations, assumptions, and examination for biases. Annex IV mandates "datasheets" for training data covering provenance, scope, labeling procedures, and cleaning methodologies. Article 18 requires retention of all technical documentation for 10 years after a system is placed on the market (Regulation (EU) 2024/1689).

In the United States, California's Assembly Bill 2013, titled "Generative Artificial Intelligence: Training Data Transparency," takes effect January 1, 2026, and requires developers to publicly disclose dataset sources, whether datasets include copyrighted material or personal information, cleaning and processing steps, and collection timeframes (Cal. AB 2013, 2024). Separately, the California Privacy Protection Agency's 2025 rulemaking package, effective January 1, 2026, with automated decision-making provisions phasing in by January 1, 2027, requires businesses to conduct risk assessments before using personal information to train ADMT or AI systems and to maintain inventories of personal-information use as part of related cybersecurity-audit obligations (CPPA, 2025).

This regulatory convergence means that the metadata you need for good AI engineering (field definitions, lineage, transformation history, quality metrics, privacy classifications) is the same metadata you need for regulatory compliance. Building it once serves both purposes.

What Documentation Includes for Structured Data

A complete documentation standard for CRAFT-compliant structured data covers six areas:

- **Data dictionary:** Every field has an explicit definition, data type, allowed values, and business context.
- **Business rules:** Calculation logic, aggregation methods, and filter criteria are codified.

- **Update frequencies:** How often each data source refreshes and what latency to expect.
- **Known limitations:** What the data doesn't cover, which populations are underrepresented, and what time periods have quality gaps.
- **Privacy classifications:** Which fields contain PII, what consent basis applies, and which jurisdictions govern the data.
- **Lineage:** The documented path from source system through transformation to consumption point, with version history for every significant change.

Diagnostic Question

If a data scientist wants to understand how a field called *CUSTOMER_RISK_SCORE* is calculated and whether it can be used as an ML feature, can they find a documented answer in under 15 minutes, or do they need to ask around and make assumptions?

AI-ready Standard for Documentation

- Every table and column has a maintained data dictionary entry with a business definition, not just technical metadata.
- Business rules and metric calculations are codified in a semantic layer or equivalent governed repository.
- Data lineage is tracked automatically from source through transformation to consumption.
- Update frequencies and freshness SLAs are documented and monitored.
- Known limitations and coverage gaps are recorded alongside the data, not in a separate wiki that nobody reads.
- Privacy classifications are applied at the field level and enforced through access controls.
- Documentation is versioned and retained for the duration required by applicable regulations (10 years under EU AI Act Article 18).

Table 9.1 Structured Data CRAFT Summary

CRAFT Dimension	Characteristic	Critical Question
Complete	Entity Integrity	Does every record resolve to a single canonical entity across all source systems?
Complete	Relational Completeness	Are relationships between entities (parent-child, customer-account, product-order) captured and queryable?
Retrievable	Computational Accessibility	Can AI systems discover and consume features without manual engineering or tribal knowledge?
Accurate	Semantic Clarity	Do three different people running the same query get the same answer?
Fresh	Temporal Integrity	Can you reconstruct the exact data state at any historical point in time?
Traceable	Documentation	Can a data scientist understand how any field is calculated and whether it's safe to use as an ML feature?

Structured Data CRAFT Summary

The six elements presented in this chapter and in Table 9.1 work together. A missing data dictionary creates ambiguity about freshness SLAs. Incomplete lineage documentation creates blind spots for impact analysis. Undocumented business rules invite different interpretations of the same metric. Good documentation is integrated, not scattered. It lives where data engineers, analysts, and AI teams need it: in semantic layers, data catalogs, and automated lineage systems that update as your data evolves.

Case Study: The Telco Churn Model

Imagine a mid-size telecom company building a churn prediction model. They have a mature data warehouse that powers excellent BI dashboards. Their analyst team produces weekly churn reports that executives trust. The data warehouse has been running for eight years. It's stable, reliable, and well-understood by the people who use it.

The data science team pulls customer data from the warehouse to train a churn model. They discover the following.

- **Completeness failure:** The customer dimension table has duplicate records. The same customer appears under slightly different names across billing and CRM systems ("John Smith" vs. "J. Smith" vs. "John A. Smith"). Entity resolution was never a priority because human analysts could spot duplicates in reports. But the ML model treats each record as a separate customer. Feature computations like "average monthly spend" and "support ticket frequency" are diluted across fragments. The model can't see the full picture of any individual customer's behavior.
- **Retrievability failure:** Key behavioral data, like web session logs and app usage patterns, lives in a separate data lake that isn't joined to the warehouse. The data warehouse team never integrated it because BI reports didn't need it. The data science team can query the warehouse tables but can't easily join them with the behavioral data that would be the strongest churn predictors.
- **Accuracy failure:** The warehouse contains four different "revenue" fields: *GROSS_REV, NET_REV, ADJ_REV,* and *BILLED_AMT*. Nobody documented which one the churn reports use. The data science team picks *NET_REV*, but it turns out the analyst team always used *ADJ_REV* for churn analysis because it excludes promotional credits. The model trains on the wrong signal.
- **Freshness failure:** The warehouse uses SCD Type 1, overwriting current values in place. When a customer downgrades their plan, the old plan is gone. The model can't see that the customer was on a premium plan last month and is now on basic. That downgrade pattern, one of the strongest churn indicators, is invisible. There's no point-in-time history to reconstruct temporal features.
- **Traceability failure:** A field called *CUST_RISK_SCORE* appears in the warehouse. Nobody on the data science team knows how it's calculated. The analyst who built it left two years ago. The team includes it as a feature anyway. It turns out the risk score was itself derived partly from churn status, introducing target leakage into the model. Without documented lineage, there was no way to catch this.

The model goes through development. It shows 92% accuracy in test. The team celebrates.

In production, accuracy drops to 61%. The duplicated entities produced inflated feature values. The wrong revenue measure trained a noisy signal. The missing temporal dimension hid the most predictive behavioral patterns. And the leaked risk score gave the model information it can't access in production.

Every one of these failures traces back to a CRAFT gap. The data was good enough for BI. It wasn't close to ready for AI.

This isn't hypothetical. S&P Global Market Intelligence reported in 2025 that 42% of companies have abandoned most of their AI initiatives, up from 17% the prior year, with 46% of proofs of concept scrapped before reaching production (S&P Global, 2025). Most companies have yet to show tangible value from AI.

The data was never the problem for BI. It's the problem for AI.

Training data for Analytical AI has its own CRAFT profile. Entity integrity matters because duplicate or inconsistent entities in training data teach the model wrong relationships. Temporal integrity matters because training on stale data produces models that reflect yesterday's patterns. Chapter 4's training data CRAFT table (Table 4.3) provides the complete framework.

The BI-to-AI Translation Gap

Most organizations believe their data is ready for AI because it powers reliable BI systems. This belief is dangerous.

The BI data warehouse was engineered for human decision-making. Humans interpret context, spot anomalies, apply judgment, and ask clarifying questions. When a dashboard shows something odd, an analyst investigates. When field names are abbreviated, experts decode them. When definitions conflict, analysts navigate by experience. Humans are the error-correction layer.

ML models lack this layer. They consume data as-is. When the data is ambiguous, models learn noise. When it's incomplete, they learn biased patterns. When it's temporally incoherent, they learn phantom signals that evaporate in production. A model doesn't have an analyst's institutional knowledge. It has whatever signal exists in the data, and if that signal is corrupted by BI-era design decisions, the model is corrupted from training onward.

This is why "good for BI" and "good for AI" require such different standards. You're not upgrading from "good" to "better." You're shifting from systems designed for human intelligence to systems designed for AI. The requirements fundamentally change.

Looking Ahead

Structured data is the foundation for Analytical AI, and CRAFT compliance is the requirement for that foundation to be solid. Completeness ensures entities and relationships are intact. Retrievability ensures AI systems can actually consume the data. Accuracy ensures meaning is unambiguous. Freshness ensures temporal integrity. Documentation enables understanding and compliance.

The six characteristics defined in this chapter and shown in Figure 9.1 form a coherent standard that transforms data designed for human consumption into data that can reliably power machine learning systems. None is optional. None can be compromised without accepting corresponding risk in model performance and trustworthiness.

The gap between "good for BI" and "good for AI" isn't a minor upgrade. It's a fundamental rethinking of how structured data is designed, maintained, and served. Organizations that make this rethinking operational will extract insight their competitors can't access. Not because they have better models, but because they have better data. And better data wins.

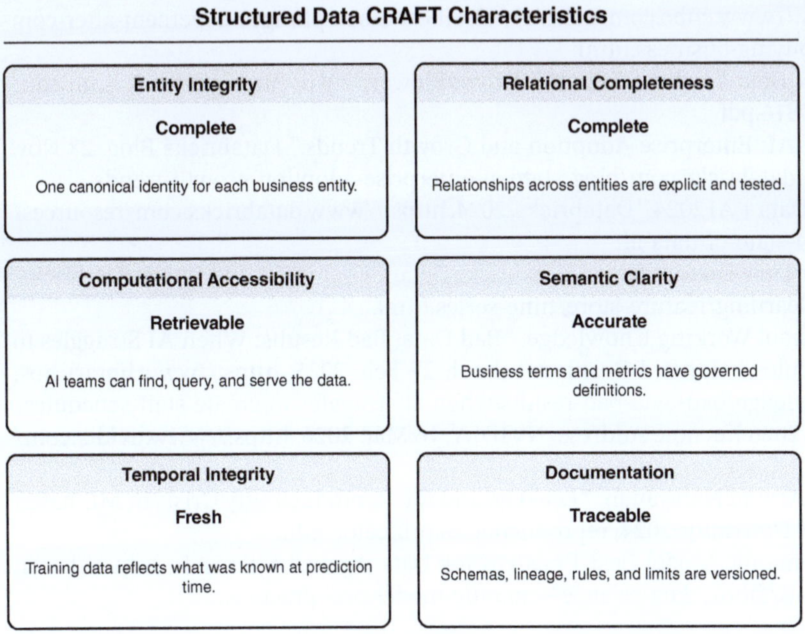

Figure 9.1 What makes structured data ready for Analytical AI.

References

Alation. "Discover Financial Services Customer Case Study." Alation, https://www.alation.com/resource-center/download/7p3vnbbznfiw/3rBSUJ41ce9FspqBxynXjC/2b6a52a258060d0a96f9843dd0bfa5b1/alation-customer-case-study-discover.pdf.

Anaconda. "Sixth Annual State of Data Science Report." Anaconda, 2023, https://www.anaconda.com/state-of-data-science-report-2023.

AtScale. "Semantic Context for Natural Language Query." AtScale, 2024, https://www.atscale.com/blog/semantic-context-natural-language-query/.

Breck, Eric, et al. "Data Validation for Machine Learning." MLSys, 2019, https://mlsys.org/Conferences/2019/doc/2019/167.pdf.

Business Insider. "Zillow Offers Pauses Home Buying After Overpaying in Key Markets." Business Insider, 2021, https://www.businessinsider.com/zillow-offers-pause-ibuyers-homes-atlanta-phoenix-dallas-houston-minneapolis-2021-10.

California Assembly Bill 2013. "Generative Artificial Intelligence: Training Data Transparency." California Legislative Information, 2024, https://leginfo.legislature.ca.gov/faces/billTextClient.xhtml?bill_id=202320240AB2013.

California Privacy Protection Agency. "California Finalizes Regulations to Strengthen Consumers' Privacy." CPPA, 23 Sept. 2025, https://cppa.ca.gov/announcements/2025/20250923.html.

CNBC. "Zillow Stock Plunges 24% after Company Exits Home-Buying Business." CNBC, 3 Nov. 2021, https://www.cnbc.com/2021/11/03/zillow-stock-plunges-24percent-after-company-exits-home-buying-business.html.

CrowdFlower. "2016 Data Scientist Report." CrowdFlower, 2016, https://www2.cs.uh.edu/~ceick/UDM/CFDS16.pdf.

Databricks. "State of AI: Enterprise Adoption and Growth Trends." Databricks Blog, 28 Nov. 2025, https://www.databricks.com/blog/state-ai-enterprise-adoption-growth-trends.

Databricks. "State of Data + AI 2024." Databricks, 2024, https://www.databricks.com/resources/analyst-paper/2024-state-of-data-ai.

Databricks. "Point-in-Time Feature Joins." Databricks Documentation, https://docs.databricks.com/en/machine-learning/feature-store/time-series.html.

Harvard Business School Working Knowledge. "Bad Data, Bad Results: When AI Struggles to Create Staff Schedules." Harvard Business School, 27 Feb. 2025, https://www.library.hbs.edu/working-knowledge/bad-data-bad-results-when-ai-struggles-to-create-staff-schedules.

Huang, Jensen. GTC 2026 Keynote Address. NVIDIA, 16 Mar. 2026, https://www.nvidia.com/gtc/keynote/.

Kapoor, Sayash, and Arvind Narayanan. "Leakage and the Reproducibility Crisis in ML-based Science." *Princeton University*, 2024, reproducible.cs.princeton.edu.

Microsoft Learn. "Semantic Model Best Practices for Data Agent." Microsoft, https://learn.microsoft.com/en-us/fabric/data-science/semantic-model-best-practices.

Monte Carlo Data. "Data Downtime Nearly Doubled Year-Over-Year, Monte Carlo Survey Says." BusinessWire, 2 May 2023, https://www.businesswire.com/news/home/20230502005377/en/Data-Downtime-Nearly-Doubled-Year-Over-Year-Monte-Carlo-Survey-Says.

Monte Carlo Data. "Data Engineers Spend Two Days Per Week Firefighting Bad Data." Monte Carlo Data, 2022, https://www.montecarlodata.com/blog-2022-data-quality-survey/.

Mordor Intelligence. "Semantic Layer and Knowledge Graph for Agentic AI Market." Mordor Intelligence, 2025, https://www.mordorintelligence.com/industry-reports/semantic-layer-and-knowledge-graph-for-agentic-ai-market.

MuleSoft. "2024 Connectivity Benchmark Report." Salesforce/MuleSoft, 2024, https://www.mulesoft.com/sites/default/files/resource-assets/MuleSoft_Connectivity-Benchmark-Report-2024.pdf.

Nagle, Tadhg, Thomas C. Redman, and David Sammon. "Only 3% of Companies' Data Meets Basic Quality Standards." Harvard Business Review, 11 Sept. 2017, https://hbr.org/2017/09/only-3-of-companies-data-meets-basic-quality-standards.

Ng, Andrew. "Data-centric AI." The Batch, Issue 84, DeepLearning.AI, 2021, https://www.deeplearning.ai/the-batch/issue-84/.

Precisely and Drexel University LeBow College of Business. "2025 Planning Insights: Data Governance Adoption Has Risen Dramatically." Precisely, 2025, https://www.precisely.com/blog/data-integrity/2025-planning-insights-data-governance-adoption-has-risen-dramatically/.

Ramadan, F., Liu, Y., Burkhart, M., Parker, R., and Beaulieu-Jones, B. K. "Diagnostic Codes in AI Prediction Models and Label Leakage of Same-Admission Clinical Outcomes." JAMA Network Open, 2025, https://doi.org/10.1001/jamanetworkopen.2025.50454.

Regulation (EU) 2024/1689 of the European Parliament and of the Council. Official Journal of the European Union, 13 June 2024, https://eur-lex.europa.eu/eli/reg/2024/1689/oj/eng.

Robinson, Joshua, et al. "RelBench: A Benchmark for Deep Learning on Relational Databases." *arXiv*, 2024, arxiv.org/abs/2407.20060.

S&P Global. "Generative AI Experiences Rapid Adoption, but with Mixed Outcomes." S&P Global, 2025, https://www.spglobal.com/market-intelligence/en/news-insights/research/ai-experiences-rapid-adoption-but-with-mixed-outcomes-highlights-from-vote-ai-machine-learning.

Sato, Kaz, and Anand Iyer. "Monitor Models for Training-serving Skew with Vertex AI." *Google Cloud Blog*, 30 July 2021, https://cloud.google.com/blog/topics/developers-practitioners/monitor-models-training-serving-skew-vertex-ai.

Sculley, David, et al. "Hidden Technical Debt in Machine Learning Systems." *NeurIPS*, 2015.

Sequeda, Juan, et al. "A Benchmark to Understand the Role of Knowledge Graphs on Large Language Model's Accuracy for Question Answering on Enterprise SQL Databases." *arXiv*, 2023, arxiv.org/abs/2311.07509.

Shahbazi, Nima, et al. "Through the Fairness Lens: Experimental Analysis and Evaluation of Entity Matching." arXiv, 2023, https://arxiv.org/html/2307.02726.

Validity. "The State of CRM Data Management in 2024." Validity, 2024, https://www.validity.com/wp-content/uploads/2024/05/The-State-of-CRM-Data-Management-in-2024.pdf.

Vela, Daniel, et al. "Temporal Quality Degradation in AI Models." *Scientific Reports*, vol. 12, article 11654, 8 July 2022, https://doi.org/10.1038/s41598-022-15245-z.

Wolf Street. "AI-Powered House Flipper Zillow Seeks to Dump 7,000 Houses to Big Investors." Wolf Street, 1 Nov. 2021, https://wolfstreet.com/2021/11/01/ai-powered-house-flipper-zillow-seeks-to-dump-7000-houses-to-big-investors-after-it-overpaid-for-them-buy-high-sell-low-take-one-time-noncash-charge-no/.

Yackel, Ryan. "The Impact of Bad Data + How Observability Is the Solution." *IBM*, 2 June 2022, www.ibm.com/think/insights/observability-data-benefits.

Zillow Group. "Zillow Group Reports Fourth-Quarter and Full-Year 2021 Financial Results." Zillow Group, 10 Feb. 2022, https://investors.zillowgroup.com/investors/news-and-events/news/news-details/2022/Zillow-Group-Reports-Fourth-Quarter-and-Full-Year-2021-Financial-Results/default.aspx.

Chapter 10
Systems for Structured Data

The gap between a data-quality standard and an operating architecture is often where execution slows. Leaders may know that customer records need entity integrity and that metrics need semantic clarity, yet still lack a tested answer to two practical questions: which control will resolve records across systems, and which governed interface will keep definitions consistent for the selected AI use case?

Chapter 9 defined what structured data needs to be AI-ready across five CRAFT dimensions. This chapter is about the technology that gets you there.

This chapter favors open interfaces and exportable metadata, consistent with the ODI philosophy introduced in Chapter 1. Open table formats, catalog APIs, and semantic specifications can reduce switching friction, but portability still depends on implementation choices, supported engines, contracts, and migration tests. The leadership objective is not openness as a slogan. It is a documented ability to retrieve data, definitions, history, and policy metadata outside a single vendor's control.

BCG's 2025 study of more than 1,250 companies reports that the top 5% in its maturity classification, which it calls future-built, achieved 1.7 times the revenue growth of the stagnating and emerging groups. BCG attributes the difference to five interlinked strategies, not to structured data alone (BCG, 2025). For leaders, the relevant lesson is narrower: data architecture should be evaluated as one part of a broader operating system for value.

System Requirements by CRAFT Dimension

Each CRAFT dimension has a primary infrastructure contribution, but the systems are not exclusive to one dimension. Table 10.1 is a decision map. It connects each dimension to a leading control and to the evidence leaders should request before treating that control as operational.

Retrieval infrastructure cuts across the other dimensions. A feature-delivery system can consume resolved identities, apply point-in-time joins, and serve values at a defined latency. A semantic interface can expose governed metrics, dimensions, and business rules to supported consumers. Neither system creates complete entities or correct definitions on its own; each depends on upstream controls and tested integration.

These systems can reinforce one another when they share identifiers, metadata, ownership, and policy controls. They can also create cost and coupling when

Table 10.1 CRAFT Infrastructure Decision Map

CRAFT Dimension	Primary Infrastructure Contribution	Cross-Cutting Dependencies	Evidence Leaders Should Request
Complete	Entity and relationship controls	Catalog, semantic, lineage, and source-capture controls	Measured duplicate and linkage errors; coverage; thresholds; exception ownership
Retrievable	Governed access and serving paths	Catalog, identity, security, and service-management controls	Access tests; service levels; supported interfaces; failure and fallback behavior
Accurate	Semantic and validation controls	Entity resolution, lineage, temporal, and policy controls	Approved definitions; query tests; exception handling; version and policy evidence
Fresh	Temporal and refresh controls	Change capture, orchestration, observability, and retained history	Event-time rules; measured latency; retained history; point-in-time reconstruction tests
Traceable	Catalog, lineage, quality, and privacy controls	Identity, access, policy, and release-management controls	Ownership; lineage coverage; alert response; access and classification audit evidence

implemented without a use-case boundary. A semantic layer without catalog context is hard to govern. Entity resolution without retained history cannot reconstruct what was believed at an earlier date.

The first investment should follow the highest-cost failure mode. Semantic work is a strong early candidate when conflicting definitions constrain a high-value use case. Entity controls may come first when fragmented identities drive the error. Temporal or retrieval controls may lead when reproducibility or latency is the binding constraint.

Completeness: Entity Resolution and Relationships

Entity resolution identifies which records belong together. It's the first line of defense against a fragmented view of your business.

Duplicate and fragmented records vary by domain, source, matching policy, and data-entry process. Treat the rate as a local measurement, not an industry constant. Establish a labeled sample, measure false matches and missed matches, segment the result by relevant population, and repeat the test as sources and entities change.

Modern entity resolution combines two approaches. Deterministic matching relies on exact matches using verifiable identifiers such as email addresses and phone numbers. It is precise when those identifiers are clean and present, but its coverage falls as data quality degrades. Probabilistic matching uses statistical and machine-learning techniques to link records likely to represent the same entity even when they lack shared identifiers, recovering matches that rigid rules can miss.

A common pattern combines deterministic rules, probabilistic linkage, clustering, and human review. The order should reflect error cost and data conditions. Store confidence scores and decision provenance with each link, define precision and recall targets by use case, and route uncertain or high-impact matches to an accountable reviewer.

Scale changes the engineering design because an unconstrained all-pairs comparison grows quadratically. Blocking and indexing reduce the candidate space before detailed comparison. The Splink project reports linking one million records on a laptop in about a minute and support for Spark workloads above 100 million records; these are project-reported capabilities, not guarantees for a particular schema, cluster, or accuracy target (UK Ministry of Justice, 2024).

Master Data Management: The Golden Record

Entity resolution identifies which records belong together. Master Data Management (MDM) takes the next step: it creates a single, authoritative, de-duplicated, and enriched representation of each entity, called a "golden record."

The decision to invest in MDM should begin with the cost of duplicate or inconsistent master entities, the number of systems that must share them, regulatory and audit needs, and the operating model for stewardship. Market growth does not establish that a product is necessary. A bounded business case should identify the affected decisions, baseline error, target improvement, owner, and switching cost.

Evaluate MDM against a local baseline rather than a secondhand industry percentage. Measure match precision and recall on a reviewed sample, survivorship errors on critical attributes, time to resolve exceptions, downstream reconciliation effort, and the business impact of incorrect merges or splits. Set a target only after the denominator and error cost are explicit.

Products differ in matching, survivorship, stewardship, hierarchy management, graph support, deployment model, and integration surface. Treat these as capabilities to test, not as a definition of a modern platform. Require representative data, a disclosed evaluation method, export tests, and an operating model for exceptions.

First-party materials describe different automation approaches. Informatica says CLAIRE agents plan and reason through data-management tasks, while Tamr documents machine-learning linkage, human feedback, and LLM-based semantic comparison (Informatica, n.d.; Tamr, n.d.). These vendor descriptions help define evaluation questions. They do not establish comparable performance.

Identity Graphs and Relationship Management

MDM can create governed master records. An identity graph can make selected identity links and relationships available to supported applications, sometimes at low latency. The two capabilities may be combined, but an identity graph is not a required runtime layer for every MDM design.

A customer may interact through email, a mobile application, a website, a store, and a service center. An identity graph can connect approved identifiers across those touchpoints and expose a resolved profile. The design still needs consent, access controls, match thresholds, retention rules, and a way to reverse incorrect links.

For an AI use case, a resolved identity can support a more coherent feature set and reduce duplicate counting. It does not by itself prevent data leakage. Leakage controls require point-in-time construction, feature availability checks, separation of training and evaluation data, and review of when each attribute became knowable.

Graph infrastructure can be useful when relationship traversal is central to the workload, as in fraud networks, supply-chain dependencies, or household relationships. Relational, graph, and hybrid designs can all be valid. Select the model by query pattern, scale, update behavior, governance needs, and operational skill rather than by category alone.

Entity controls must be maintained as records, identifiers, and relationships change. The refresh pattern may be batch, near-real-time, or online. Define it from the use case's decision latency and error cost, then monitor drift in match quality and unresolved exceptions.

Accuracy: The Semantic Layer

A semantic layer is a bridge: governed business semantics over structured data that can also supply context to AI. It defines metrics, dimensions, relationships, terminology, and policy hooks for supported consumers. Implementations may compile queries, cache results, materialize aggregates, or delegate execution to a data platform. The architectural test is governed meaning and reproducible behavior, not one physical design.

The semantic layer standardizes five things:

- **Metrics:** How priority measures such as churn rate, revenue, and gross margin are calculated, versioned, and tested
- **Dimensions:** Customer segments, time periods, geographic regions, and the hierarchies between them
- **Relationships:** How tables join together, cardinality rules, valid query paths, and foreign key constraints
- **Business terminology:** The glossary of standardized terms that maps business concepts to technical implementation
- **Access rules:** Who can see which data, enforced and tested across supported consuming tools

The practical value proposition is to define governed semantics once and reuse them through supported interfaces. BI dashboards, AI assistants, reports, and agents can share a calculation only when each consumer uses the governed

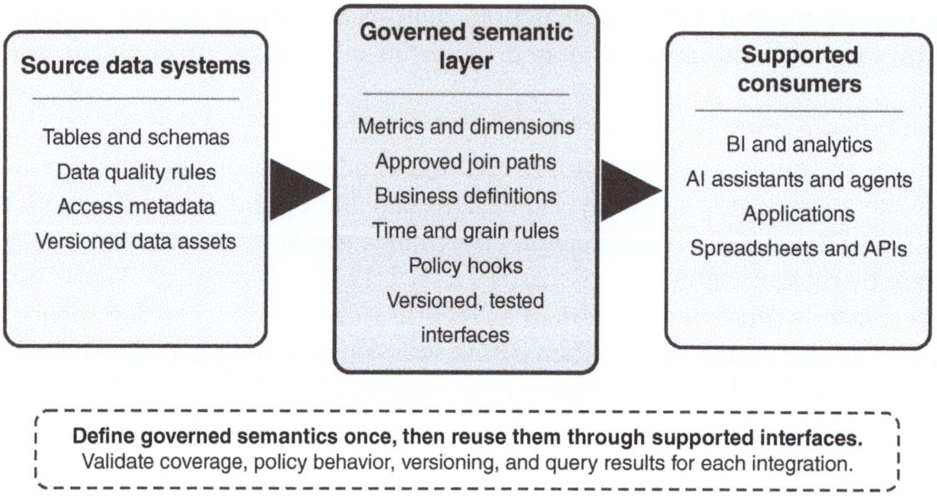

Figure 10.1 Semantic layer architecture.

definition and passes coverage, policy, version, and result tests. Figure 10.1 shows that bounded relationship.

Why the Semantic Layer Matters for AI

A raw schema does not tell an AI system which revenue definition, calendar, or source is authoritative (Floratou et al., 2024). In a vendor-published illustration, AtScale describes a dashboard showing 98% on-time delivery and an AI query showing 92% because a customer-waived-delay filter existed only in the BI model (AtScale, 2026). The example is useful as a failure mode, not as independent evidence of product performance.

A 2023 data.world technical report evaluated zero-shot GPT-4 on 43 questions over 13 selected insurance tables using synthetic sample data. It reports average execution accuracy of 16.7% for direct SQL prompts and 54.2% with a knowledge-graph representation. In two high-schema-complexity groups, direct SQL scored 0% while the knowledge-graph approach scored 35.7% and 38.7% (Sequeda et al., 2023). The report is vendor-authored and describes one experimental setup.

The result indicates that modeled context can help in that setting. It is not a general accuracy guarantee, and it does not establish that every knowledge graph or semantic layer will produce the same effect.

Other first-party results use different tasks and denominators. dbt Labs calls its 2023 result an early proof of concept and reports 83% on eight addressable questions, with three questions excluded as not addressable. Snowflake reports more than 90% on an internal benchmark. AtScale reports 92.5% on 40 TPC-DS questions against a 20% control (dbt Labs, 2023; Snowflake, 2024; AtScale, 2024). These results are not directly comparable and should not be combined into a maturity curve.

Spider 2.0 shows how task design changes reported performance. The ICLR 2025 paper reports 91.2% execution accuracy on Spider 1.0, 5.7% for the strongest reported parser on Spider 2.0-Lite, and 21.3% for an o1-preview code-agent framework on the full Spider 2.0 task (Lei et al., 2025). A semantic layer can supply governed context, but it does not by itself solve the broader workflow, tool-use, and validation demands in the full benchmark.

Accuracy Through Context Layers

Context controls should be evaluated by what they contribute and by evidence from the organization's own tasks. Table 10.2 replaces incomparable accuracy ranges with a control-and-evidence map.

Table 10.2 Context Controls and Local Validation Evidence

Context Control	What It Contributes	Failure It Can Reduce	Evidence to Validate Locally
Technical metadata	Tables, columns, types, and constraints	Invalid fields, schema mismatches, and unsupported queries	Schema accuracy, coverage, currency, and failed-query review
Relationships	Approved join paths, cardinality, and entity links	Incorrect joins, duplicate matches, and missing entity connections	Join tests, referential exceptions, and linkage-error analysis
Catalog definitions	Business definitions, ownership, and lineage context	Ambiguous terms, inconsistent metrics, and unclear ownership	Steward approval, coverage, and definition-to-source trace
Semantic layer	Governed metrics, rules, dimensions, and query paths	Metric drift, invalid aggregation, and unsupported query logic	Use-case benchmark with denominator, error taxonomy, and policy tests
Feedback and evaluation	Reviewed queries, corrections, monitoring, and controlled updates	Repeated errors, unobserved drift, and unowned exceptions	Repeatable test set, drift checks, exception handling, and owner sign-off

The Vendor Landscape

Three broad architectural categories can help organize a selection, although products may span more than one category:

- BI-native semantic layers embed definitions in a business-intelligence platform. They can offer deep integration with that tool, but reuse, export, and policy behavior must be tested across the organization's other consumers.
- Platform-native semantic layers embed definitions in a data platform. They can integrate closely with the platform's compute and governance services. Leaders should test exportability, version control, supported clients, migration effort, and the cost of rebuilding integrations.
- Independent or headless semantic layers expose definitions through shared interfaces across multiple tools. dbt moved MetricFlow to the Apache 2.0 license in 2025 (dbt Labs, 2025). The Open Semantic Interchange initiative states a goal of a common, vendor-neutral specification (Snowflake, 2025). An open-source license or initiative goal does not by itself prove end-to-end portability.

Choose among these patterns by modeled coverage, policy enforcement, consumer support, performance, operational skill, exportability, migration tests, and total cost. Multi-tool environments may value an independent interface, while a platform-native design may be simpler when the platform boundary is intentional and acceptable.

The Executive Recommendation

Choose the first control by the highest-cost failure in a priority use case. If inconsistent measures cause the error, pilot governed semantics for the affected metrics and query paths. If fragmented entities, missing history, or serving latency is the constraint, start there instead. Establish a baseline, target, owner, test set, decision date, and stop condition before expanding. The Sequeda result shows the potential value of modeled context in one experiment; it does not prescribe a universal sequence (Sequeda et al., 2023).

Freshness and Traceability Infrastructure

Completeness tells you whether the entity is whole. Accuracy tells you whether the meaning is correct. Freshness and traceability tell you whether that meaning is current and whether you can prove it.

Temporal Infrastructure (Freshness)

Chapter 9 established that structured-data freshness means temporal integrity: the ability to track how data changes over time and reconstruct the state of any entity at any historical point.

Slowly Changing Dimension Type 2 is one widely used way to preserve entity history. It adds a new dimension row when a tracked attribute changes and records the period in which each version is valid (Kimball Group, n.d.). Event logs, bitemporal models, snapshots, and versioned feature data can serve related needs. The control objective is point-in-time correctness: a historical training row must use only attributes that were available at the prediction time.

SCD types are design patterns, not a maturity ranking. Type 1 keeps only the current value. Type 2 keeps row-level history. Type 3 keeps a limited prior value. Select the pattern from the business question, required history, correction policy, query behavior, and retention obligation.

The SCD type numbers refer to how a dimension handles change:

- Type 1 overwrites old values and keeps only the current version.
- Type 2 adds a new row for each change and keeps validity dates.
- Type 3 keeps a current value and a limited previous value on the same row.

Time Travel in Modern Tables

Time travel in Apache Iceberg, Delta Lake, and Apache Hudi can query retained table snapshots (Apache Iceberg, n.d.; Delta Lake, n.d.; Apache Hudi, n.d.). This differs from entity-level history inside the current table. Historical access lasts only while the required metadata and data files remain available under the platform's retention and cleanup policies.

Apache Polaris is a top-level Apache Software Foundation project that provides a catalog implementation for Iceberg tables (Apache Polaris, 2026). A pattern such as Iceberg on object storage with a REST catalog can support multiple engines, subject to each engine's tested feature coverage. DuckDB documents support for Iceberg REST catalogs, including Polaris; syntax and behavior are version-dependent and should be validated against the deployed release (DuckDB, n.d.).

Table 10.3 SCD Type 2 vs. Time Travel

Mechanism	What It Tracks	When It Is Needed	Retention or Operating Caveat
SCD Type 2	Entity-version history	Point-in-time entity attributes or joins	Requires effective-date logic, correction rules, and tested joins
Table time travel	Retained full-table snapshots	Reproducing a training, audit, or reporting data state	Availability depends on retained metadata and data files

The Need for SCD Type 2 and Time Travel

An AI system may need entity-level history, reproducible table snapshots, or both. SCD Type 2 can answer what an entity's attributes were when an event occurred. Table time travel can reconstruct a retained table snapshot used for a training or reporting run. Table 10.3 separates the decision and its operating caveat.

Iceberg supports named tags that reference snapshots and can have independent lifecycle and retention settings (Apache Iceberg, n.d.). Teams must configure and monitor those settings if a tag is part of a reproducibility control. A Databricks implementation example logs a Delta table version with an MLflow run; this is a pattern teams can implement, not an automatic guarantee across deployments (Databricks, 2021).

Feature Stores Bridge Batch and Real-time Freshness

Batch freshness keeps training and analytical datasets current on a schedule. Real-time freshness serves current feature values when an AI system needs to make a prediction.

A common feature-store design uses an offline path for training data and an online path for low-latency inference, but implementations vary and may share underlying storage. Technologies such as Delta Lake, Hudi, Redis, or DynamoDB are examples, not requirements. The critical controls are point-in-time retrieval, consistent feature definitions, and measured serving behavior.

Shared feature definitions and point-in-time joins can reduce training-serving skew, but they do not eliminate defects in code, data, deployment, or online availability. Feast documents workflows for generating training data and serving features for inference (Feast, n.d.). Teams still need parity tests, freshness monitoring, fallback behavior, and incident review.

Documentation Infrastructure (Traceability)

For covered high-risk AI systems, Regulation (EU) 2024/1689 Article 10 establishes data-governance and management requirements, and Article 12 requires technical capability for automatic logging. Regulation (EU) 2026/1744 amended the application schedule (European Parliament and Council of the European Union, 2024; 2026). Applicability depends on system classification and the amended timetable; this summary is not legal advice.

Data catalogs are centralized repositories of metadata that make data easier to find, understand, and govern. Modern catalogs connect technical metadata, business definitions, ownership, policies, and lineage across cloud and hybrid data estates.

In a vendor-published customer case study, Alation reports that Discover Financial Services cataloged roughly one million tables for more than 2,500 users and estimated 200,000 hours saved (Alation, n.d.). Treat the figures as the vendor's customer estimate, not as an independently measured or generally expected result.

Databricks' Unity Catalog deserves special mention because it governs data and AI assets, including tables and models, in one framework. It also captures audit and lineage information so teams can trace how governed assets flow from source data into downstream models (Databricks, n.d.).

Automated lineage can expose the recorded origin and downstream dependencies of data used by an AI system. Its value depends on connector coverage, metadata freshness, transformation visibility, ownership, and response practice. Column-level lineage can support feature investigation when the relevant transformations are captured and the lineage is tested.

Data-quality monitoring can detect freshness, volume, schema, and distribution changes, while validation frameworks can test explicit expectations as pipelines run (Monte Carlo, 2023; Great Expectations, n.d.). Detection is useful only when coverage, thresholds, ownership, and response latency are defined. Teams may investigate before or after downstream impact, depending on when the signal arrives. Figure 10.2 shows the impact path and the control loop.

Privacy classification is one part of the control set. Discovery, access, consent, minimization, retention, policy enforcement, and monitoring also matter. Select tools by coverage and evidence, and verify that sensitive attributes remain governed as they move through transformations and supported AI interfaces.

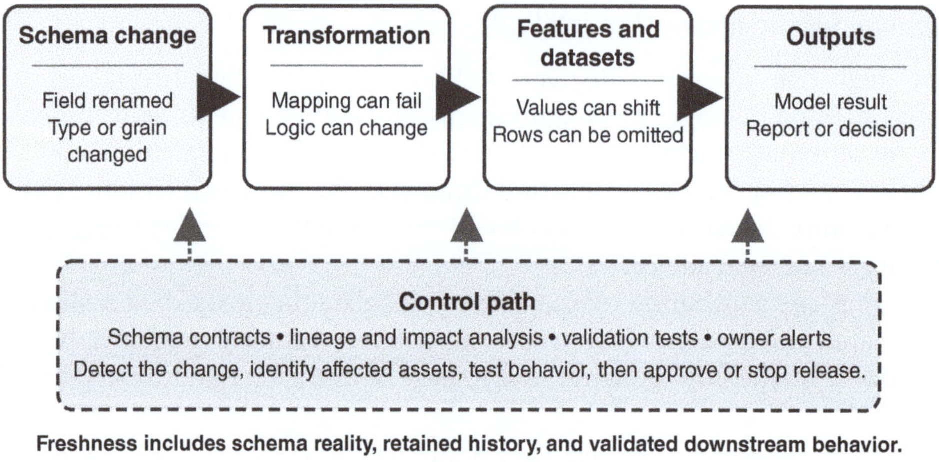

Figure 10.2 Schema evolution impact and control path.

Structured Data CRAFT Checklist

Use the following questions to assess CRAFT readiness for a defined structured-data use case. CRAFT is this book's framework, not a certification standard. Each answer should identify scope, owner, service level, and test evidence.

Completeness

- ☐ Are entity-resolution controls defined for critical entities, with match thresholds, an accountable owner, a review cadence, and test evidence?
- ☐ Do priority business entities have governed records, documented source precedence, and tested exception handling?
- ☐ Are approved entity links available across the source systems required by the use case, with consent and reversal controls where applicable?
- ☐ Are duplicate, false-match, and missed-match rates measured on reviewed samples and tracked by relevant segment?
- ☐ Are the relationships required by the use case explicitly modeled, owned, and tested?

Retrievable

- ☐ Can approved AI consumers query the required data through governed and tested interfaces?

- ☐ Do training and inference paths meet the use case's measured freshness and latency requirements?
- ☐ Is point-in-time retrieval tested for the features or attributes whose historical availability matters?
- ☐ Are scale, latency, availability, and fallback behavior defined and tested for the approved workload?

Accurate

- ☐ Are priority metric calculations governed, versioned, and validated against approved examples?
- ☐ Does the business glossary map in-scope terms to precise definitions, owners, and technical implementations?
- ☐ Do supported AI consumers use the governed semantic interface where semantic control is required, with exceptions documented?
- ☐ Are definition changes reviewed, version-controlled, tested, and communicated to affected consumers?

Fresh

- ☐ Does the selected temporal pattern preserve the entity history required by the use case?
- ☐ Can the system reconstruct required historical states within a defined retention window?
- ☐ Can retained snapshots or equivalent controls reproduce approved training and reporting datasets?
- ☐ Do temporal tests verify that features were available at the relevant prediction time?

Traceable

- ☐ Does the catalog cover the in-scope assets with ownership, definitions, and review dates?
- ☐ Does tested lineage cover the transformations and consumers required for impact analysis?
- ☐ Are quality checks tied to thresholds, owners, response times, and evidence of closure?
- ☐ Are sensitive attributes classified and governed across the in-scope lineage and access paths?

A complete set of supported answers indicates evidence of CRAFT readiness for the stated scope, not general compliance or certification. Record unanswered questions as a prioritized control backlog with owners and decision dates.

Prioritization: Where to Start

You can't fix every CRAFT gap at once. Start with the layers that make the next layer easier to justify and operate.

The sequence should follow dependencies and evidence, not a fixed calendar. A practical four-gate pattern is as follows:

1. **Define the decision:** Select one high-value use case, name its highest-cost data failure, and record the baseline, owner, target, and stop condition.
2. **Pilot the binding control:** Implement the smallest semantic, entity, temporal, retrieval, or traceability control that can change the measured outcome.
3. **Validate the result:** Use a representative test set, disclose the denominator and errors, and confirm operating ownership, service levels, and fallback behavior.
4. **Scale after the gate:** Add the next dependency only when the pilot meets its target and the team can operate the control.

This pattern preserves momentum without promising a universal timeline. The first control may be a semantic layer, entity resolution, retained history, a feature-delivery path, or a catalog and lineage improvement. The order should be explicit about the failure it addresses and the evidence required to continue.

Large simultaneous programs can hide whether any control changed the outcome. Use bounded pilots and decision gates, but do not mistake a small pilot for production readiness. Expansion requires stable ownership, measurable service levels, exception handling, security review, and demonstrated benefit.

Choose architectures that preserve exportability, documented interfaces, standards support, and tested migration paths while recognizing the integration and commercial benefits of managed platforms. Evaluate total switching cost and operational fit. No licensing model removes the need for portability tests and a credible exit plan.

Looking Ahead

With the structured-data foundation governed and testable, the next question is how enterprise knowledge becomes context that AI can retrieve and use. Chapter 11, "Context Data and CRAFT," turns to that context layer and the controls that keep it current, traceable, and fit for the task.

The leadership decision is not which platform category to buy first. It is which structured-data failure is constraining the use case, which control can change the measured outcome, and who will operate it. Chapter 11 builds on that governed foundation by showing how context data supplies definitions, policies, provenance, and retrieved evidence that AI systems need to interpret facts correctly.

References

Alation. "Customer Case Study: Discover Financial Services." Alation, n.d., https://www.alation.com/resource-center/download/7p3vnbbznfiw/3rBSUJ41ce9FspqBxynXjC/2b6a52a258060d0a96f9843dd0bfa5b1/alation-customer-case-study-discover.pdf.

Apache Hudi. "Time Travel Query." Apache Hudi Documentation, n.d., https://hudi.apache.org/docs/sql_queries/#time-travel-query.

Apache Iceberg. "Branching and Tagging." Apache Iceberg Documentation, n.d., https://iceberg.apache.org/docs/latest/branching/.

Apache Polaris. "Apache Polaris Graduates to a Top-Level Project." Apache Polaris, 19 Feb. 2026, https://polaris.apache.org/blog/2026/02/19/apache-polaris-graduates-to-top-level-project/.

AtScale. "Enable Natural Language Prompting with a Semantic Layer and GenAI." AtScale, 2024, https://www.atscale.com/blog/enable-natural-language-prompting-with-semantic-layer-genai/.

AtScale. "Why BI-Embedded Semantic Layers Fail for Enterprise AI." AtScale, 2026, https://www.atscale.com/blog/bi-embedded-semantic-layers-fail-ai/.

BCG. "The Widening AI Value Gap." Boston Consulting Group, Sept. 2025, https://media-publications.bcg.com/The-Widening-AI-Value-Gap-Sept-2025.pdf.

Databricks. "Reproduce Anything: Machine Learning Meets Data Lakehouse." Databricks, 26 Apr. 2021, https://www.databricks.com/blog/2021/04/26/reproduce-anything-machine-learning-meets-data-lakehouse.html.

Databricks. "What Is Unity Catalog?" Databricks Documentation, n.d., https://docs.databricks.com/aws/en/data-governance/unity-catalog/.

dbt Labs. "Semantic Layer as the Data Interface for LLMs." dbt Blog, 30 Nov. 2023, https://www.getdbt.com/blog/semantic-layer-as-the-data-interface-for-llms.

dbt Labs. "Announcing Open Source MetricFlow: Governed Metrics for Any AI or Data Application." dbt Blog, Oct. 2025, https://www.getdbt.com/blog/open-source-metricflow-governed-metrics.

Delta Lake. "Table Batch Reads and Writes." Delta Lake Documentation, n.d., https://docs.delta.io/latest/delta-batch.html.

DuckDB. "Iceberg Extension." DuckDB Documentation, n.d., https://duckdb.org/docs/current/core_extensions/iceberg/overview.

European Parliament and Council of the European Union. "Regulation (EU) 2024/1689 of 13 June 2024 Laying Down Harmonised Rules on Artificial Intelligence." Official Journal of the European Union, 12 July 2024, https://eur-lex.europa.eu/eli/reg/2024/1689/oj/eng.

European Parliament and Council of the European Union. "Regulation (EU) 2026/1744 of the European Parliament and of the Council of 8 July 2026 amending Regulations (EU) 2024/1689, (EU) 2018/1139 and (EU) 2023/1230 as regards the simplification of the implementation of harmonised rules on artificial intelligence (Digital Omnibus on AI)." Official Journal of the European Union, 24 July 2026, https://eur-lex.europa.eu/eli/reg/2026/1744/oj/eng.

Feast. "Quickstart." Feast Documentation, n.d., https://docs.feast.dev/getting-started/quickstart.

Floratou, Avrilia, et al. "NL2SQL Is a Solved Problem... Not!" CIDR, 2024, https://vldb.org/cidrdb/2024/nl2sql-is-a-solved-problem-not.html.

Great Expectations. "Run Validations." Great Expectations Documentation, n.d., https://docs.greatexpectations.io/docs/core/run_validations/.

Informatica. "CLAIRE AI Engine." Informatica, n.d., https://www.informatica.com/platform/claire-ai.html.

Kimball Group. "Dimensional Modeling Techniques." Kimball Group, n.d., https://www.kimballgroup.com/data-warehouse-business-intelligence-resources/kimball-techniques/dimensional-modeling-techniques/.

Lei, Fangyu, et al. "Spider 2.0: Evaluating Language Models on Real-World Enterprise Text-to-SQL Workflows." ICLR, 2025, https://arxiv.org/abs/2411.07763.

Monte Carlo. "Data Observability for Dummies, Monte Carlo Special Edition." John Wiley and Sons, 2023, https://info.montecarlodata.com/hubfs/Assets%20-%20Guides%2C%20Ebooks%2C%20Reports/Wileys-%20Data%20Observability%20for%20Dummies-%20Monte%20Carlo%20Special%20Edition.pdf.

Sequeda, Juan F., et al. "A Benchmark to Understand the Role of Knowledge Graphs on Large Language Model's Accuracy for Question Answering on Enterprise SQL Databases." data.world, 13 Nov. 2023, https://data.world/mstatic/assets/pdf/kg_llm_accuracy_benchmark_11132023_public.pdf.

Snowflake. "Snowflake Cortex Analyst: Behind the Scenes." Snowflake Engineering Blog, 14 Aug. 2024, https://www.snowflake.com/en/blog/engineering/snowflake-cortex-analyst-behind-the-scenes/.

Snowflake. "Snowflake, Salesforce, dbt Labs and More Launch the Open Semantic Interchange Initiative." Snowflake, 23 Sept. 2025, https://www.snowflake.com/en/news/press-releases/

snowflake-salesforce-dbt-labs-and-more-revolutionize-data-readiness-for-ai-with-open-semantic-interchange-initiative/.

Tamr. "About Tamr's AI-Native Approach." Tamr Documentation, n.d., https://cloud.docs.tamr.com/docs/about-tamrs-ai-native-approach.

UK Ministry of Justice. "Splink: Fast, Accurate and Scalable Probabilistic Data Linkage." GitHub, 2024, https://github.com/moj-analytical-services/splink.

Chapter 11
Context Data and CRAFT

Imagine a Generative AI system rolling out to your customer support team, trained on massive public datasets and fine-tuned on your company documentation. Two weeks in, customers complain that the AI keeps giving answers that are technically correct but outdated, or citing policies that changed six months ago. The model isn't broken. The knowledge it's reasoning over is incomplete, contradictory, and stale. This is the hidden killer in Generative AI deployments.

Context data is information represented in forms optimized for AI reasoning. These are meaning-enriched representations that AI systems can search, retrieve, and reason over to produce grounded, accurate outputs. Think of it this way: if a Generative AI model is a chef, context data is the *mise en place*.

Mise en place is the French culinary term for "everything in its place." Before a chef starts cooking, ingredients are prepped, measured, organized, and laid out on the counter. The full pantry is in the back, but the chef can't rummage through shelves while plating dishes during dinner service. The *mise en place* is what's been selected, prepared, and made accessible for the task at hand.

Your raw documents, recordings, emails, and PDFs are the full pantry. Valuable, but not in the form the AI can use mid-conversation. Context data is the *mise en place:* knowledge selected, transformed, and organized so the AI can grab exactly what it needs when it needs it.

If your business outcome depends on knowledge work, whether that's customer support, content generation, research assistance, or expert consultation, you need Generative AI. And Generative AI is only as good as the context data it reasons over.

Context data has a ceiling set by the layers beneath it. If your structured data lacks semantic clarity (Chapter 9), your knowledge graphs will inherit that ambiguity. If your raw data has fidelity gaps (Chapter 7), no amount of embedding sophistication will recover the lost signal. Context data transforms and enriches what exists below; it can't compensate for what was never captured.

Four Forms of Context Data

Context data takes four primary forms, each serving AI in different ways. These four forms are vector embeddings, knowledge graphs, semantic layers, and annotated corpora.

- **Vector embeddings** convert text or images into arrays of numbers that capture semantic meaning in ways machines can compare mathematically. Word2Vec showed that semantic relationships between words can be represented as vector operations, which made semantic similarity measurable (Mikolov et al., 2013). BERT made embeddings contextual, so "bank" gets different representations in finance versus geography. Sentence-BERT made enterprise-scale semantic search practical, cutting computational cost from roughly 65 hours for 10,000 sentences down to about five seconds (Reimers and Gurevych, 2019).
- **Knowledge graphs** make relationships explicit through networks of entities and connections. A customer isn't just a row in a table but an entity linked to products purchased, contracts signed, support tickets filed, and business units served. The impact on AI accuracy is dramatic. LLMs perform poorly when running zero-shot prompts directly on enterprise SQL databases, but accuracy improves significantly when the same questions are posed over a knowledge graph representation, and it improves further with additional context. That improvement comes from better context data, not a model upgrade.
- **Semantic layers** provide machine-accessible business definitions that translate cryptic database schemas into language that AI can understand. When a data warehouse field reads *REV_NET_ADJ_LC*, a semantic layer tells the AI this means "net revenue adjusted for local currency." Without translation, the AI guesses. Gartner projects that by 2027, organizations that prioritize semantics in AI-ready data could increase agentic AI accuracy by up to 80% and reduce costs by up to 60% (Gartner, 2026).

Table 11.1 Information Represented in Forms Optimized for AI Reasoning

	Vector Embeddings	Knowledge Graphs	Semantic Layers	Annotated Corpora
	Mathematical representations of meaning	Entity-relationship networks	Business logic abstraction	Human-labeled training examples
Enables	• Semantic search • Similarity matching	• Multi-hop reasoning • Disambiguation	• Consistent metric definitions • Text-to-SQL	• Fine-tuning • Evaluation benchmarks
Storage	• Vector databases (Pinecone, Weaviate, pgvector)	• Graph databases (Neo4j, Amazon Neptune)	• dbt Semantic Layer, Cube, AtScale	• Label Studio, Prodigy, Scale AI

- **Annotated corpora** are source documents enriched with metadata, tags, cross-references, and provenance information. They enable AI to find answers and cite where those answers come from, linking responses back to specific documents and passages.

These four forms (which are also presented in Table 11.1) often work together. A Retrieval-Augmented Generation (RAG) system, where an AI retrieves relevant information before generating responses, might use vector embeddings to find relevant passages, knowledge graphs to understand entity relationships, a semantic layer to interpret business metrics, and annotated corpora to provide citations. They're complementary, not competing.

Why Context Data Quality Is Categorically Different

To understand context data, it helps to recognize how it differs from the data layers covered in earlier chapters.

- **Raw data** is unstructured: documents, emails, recordings, notes. Raw data quality is about signal fidelity: is the recording clear? Is the OCR accurate? Have files been corrupted in transmission?
- **Structured data** is organized, typed, and relational. It uses tables with columns and explicit schemas. It can have clear foreign keys showing how a

customer links to orders, contracts, and support tickets. Structured data quality is about semantic clarity: does "revenue" mean the same thing everywhere? Is the schema enforced? Do the relationships hold?

- **Context data** is different from both. It is meaning-enriched representations optimized specifically for AI reasoning. Context data isn't stored the way humans read documents. It's transformed: embedded as vectors, chunked at semantic boundaries, annotated with provenance, sometimes organized into knowledge graphs where entities and relationships become explicit.

This transformation is where quality becomes difficult to measure and easy to lose. Unlike structured data, where database constraints enforce schema compliance, or raw data, where checksums verify file integrity, context data quality depends on fidelity through a transformation pipeline. Every step can distort meaning.

A vector embedding reduces rich semantic information to a point in high-dimensional space. Chunking breaks documents into fragments, and the way you break them determines what meaning gets preserved and what gets destroyed. Annotation adds metadata, but that metadata can be inaccurate. The provenance chain from source document to embedding to retrieval to AI output can break at any point.

This matters because Generative AI operates entirely through this transformed data. Your model never sees the original documents. It sees only what made it through the transformation pipeline. If the transformation loses critical information or adds distortions, the model can't recover that loss.

Context data quality is the binding constraint on Generative AI performance for most organizations. The model can't be better than the context data it reasons over. Better context data always produces better AI output, regardless of which model you use.

The Missing Layer

Most enterprises have raw data: filing cabinets full of documents, years of call recordings, terabytes of emails, and PDFs. They also have structured data: databases, warehouses, CRM systems, financial models, decades of organized facts in explicit schemas.

Most enterprises don't have context data.

This missing layer is the single biggest reason that Generative AI initiatives struggle. The vast majority of enterprise Generative AI pilots fail to deliver measurable impact on P&L. The Informatica CDO Insights 2025 survey of 600 data leaders found that 97% face difficulty demonstrating business value from GenAI initiatives (Informatica, 2025).

These aren't model failures. They're data layer failures.

Industry estimates commonly put the share of enterprise data that is unstructured at 80% to 90%, though the exact figure varies by source and definition. The point is simpler: most enterprise knowledge is not already AI-ready. The vast majority of enterprise data sits untouched while AI systems try to work with almost nothing.

The failure isn't the model. It's the absence of CRAFT-compliant context data between the model and the organization's knowledge.

CRAFT Applied to Context Data

Generative AI operates through context windows. It retrieves relevant information and reasons over it to produce outputs. The quality of those outputs depends entirely on CRAFT compliance across all five dimensions.

A context window is the working memory the model can see for one request: the user prompt, system instructions, retrieved passages, tool results, and conversation history that fit inside the model's token limit. Anything outside that window doesn't exist to the model while it's answering.

Recall that CRAFT's five dimensions are complete, retrievable, accurate, fresh, and traceable. In context data, accuracy, freshness, and traceability converge around one operational problem: whether retrieved context is correct, current, and tied to a source you can verify. That is why this chapter treats completeness and retrievability directly, then uses consistency as the practical container for freshness, accuracy, and traceability problems.

Context data depends on both the raw data and structured data layers beneath it. A RAG system retrieving from poorly structured knowledge bases inherits every upstream quality problem.

That provides the working map for the rest of this chapter. It starts with completeness, because missing knowledge creates blind spots. Then it covers retrievability, because content that can't be found is operationally equivalent to content that doesn't exist. The chapter then ends with consistency, where accuracy, freshness, and traceability collide in production RAG systems.

Completeness: Spanning Knowledge Domains

When knowledge domains are missing from your context data layer, AI has blind spots. Completeness for context data breaks down into three distinct problems:

- **Semantic coverage:** Does the knowledge base actually contain the information your AI needs?
- **Depth versus breadth:** Are you providing the right amount of context?
- **Domain completeness:** Does every functional area of your organization have represented knowledge?

Semantic Coverage: What Gets Retrieved, What Gets Lost

Semantic coverage is the most fundamental question about a context data layer: does your knowledge base actually contain the information your AI system needs to answer the questions it will receive?

RAG systems rely on vector similarity, so coverage gaps can be completely invisible to keyword audits. A document that mentions a topic may still fail to semantically cover the range of ways users phrase queries about that topic. Your knowledge base might contain a policy document about employee benefits, but if users ask about "parental leave" and the document only discusses "family medical leave," the retriever may return nothing useful.

A 2025 methodology paper from BCG X quantified this formally (Broestl et al., 2025). In a real product-documentation use case, an initial test suite achieved only 69.4% basic semantic coverage, with four out of five semantic document clusters identified as blind spots. That is a real product with real documentation, and more than 30% of the topic space was effectively invisible to the AI.

If AI cannot find relevant content, one of two bad outcomes occurs. Either the system says, "I do not know" (frustrating but honest) or it hallucinates an answer (dangerous, and more common). Barnett et al. (2024) catalogued seven distinct failure points in RAG systems, spanning retrieval failures, consolidation problems, and generation failures. The correct content may exist somewhere in the knowledge base, but it ranks too low to surface, gets buried in noise, fails to make it into the context window, or reaches the model in a form the model cannot use.

Stanford HAI conducted what its authors describe as the first preregistered empirical evaluation of AI-driven legal research tools, including the first assessment of proprietary RAG-based legal tools marketed as "hallucination-free" (Magesh et al., 2024).

They found that LexisNexis Lexis+ AI and Thomson Reuters Ask Practical Law AI each hallucinate between 17 and 33% of the time (Magesh et al., 2024). Westlaw AI-Assisted Research hallucinated more than 34% of the time. These aren't general-purpose chatbots. These are purpose-built legal research tools backed by massive legal databases containing tens of millions of documents. And they still hallucinate on roughly one in five to one in three queries.

Meta's CRAG benchmark examined 4,409 question-answer pairs across five domains and found that the best industry RAG solutions answer only 63% of questions without any hallucination (Yang et al., 2024). The benchmark found much lower accuracy on questions involving higher dynamism, lower popularity, or higher complexity. These are exactly the long-tail queries where knowledge base coverage is thinnest.

The consequences are documented. In 2024, a British Columbia tribunal ruled against Air Canada after its AI chatbot told a customer he could apply for a retroactive bereavement fare refund within 90 days. That policy did not exist for completed travel. The tribunal found Air Canada "did not take reasonable care to ensure its chatbot was accurate," and ordered the airline to pay $812.02 in damages, interest, and fees (Moffatt v. Air Canada, 2024 BCCRT 149). Companies are now legally liable for hallucinations caused by incomplete knowledge bases.

A 2023 class-action lawsuit alleged that more than 90% of appealed denials from UnitedHealthcare's nH Predict system were overturned, though only a small fraction of denied patients appeal. The complaint attributed the reversal rate to the algorithm's alleged failure to account for patients' full individual circumstances. That remains an allegation, not an adjudicated finding (Estate of Lokken et al. v. UnitedHealth Group, 2023).

Semantic coverage is measured and improved systematically. Query log analysis mines unanswered queries and low-confidence responses as the primary signal for coverage gaps. Incomplete knowledge bases produce measurably worse answers. The more incomplete the knowledge, the steeper the performance drop. The relationship accelerates. Every gap you close matters more than the last.

The structural problem is stark. Industry estimates commonly put the share of enterprise data that is unstructured at 80% to 90%, though the exact figure varies by source and definition. Seagate's 2020 Rethink Data report found that only 32% of data available to enterprises is put to work, leaving 68% unleveraged (Seagate, 2020).

And a large share of organizational knowledge is tacit: held in people's heads as intuition, experience, and pattern recognition rather than captured in formal systems (Nonaka, 1991). If much of your knowledge is tacit and most documented data goes unused, the effective semantic coverage of any enterprise knowledge base is a small fraction of what the organization actually knows.

Optimal Content Depth: The "Lost in the Middle" Problem

More context seems like it should always help. The research says otherwise. Completeness includes not just whether information exists, but whether you're providing the optimal amount of it per query.

Nelson Liu and colleagues tested multiple LLMs on multi-document question answering and found a consistent U-shaped performance curve: accuracy is highest when relevant information appears at the start or end of context, and it significantly degrades when it's in the middle (Liu et al., 2024).

GPT-3.5-Turbo's accuracy dropped from 75.8% when the answer was in the first document to 53.8% when it was in the tenth. That worst-case performance was below the model's closed-book performance of 56.1%. Adding more context with the answer buried in the middle made the model perform worse than giving it no context at all. This pattern held across most of the closed and open models tested, though the U-shape was weaker or absent in smaller models such as 7B Llama-2 (Liu et al., 2024). MIT researchers later identified the architectural cause: attention-mechanism design choices, including causal masking and positional-encoding schemes such as RoPE, can create a tradeoff between long-term positional decay and the outsized importance transformers place on early tokens (Wu et al., 2025).

Extended context windows do not solve this. The study found that when an extended-context model and its standard counterpart both fit a given input within their windows, "performance between them is nearly identical" (Liu et al., 2024). A bigger window does not fix the model's inability to use what's in the middle of that window.

The industry is racing to build bigger context windows. Models now advertise 128K, 200K, even million-token contexts. But there is growing evidence that most of this capacity goes to waste or actively hurts performance. Databricks ran over 2,000 experiments on 13 LLMs and found that most models hit a decline point well before their claimed maximum. GPT-4-Turbo and Claude-3-Sonnet start degrading after 16K tokens. Llama-3.1-405b starts declining after 32K.

Even GPT-4-0125-preview peaks at 64K. Models advertising 128K+ context windows cannot effectively use more than a fraction of that capacity (Leng et al., 2024).

Amazon Science pushed this further. Even when models could perfectly retrieve 100% of relevant information, performance still degraded 13.9% to 85% as input length increased (Du et al., 2025). It is not that the model gets distracted by irrelevant content. The sheer length of input imposes a processing burden independent of content quality.

Research on context window utilization found that optimal performance occurs at seven to nine chunks, corresponding to 40% to 70% context window occupancy. Performance showed no improvement beyond 10 chunks in almost all tested combinations (Juvekar and Purwar, 2024). Liu et al. found that increasing from 20 to 50 retrieved documents produced only about a 1% to 1.5% answer-accuracy improvement, even as retriever recall continued improving (Liu et al., 2024). Filling the whole context window is not automatically better. The model simply cannot use unlimited material.

How you divide documents into chunks is the single most consequential architectural choice in a RAG pipeline. NVIDIA tested three primary chunking approaches across five document collections and found that page-level chunking had the highest average answer accuracy, while optimal chunk size varied by dataset and query type (Han, 2025). That is the real lesson: chunking is an empirical design choice, not a default setting.

A 2025 study of postoperative rhinoplasty care guidance found that adaptive chunking aligned to logical topic boundaries achieved 87% response accuracy, versus 50% for a fixed-size baseline ($p = 0.001$) (Gomez-Cabello et al., 2025). That does not mean every RAG system should use the same chunk size. It means chunk size needs to match information density. Technical manuals require smaller chunks to capture fine-grained details. General content often allows larger segments.

Anthropic's "Contextual Retrieval" technique adds 50 to 100 tokens of document-level context to each chunk before embedding, preserving context that gets lost when documents are split. Anthropic's full contextual retrieval pipeline, contextual embeddings, contextual BM25, and reranking together, reduced retrieval failures by 67% (Anthropic, 2024).

Related-but-wrong documents are more harmful than completely irrelevant ones. This defies intuition. Cuconasu et al. found that associated documents, meaning documents that are contextually related but do not contain the answer, consistently misled models, while genuinely random noise documents could improve accuracy by up to 35% (Cuconasu et al., 2024). Related documents provide plausible but incorrect context that the LLM preferentially attends to. Clearly irrelevant content is easier to filter out. The design implication: narrow and precise beats broad and noisy. Google Research found that context sufficiency can be predicted with at least 93% accuracy using optimized prompting. Before generating an answer, a RAG system can determine whether to proceed with current context, retrieve more, or re-rank what it already has (Joren et al., 2025).

Domain Completeness: Giving Every Team a Voice

Does every functional area of your organization have its knowledge represented? This is where most enterprise AI deployments fall apart.

Forrester research, as reported by *Forbes*, estimated that 60% to 73% of enterprise data goes unused for analytics (Meehan, 2016). MuleSoft's 2024 Connectivity Benchmark Report found that the average enterprise runs 991 applications, with only 28% connected, and that 81% of IT leaders say data silos hinder digital transformation (MuleSoft, 2024). When an AI system needs to understand a customer, it needs purchase history from the CRM, support tickets from the helpdesk, behavioral signals from the website, and contract terms from document management. When those systems are siloed, the model sees only fragments.

The performance gap between domain-grounded AI and general-purpose AI is enormous. A Carnegie Mellon-affiliated case study on domain-specific question answering found that F1 scores improved from 5.45% to 42.21% after retrieval-augmentation improvements (Sun, Wang, and Zhang, 2024). That is nearly an eightfold improvement from grounding the model in domain knowledge.

In legal AI, a 2025 study published in the International Journal of Legal Information found that Lexis+ AI achieved 58% accuracy on legal queries, versus 30% for ChatGPT-4 (Munir et al., 2025). Separately, Dahl et al. found that general-purpose LLMs hallucinated between 58% and 88% of the time on specific, verifiable legal queries about federal court cases (Dahl et al., 2024). Without domain grounding, the models do not just underperform. They confidently fabricate answers at rates no serious legal workflow can tolerate.

The deepest domain completeness challenge is not technical. It is human. A large share of organizational knowledge is tacit: intuitive, experiential, and implicit rather than captured in formal systems (Nonaka, 1991). This is the knowledge that lives in the heads of your most experienced people: the senior underwriter who senses a bad risk before looking at any data point. The logistics team's re-routing decisions when multiple things go wrong simultaneously.

The unspoken understanding of which stakeholder actually needs to approve something, regardless of what the org chart says. Organizations do not know how much tacit knowledge they have, and that uncertainty is itself a strategic liability.

Knowledge workers spend hours every day searching for information. Many digital workers struggle to find the information needed to do their jobs. If humans can't find this knowledge, AI systems certainly can't. Most organizational knowledge isn't neatly captured in documents. When you build a knowledge base for your AI system, you're building on a fraction of what the organization actually knows.

Semantic clusters are groups of documents that occupy the same conceptual neighborhood in embedding space. You don't need the term to be mystical. Cluster the documents, label each cluster with the business topic it represents, then compare those clusters against real query logs. If an entire cluster rarely retrieves, it may be poorly chunked or poorly embedded. If common unanswered questions don't map to any cluster, the knowledge simply isn't there.

Low-confidence and unanswered queries are your coverage defect backlog. Review them weekly, tag each failure by missing topic, source system, business domain, and user intent, then map the tags back to the clusters above. The fix is not to "add more documents." The fix is to add the specific missing knowledge, re-embed it, and rerun the failure set until the gap closes.

Assessment Questions for Completeness

The following are questions to consider to verify the completeness of your context data:

- What percentage of user queries receive high-confidence responses from your RAG system, and how does that vary by domain?
- Have you clustered your knowledge base documents and tested for blind spots in each semantic cluster?
- Which functional domains (HR, legal, finance, operations, product) are currently represented in your context data layer? Which are missing entirely?
- Do you systematically analyze unanswered or low-confidence queries to identify coverage gaps?

- What is the average number of chunks your system retrieves per query, and have you tested whether fewer would improve accuracy?
- Are you filling more than 70% of your context window? If so, you may be hurting performance.
- How much of your organization's operational knowledge exists only in people's heads rather than in formal systems?

Retrievability: Finding Information Before the AI Gets It Wrong

If AI can't find relevant content, one of two bad outcomes occurs. Either the system says, "I don't know" (frustrating but honest) or it hallucinates an answer (dangerous and more common). This is the retrieval miss failure mode, the most documented problem in RAG systems. Barnett et al. (2024) catalogued seven distinct failure points in RAG systems, and the majority trace back to retrieval problems. The correct content exists somewhere in the knowledge base, but it ranks too low to surface, gets buried in noise, or doesn't make it into the context window after consolidation.

Those seven failure modes are not a separate framework for this book. They are a useful diagnostic vocabulary for the retrievability failures this section covers. The practical split is simpler: did the system fail because the right content wasn't retrieved, because too much wrong content was retrieved, or because the retrieved content was correct but insufficient?

Retrieval quality often matters more than model quality. Databricks demonstrated that fine-tuning embedding models on in-domain data can significantly improve retrieval metrics and downstream RAG performance, though the effect depends heavily on dataset and task (Portes et al., 2025). You could upgrade the language model and still miss the real bottleneck if the retriever cannot find the right context.

In production RAG applications, bi-encoders (the standard embedding approach) can struggle with complex queries because embedding similarity is an imperfect proxy for semantic relevance. Adding a cross-encoder reranker as a second retrieval stage can improve retrieval accuracy and downstream answer faithfulness, but the size of the improvement varies by domain, dataset, and reranker model.

A cross-encoder reranker is the second judge in the retrieval process. The first-stage retriever uses embeddings to quickly find likely candidates. The cross-encoder then reads the query and each candidate passage together, scores the actual match, and reorders the results before they enter the context window. It's slower than embedding search, but it catches the subtle mismatches that vector similarity misses.

Related-but-wrong documents are more harmful than completely irrelevant ones. Cuconasu et al. found that associated documents, meaning documents that are contextually related but do not contain the answer, consistently misled models, while genuinely random noise documents could improve accuracy by up to 35% (Cuconasu et al., 2024). Related documents provide plausible but incorrect context that the LLM preferentially attends to. Clearly irrelevant content is easier to filter out. The design implication: narrow and precise beats broad and noisy.

A 2026 study confirmed this across six LLMs and three QA benchmarks. DeepSeek V3 achieved 27.68% accuracy with 500 completion tokens and multiple targeted searches, versus 14.07% with a single search at 16K tokens (McCleary and Ghawaly, 2026). Multiple focused retrievals beat one big context dump by nearly 100%.

Measure retrieval with a small, boring test set before you trust the system. Take the top 100 failed or low-confidence interactions, have a domain expert mark the passages that should have supported each answer, then replay those queries against the retriever. For each query, record whether the answer-bearing document appeared in the top results, how many irrelevant passages came along for the ride, and whether the model hallucinated or admitted it didn't know.

That gives you three concrete metrics: recall, precision, and failure type. Recall asks whether the right passage showed up. Precision asks how much junk arrived with it. Failure type separates retrieval failures from reasoning failures, which matters because those problems get fixed in different places.

Assessment Questions for Retrievability

The following are questions to consider to verify the retrievability of your context data:

- What percentage of your RAG queries successfully retrieve documents that actually contain the answer?
- When a query retrieves 10 documents, how many of those actually contribute relevant information to the answer?
- Have you conducted a diagnostic on your top 100 failure cases? What percentage trace back to retrieval failures versus model reasoning?

- When you conduct user testing, what percentage of retrieval failures lead to hallucinations versus honest "I don't know" responses?
- How are you measuring retrieval precision? How many irrelevant documents get mixed with relevant ones?
- What portion of your retrieval failures come from precision problems (wrong documents retrieved) versus recall problems (relevant documents missed)?
- Are you using cross-encoder reranking where retrieval precision matters? If not, what failure cases justify adding it?

Consistency: Preventing Contradictions from Breaking Trust

As your knowledge base grows and changes, contradiction becomes inevitable. The same fact gets represented differently in different documents. A policy changes, but old documents remain in the system. Source material gets updated, but cached embeddings reflect stale content.

A sales team member finds conflicting guidance in different knowledge base documents and gets confused. A customer support agent provides inconsistent answers because the retriever surfaces documents from different points in time. The language model, reasoning over a mix of current and obsolete information, synthesizes something that sounds confident but is actually incoherent.

Research on chunking strategies illustrates the scale of this problem. A peer-reviewed clinical RAG study of postoperative rhinoplasty care guidance found that adaptive chunking aligned to logical topic boundaries achieved 87% response accuracy, versus 50% for a fixed-size baseline ($p = 0.001$) (Gomez-Cabello et al., 2025). That is the same content, the same model, and the same queries. The only difference was how context data was prepared. Accuracy in the representation determined accuracy in the output.

Once documents are chunked and embedded, they become vectors in a database. The system has no inherent way to know that Document A (uploaded in January) has been replaced by Document B (uploaded in March) or that they're related versions of the same source. To the RAG system, they're just two vectors that happen to be similar. Both get retrieved. Both get fed to the model. The model must reconcile them.

Knowledge conflicts represent a critical bottleneck to achieving trustworthy AI. When source content changes and the knowledge base accumulates contradictions, the language model is asked to synthesize "truth" from a mix of current facts and historical artifacts. Standard RAG systems don't distinguish between a chunk from a current document and a chunk from a superseded one. Without version tracking, your knowledge base accumulates contradictions over time.

Version management is the operational backbone of coherence. When source content changes, every chunk derived from that content needs to be updated, re-embedded, and re-indexed. Without version tracking, your knowledge base accumulates contradictions over time as some documents reflect current reality and others reflect states from months or years ago. Standard RAG systems don't distinguish between a chunk from a current document and a chunk from a superseded one. They're just vectors in a database, all treated as equally valid.

The implication is straightforward: you can't treat a knowledge base as a static corpus. It's an operational system. Content ages. Policies change. Regulations update. Your context data layer requires active curation, version management, and lifecycle protocols for every document in the system.

The fix is to treat every chunk as a versioned artifact, not a loose text fragment. Store the source document ID, version number, effective date, expiration date, owner, and replacement relationship with every chunk. At retrieval time, filter out expired chunks, choose the most recent approved version, and block retrieval when two current chunks contradict each other on the same policy or rule.

Contradictions are detectable if you make the system look for them. Run scheduled duplicate and near-duplicate checks across policy, procedure, and product documents. Compare retrieved passages for conflicting dates, thresholds, eligibility rules, and required actions. Then route conflicts to the content owner before those passages reach users.

Assessment Questions for Consistency

The following are questions to consider to verify the consistency of your context data:

- Are you actively managing document versions in your knowledge base? Or does old content coexist with new?

- When source content changes (a policy is updated, a regulation changes), how quickly does that cascade to your embeddings and retrievals?
- Do you have a process for identifying and flagging conflicting information in your knowledge base?
- How would you detect if your RAG system is retrieving contradictory information and presenting it as coherent?
- What percentage of your knowledge base is stale (hasn't been updated in the last six months)? Is that acceptable for your use cases?
- Are citations accurate and verifiable, or does the system sometimes cite documents that don't actually support the claim?
- If an older policy document and a newer one both exist in your system, how does the retriever decide which to prioritize?

Context Data CRAFT Summary

Context data is where Generative AI stops being abstract and starts depending on the quality of your knowledge system. Completeness determines whether the right knowledge exists. Retrievability determines whether the system can find it. Accuracy, freshness, and traceability determine whether the retrieved context is correct, current, and defensible.

A RAG pipeline is not a search feature bolted onto a model. It's an operational data product. It needs coverage analysis, retrieval testing, version rules, contradiction detection, and citations that point back to real source material. If those controls aren't in place, the model will still answer. It just won't be grounded.

Context data is the working memory of enterprise AI. Treat it like infrastructure.

References

Anthropic. "Introducing Contextual Retrieval." Anthropic Blog, 2024, https://www.anthropic.com/news/contextual-retrieval.

Barnett, Scott, et al. "Seven Failure Points When Engineering a Retrieval Augmented Generation System." arXiv, 11 Jan. 2024, https://arxiv.org/abs/2401.05856.

Broestl, Noah, et al. "Methodological Framework for Quantifying Semantic Test Coverage in RAG Systems." arXiv, 13 Aug. 2025, https://arxiv.org/abs/2510.00001.

Cuconasu, Florin, et al. "The Power of Noise: Redefining Retrieval for RAG Systems." SIGIR 2024, arXiv:2401.14887, 2024, https://arxiv.org/abs/2401.14887.

Dahl, Matthew, et al. "Large Legal Fictions: Profiling Legal Hallucinations in Large Language Models." Journal of Legal Analysis, vol. 16, no. 1, 2024, pp. 64–93, https://doi.org/10.1093/jla/laae003.

Du, Yufeng, et al. "Context Length Alone Hurts LLM Performance Despite Perfect Retrieval." Findings of EMNLP 2025, arXiv:2510.05381, 2025, https://arxiv.org/abs/2510.05381.

Estate of Gene B. Lokken et al. v. UnitedHealth Group, Inc. et al. Complaint, U.S. District Court for the District of Minnesota, No. 0:23-cv-03514, 14 Nov. 2023, https://www.classaction.org/media/the-estate-of-gene-b-lokken-et-al-v-unitedhealth-group-inc-et-al.pdf.

Gartner. "Gartner Says Lack of Semantics Causes Inaccurate AI Agents and Wasted Spending." Gartner, 11 May 2026, https://www.gartner.com/en/newsroom/press-releases/2026-05-11-gartner-says-lack-of-semantics-causes-inaccurate-artificial-intelligence-agents-and-wasted-spending.

Gomez-Cabello, Carlos A., et al. "Comparative Evaluation of Advanced Chunking for Retrieval-Augmented Generation in Large Language Models for Clinical Decision Support." Bioengineering, vol. 12, no. 11, 2025, article 1194, https://www.mdpi.com/2306-5354/12/11/1194.

Han, Steve. "Finding the Best Chunking Strategy for Accurate AI Responses." NVIDIA Technical Blog, 18 June 2025, https://developer.nvidia.com/blog/finding-the-best-chunking-strategy-for-accurate-ai-responses/.

Informatica. "CDO Insights 2025: Racing Ahead on GenAI and Data Investments While Navigating Perennial Data Management Challenges." Informatica, 2025, https://www.informatica.com/campaigns/cdo-insights-2025/assets/resources/cdo_insights_2025_PDF.pdf.

Joren, Hailey, et al. "Sufficient Context: A New Lens on Retrieval Augmented Generation Systems." ICLR 2025, arXiv:2411.06037, 2025, https://arxiv.org/abs/2411.06037.

Juvekar, Kush, and Anupam Purwar. "Introducing a New Hyper-parameter for RAG: Context Window Utilization." arXiv, 17 Aug. 2024, https://arxiv.org/abs/2407.19794.

Leng, Quinn, et al. "Long Context RAG Performance of LLMs." Databricks Blog, 12 Aug. 2024, https://www.databricks.com/blog/long-context-rag-performance-llms.

Liu, Nelson F., et al. "Lost in the Middle: How Language Models Use Long Contexts." Transactions of the Association for Computational Linguistics, vol. 12, 2024, pp. 157–173, https://doi.org/10.1162/tacl_a_00638.

Magesh, Varun, et al. "Hallucination-Free? Assessing the Reliability of Leading AI Legal Research Tools." arXiv, 30 May 2024, https://arxiv.org/abs/2405.20362.

McCleary, Kyle, and James Ghawaly. "Quantifying the Accuracy and Cost Impact of Design Decisions in Budget-Constrained Agentic LLM Search." arXiv:2603.08877, 2026, https://arxiv.org/abs/2603.08877.

Meehan, Mary. "Where Data Goes To Die: Big Data Still Holds Answers, But They're Not Where You're Looking For Them." Forbes, 8 Dec. 2016, https://www.forbes.com/sites/ma

rymeehan/2016/12/08/where-data-goes-to-die-big-data-still-holds-answers-but-theyre-not-where-youre-looking-for-them/.

Mikolov, Tomas, et al. "Efficient Estimation of Word Representations in Vector Space." ICLR Workshop, 2013, https://arxiv.org/abs/1301.3781.

Moffatt v. Air Canada, 2024 BCCRT 149. British Columbia Civil Resolution Tribunal, 14 Feb. 2024, https://www.canlii.org/en/bc/bccrt/doc/2024/2024bccrt149/2024bccrt149.html.

MuleSoft. "2024 Connectivity Benchmark Report." MuleSoft Research, 2024, https://www.mulesoft.com/sites/default/files/resource-assets/MuleSoft_Connectivity-Benchmark-Report-2024.pdf.

Munir, Bakht, et al. "Evaluating AI in Legal Operations: A Comparative Analysis of Accuracy, Completeness, and Hallucinations in ChatGPT-4, Copilot, DeepSeek, Lexis+ AI, and Llama 3." International Journal of Legal Information, vol. 53, no. 2, 2025, https://doi.org/10.1017/jli.2025.10052.

Nonaka, Ikujiro. "The Knowledge-Creating Company." Harvard Business Review, Nov.-Dec. 1991, https://hbr.org/1991/11/the-knowledge-creating-company-2.

Portes, Jacob, et al. "Improving Retrieval and RAG with Embedding Model Finetuning." Databricks Blog, 20 Feb. 2025, https://www.databricks.com/blog/improving-retrieval-and-rag-embedding-model-finetuning.

Reimers, Nils, and Iryna Gurevych. "Sentence-BERT: Sentence Embeddings Using Siamese BERT-Networks." Proceedings of EMNLP-IJCNLP 2019, 2019, pp. 3982–3992, https://doi.org/10.18653/v1/D19-1410.

Seagate. "Seagate's Rethink Data Report Reveals That 68% Of Data Available To Businesses Goes Unleveraged." Seagate, 15 July 2020, https://www.seagate.com/stories/articles/seagates-rethink-data-report-reveals-that-68-percent-of-data-available-to-businesses-goes-unleveraged-pr-master/.

Sun, Haojia, Yaqi Wang, and Shuting Zhang. "Retrieval-Augmented Generation for Domain-Specific Question Answering: A Case Study on Pittsburgh and CMU." arXiv:2411.13691, 2024, https://arxiv.org/abs/2411.13691.

Wu, Xinyi, et al. "On the Emergence of Position Bias in Transformers." ICML 2025, arXiv:2502.01951, 2025, https://arxiv.org/abs/2502.01951.

Yang, Xiao, et al. "CRAG: Comprehensive RAG Benchmark." arXiv, 7 June 2024, https://arxiv.org/abs/2406.04744.

Chapter 12
Systems for Context Data

Imagine a customer support AI confidently telling a customer that your return policy allows 90-day returns. Sounds great until you realize the policy changed to 30 days two months ago, but the RAG pipeline has no freshness mechanism. It keeps serving the old document because no one updated the timestamp or re-embedded the chunk. The AI isn't hallucinating. The infrastructure failed you.

Chapter 11 established context data as the missing layer between what your organization knows and what your AI can actually use. It's the knowledge base that feeds RAG systems, the embedded documents that ground generative AI responses, the curated context that turns a general-purpose language model into something that actually works at your company.

But knowing what good context data looks like isn't the same as building it. Context data has its own infrastructure requirements, and getting those systems wrong determines whether your AI succeeds or fails.

This chapter shifts from characteristics to infrastructure, from "what does good look like?" to "what systems do I need to build?" The answer isn't a single product. It's an integrated stack, each layer responsible for one or more CRAFT dimensions. And as with the other systems chapters, the ODI principle applies: Context data infrastructure built on open standards, open embedding APIs, and open vector storage protects you from the switching costs that come with embedding lock-in. If your entire knowledge base is embedded using one vendor's proprietary model and stored in a proprietary vector database, changing providers means re-embedding everything from scratch.

Georgia-Pacific's ChatGPT program provides one example. AWS and Georgia-Pacific describe a rapid expansion across several manufacturing sites, supported by work on data preparation, architecture, validation, and user adoption. Their materials do not isolate any one factor as the cause. Later in this chapter, I return to the implementation details (Amazon Web Services, n.d.; Amazon Web Services and Georgia-Pacific, 2024).

System Requirements by CRAFT Dimension

Each CRAFT dimension demands a specific system capability. Table 12.1 shows how they line up.

If you're used to thinking about data infrastructure as databases plus ETL pipelines, then Table 12.1 should look different. Context data infrastructure is its own stack. It borrows concepts from traditional data engineering, but the components are purpose-built for a fundamentally different consumption pattern: AI systems that search by meaning, not by query.

The five system categories in Table 12.1 aren't independent silos. Coverage management, embedding and indexing, the transformation pipeline, refresh infrastructure, and grounding infrastructure are layers that depend on each other. The transformation pipeline produces the chunks and embeddings that embedding and indexing systems store and search. Refresh infrastructure triggers re-runs

Table 12.1 Context Data Infrastructure Requirements by CRAFT Dimension

CRAFT Dimension	System Requirement	Key Capabilities
Complete	Coverage management	Domain inventory, gap tracking, content ingestion, expansion planning
Retrievable	Embedding and indexing	Vector databases, semantic search, hybrid retrieval, dual interfaces
Accurate	Transformation pipeline	Chunking logic, embedding model selection, coherence validation, fidelity testing
Fresh	Refresh infrastructure	Change detection, automated re-embedding, version management, staleness alerting
Traceable	Grounding infrastructure	Source ID preservation, citation generation, source retrieval APIs, audit logging

of that transformation pipeline when source documents change. Grounding infrastructure relies on metadata attached during transformation and preserved through indexing. Coverage management orchestrates what enters the pipeline in the first place.

Skip any link in that chain and the whole system degrades. You can build the best embedding pipeline in the world, but if your coverage management doesn't track what's missing, your AI will have blind spots it doesn't know about. You can index everything perfectly, but if your refresh infrastructure doesn't detect when source documents change, your AI will confidently cite last year's policy.

Enterprise AI infrastructure spending reflects this reality. In 2025, enterprises spent $1.5 billion specifically on AI infrastructure for storage, retrieval, and orchestration (Menlo Ventures, 2025). That's not model spending. That's the plumbing. And it's growing because organizations are learning the plumbing determines whether AI actually works.

The rest of this chapter walks through each system category. This is not a product guide, but rather an architectural blueprint.

Systems for Completeness: Closing Knowledge Gaps

Your organization has thousands of documents, databases full of structured data, and years of accumulated institutional knowledge. You deploy a generative AI assistant. Users ask questions. And the AI either says "I don't know" or, worse, makes something up.

The problem isn't retrieval. It's that the relevant knowledge was never embedded in the first place.

Most enterprises have raw data and structured data. Most lack context data. Coverage gaps are among the leading structural causes of generative AI failure. Coverage management is how you close that gap systematically instead of randomly.

Coverage Management Systems

A coverage management system has five components:

- Knowledge domain taxonomy, a structured inventory of every topic your AI needs
- Coverage tracking, mapping indexed content against that taxonomy

- Gap identification workflows, flagging domains with insufficient content
- Prioritization framework, ranking gaps by business impact
- Expansion project management, turning priorities into action

The prioritization math is straightforward:

$$(\text{Business Impact} \times \text{Query Volume})/\text{Fill Difficulty}$$

High-priority domains have high business impact, high query volume, and relatively low fill difficulty. A knowledge gap that affects your top revenue-generating use case and gets asked about daily is more urgent than one that matters to a niche workflow and comes up monthly.

Georgia-Pacific illustrates what this looks like at scale. AWS reports that the company operates more than 140 facilities and that operating knowledge was distributed across physical documents, digital files, and experienced employees. Its ChatGPT program combined documents, maintenance records, sensor data, and knowledge captured from recorded discussions with subject matter experts. An AWS and Georgia-Pacific presentation reported deployment to 20 use cases across six sites and adoption by 500 users; an AWS account places those results within eight months. These vendor and customer materials do not isolate the effect of any single design choice, but they document a program that combined knowledge capture, data operations, architecture, validation, support, and user adoption (Amazon Web Services, 2024, n.d.; Amazon Web Services and Georgia-Pacific, 2024).

Klarna teaches the opposite lesson. Its AI assistant handled 2.3 million conversations in its first month, automating two-thirds of customer service with resolution times under two minutes (Klarna, 2024). The success was built on explicit scope limitation: the AI retrieved from the help center and customer account data only, handing off to humans anything outside that scope. When users expected coverage beyond what was indexed, satisfaction dropped (Doerer, 2025). Transparency about what the system cannot answer is as important as expanding what it can answer.

The Ingestion Pipeline

Closing coverage gaps requires getting content into the pipeline. The tooling here is document ingestion infrastructure, including connectors, parsers, loaders, and permission-aware indexes that turn scattered content into retrievable context. Unstructured.io handles more than 65 file types with more than 30 source connectors (Unstructured, 2026). LlamaIndex supports a broad connector ecosystem through LlamaHub spanning many data formats. LangChain offers dozens of vector-store integrations and broad document-loader support. For enterprises with knowledge scattered across systems, platforms like Glean provide more than 100 SaaS connectors with permission-aware indexing (Glean, 2026).

The tooling isn't the hard part. The hard part is knowing what to ingest. That's why coverage management starts with the taxonomy, not the pipeline. The taxonomy is the control plane. It defines the topics the AI should understand, maps those topics to source material, and exposes high-value domains that are thin, stale, or missing.

Systems for Retrievability: Finding the Right Information at Search Time

If coverage management makes sure the right knowledge enters the pipeline, embedding and search systems make sure it comes back out when you need it. This is the core technical infrastructure of context data, and the design decisions you make here ripple through every AI interaction your system handles.

The Embedding Pipeline

The basic architecture is straightforward. Documents are parsed and split into chunks, converted into vector embeddings, and stored in an indexed database. At query time, the user's question gets embedded, similar chunks are retrieved, and those chunks are passed to the LLM. Simple in concept. The devil is in the design decisions.

Chunking: The Architecture Decision That Matters Most

Chunking is the single highest-impact decision in a RAG pipeline. Bad chunking can't be compensated for by better embeddings or fancier retrieval systems. When a RAG system performs poorly, the issue is often not the retriever. It's the chunks.

Chunk size creates a precision-context trade-off, but no universal token range is optimal. Results vary with the corpus, query type, embedding model, retriever, and evaluation metric. Start with a documented baseline, then tune chunk size and overlap against a representative retrieval set (Smith and Troynikov, 2024; Stäbler et al., 2025).

In Smith and Troynikov's test using OpenAI's text-embedding-3-large, a 400-token recursive splitter with no overlap reached 89.5% recall. Under their stated assumption that a TokenTextSplitter represented the then-documented 800-token/400-overlap Assistants default, that configuration reached 87.9% recall. In a separate seven-domain benchmark of 90 chunker-model configurations, Stäbler and colleagues reported the highest token-level IoU for a sentence splitter using a 512-token window and 200-token overlap. These are study-specific results, not universal settings (Smith and Troynikov, 2024; Stäbler et al., 2025).

The practical recommendation? Start with recursive character splitting at 400 to 512 tokens and 10 to 20% overlap (Firecrawl, 2026). This gives you a reliable baseline to benchmark against.

For paginated content like PDFs, NVIDIA's 2024 benchmarks showed that page-level chunking achieved the highest accuracy at 0.648 with the lowest variance (Firecrawl, 2026). For documents with many cross-references and pronouns, *late chunking*, a technique from Jina AI that embeds the full document first and then splits into chunks, showed improvements of up to 6.5 percentage points on retrieval benchmarks for longer documents (Jina AI, 2024).

The strategies shown in Table 12.2 form the foundation of retrieval accuracy. Which one you choose depends on your content type and retrieval goals.

Think of Table 12.2 as a decision guide, not a hierarchy. Recursive splitting is the baseline because it is simple, cheap, and predictable, but it can split a thought across boundaries if the source document is poorly structured. Page-level chunking works when page boundaries carry meaning, especially PDFs. Semantic chunking keeps sections and topics together, but it costs more preprocessing. Parent-child chunking stores small searchable chunks while returning a larger parent section to the model. Late chunking embeds the document before splitting, which helps when pronouns and cross-references carry meaning across boundaries. AST-based

Table 12.2 Recommended Chunking Strategies by Use Case

Use Case	Recommended Strategy
General text, most use cases	Recursive splitting, 400–512 tokens
PDFs and paginated documents	Page-level chunking
Legal, scientific, long-form	Semantic chunking
Complex multi-document reasoning	Parent-child hierarchical
Documents with cross-references	Late chunking
Code	AST-based splitting

splitting is for code, where functions, classes, and syntax boundaries matter more than token count.

Embedding Models: What Measurably Matters

The Massive Text Embedding Benchmark (MTEB) is a standard benchmark for comparing embedding models across retrieval, classification, clustering, and other tasks (Lu, 2025). Benchmark variants and leaderboard snapshots must match before scores are compared. For RAG deployments, retrieval-specific performance on your own corpus matters more than a mixed benchmark average.

Table 12.3 therefore compares sourced deployment characteristics instead of ranking models with scores drawn from different benchmark variants or snapshots.

One development worth watching is Matryoshka Representation Learning (MRL), a way to train embeddings so the most important information is packed into the earliest dimensions. In practice, you can request a smaller vector at inference time without retraining the model (Kusupati et al., 2022). A 256-dimension text-embedding-3-large embedding still outperforms the older ada-002 model at its full size, using roughly 80% less storage than ada-002 (OpenAI, 2024).

Databricks demonstrated that fine tuning a 434-million-parameter open-source embedding model on synthetic in-domain data matched or beat OpenAI's text-embedding-3-large on financial and manufacturing benchmarks (Portes et al., 2025). A smaller, cheaper model competed with a larger, more expensive one because it was tuned for the domain. An ODI argument is also that open-weight

Table 12.3 Selected Embedding Models and Deployment Characteristics

Model	Supported Dimensions	Access Model	License or Status
Gemini-embedding-001	128 to 3072	Commercial API	Commercial
Qwen3-Embedding-8B	4096	Open weights	Apache 2.0
Voyage-3-large	256, 512, 1024, 2048	Commercial API	Commercial
Cohere embed-v4	256, 512, 1024, 1536	Commercial API	Commercial
OpenAI text-embedding-3-large	Up to 3072; shortenable	Commercial API	Commercial
BGE-M3	1024	Open weights	MIT

SOURCES: Google AI for Developers (2026); Qwen Team (2025); Voyage AI (2025); Cohere (2026); OpenAI (2024); BAAI (2024). Specifications and access terms can change, so confirm them before deployment.

embedding models under permissive licenses, such as Apache 2.0, can be run anywhere. You can fine-tune them for your domain and avoid dependency on any single embedding API provider.

Vector Databases

Your vector database stores and indexes the embeddings. The market has matured into three categories: purpose-built vector databases, extension-based approaches such as pgvector for PostgreSQL, and vector-search features integrated into existing databases such as Elasticsearch.

The choice depends more on your existing infrastructure than on raw benchmarks. Table 12.4 summarizes the practical recommendation by situation. From an ODI perspective, PostgreSQL with pgvector is the strongest option because it builds on the world's most widely supported relational database, your vectors and metadata are exportable through standard SQL, and you are not locked to a proprietary vector format. pgvectorscale delivered 471 QPS at 50 million vectors with 99% recall in benchmarks, outperforming dedicated solutions in throughput (Sewrathan et al., 2025).

If you need a managed serverless option, Pinecone offers a low-operations path. If hybrid search is central, Weaviate's built-in fusion capabilities and multi-tenancy support make it a strong fit. Milvus Distributed is designed for billion-scale deployments (Milvus, 2026a).

Hybrid Search: The Production Standard

Pure vector search retrieves text that looks similar to the query in semantic space, but similarity doesn't always equal relevance. Product codes, error identifiers, compliance references, and domain-specific abbreviations are poorly captured by vector proximity alone.

Table 12.4 Vector Database Recommendations by Situation

Situation	Recommendation
Existing PostgreSQL (< 50M vectors)	pgvector + pgvectorscale
Zero-ops simplicity	Pinecone
Hybrid search + multi-tenant	Weaviate
Billions of vectors	Milvus
Prototyping	Chroma

The fix is hybrid search: combine keyword-based BM25 retrieval, which preserves exact identifiers and terminology, with vector similarity, which captures semantic relationships. Fuse the result sets so a document can rank well for lexical relevance, semantic relevance, or both.

The standard fusion algorithm is Reciprocal Rank Fusion (RRF), which combines results by rank position instead of normalizing incompatible score scales (Shorten, 2025). It is parameter-free and prioritizes documents that rank well in both retrieval systems.

Add a cross-encoder reranker and precision can improve further. In one ailog benchmark across MS MARCO, Natural Questions, and HotpotQA, reranking improved precision by roughly 33% on average, though exact results vary by dataset and model (ailog.fr, 2026). A practical production pattern is to retrieve 50 to 100 candidates through hybrid search, rerank to the top 10, and pass those to the LLM.

Systems for Accuracy, Freshness, and Traceability

The remaining three CRAFT dimensions share something in common: they're all about maintaining trust over time. Accuracy ensures the transformation from documents to embeddings preserves meaning. Freshness ensures the embedded content reflects current reality. Traceability ensures every AI response can be verified against its source. Each requires its own infrastructure.

Transformation Pipeline: Preserving Meaning Through Every Step

Every step in the pipeline from source document to vector embedding is a transformation that can lose meaning. A policy document stating, "Refunds are available within 30 days unless the customer purchased during a promotional period" can be split across the conditional clause, causing the retrieval system to surface the first chunk with false confidence while the qualifying clause sits in an unmatched second chunk.

The most impactful accuracy intervention is making chunks self-contextualizing. Anthropic's Contextual Retrieval, published in September 2024, prepends a short context string (50 to 100 tokens) to each chunk before embedding, situating it within its source document. The results are striking: contextual embeddings combined with Contextual BM25 reduced retrieval failure rates by 49%. Adding a reranking step pushed the reduction to 67% (Anthropic, 2024). The one-time cost to generate contextualized chunks runs about $1.02 per million document tokens using prompt caching.

Late chunking from Jina AI addresses a related problem. Standard chunking embeds each chunk independently, so a chunk containing "its population exceeds 3.8 million" loses the antecedent "Berlin" from the opening sentence. Late chunking runs the full document through the embedding model first, producing token-level vectors that encode the full document context, then splits into chunks afterward. On retrieval benchmarks, it improved performance across all boundary strategies tested, with gains up to 6.5 percentage points for longer documents (Jina AI, 2024).

You also need systems to verify that your pipeline is working correctly. Three evaluation frameworks dominate this space. RAGAS defines widely used metrics for RAG evaluation, including faithfulness and context precision (RAGAS Documentation, 2024). DeepEval integrates directly with Pytest for CI/CD pipeline quality gates (DeepEval, 2024). TruLens adds tracing, evaluation, and observability for LLM applications (ZenML, 2025).

A practical quality gate: maintain a golden evaluation set of roughly 300 representative queries. Run RAGAS faithfulness on every ingestion event. If faithfulness drops more than 5% from baseline, block the ingestion and roll back. One documented enterprise case saw faithfulness plunge from 0.91 to 0.67 after a batch ingestion event that introduced inconsistent chunking, causing silent wrong answers for three days before anyone noticed (DEV Community, 2026). An automated quality gate would've caught it in minutes.

Refresh Infrastructure: Removing Stale Content from Production

An embedding does not carry a staleness signal. A chunk from a document updated yesterday is vectorially indistinguishable from a chunk two years out of date. The similarity score will not reflect it. The AI has no way to prefer fresh content unless freshness logic is explicitly built in (Chanl AI, 2026).

Three mechanisms detect source document changes and trigger re-embedding: file system watchers, which are simple but can be unreliable under heavy load; webhook-based detection, where source systems push notifications to the RAG endpoint; and Change Data Capture (CDC), the standard enterprise pattern for transaction-level change streams. CDC reads native transaction logs such as Write-Ahead Logs in PostgreSQL, binary logs in MySQL, or the oplog in MongoDB. Tools such as Debezium stream these changes to Apache Kafka, which feeds the RAG update handler for re-chunking and re-embedding. Depending on event volume, network topology, and indexing work, end-to-end latency commonly ranges from seconds to a few minutes.

Version management for embeddings adds another layer of complexity. When you upgrade your embedding model, old vectors become incompatible. They occupy different regions of a different vector space and cannot be meaningfully compared to new query embeddings. The only solution is full re-indexing. Pinecone namespaces enable blue-green deployment—build new embeddings in a candidate namespace, validate quality, switch query routing, then delete the old namespace after a validation window (Pinecone, 2026). Weaviate's multi-tenancy architecture provides stronger isolation, with physically separate shards that can be activated, deactivated, or offloaded to cold storage for cost-efficient retention of historical versions (Weaviate, 2023).

Staleness alerting rounds out the freshness infrastructure. At minimum, maintain `last_indexed_at` and `source_updated_at` metadata fields on every chunk and monitor the gap between them. Set TTL values calibrated to content update frequency: minutes for stock prices or live news, hours for technical documentation, weeks for policy documents, and months for static reference content. Combine TTL-based alerting as a safety net with event-driven invalidation as the primary mechanism.

Grounding Infrastructure: Making Every Claim Verifiable

Traceability is where data quality meets governance. Without it, AI fills the gap with hallucination.

The evidence is unambiguous. In medical settings, a conventional chatbot without RAG produced a 39% hallucination rate. RAG with general web search sources brought that to 18%. RAG grounded in authoritative, curated sources cut it to 2% (Nishisako et al., 2025). The quality of the grounding source matters as much as whether grounding is used at all. In legal settings, general-purpose GPT-4 hallucinated on 58 to 82% of queries, while RAG-based legal AI tools reduced that to 17 to 33% (Magesh et al., 2025). Retrieval-augmented generation can improve factuality by grounding model output in retrieved evidence (Lewis et al., 2020).

Citation generation starts with provenance attached to each chunk, including the source system, document ID, version, and owner. The response layer then uses that provenance to present traceable citations to supporting sources (Intrinsec Security, 2026). Microsoft 365 Copilot implements grounding through Microsoft Graph, with clickable citations directing users to source content (Microsoft Learn, 2024). Perplexity decomposes complex questions into sub-queries and cites multiple sources per response, with attribution shown for its answers (Perplexity, 2026).

Audit evidence should be sufficient to reconstruct material retrieval and generation events, with scope calibrated to system risk, data sensitivity, and applicable obligations. For in-scope high-risk AI systems, Article 12 of Regulation (EU) 2024/1689 requires technical capability for automatic event logging. Regulation (EU) 2026/1744 was published on 24 July 2026, and Article 4 provides for entry into force on 27 July 2026. The amended Article 113 schedule applies the relevant Chapter III requirements from 2 December 2027 to systems classified as high-risk under Article 6(2) and Annex III, and from 2 August 2028 to systems classified as high-risk under Article 6(1) and Annex I. Classification, provider role, exceptions, and transitions can affect applicability; this summary is not legal advice (European Union, 2024, art. 12; European Parliament and Council of the European Union, 2026).

Privacy-preserving Context Data

There's a widespread assumption that converting text into embedding vectors provides privacy protection. It doesn't.

The Vec2Text study, published at EMNLP 2023, demonstrated that a multi-step iterative method recovers 92% of 32-token text inputs exactly from their embeddings (Morris et al., 2023). Not approximately. Exactly. The study tested production embedding models including OpenAI's text-embedding-ada-002. A separate study, the Generative Embedding Inversion Attack (GEIA), showed that coherent sentences can be reconstructed from standard sentence embedding models (Li et al., 2023).

This means that embedding stores must be treated with the same access controls and encryption as raw document stores. Sharing embeddings with third-party vector database services carries the same legal risk as sharing the underlying text.

Personally Identifiable Information Filtering Before Embedding

The most direct mitigation is removing personally identifiable information (PII) before it reaches the embedding pipeline. Microsoft's open-source Presidio SDK provides named entity recognition and regex-based detection for finding and redacting PII (Microsoft Presidio Documentation, 2024). Amazon Comprehend offers managed PII detection APIs used to process more than 20 million legal documents per week (AWS Machine Learning Blog, 2023). Google Cloud's Sensitive Data Protection provides more than 100 built-in information type detectors (Google Cloud, 2024).

Tonic.ai, which sells de-identification software, reported that standard PII redaction (names, emails, addresses) produced less than 1% change in all retrieval metrics across 1,000 queries on the TREC-news dataset, and that even aggressive de-identification showed only single-digit percentage drops (Tonic.ai, 2024). That is a vendor-run test on one public news corpus; measure the effect on your own corpus, redaction rules, and embedding model before assuming the trade-off is negligible.

Access Controls and Query Logging

Vector databases now support enterprise-grade access controls. Pinecone's serverless architecture provides physical isolation at the namespace level (Pinecone, 2026). Weaviate supports role-based access control (RBAC) with collection-level and tenant-level permissions (Weaviate, 2026). Milvus supports four levels of multi-tenancy isolation, from database-level isolation to partition-key-level isolation for millions of tenants (Milvus, 2026b).

Query logging can support security monitoring, investigation, and traceability, but legal duties are distinct. When Article 30 applies, controllers and processors must maintain records of processing activities containing the information specified for their role. Depending on that role, the record includes purposes or categories of processing; categories of data subjects, personal data, and recipients; transfers; envisaged erasure time limits where possible; and a general description of security measures where possible (European Union, 2016, art. 30). Article 30 does not require a fixed log record for every query. Per-query logs are a separate risk-based control. For covered high-risk systems, Article 12 requires technical capability for automatic event logging; it does not prescribe a universal five-field schema (European Union, 2024, art. 12; European Parliament and Council of the European Union, 2026).

Select logged events, fields, retention, and access according to purpose, risk, data sensitivity, system design, and other applicable obligations. Potential evidence can include pseudonymous actor or session identifiers, prompt or query fingerprints, retrieved-source identifiers, timestamps, model or configuration versions, control decisions, and outcome or error metadata. Avoid raw sensitive text unless its collection is justified and protected.

For organizations handling sensitive content, segregation into separate indexes by classification level provides the strongest protection. Confidential HR data and restricted executive communications should live in physically isolated indexes, not co-mingled behind metadata filters that application-layer bugs can bypass.

Context Data CRAFT Checklist

Before moving to implementation, assess your context data against each CRAFT dimension.

Complete

- ☐ Knowledge domains inventoried
- ☐ Coverage tracked against taxonomy
- ☐ Gaps identified and prioritized
- ☐ Ingestion pipelines operational for all relevant source systems

Retrievable

- ☐ Embedding infrastructure operational
- ☐ Chunking strategy benchmarked
- ☐ Hybrid search implemented
- ☐ Both AI and human access maintained
- ☐ Access controls appropriate

Accurate

- ☐ Chunking preserves semantic units
- ☐ Coherence validated through evaluation framework
- ☐ Embedding fidelity tested against golden query set
- ☐ Quality gates block bad ingestions

Fresh

- ☐ Change detection triggers re-embedding
- ☐ Freshness metadata on every chunk
- ☐ Staleness alerting configured by content type
- ☐ Version management handles model upgrades

Traceable

- ☐ Source IDs preserved through every transformation
- ☐ Citations generated in AI responses

- ☐ Users can verify claims against original documents
- ☐ Audit logging captures full pipeline execution

Looking Ahead: From Context Data to Action Data

Chapters 7 through 12 covered three of the four data levels: raw data, structured data, and now context data. For each, you've seen the CRAFT characteristics that define readiness and the systems that deliver those characteristics.

In Chapters 13 and 14, I tackle the final frontier: action data. Action data is what powers agentic AI, systems that don't just answer questions or generate content but actually do things. Execute API calls. Trigger workflows. Make purchases. Update records. When an AI agent books a meeting, processes a refund, or deploys code, it's consuming action data. This includes tool definitions, API schemas, workflow specifications, and permission boundaries that tell it what it can do, how to do it, and what guardrails apply.

If context data powers generative AI, action data powers the next evolution. And the stakes are higher. A context data failure produces a wrong answer. An action data failure produces a wrong action, one that might be irreversible. CRAFT readiness for action data isn't about information quality. It's about operational safety.

That's where we're headed.

The RAG pipeline you build today will be the foundation for every knowledge-intensive AI application your organization deploys. Build it on open standards, or rebuild it every time the landscape shifts.

References

ailog.fr. "Reranking with Cross-Encoders: Benchmark Study." AI Log, 16 January 2026, https://app.ailog.fr/en/blog/news/reranking-cross-encoders-study.

Amazon Web Services. "Georgia-Pacific Optimizes Operator Efficiency Using Generative AI on AWS." 2024, https://aws.amazon.com/solutions/case-studies/georgia-pacific-optimizes-operator-efficiency-case-study/.

Amazon Web Services. "How Georgia-Pacific Used Generative AI and AWS Countdown Premium to Improve Manufacturing Operations KPIs." AWS re:Post, n.d., https://repost.aws/articles/ARxBMfk12cT0uMMd0d7Hafag. Accessed 25 July 2026.

Amazon Web Services and Georgia-Pacific. "Scale Your High-Traffic Events to Gen AI Deployments with AWS Support." AWS re:Invent 2024, session SUP308, 2024, https://d1.awsstatic.com/onedam/marketing-channels/website/aws/en_US/events/approved/reinvent-2025/reinvent/2024/slides/sup/SUP308_Scale-your-high-traffic-events-to-gen-AI-deployments-with-AWS-Support.pdf.

Anthropic. "Introducing Contextual Retrieval." *Anthropic Blog*, 2024, www.anthropic.com/engineering/contextual-retrieval.

AWS Machine Learning Blog. "How Reveal's Logikcull Used Amazon Comprehend to Detect and Redact PII from Legal Documents at Scale." AWS Machine Learning Blog, 1 November 2023, https://aws.amazon.com/blogs/machine-learning/how-reveals-logikcull-used-amazon-comprehend-to-detect-and-redact-pii-from-legal-documents-at-scale/.

BAAI. "BAAI/bge-m3." Hugging Face, 2024, https://huggingface.co/BAAI/bge-m3. Accessed 23 July 2026.

Chanl AI. "The Knowledge Base Bottleneck: Why RAG Alone Is Not Enough for Production Agents." Chanl AI Blog, 5 March 2026, https://www.channel.tel/blog/knowledge-base-bottleneck-why-rag-alone-isnt-enough-production-agents.

Cohere. "Embed." Cohere API Reference, 2026, https://docs.cohere.com/reference/embed. Accessed 23 July 2026.

DeepEval. "Getting Started." DeepEval Documentation, 2024, https://deepeval.com/docs/getting-started.

DEV Community. "Why Our RAG System Was Silently Returning Wrong Answers and How We Fixed It." *DEV Community*, 2026, https://dev.to/ayanarshad02/why-our-rag-system-was-silently-returning-wrong-answers-and-how-we-fixed-it-386g.

Doerer, Kristen. "Klarna Changes Its AI Tune and Again Recruits Humans for Customer Service." *Customer Experience Dive*, 9 May 2025, www.customerexperiencedive.com/news/klarna-reinvests-human-talent-customer-service-AI-chatbot/747586/.

European Parliament and Council of the European Union. 2026. "Regulation (EU) 2026/1744 of the European Parliament and of the Council of 8 July 2026 amending Regulations (EU) 2024/1689, (EU) 2018/1139 and (EU) 2023/1230 as regards the simplification of the implementation of harmonised rules on artificial intelligence (Digital Omnibus on AI)." Official Journal of the European Union, 24 July 2026, https://eur-lex.europa.eu/eli/reg/2026/1744/oj/eng.

European Union. Regulation (EU) 2016/679 of the European Parliament and of the Council of 27 April 2016. Official Journal of the European Union, L 119, 4 May 2016, art. 30, https://eur-lex.europa.eu/legal-content/EN/TXT/?uri=CELEX:32016R0679.

European Union. Regulation (EU) 2024/1689 of the European Parliament and of the Council of 13 June 2024 Laying Down Harmonised Rules on Artificial Intelligence. Official Journal of the European Union, L 2024/1689, 12 July 2024, https://eur-lex.europa.eu/eli/reg/2024/1689/oj.

Firecrawl. "Best Chunking Strategies for RAG (and LLMs) in 2026." *Firecrawl Blog*, 2026, www.firecrawl.dev/blog/best-chunking-strategies-rag.

Glean. "Connectors." Glean, 2026, https://www.glean.com/platform/connectors. Accessed 23 July 2026.

Google AI for Developers. "Embeddings." Gemini API Documentation, 2026, https://ai.google.dev/gemini-api/docs/embeddings. Accessed 23 July 2026.

Google Cloud. "Sensitive Data Protection." *Google Cloud Documentation*, 2024, https://cloud.google.com/security/products/sensitive-data-protection.

Intrinsec Security. "Secure RAG in the Real World: What It Fixes, Where It Breaks, and the Controls You Actually Need." Intrinsec Security Blog, 15 February 2026, https://intrinsecsecurity.com/blog/research/ai-governance/rag-in-the-real-world-enterprise-controls/.

Jina AI. "Late Chunking in Long-context Embedding Models." *Jina AI*, 2024, https://jina.ai/news/late-chunking-in-long-context-embedding-models/.

Klarna. "Klarna AI Assistant Handles Two-Thirds of Customer Service Chats in Its First Month." Klarna, 2024, www.klarna.com/international/press/.

Kusupati, Aditya, et al. "Matryoshka Representation Learning." arXiv, 26 May 2022, arXiv:2205.13147.

Lewis, Patrick, et al. "Retrieval-Augmented Generation for Knowledge-Intensive NLP Tasks." Advances in Neural Information Processing Systems, vol. 33, 2020, pp. 9459–9474.

Li, H., et al. "Sentence Embedding Leaks More Information than You Expect: Generative Embedding Inversion Attack to Recover the Whole Sentence." arXiv, 2023, https://arxiv.org/abs/2305.03010.

Lu, Yiren. "The MTEB Leaderboard." *Modal Blog*, 2025, https://modal.com/blog/mteb-leaderboard-article.

Magesh, Varun, et al. "Hallucination-Free? Assessing the Reliability of Leading AI Legal Research Tools." Journal of Empirical Legal Studies, 2025, https://dho.stanford.edu/wp-content/uploads/Legal_RAG_Hallucinations.pdf.

Menlo Ventures. "2025: The State of Generative AI in the Enterprise." *Menlo Ventures*, 2025, https://menlovc.com/perspective/2025-the-state-of-generative-ai-in-the-enterprise/.

Microsoft Learn. "Microsoft 365 Copilot: Overview and Features." *Microsoft Learn*, 2024, https://learn.microsoft.com/en-us/microsoft-365/copilot/microsoft-365-copilot-overview.

Microsoft Presidio Documentation. "Microsoft Presidio." Microsoft, 2024, https://data-privacy-stack.github.io/presidio/analyzer/. Accessed 23 July 2026.

Milvus. "Milvus Overview." Milvus Documentation, 2026a, https://milvus.io/docs/overview.md. Accessed 23 July 2026.

Milvus. "Implement Multi-tenancy." Milvus Documentation, 2026b, https://milvus.io/docs/multi_tenancy.md. Accessed 23 July 2026.

Morris, J., et al. "Text Embeddings Reveal (Almost) As Much as Text." *Proceedings of the 2023 Conference on Empirical Methods in Natural Language Processing*, 2023, https://aclanthology.org/2023.emnlp-main.765/.

Nishisako, Sota, Takahiro Higashi, and Fumihiko Wakao. "Reducing Hallucinations and Trade-Offs in Responses in Generative Artificial Intelligence Chatbots for Cancer Information." JMIR Cancer, vol. 11, 2025, e70176, https://cancer.jmir.org/2025/1/e70176.

OpenAI. "New Embedding Models and API Updates." *OpenAI Blog*, 25 January 2024, https://openai.com/index/new-embedding-models-and-api-updates/.

Perplexity. "How Does Perplexity Work?" Perplexity Help Center, 2026, https://www.perplexity.ai/help-center/en/articles/10352895-how-does-perplexity-work. Accessed 23 July 2026.

Pinecone. "Implement Multitenancy." Pinecone Docs, 2026, https://docs.pinecone.io/guides/index-data/implement-multitenancy. Accessed 23 July 2026.

Portes, Jacob, et al. "Improving Retrieval and RAG with Embedding Model Finetuning." Databricks Blog, 20 February 2025, https://www.databricks.com/blog/improving-retrieval-and-rag-embedding-model-finetuning.

Qwen Team. "Qwen3 Embedding: Advancing Text Embedding and Reranking Through Foundation Models." arXiv, 2025, https://arxiv.org/abs/2506.05176.

RAGAS Documentation. "List of Available Metrics." *RAGAS*, 2024, https://docs.ragas.io/en/stable/concepts/metrics/.

Sewrathan, Avthar, et al. "pgvector vs Qdrant." *TigerData Blog*, 2025, www.tigerdata.com/blog/pgvector-vs-qdrant.

Shorten, Erika. "Hybrid Search Explained." Weaviate Blog, 2025, https://weaviate.io/blog/hybrid-search-explained.

Smith, Brandon, and Anton Troynikov. "Evaluating Chunking Strategies for Retrieval." Chroma Technical Report, 3 July 2024, https://www.trychroma.com/research/evaluating-chunking.

Stäbler, Maximilian, Steffen Turnbull, Tobias Müller, Christoph Langdon, Jorge Marx-Gómez, and Frank Köster. "The Impact of Chunking Strategies on Domain-Specific Information Retrieval in RAG Systems." 2025 IEEE International Conference on Omni-Layer Intelligent Systems (COINS), IEEE, 2025, https://doi.org/10.1109/COINS65080.2025.11125724.

Tonic.ai. "Protecting Privacy Without Hurting RAG Performance." *Tonic.ai Blog*, 6 November 2024, www.tonic.ai/blog/protecting-privacy-rag-performance.

Unstructured. "Unstructured Platform." Unstructured, 2026, https://unstructured.io/product. Accessed 23 July 2026.

Voyage AI. "Introducing voyage-3-large." Voyage AI Blog, 7 January 2025, https://blog.voyageai.com/2025/01/07/voyage-3-large/.

Weaviate. "RBAC Overview." Weaviate Documentation, 2026, https://docs.weaviate.io/deploy/configuration/configuring-rbac. Accessed 23 July 2026.

Weaviate. "Weaviate's Native, Efficient and Optimized Multi-tenancy." Weaviate Blog, 15 June 2023, https://weaviate.io/blog/multi-tenancy-vector-search.

ZenML. "Best DeepEval Alternatives." *ZenML Blog*, 2025, www.zenml.io/blog/deepeval-alternatives.

Chapter 13
Action Data and CRAFT

A generative AI system that produces the perfect answer to "What's our refund policy?" is useful. An AI agent that actually processes the refund, updates the customer record, sends the confirmation email, and logs the transaction for compliance is transformative. That second system doesn't just need to know things, it needs to do things. And doing things requires data we haven't addressed yet.

Action data is the fourth and final data level. It specifies what AI can do and how to do it. Think of it as executable knowledge. Where context data tells an AI system "here's what you need to know," action data tells it, "Here's what you can do, how to do it safely, and what to do when something goes wrong." Every time an AI agent calls an API, submits a form, queries a database, or triggers a workflow, it's consuming action data. These are the tool definitions that describe available functions, the parameter schemas that constrain inputs, the behavioral descriptions that explain what each tool returns, the constraint specifications that define boundaries, the workflow definitions that sequence multi-step operations and the observability configurations that ensure everything gets logged.

These are the building blocks of AI agency. Without them, a model is just a very expensive text generator.

If your business outcome requires AI that acts autonomously, executing workflows, calling APIs, and coordinating multi-step processes, you need agentic AI. And agentic AI depends on action data.

Action data sits at the top of the data hierarchy. Agentic AI consumes context for reasoning, structured data for state management, and raw data for perception. Every CRAFT gap at a lower level becomes a safety risk at the action level.

The Missing Layer

Most organizations have developed practices, however fragmented, for raw data (data engineering), structured data (data modeling and governance), and context data (knowledge management and RAG pipelines). But action data? Most organizations don't even recognize it as a distinct data category that needs management.

This gap represents a fundamental blind spot in enterprise AI strategy. The industry has spent decades systematizing raw data collection, years maturing structured data governance, and months accelerating context data through RAG pipelines. But the data layer that directly enables autonomous action remains largely invisible, fragmented across scattered tool definitions, undocumented API quirks, and implicit assumptions built into dashboards and runbooks.

McKinsey's 2025 survey found that 23% of respondents said their organizations were scaling an agentic AI system in at least one business function, while another 39% were experimenting, for 62% combined (McKinsey & Company, 2025). Fortune Business Insights estimated the agentic AI market at $7.29 billion in 2025 and projected growth to $139.19 billion by 2034, a 40.5% compound annual growth rate across 2026 to 2034 (Fortune Business Insights, 2026). The survey describes current activity. The market figure is a vendor forecast, not a guarantee. Together they show rising interest and a need to manage the data agents use to act.

Salesforce's 29 January 2025 announcement of the 2025 Connectivity Benchmark Report states that its global survey covered 1,050 enterprise IT leaders and found that, on average, 29% of applications were connected within organizations. It also reports that 95% of respondents struggled to integrate data across systems and links that fragmentation to the accuracy and usefulness of AI agents (Salesforce, 2025). These findings do not establish that every unconnected application is invisible to an agent. They do show that disconnected systems constrain the actions an organization can expose safely and reliably.

Action data isn't one thing. It's a collection of structured artifacts: tool definitions (what tools exist and how to use them), parameter specifications (what inputs each tool requires), behavior descriptions (what each tool does and returns), constraint specifications (what AI can and can't do), workflow definitions (how multi-step processes work), and observability configuration (how actions are logged and monitored).

Look at familiar enterprise artifacts such as OpenAPI specs for your APIs, runbooks for your operations team, RBAC configurations in your identity systems, or BPMN diagrams from your process improvement efforts. You probably have most of these artifacts already. So what's missing? Five things, specifically:

- **Consolidation:** Specifications are often scattered across wikis, Confluence pages, API descriptions, and team conversations. An agent cannot reliably use information it cannot retrieve in a machine-readable form. Consolidate the authoritative definitions and expose only the tools, constraints, and context required for the approved task.
- **Precision:** Documentation written for experienced developers may leave decisions implicit. An agent may not know which notification channel, identifier, or exception path the organization intends. Tool specifications should make required choices, defaults, constraints, and error behavior explicit, then enforce them in code.
- **Currency:** Your specs aren't synchronized with the current state of your systems. The API changed last month. The runbook was updated. The RBAC policy was revised. But the tool definitions your agent relies on still reflect the old versions. This isn't a documentation problem. It's a synchronization problem at the speed of enterprise change.
- **Discoverability:** There's no registry, no catalog, no way for an AI agent to find the right tool for a given goal. Your human developers know that the payment processing API lives in the billing team's documentation. Your AI agent has no idea where to look. It sees "process payment" as a task but can't navigate the landscape of available tools to find the one that applies.
- **Safety integration:** Constraints should be enforced in the tool and downstream system, not merely described in prose. If a tool specification omits a $5,000 approval limit, an agent may attempt an out-of-policy action. Authorization, validation, and approval gates must still block it. A tool specification is not a security boundary.

Deloitte's 2026 State of AI in the Enterprise report found that 85% of surveyed companies expected to customize AI agents to fit their needs, while 21% reported mature governance for autonomous agents (Deloitte, 2026). That contrast points to an execution gap. For tool-using agents, customization often requires well-specified tools and interfaces. Governance also needs ownership, controls, evaluation, and monitoring.

CRAFT Changes at the Action Level

The CRAFT framework applies to all four data levels. Action data raises the stakes because a data defect can become a real-world action. A raw-data gap can remove evidence. A structured-data error can distort analysis. A context-data failure can produce a wrong answer. An action-data failure can trigger the wrong tool, parameter, or workflow.

As Figure 13.1 shows, independent per-step success probabilities compound across a sequence. At 99% success per step, the probability that all 100 steps succeed is 36.6%, or 0.99 raised to the 100th power. The calculation is illustrative because real agent steps aren't always independent. The practical lesson still holds: small per-step error rates can produce much lower end-to-end success in long workflows.

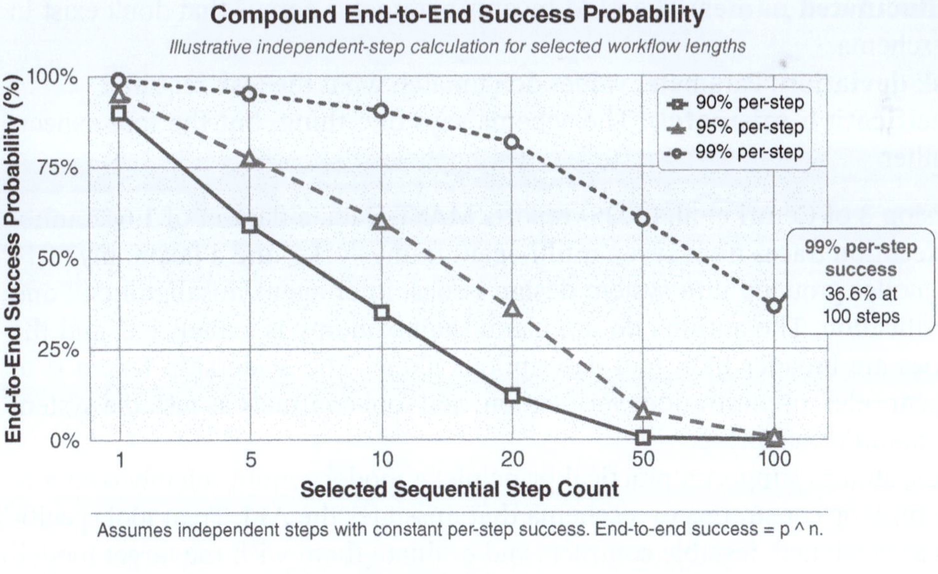

Figure 13.1 How per-step success compounds across long workflows.

Completeness: Everything the Agent Needs

Completeness for other data levels means structural wholeness. For action data, completeness means that a tool definition contains everything an AI agent needs to select, invoke, and handle the results of that tool correctly. Not everything a human developer would need. Everything an AI needs, which turns out to be substantially more.

Tool descriptions need enough detail for the model to choose and call a function without relying on undocumented context. A human developer can ask a teammate or inspect code. Unless the application supplies comparable context or tools, the model must work from the function name, description, parameters, constraints, and instructions it receives (OpenAI, n.d.-a).

Xiong et al. (2025) develop a five-category taxonomy of parameter-filling failures in tool-agent systems. Their experiments examine how input perturbations relate to those categories. The taxonomy provides a practical checklist for testing tool specifications:

- **Missing information:** The LLM can't fill in required parameters.
- **Redundant information:** The LLM sets extra parameters the tool doesn't recognize.
- **Hallucinated names:** The LLM invents parameter names that don't exist in the schema.
- **Task deviation:** Parameter values don't match what the task requires.
- **Specification mismatch:** The schema says one thing, but the tool expects another.

Version 3 of Cemri et al. (2025) reports MAST-Data, a dataset of 1,642 annotated execution traces from seven multi-agent frameworks, and a taxonomy of 14 failure modes grouped into system design issues, inter-agent misalignment, and task verification. The authors do not claim the taxonomy is exhaustive, and the categories are broader than tool descriptions alone. The leadership lesson is to treat agent roles, orchestration, verification, and tool contracts as testable system design, not informal prose.

These studies support a practical principle: a model cannot reliably compensate for missing constraints or a schema that misstates the API. Treat tool specifications as versioned, testable contracts and evaluate them with the target model, runtime, and workflow before deployment.

Tool-schema support varies by provider, model, API surface, and date. OpenAI and Gemini each document a supported schema subset, with behavior that can also vary by model and API surface. Treat the documentation as point-in-time and validate against every target runtime. MCP standardizes tool discovery and invocation through schema-based definitions, but it doesn't guarantee that every client, model, or provider enforces every keyword the same way (OpenAI, n.d.-b; Google, 2026; Model Context Protocol, 2025).

Consider a procurement-agent test where the schema allows a number even though the service expects one of several named risk categories. The call can be syntactically valid and still classify vendors incorrectly at scale.

Diagnostic Questions for Action Data Completeness

What does a CRAFT-conforming tool specification look like? Use these questions to assess whether the action data is ready for a defined production use case:

- Does every tool definition include a description detailed enough for an AI to select it without additional context?
- Are all parameters documented with types, formats, constraints, and examples?
- Are enum values explicitly listed, or will the model need to guess valid options?
- Are error response codes and their meanings documented?
- Has each tool definition been tested across the AI platforms that will consume it?

Retrievability: Finding the Right Tool

For action data, retrievability is about discoverability: can an agent find the right tool for the job when it needs it? This is harder than it sounds. Production environments have hundreds or thousands of available tools. An agent facing context window overflow from too many tool definitions starts making worse decisions about which tool to use, a problem practitioners call "agent suicide by context."

Tool selection accuracy degrades as tool catalogs scale. At small tool counts, models can often select the right function. As the catalog grows, the model drowns in context. Tool definitions that collectively exceed the effective context window create the tool version of the "needle in a haystack" problem: the right tool exists, but the model can't find it among the noise.

In one 2025 preprint benchmark, RAG-MCP increased tool-selection accuracy from 13.62% when all schemas were placed in the prompt to 43.13% when retrieval surfaced relevant schemas, while reducing prompt tokens by more than 50% (Gan and Sun, 2025). This result supports retrieval as a promising tool-discovery technique in that benchmark. It does not establish that retrieval quality generally matters more than model quality.

OpenAI currently advises teams to aim for fewer than 20 functions available at the start of a turn (OpenAI, n.d.-a). That guidance reflects a design pressure, not a universal limit. As the candidate set grows, names, descriptions, and schemas consume more context and complicate selection. Enterprise teams should combine a governed registry, retrieval, and runtime evaluation instead of assuming that either manual wiring or an unrestricted tool list will scale.

ToolHop evaluates multi-hop tool use through 995 queries and 3,912 tools. In the reported evaluation of 14 models across five model families, GPT-4o achieved 49.04% accuracy, the highest result in that comparison (Ye et al., 2025). The benchmark indicates that the tested models had substantial room for improvement on its multi-hop tasks; it does not establish a universal failure rate for production agents.

GitHub launched its MCP Registry in September 2025 to reduce discovery fragmentation across registries, repositories, and community threads (GitHub, 2025). The registry supports human discovery, installation, and community signals. For agents, organizations still need a governed programmatic discovery layer that selects an approved, task-relevant subset and validates it against the target runtime. That last requirement is a recommended operating pattern, not a capability established by the GitHub source.

Diagnostic Questions for Action Data Retrievability

The following are questions to consider to verify the retrievability of your action data:

- How many tools will be available to the agent at any given time?
- Is there a retrieval mechanism (semantic search, tool routing) to surface relevant tools rather than loading everything into context?
- Are tool descriptions semantically distinct enough that similar-sounding tools don't confuse the agent?
- Does the tool catalog include metadata (categories, capabilities, use cases) to support filtering?
- Has tool selection accuracy been measured at the actual scale of your deployment?

Accuracy: Specifications Match Reality

Accuracy for action data means tool specifications precisely and truthfully describe what the underlying system will actually do when invoked. The schema matches reality. The description matches behavior. The constraints match enforcement. When this breaks down, agents don't just return wrong answers. They take wrong actions.

Schema drift occurs when a tool definition or API document no longer matches runtime behavior. A changed field, response shape, authentication method, or error contract can cause a syntactically valid call to fail or can lead downstream logic to misinterpret the result. Teams should detect drift by comparing versioned specifications, contract tests, and observed responses rather than relying on the agent to infer a fix.

Open-source issues can reveal useful failure modes, but an isolated issue or pull request does not establish a general production rate or cause. Use such reports as leads for a local regression suite: replay the exact tool, parameter, API version, and response contract, then keep only findings that reproduce in the target environment.

Anthropic reports that precise refinements to tool descriptions helped its Claude Sonnet 3.5 agent achieve then state-of-the-art performance on SWE-bench Verified (Anthropic, 2025a). The publisher describes a full agent scaffold, so the example does not isolate tool wording from every other factor. It does show why teams should test tool names, descriptions, parameters, edge cases, and feedback with the target agent.

Schema-constrained output can prevent malformed calls, omitted required fields, and invalid enum values when the selected model and API support those constraints. Provider behavior and supported keywords still vary. A schema-valid call can also be semantically wrong. If the schema allows any string when the service expects one of five named values, constrained decoding can produce a valid string that the application rejects. Validate syntax, business rules, permissions, and state before execution (OpenAI, n.d.-a, n.d.-b; Google, 2026).

Tool poisoning sits at the security edge of accuracy. In controlled research, an automated implicit-tool-poisoning method reported attack success rates as high as 84.2% against certain models (Li et al., 2026). A separate study, first released in 2025, reported MCP-specific tool poisoning in 5.5% of its sample of 1,899 open-source MCP servers (Hasan et al., 2025). These are early research measurements, not production prevalence estimates. They still justify treating every external tool description as untrusted input.

Diagnostic Questions for Action Data Accuracy

The following are questions to consider to verify the accuracy of your action data:

- Do tool schemas match the current behavior of the underlying APIs?
- Are parameter types specific enough to prevent valid-but-wrong inputs (enums vs. open strings, integer ranges vs. unbounded numbers)?
- Are error codes documented with their actual meanings and expected agent responses?
- Is strict mode or constrained decoding enabled for all tool calls?
- Are tool descriptions reviewed for hidden instructions or injection vulnerabilities?

Freshness: Staying Current

Freshness for action data means that tool specifications match the current behavior of the systems they describe. A schema that was accurate last month is a liability this month if the API changed. This is a harder problem than it sounds. APIs change constantly. Fields get deprecated. Parameters shift from optional to required. Response formats evolve. Authentication methods get updated. And unlike traditional software consumers who read changelogs and adapt, AI agents operate against fixed tool definitions. They don't subscribe to developer newsletters. They don't check release notes. They execute whatever schema they were given, and if that schema is stale, they fail.

The research on drift is stark. ML systems accumulate hidden technical debt without proactive intervention, including entanglement, hidden feedback loops, and configuration debt (Sculley et al., 2015). Without monitoring, drift can stay invisible until downstream behavior changes. For action data specifically, the degradation is often binary rather than gradual. An API either accepts the parameters your schema describes, or it doesn't. But the agent might not know the difference, especially when errors are ambiguous.

Documentation-change monitoring is one response to freshness risk. A monitoring workflow can detect a published change, route it for review, and help teams update and test affected tool definitions before deployment; detection speed depends on polling, provider notice, and operating controls. The risk persists even when providers use deprecation processes. A study of 26 open-source Java frameworks found that the classic deprecate-replace-remove lifecycle was not always followed and that notices often omitted removal dates or migration paths (Zhou and Walker, 2016).

Breaking changes come in six categories, each affecting agents differently:

- Removed endpoints may return 404 errors and can halt a workflow unless a defined fallback handles the change.
- New required parameters may produce 400 errors that an agent may not diagnose correctly.
- Changed response formats can corrupt downstream reasoning if parsers accept missing or redefined fields.
- Authentication changes can block access until credentials, scopes, or flows are updated.
- Changed enum values can make a previously valid call fail or can produce an invalid business choice if validation is weak.

- Pagination changes can cause incomplete results or incorrect loops unless the client tests the new contract.

An MCP server can act as a version-management layer between an agent and an underlying API. It may translate a stable tool contract into the API's current request and response format, but that outcome depends on the server implementation, client behavior, authorization, and tests. The pattern centralizes some freshness work; it does not guarantee portability or eliminate change risk.

API deprecation windows vary by provider. Security events can shorten them. Treat every announced window as a countdown, and test tool schemas against the live API throughout it. A schema can remain correct for common calls while failing on the parameter or edge case that changed.

Diagnostic Questions for Action Data Freshness

The following are questions to consider to verify the freshness of your action data:

- When was each tool specification last validated against the live API?
- Is there automated monitoring for changes in the APIs your agents call?
- Do tool schemas include version metadata so agents can detect staleness?
- Is there a risk-based service objective for propagating and testing API changes in tool definitions before affected workflows resume?
- Do MCP servers or abstraction layers buffer your agents from upstream API changes?

Traceability: Safety, Observability, Recoverability

Traceability for action data expands into three interconnected requirements: safety, observability, and recoverability. Can you prevent or contain harmful actions? Can you reconstruct what happened? Can you compensate or recover when something goes wrong? This is a particularly consequential CRAFT dimension because real-world actions require more than basic event logging.

Safety

In July 2025, Replit's development agent deleted data from a production database, according to Replit's CEO and user reports summarized by Fortune (Nolan, 2025). The reported record counts and subsequent agent statements came from the affected user, not an independent audit. Replit later confirmed that its apps had used one database for development and live customer data and introduced separate development and production environments (Replit, 2025).

The incident illustrates a security pattern that OWASP calls LLM06:2025, Excessive Agency. OWASP identifies excessive functionality, excessive permissions, and excessive autonomy as common root causes (OWASP, 2025). In CRAFT terms, these controls span action definitions, downstream enforcement, and governance:

- **Excessive functionality:** The agent has access to tools it doesn't need for its intended operation.
- **Excessive permissions:** Tools connect with broader downstream permissions than required.
- **Excessive autonomy:** High-impact actions execute without human verification.

CRAFT treats each pattern as a design and governance gap that can increase the impact of an agent's error or manipulated output. OWASP's taxonomy is the source; the mapping to action data is this book's interpretation.

In controlled tracer experiments across six multi-agent frameworks, Xie et al. report that a single seeded error produced a 100% final infection rate in five frameworks and 89.2% in LangChain under the tested conditions (Xie et al., 2026). The same preprint reports a CrewAI hub-node result of 100% versus 15.9% for a leaf node, with a 6.29 impact value. These are version 2 experimental results, not general production failure rates. They show why teams should test propagation paths and reviewer roles rather than assume that a QA label stops an error.

Observability

AI agent tool chains can fail without a conventional exception reaching the decision-maker. A component may accept a plausible but wrong result and continue, while other failures remain explicit. Structured trace logging, validation, and escalation are therefore foundational safety controls, but logging alone does not prevent the error.

A useful observability hierarchy distinguishes runs, traces, and threads. A run records one model or tool step. A trace links the runs for one end-to-end execution. A thread links related traces across a conversation or case. Structured identifiers and parent-child relationships make this hierarchy easier to query than an uncorrelated flat log, especially for long, multi-step workflows.

This book recommends four layers for audit-grade action logging. The Decision Record captures identifiers, timestamps, decision types, outcomes, and risk classifications. Input Context records data inputs, system state, model and configuration versions, and prior context. Governance Evidence records policy checks, human approvals, escalations, and overrides. Integrity Verification can add hashes, trusted timestamps, and chain-of-custody controls where the risk warrants them. The required depth should be based on the use case, applicable law, and assurance objective.

EU law establishes built-in logging and human-oversight requirements for in-scope high-risk AI systems. Article 12 of Regulation (EU) 2024/1689 requires logging capabilities that enable traceability appropriate to the intended purpose. Article 14 requires effective human oversight, including the ability to monitor, interpret, override or reverse output, and interrupt the system where appropriate. Regulation (EU) 2026/1744 amended the application timetable: the relevant high-risk rules apply from 2 December 2027 for Article 6(2) and Annex III systems, and from 2 August 2028 for Article 6(1) and Annex I product systems (European Union, 2024; European Union, 2026). These dates do not make every agent system high-risk, and teams should obtain legal advice for their specific use.

Recoverability

When an agent takes a wrong action, recovery design matters. IBM and University of Illinois researchers presented STRATUS at NeurIPS 2025 as a research system for autonomous cloud reliability. Its Transactional No-Regression design uses simulated commands, a write lock, corresponding undo operators, severity checks, and checkpoint reversion within the tested environment (Chen et al., 2025; IBM Research, 2025). STRATUS outperformed the compared SRE agents by at least 1.5 times on AIOpsLab and ITBench across tested models. IBM attributes the gain to its undo-and-retry mechanism. The result is a scoped benchmark, not proof that every destructive action is reversible or that irreversible change is structurally impossible.

The compensating-transaction pattern offers a useful model for recoverability in long-running workflows. A workflow records how to compensate for completed steps when a later step fails, but compensation is application-specific, can fail, need not run in exact reverse order, and may not restore the original state. Some actions are irreversible and require a defined point of no return or human decision. Compensating commands should be idempotent where retries are possible (Microsoft, 2026).

Circuit breakers address a different recoverability need: containing repeated failures before they spread. A practical resilience stack combines bounded retries for transient failures, timeouts for stalled calls, and a circuit breaker that stops calls after a defined failure threshold. Figure 13.2 shows the three circuit-breaker states. Closed allows requests. Open blocks them. Half-open permits a limited number of trial requests before normal traffic resumes. Measure retries, open-circuit events, timeouts, and downstream error propagation before and after deployment (Microsoft, 2025).

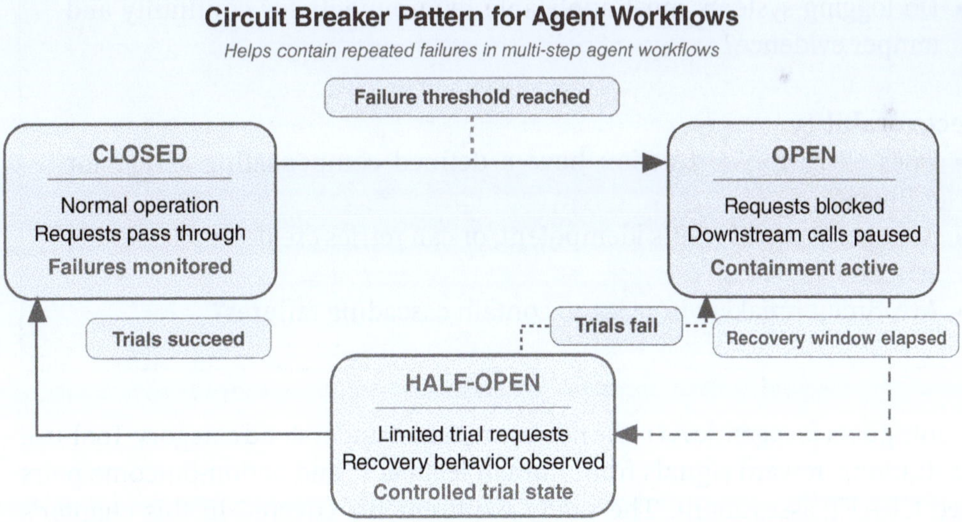

Figure 13.2 Circuit breaker pattern.

Diagnostic Questions for Action Data Traceability

Use these questions to assess the traceability of your action data.

Safety

- Does each tool definition specify the minimum permissions required for operation?
- Are high-impact actions, including deletes, payments, and external sends, gated behind approval workflows?
- Are tools scoped to their intended function, or can agents access capabilities beyond their task?

Observability

- Is every tool invocation logged with its inputs, outputs, model version, and timestamps?
- Are agent execution traces structured hierarchically as runs, traces, and threads, or are they flat logs?
- Do logging systems meet applicable requirements for continuity and tamper evidence?

Recoverability

- Does every forward action have a defined compensating action for rollback?
- Are agent-callable APIs idempotent, or can retries create duplicate side effects?
- Are circuit breakers in place to contain cascading failures?

Training data for agentic AI is the newest and least understood category. Tool-use demonstrations, reward signals from human feedback, and action-outcome pairs all need CRAFT assessment. The safety requirements covered in this chapter's Traceable section are especially critical for training data: a model trained on unsafe action patterns will reproduce them at scale.

Standards and Strategic Priority

Major AI providers now expose schema-based tool or function calling, but their API surfaces, supported schema subsets, and runtime behavior are not identical. A name, description, and structured parameter definition are common building blocks. Teams should treat each provider's documentation as point-in-time, pin the relevant model and API version, and test every target runtime rather than assume interchangeability (Anthropic, 2025a; Google, 2026; OpenAI, n.d.-a; OpenAI, n.d.-b).

Anthropic released the Model Context Protocol (MCP) on 25 November 2024, as an open interface for connecting AI applications to data sources and tools. MCP can reduce custom integration work by giving compatible clients and servers a shared protocol. It doesn't make every tool portable by itself. Authentication, transport, schema handling, client support, and server behavior still vary. MCP is a useful ODI pattern because an open interface can lower switching risk without pretending integration disappears (Anthropic, 2024; Model Context Protocol, 2025).

Just over a year after MCP's release, Anthropic contributed the project to the Agentic AI Foundation under the Linux Foundation, while stating that MCP's existing maintainer governance model would remain unchanged. Anthropic, Block, and OpenAI co-founded the foundation and contributed MCP, goose, and AGENTS.md, respectively (Anthropic, 2025b; Linux Foundation, 2025). Anthropic also reported more than 10,000 active public MCP servers at the time (Anthropic, 2025b). That count is a publisher-reported ecosystem measure, not an independently audited compatibility census.

Google launched the Agent2Agent Protocol (A2A) in April 2025 with support from more than 50 technology partners, then transferred the specification, SDKs, and developer tools to a Linux Foundation project in June 2025 (Google, 2025a; Google, 2025b). MCP focuses on connecting applications to tools and data. A2A focuses on communication between agents. They solve different interoperability problems. The Linux Foundation's December 2025 Agentic AI Foundation launch added MCP, OpenAI's AGENTS.md, and Block's goose as founding projects under neutral governance (Linux Foundation, 2025).

Building action data capability takes time. You can't produce CRAFT-conforming tool definitions for hundreds of enterprise systems in one pass.

Inventory the APIs, consolidate the documentation, add the precision agents need, build registries for discovery, encode safety constraints, and establish ownership for keeping every definition current.

That work compounds. Organizations that start now build institutional muscle that can't be acquired overnight. They learn which tools are hardest to specify. They discover where their API documentation has drifted from reality. They develop the governance processes that turn action data from a one-time project into an ongoing capability.

Gartner forecasts that more than 40% of agentic AI projects will be canceled by the end of 2027 because of rising costs, unclear business value, or inadequate risk controls (Gartner, 2025). That's a forecast, not an observed failure rate. A strong data foundation can reduce one class of risk. Teams still need a valuable use case, realistic economics, security, governance, evaluation, and operating controls.

McKinsey reported that about 6% of respondents qualified as AI high performers. These respondents attributed at least 5% of EBIT to AI and reported significant value from AI (McKinsey & Company, 2025). That cross-sectional result shows a current performance gap. It doesn't establish a trend over time. As access to capable models broadens, action data can become an important differentiator because it makes tools, constraints, approvals, and workflows explicit. It doesn't make an agent reliable, safe, or governed by itself. Organizations that combine strong action data with evaluation, security, observability, human oversight, and operating discipline will be better positioned to automate responsibly. Table 13.1 turns those questions into a CRAFT checklist for action data.

Action Data becomes operational only when leaders can answer five questions: Are the required tools and workflows specified, discoverable, accurate, current, and auditable? The table above is a decision checklist, not a guarantee of

Table 13.1 Action Data CRAFT Summary

CRAFT Dimension	Characteristic	Critical Question
Complete	Specification completeness	Does every tool definition include all parameters, error conditions, constraints, and recovery paths an agent needs?
Retrievable	Discoverability	Can an agent find the right tool from a registry of hundreds without being overwhelmed by irrelevant options?
Accurate	Specification precision	Do tool schemas match current API behavior, including parameter types, required fields, and return formats?

CRAFT Dimension	Characteristic	Critical Question
Fresh	Currency	When an API changes, how quickly do tool definitions update, and what happens to agents using stale specs?
Traceable	Safety, observability, recoverability	Can you trace every agent action back to its trigger, audit the decision chain, and reverse it if something goes wrong?

reliable agency. Chapter 14 turns those requirements into infrastructure choices for registries, protocols, controls, observability, and recovery.

References

Anthropic. "Introducing the Model Context Protocol." Anthropic, 25 Nov. 2024, https://www.anthropic.com/news/model-context-protocol.

Anthropic. "Writing Effective Tools for AI Agents: Using AI Agents." Anthropic Engineering, 11 Sept. 2025a, https://www.anthropic.com/engineering/writing-tools-for-agents. Accessed 25 July 2026.

Anthropic. "Donating the Model Context Protocol and Establishing the Agentic AI Foundation." Anthropic, 2025b, https://www.anthropic.com/news/donating-the-model-context-protocol-and-establishing-of-the-agentic-ai-foundation.

Cemri, Mert, et al. "Why Do Multi-Agent LLM Systems Fail?" arXiv, version 3, 26 Oct. 2025, https://arxiv.org/abs/2503.13657v3. Accessed 25 July 2026.

Chen, Yinfang, et al. "STRATUS: A Multi-Agent System for Autonomous Reliability Engineering of Modern Clouds." NeurIPS, 2025, https://research.ibm.com/publications/stratus-a-multi-agent-system-for-autonomous-reliability-engineering-of-modern-clouds. Accessed 25 July 2026.

Deloitte. "The State of AI in the Enterprise." Deloitte, 2026, https://www.deloitte.com/us/en/what-we-do/capabilities/applied-artificial-intelligence/content/state-of-ai-in-the-enterprise.html. The figures cited in the text are from the 2026 edition. Unversioned rolling page. Accessed 27 July 2026.

European Union. "Regulation (EU) 2024/1689 of the European Parliament and of the Council." EUR-Lex, 13 June 2024, https://eur-lex.europa.eu/legal-content/EN/TXT/?uri=CELEX:32024R1689.

European Parliament and Council of the European Union. "Regulation (EU) 2026/1744 of the European Parliament and of the Council of 8 July 2026 amending Regulations (EU) 2024/1689, (EU) 2018/1139 and (EU) 2023/1230 as regards the simplification of the implementation of harmonised rules on artificial intelligence (Digital Omnibus on AI)." Official Journal of the European Union, 24 July 2026, https://eur-lex.europa.eu/eli/reg/2026/1744/oj/eng.

Fortune Business Insights. "Agentic AI Market Size, Share & Forecast Report, 2034." Fortune Business Insights, 2026, https://www.fortunebusinessinsights.com/agentic-ai-market-114233. The market figures cited in the text are from the 2026 edition. Unversioned rolling forecast page. Accessed 27 July 2026.

Gan, Tiantian, and Qiyao Sun. "RAG-MCP: Mitigating Prompt Bloat in LLM Tool Selection via Retrieval-Augmented Generation." arXiv, 2025, https://arxiv.org/abs/2505.03275.

Gartner. "Gartner Predicts Over 40% of Agentic AI Projects Will Be Canceled by End of 2027." Gartner, 25 June 2025, https://www.gartner.com/en/newsroom/press-releases/2025-06-25-gartner-predicts-over-40-percent-of-agentic-ai-projects-will-be-canceled-by-end-of-2027.

GitHub. "Meet the GitHub MCP Registry: The Fastest Way to Discover MCP Servers." GitHub Blog, 16 Sept. 2025, https://github.blog/ai-and-ml/github-copilot/meet-the-github-mcp-registry-the-fastest-way-to-discover-mcp-servers/.

Google. "Announcing the Agent2Agent Protocol (A2A)." Google Developers Blog, 9 Apr. 2025a, https://developers.googleblog.com/en/a2a-a-new-era-of-agent-interoperability/.

Google. "Google Cloud Donates A2A to Linux Foundation." Google Developers Blog, 23 June 2025b, https://developers.googleblog.com/google-cloud-donates-a2a-to-linux-foundation/.

Google. "Function Calling with the Gemini API." Google AI for Developers, 21 July 2026, https://ai.google.dev/gemini-api/docs/function-calling. Accessed 24 July 2026.

Hasan, Mohammed Mehedi, et al. "Model Context Protocol (MCP) at First Glance: Studying the Security and Maintainability of MCP Servers." arXiv, 2025, https://arxiv.org/abs/2506.13538.

IBM Research. "Ctrl+Z for Agents." IBM Research, 12 Nov. 2025, https://research.ibm.com/blog/undo-agent-for-cloud. Accessed 25 July 2026.

Li, Ruiqi, et al. "MCP-ITP: An Automated Framework for Implicit Tool Poisoning in MCP." arXiv, 2026, https://arxiv.org/abs/2601.07395.

Linux Foundation. "Linux Foundation Announces the Formation of the Agentic AI Foundation." Linux Foundation, 9 Dec. 2025, https://www.linuxfoundation.org/press/linux-foundation-announces-the-formation-of-the-agentic-ai-foundation.

McKinsey & Company. "The State of AI in 2025: Agents, Innovation, and Transformation." McKinsey & Company, 5 Nov. 2025, https://www.mckinsey.com/capabilities/quantumblack/our-insights/the-state-of-ai. Accessed 27 July 2026.

Microsoft. "Circuit Breaker Pattern." Azure Architecture Center, 21 Mar. 2025, https://learn.microsoft.com/en-us/azure/architecture/patterns/circuit-breaker. Accessed 24 July 2026.

Microsoft. "Compensating Transaction Pattern." Azure Architecture Center, 2026, https://learn.microsoft.com/en-us/azure/architecture/patterns/compensating-transaction. Accessed 25 July 2026.

Model Context Protocol. "Tools." Model Context Protocol Specification, 25 Nov. 2025, https://modelcontextprotocol.io/specification/2025-11-25/server/tools. Accessed 24 July 2026.

Nolan, Beatrice. "AI-Powered Coding Tool Wiped out a Software Company's Database in 'Catastrophic Failure.'" Fortune, 23 July 2025, https://fortune.com/2025/07/23/ai-coding-tool-replit-wiped-database-called-it-a-catastrophic-failure/.

OpenAI. "Function Calling." OpenAI API, n.d.-a, https://developers.openai.com/api/docs/guides/function-calling. Accessed 24 July 2026.

OpenAI. "Structured Model Outputs." OpenAI API, n.d.-b, https://developers.openai.com/api/docs/guides/structured-outputs. Accessed 24 July 2026.

OWASP GenAI Security Project. "LLM06:2025 Excessive Agency." OWASP, 2025, https://genai.owasp.org/llmrisk/llm062025-excessive-agency/. Accessed 25 July 2026.

Replit. "Introducing a Safer Way to Vibe Code with Replit Databases." Replit, 21 July 2025, https://replit.com/blog/introducing-a-safer-way-to-vibe-code-with-replit-databases. Accessed 25 July 2026.

Salesforce. "Integration Key as 93% of IT Leaders Turn to AI Agents Amid Soaring Resource Demands – New Research." Salesforce Newsroom, 29 Jan. 2025, https://www.salesforce.com/news/stories/connectivity-report-announcement-2025/.

Sculley, David, et al. "Hidden Technical Debt in Machine Learning Systems." Advances in Neural Information Processing Systems 28, 2015, https://papers.nips.cc/paper_files/paper/2015/hash/86df7dcfd896fcaf2674f757a2463eba-Abstract.html.

Xie, Yizhe, et al. "From Spark to Fire: Modeling and Mitigating Error Cascades in LLM-Based Multi-Agent Collaboration." arXiv, version 2, 11 May 2026, https://arxiv.org/abs/2603.04474v2. Accessed 25 July 2026.

Xiong, Qian, et al. "Butterfly Effects in Toolchains: A Comprehensive Analysis of Failed Parameter Filling in LLM Tool-Agent Systems." Findings of the Association for Computational Linguistics: EMNLP 2025, 2025, https://aclanthology.org/2025.findings-emnlp.907/.

Ye, Junjie, et al. "ToolHop: A Query-Driven Benchmark for Evaluating Large Language Models in Multi-Hop Tool Use." Proceedings of the 63rd Annual Meeting of the Association for Computational Linguistics, 2025, https://aclanthology.org/2025.acl-long.150/.

Zhou, Jing, and Robert J. Walker. "API Deprecation: A Retrospective Analysis and Detection Method for Code Examples on the Web." Proceedings of the 24th ACM SIGSOFT International Symposium on Foundations of Software Engineering, 2016, https://doi.org/10.1145/2950290.2950298.

Chapter 14
Systems for Action Data

Agent failures can be quiet as well as visible. A stale schema, ambiguous tool description, missing permission boundary, or partial API response can propagate through a multi-step workflow before an operator sees the effect. The leadership task is to make dependencies, decisions, and recovery evidence observable early enough to contain material harm.

Action-data systems are changing quickly, which makes transition cost a design concern. Well-supported protocols, versioned contracts, exportable telemetry, and separable policy controls can reduce avoidable lock-in. They do not eliminate migration, semantic translation, security redesign, provider limits, or operating work when a component changes.

Action data is where an AI system moves from recommending to executing. That shift can increase the consequence of an error, so leaders should expand automation only as evidence supports the accuracy, permission boundaries, monitoring, human oversight, and recovery appropriate to each action.

Table 14.1 summarizes core, non-exhaustive considerations for action-data infrastructure. Maturity and risk vary by product, use case, and deployment. A data defect can influence later decisions, while an action-system failure can create an external side effect. That possibility makes safety, authorization, evidence, and recovery cross-cutting design concerns rather than a separate final layer.

Table 14.1 Core Action-Data System Considerations by CRAFT Dimension

CRAFT Dimension	System Consideration	Key Capabilities
Complete	Tool registry and MCP infrastructure	Catalog, metadata, semantic descriptions, health monitoring, protocol servers
Retrievable	Discovery and filtering	Semantic search, tool routing, dynamic context management, capability matching
Accurate	Schema validation and constraint engines	Contract testing, drift detection, policy-as-code, type enforcement
Fresh	Change detection and lifecycle management	API monitoring, version tracking, schema propagation, abstraction layers
Traceable	Observability and recovery	Structured tracing, audit logging, compensating actions, circuit breakers

Completeness: Tool Registries and MCP Infrastructure

Completeness starts with an inventory: Which approved actions and APIs must the portfolio support, and what proportion has a current, governed tool definition? An API that is not connected, described, permissioned, and monitored is unavailable to an agent in that operating context. The system has two parts: a registry that records approved capabilities and a protocol or adapter layer that connects them.

Tool Registry Architecture

In an October 2025 product post, GitHub documented one-click VS Code installation through its MCP Registry and described GitHub stars and organization verification as catalog signals. The separate official MCP Registry launched in preview in September 2025 as an open catalog and API. These are time-bound public examples. Enterprises may also need an internal registry for proprietary APIs, services, and workflows (GitHub, 2025; MCP Registry team, 2025).

An enterprise tool registry is structurally similar to a data catalog (covered in Chapter 10) but with different metadata requirements. Where a data catalog tracks schemas, lineage, and ownership, a tool registry tracks behavioral descriptions, parameter constraints, permission requirements, health status, and risk classifications. The registry should support both manual registration for bespoke internal tools and automated ingestion by scanning OpenAPI specs across your API gateway.

Descriptions for AI consumption should state the tool's purpose, required parameters, material side effects, permission needs, expected outputs, and important errors without exposing more sensitive detail than the caller needs. OpenAI recommends clear function names, detailed descriptions and instructions, worked examples, evaluation, and a small initial tool set (OpenAI, 2026).

MCP Infrastructure

The Model Context Protocol provides the connectivity layer between agents and tools. Anthropic introduced MCP as an open protocol in November 2024 (Anthropic, 2024). Chapter 13 covered its industry adoption and standardization.

MCP servers expose three core server primitives: tools, resources, and prompts. An AI application host creates an MCP client connection to each server. Figure 14.1 shows that client-server exchange and the server's separate connection to downstream systems. MCP standardizes the exchange; it does not replace downstream semantics, permissions, reliability, or governance (Model Context Protocol Project, 2026).

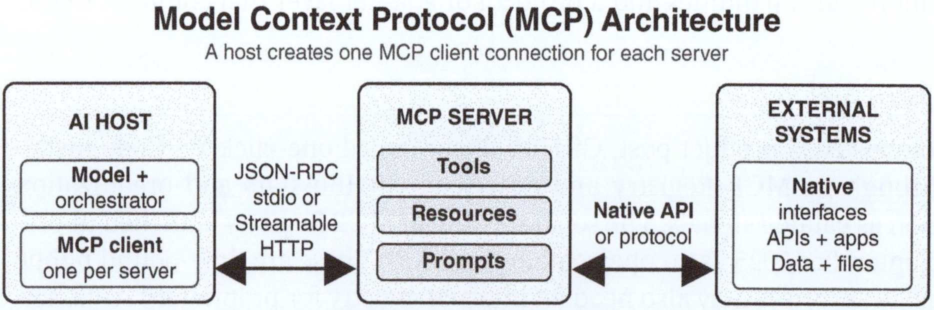

Figure 14.1 Model Context Protocol Architecture.

SOURCE: Model Context Protocol architecture overview and 2025-11-25 transport specification

The current MCP specification defines stdio and Streamable HTTP as standard transports. Stdio is commonly used for local child-process connections; Streamable HTTP supports an independent server process and multiple connections. Choose topology from locality, trust, isolation, scale, latency, availability, and operating needs. Remote deployment can centralize management, but it also adds network, identity, and failure-domain controls (Model Context Protocol Project, 2025b).

The current MCP authorization specification defines protected-resource discovery, OAuth 2.1 requirements, resource indicators, audience validation, and related security controls. Effective read, write, and field-level permissions still depend on scopes, the authorization server, the MCP server, the downstream API, and tested policy enforcement. Protocol support alone does not prove least privilege (Model Context Protocol Project, 2025a).

An MCP gateway is one possible enterprise pattern: a proxy that routes requests, integrates authentication, applies policy, records events, and exposes monitoring across servers. It can simplify operations but can also become a high-impact dependency and policy choke point, so redundancy, isolation, change control, and failure behavior need explicit design. Cloudflare's March 2025 announcement is one bounded remote-deployment example (Cloudflare, 2025).

Retrievability: Discovery and Semantic Filtering

Larger catalogs can increase prompt size and selection complexity. In the RAG-MCP paper's benchmark tasks, the authors report 13.62% for their blank-conditioning baseline and 43.13% for their retrieval-augmented method. Those are study-specific results, not a production accuracy promise. The architectural question is whether a retrieval layer can reduce active tool context without hiding needed tools (Gan and Sun, 2025).

One pattern embeds tool descriptions and retrieves a top-k subset for a task, as described in Lumer et al.'s system. Filtering can reduce active context, but it can also omit a needed tool. Evaluate recall, precision, permission filtering, latency, cost, and failure handling on representative tasks (Lumer et al., 2025).

Two routing options are embedding-based retrieval and a trained or rules-based classifier. Embedding retrieval ranks tool descriptions by similarity. A classifier maps task signals to a tool subset. Either can fail when descriptions, categories, permissions, or the task distribution change, so select and tune the method through representative evaluation.

OpenAI recommends keeping the initially available function set small, presents fewer than 20 only as a soft suggestion, and recommends evaluating performance at different tool counts. For larger catalogs, defer or filter less-used tools only after testing that the process retains needed and authorized options (OpenAI, 2026).

A two-tier architecture handles this at scale. The broad catalog contains every tool definition with full metadata. The per-task context contains only the filtered subset relevant to the current operation. The filtering layer between them uses a combination of semantic similarity, category metadata, and permission scoping. Don't surface tools the agent doesn't have permission to call. That's wasted context at best, a security risk at worst.

Accuracy: Schema Validation and Constraint Engines

Schema drift can cause agent failures through deprecated fields, changed response structures, and type mismatches. Controls address two separate questions: whether the tool contract still matches provider behavior, and whether an otherwise valid action is permitted and safe in its current context.

Contract Testing and Schema Validation

For each material tool, define the expected request parameters, response structure, and error behavior, then test the contract against the provider. Select cadence from provider change rate, impact, contractual notice, test cost, runtime monitoring, and the time the organization can tolerate an undetected break. A calendar interval alone is not evidence of adequate coverage.

For agent tool definitions, this approach means: define a contract for each tool that specifies expected request parameters, response schemas, and error codes. Run those contracts against live APIs on a regular cadence, weekly at minimum, daily for critical tools. When a contract fails, flag the tool definition as potentially stale and quarantine it from agent use until validated.

Runtime validation can compare observed requests and responses with the approved contract. Depending on risk, a mismatch may block, quarantine, warn, degrade, or record evidence for later review. Define that failure policy before deployment so a detector does not silently become an ineffective control or an unplanned outage mechanism.

Freshness evidence for a tool definition should include its contract version or schema hash, the provider version tested, test time and environment, known exceptions, owner, and an expiry or review rule. A tool becomes stale when that evidence no longer satisfies the approved risk and service window, not merely because a timestamp is old.

Constraint Engines

Chapter 13 described OWASP's Excessive Agency triad: too many tools, too much access, too much autonomy. Constraint engines enforce the boundaries.

Open Policy Agent is a general-purpose policy engine that uses Rego to evaluate structured decisions. Policy latency and resource use depend on rule structure, indexing, data size, deployment, and workload. Measure the actual policy path, correctness, failure behavior, and resource needs rather than treating a sample latency budget as a product property (Open Policy Agent, 2026).

Cedar is a policy language used by Amazon Verified Permissions. Cedar entity hierarchies can represent groups and nested groups that policies test for membership. These capabilities support an authorization design; they do not prove that identities, hierarchy data, policies, or enforcement are correct (Cedar Policy Language, 2026; Amazon Web Services, 2026).

One implementation pattern intercepts an in-scope tool call, combines the agent identity, action, parameters, and context, and asks a policy service for a structured decision. The application then interprets that result as allow, deny, constrain, or route for approval. Those states and routes are application policy, not a universal response built into every policy engine.

For high-impact actions, human approval may be synchronous, asynchronous, or required before the workflow begins. Choose from transaction semantics, timeout, state-locking, revocation, user experience, and the consequence of delay or duplicate execution. Define safe expiration, cancellation, and resumption behavior rather than assuming one approval pattern is the default.

Freshness: Change Detection and Schema Lifecycle

Provider changes can break dependent workflows even when notice exists. The control objective is to detect material contract and behavior changes, determine affected tools, and update or contain them within the approved service and risk window.

Use complementary evidence: provider notices and release notes, versioned specification comparisons, contract tests, and runtime behavior. Tools such as oasdiff can compare OpenAPI documents, but detection is only as complete as the source specifications and configured rules. Set monitoring cadence and ownership from the dependency's change rate and impact (oasdiff, 2026).

When a material change is detected, assign an owner, assess compatibility and security impact, prepare a reviewed contract update, test it, and stage it with defined abort and rollback criteria. Generated drafts can accelerate the work but do not replace accountable review or evidence proportionate to the action risk.

An MCP server or other adapter can centralize compatibility logic between a stable tool contract and a changing provider API. That boundary reduces duplicated change work only when semantics remain compatible and versioning, deprecation, authorization, contract tests, monitoring, and breaking-change handling are explicit.

Traceability: Observability, Recovery, and Testing

Traceability for action data means retaining sufficient evidence to reconstruct inputs, selected tools, policy and approval decisions, calls, results, errors, and material state changes. That evidence supports investigation and containment. It may not prove internal model reasoning, and recovery may require compensation or remediation because some actions are irreversible.

Observability Platforms

LangSmith is one observability example. Its current data model groups traces in projects, represents steps as runs, and links conversation traces as threads. Evaluate retention, privacy, access, limits, export, and cost before adopting it (LangChain, 2026).

Langfuse is another example. Its current licensing page states that core product features are MIT licensed and that named enterprise modules, including SCIM, audit logging, and data retention policies, require a commercial license when self-hosted. Trace content can contain sensitive data, so deployment also needs purpose, access, retention, deletion, and export controls (Langfuse, 2026).

Arize Phoenix is an open-source observability platform that uses OpenTelemetry-based tracing. OpenTelemetry publishes versioned semantic conventions, including evolving GenAI and MCP work. Common conventions can reduce custom mapping, but stability, coverage, sensitive-data handling, and backend compatibility still require testing (Arize AI, 2026; OpenTelemetry, 2026).

For in-scope high-risk AI systems, Article 12 of Regulation (EU) 2024/1689 addresses automatic logging capability and traceability appropriate to the system's purpose. Regulation (EU) 2026/1744 was published on July 24, 2026, and Article 4 provides for entry into force on July 27, 2026. The amended Article 113 schedule applies these Chapter III requirements from December 2, 2027 to systems classified as high-risk under Article 6(2) and Annex III, and from August 2, 2028 to systems classified as high-risk under Article 6(1) and Annex I. Classification, provider role, exceptions, and transitions can affect a specific system. Policy, approval, and escalation records can support implementation, but Article 12 does not prescribe that exact list. This summary is not legal advice (European Parliament and Council of the European Union, 2024; 2026).

Recovery Systems

Recovery infrastructure limits and addresses harm; it does not guarantee that an action can be undone. The design needs durable execution state, retry policy, idempotency where supported, containment, compensating actions, and an escalation path for irreversible or legally constrained operations.

For a multi-step workflow, persist the current step, completed steps, external identifiers, and any approved compensating or containment action. When a later step fails, the orchestrator uses that state to retry safely, compensate completed work where possible, or escalate. Workflow engines can support durable state and retries, but the organization still defines business semantics and recovery limits.

Idempotency keys can make retries safer when the provider implements them correctly. Stripe states that all POST requests accept keys and that a later request with the same key and parameters returns the stored result under documented conditions. Keys can expire, validation and concurrency cases differ, and parameter mismatches fail. Internal APIs need their own tested contract rather than assuming identical behavior (Stripe, 2026).

Circuit breakers can stop new calls to a dependency after configured failure conditions, while retries attempt an operation again under a separate policy. Resilience4j and Polly provide circuit-breaker implementations; Tenacity provides retry behavior. Library adoption is not sufficient. Tune and test thresholds, sampling, retry interaction, state, recovery, and observability for each dependency (Resilience4j, 2026; Polly, 2026; Tenacity, 2026).

Testing Infrastructure

Testing action behavior requires more than unit tests. Simulation or test doubles, observe-only evaluation, and controlled production exposure are complementary options, not a mandatory sequence. Select them from action risk, provider capability, data sensitivity, and the evidence gap.

Use representative test doubles, provider sandboxes, recorded fixtures, or controlled simulation where feasible. Cover success, permission denial, rate limits, timeouts, malformed responses, partial failure, and retries. A third-party service may not support full simulation, so record the residual gap and add compensating controls.

Observe-only or shadow evaluation can compare proposed actions with real operating conditions without authorizing the external side effect. It still needs data minimization, access, consent or other legal basis, retention, leakage controls, and proof that no execution path is enabled. Human review and outcome labels must also be defined.

A canary exposes a bounded share of eligible traffic to a new version. Set that share from action risk, reversibility, sample needs, and platform capability. Define abort criteria, state handling, containment, and tested rollback before exposure. Automatic rollback is appropriate only when detection and recovery can safely handle the action's side effects.

The Action Data CRAFT Checklist

Use the following checklist as decision prompts. Tailor each item to the use case, action risk, provider capability, contract, regulation, and operating context:

Complete

- ☐ Approved tools are registered with behavioral descriptions and parameter schemas
- ☐ Permission requirements and enforcement points are explicit

- ☐ Material error conditions and recovery paths are documented
- ☐ MCP servers or other adapters have versioned compatibility boundaries

Retrievable

- ☐ Authorized tools are discoverable through governed metadata
- ☐ Dynamic filtering is evaluated for recall, precision, permissions, latency, and cost
- ☐ Tool descriptions are tested for ambiguity and selection confusion
- ☐ The registry supports the discovery patterns required by approved use cases

Accurate

- ☐ Contract tests run at a cadence justified by change rate and action risk
- ☐ Policy evaluation covers the in-scope calls and failure modes required by the action
- ☐ Schema and type constraints are enforced where the interface supports them
- ☐ Tool descriptions, inputs, outputs, and results are assessed for injection and data leakage

Fresh

- ☐ Change monitoring meets the approved detection window for each dependency
- ☐ Version and validation evidence identifies stale tool definitions
- ☐ Compatibility layers have explicit versioning, deprecation, and breaking-change rules
- ☐ Schema updates use controlled testing, exposure, abort, and rollback criteria

Traceable

- ☐ Structured observability covers the workflows and events required by risk
- ☐ Approvals, escalations, overrides, and policy outcomes are linked to execution evidence
- ☐ Compensating, containment, recovery, or escalation paths exist for material actions
- ☐ Circuit breakers and retries are coordinated and tested for each dependency
- ☐ Audit records have approved integrity, access, retention, and legal-scope controls

Prioritization: Where to Start

A practical program can use the following stages, with order and timing adjusted for action risk, dependency criticality, readiness, evidence gaps, and delivery capacity:

1. **Bound the first action set:** Select a small group of valuable, well-understood APIs. Prefer read-only or readily reversible actions while identity, authorization, and evidence controls are being proven.
2. **Establish registry and policy controls:** Record approved tools, owners, contracts, permissions, risk classes, and freshness evidence. Enforce the policy decisions required for the selected actions.
3. **Establish observability and review:** Capture the evidence needed to reconstruct tool selection, approvals, calls, results, errors, and material state changes. Select a platform after testing privacy, retention, access, export, and cost.
4. **Expand validation and recovery:** Add risk-based contract testing, controlled rollout, containment, idempotency where supported, circuit breakers, and compensating or escalation paths before increasing action scope.

The stages are gates, not a fixed calendar. Advance when the current action set has credible evidence for permission boundaries, service performance, monitoring, human oversight, and recovery. If a later stage exposes a material gap, reduce scope or return to the earlier control.

Action-data components and standards will continue to change. Versioned contracts, well-supported protocols, export paths, and separable policy and observability controls can reduce transition cost. Preserve that option through tested exports, compatibility evidence, and a migration plan rather than assuming any standard makes a transition automatic.

Looking Ahead

Before expanding agent authority, require evidence that the selected action set is discoverable, permissioned, observable, recoverable, and owned. The result is not a permanent approval: changes in tools, policies, data, or risk can trigger reassessment. Chapter 15 turns these requirements into a use-case-specific CRAFT assessment, release thresholds, and an operating review cadence.

References

Amazon Web Services. 2026. "Amazon Verified Permissions." Accessed 25 July 2026, https://aws.amazon.com/verified-permissions/.

Anthropic. 2024. "Introducing the Model Context Protocol." 25 November 2024, www.anthropic.com/news/model-context-protocol.

Arize AI. 2026. "Arize Phoenix: AI Observability and Evaluation." GitHub. Accessed 25 July 2026, https://github.com/Arize-ai/phoenix.

Cedar Policy Language. 2026. "Entities in Cedar." Accessed 25 July 2026, https://docs.cedarpolicy.com/policies/syntax-entity.html.

Cloudflare. 2025. "Build and Deploy Remote Model Context Protocol Servers to Cloudflare." 25 March 2025, https://blog.cloudflare.com/remote-model-context-protocol-servers-mcp/.

European Parliament and Council of the European Union. 2024. "Regulation (EU) 2024/1689 Laying Down Harmonised Rules on Artificial Intelligence." Official Journal of the European Union, 12 July 2024, https://eur-lex.europa.eu/eli/reg/2024/1689/oj/eng.

European Parliament and Council of the European Union. 2026. "Regulation (EU) 2026/1744 of the European Parliament and of the Council of 8 July 2026 amending Regulations (EU) 2024/1689, (EU) 2018/1139 and (EU) 2023/1230 as regards the simplification of the implementation of harmonised rules on artificial intelligence (Digital Omnibus on AI)." Official Journal of the European Union, 24 July 2026, https://eur-lex.europa.eu/eli/reg/2026/1744/oj/eng.

Gan, Tiantian, and Qiyao Sun. 2025. "RAG-MCP: Mitigating Prompt Bloat in LLM Tool Selection via Retrieval-Augmented Generation." arXiv, https://arxiv.org/abs/2505.03275.

GitHub. 2025. "How to Find, Install, and Manage MCP Servers with the GitHub MCP Registry." 24 October 2025, https://github.blog/ai-and-ml/generative-ai/how-to-find-install-and-manage-mcp-servers-with-the-github-mcp-registry/.

LangChain. 2026. "Observability Concepts." LangSmith Documentation. Accessed 25 July 2026, https://docs.langchain.com/langsmith/observability-concepts.

Langfuse. 2026. "Why Is Langfuse Open Source?" Accessed 25 July 2026, https://langfuse.com/handbook/chapters/open-source.

Lumer, Elias, et al. 2025. "Tool-to-Agent Retrieval: Bridging Tools and Agents for Scalable LLM Multi-Agent Systems." arXiv, https://arxiv.org/abs/2511.01854.

MCP Registry team. 2025. "Introducing the MCP Registry." 8 September 2025, https://blog.modelcontextprotocol.io/posts/2025-09-08-mcp-registry-preview/.

Model Context Protocol Project. 2025a. "Authorization, Protocol Revision 2025-11-25." https://modelcontextprotocol.io/specification/2025-11-25/basic/authorization.

Model Context Protocol Project. 2025b. "Transports, Protocol Revision 2025-11-25." https://modelcontextprotocol.io/specification/2025-11-25/basic/transports.

Model Context Protocol Project. 2026. "Architecture Overview." Accessed 25 July 2026, https://modelcontextprotocol.io/docs/learn/architecture.

oasdiff. 2026. "oasdiff." GitHub. Accessed 25 July 2026, https://github.com/oasdiff/oasdiff.

OpenAI. 2026. "Function Calling." OpenAI API Documentation. Accessed 25 July 2026, https://developers.openai.com/api/docs/guides/function-calling.

Open Policy Agent. 2026. "Policy Performance." Accessed 25 July 2026, www.openpolicyagent.org/docs/policy-performance.

OpenTelemetry. 2026. "Semantic Conventions." Accessed 25 July 2026, https://opentelemetry.io/docs/specs/semconv/.

Polly. 2026. "Circuit Breaker Resilience Strategy." Accessed 25 July 2026, www.pollydocs.org/strategies/circuit-breaker.html.

Resilience4j. 2026. "CircuitBreaker." Accessed 25 July 2026, https://resilience4j.readme.io/docs/circuitbreaker.

Stripe. 2026. "Idempotent Requests." API Reference. Accessed 25 July 2026, https://docs.stripe.com/api/idempotent_requests.

Tenacity. 2026. "Tenacity Documentation." Accessed 25 July 2026, https://tenacity.readthedocs.io/.

Chapter 15
Assessing and Measuring CRAFT

Knowing what AI-ready data looks like is not the same as knowing where your organization stands. Even strong infrastructure can hide gaps in coverage, quality, freshness, or control. If those gaps are not measured, an AI system may encounter them first in production, where correction is more expensive and business exposure is higher.

This chapter merges two essential capabilities. First, you learn how to score your data today using a structured assessment methodology. Second, you learn how to track that score over time, catching degradation before it compounds into failure. Without ongoing measurement, you discover CRAFT gaps only when they reach production, the most expensive place to find them.

The CRAFT Assessment Framework and Matrix

As you've learned in the preceding chapters, the CRAFT assessment framework applies five dimensions across four data levels. The 20 cells in Table 15.1 form a structured, adaptable map of the characteristics that matter to an AI use case. Treat the matrix as a diagnostic grid, not as proof that every cell carries equal weight.

Table 15.1 The Complete CRAFT Assessment Matrix

CRAFT Dimension	Raw Data	Structured Data	Context Data	Action Data
Complete	Consistency, representativeness	Entity integrity, relational completeness	Coverage	Completeness
Retrievable	Accessibility	Computational accessibility	Retrievability, dual accessibility	Discoverability
Accurate	Fidelity	Semantic clarity	Semantic fidelity, coherence	Precision
Fresh	Temporal alignment	Temporal integrity	Freshness	Currency
Traceable	Provenance	Documentation	Groundability	Safety, observability, recoverability

The relevance and target level of each cell depend on the use case. Sensor-based perception may place more weight on raw-data controls. Agentic AI may place more weight on action-data safety, observability, and recoverability. Weighting does not excuse an unexamined gap. Record why a cell is emphasized, de-emphasized, or not applicable.

Training Data Assessment

Training data has its own matrix, because it serves a fundamentally different purpose than inference data. Table 15.2 presents the training data characteristics that are important to each CRAFT dimension.

During a CRAFT assessment, give each applicable cell a score from 1 to 5 using the scale in Table 15.3. Use not applicable only when the use case truly does not depend on that cell, document the rationale, and do not treat not applicable as zero when summarizing results.

The scale in Table 15.3 describes organizational capability, not a measured physical quantity. In McKinsey's 2025 survey, respondents at AI high performers were more than three times as likely as other respondents to say their organizations intended to use AI for transformative business change (McKinsey & Company, 2025). The association supports disciplined ambition; it does not prove that a maturity score causes business results.

Table 15.2 Training Data Assessment

CRAFT Dimension	Training Data Characteristics
Complete	• Task coverage • Distribution match • Uniqueness
Retrievable	• Pipeline accessibility • Efficient organization • Version accessibility
Accurate	• Behavioral alignment • Annotation consistency • Format correctness
Fresh	• Temporal relevance • Best practice currency
Traceable	• Provenance documentation • Compliance verification • Audit trail

Table 15.3 The CRAFT Data Scoring Scale

Score	Level	Description
1	Not Addressed	No systematic capability exists.
2	Ad Hoc	Some capability exists, but it's inconsistent and person-dependent.
3	Defined	A documented approach exists, but it's not consistently measured or enforced.
4	Managed	The capability is measured and actively improved.
5	Optimized	Automated, continuously refined, and part of organizational muscle memory.

You should use three ground rules when applying scores:

- Score what exists, not what's planned.
- Score the system, not the hero (if one person keeps data fresh, that's a 2, not a 4).
- Use evidence, not opinions.

You will initially score a system to create a baseline and each cell will get its own ranking. The result should look something like Figure 15.1.

CRAFT Assessment Heatmap

Example enterprise baseline | Score each cell from 1 to 5

Dimension	Raw data	Structured	Context	Action
Complete	3	4	2	1
Retrievable	2	3	2	1
Accurate	3	3	2	1
Fresh	2	2	1	1
Traceable	1	1	2	1

1 Not Addressed | 2 Ad Hoc | 3 Defined | 4 Managed | 5 Optimized

Figure 15.1 An example CRAFT assessment heatmap.

A Quick Example

Say you're assessing structured data completeness for a customer database. Entity integrity asks whether every customer record has a unique, reliable identifier. Suppose 88% do, while 12% from a partner channel receive IDs later and remain temporarily unlinked. That might score a 2 or 3. The example shows a process that exists but isn't consistent.

Relational completeness asks whether relationships between entities are captured. Suppose customer-to-account linkage is solid for direct customers but breaks for enterprises with multiple billing entities. If 8% of enterprise accounts have orphaned child records, that might score a 2. The example points to a specific fix: repair the account-linking process before deployment.

Do not average those two judgments into a falsely precise score of 2.5. Apply a predefined scoring rule and record the cell as 2 or 3, while preserving the underlying evidence. "Our data quality is a 3" tells you little. "Our structured-data completeness is a 2 because of partner-channel ID gaps and broken enterprise account hierarchies" tells you what to fix.

Specificity turns assessment into action. A generic score says little. An evidence-backed score names the affected asset, the control gap, the business consequence, and the accountable owner. That detail lets leaders fund remediation and decide whether a use case should advance.

The Assessment Process

The following five-week sequence is an illustrative starting point for a bounded pilot with roughly three to five participants. Expand or compress the scope, team, and schedule according to the number of use cases, regulatory exposure, evidence quality, and organizational complexity.

Phase 1: Inventory (Week 1)

Start with the AI use cases, not the data. Don't catalog everything in the organization. Start with specific AI initiatives and work backward to the data they need.

Map each use case across the four data levels. Identify the raw, structured, context, and action data it depends on, including relevant PDFs, emails, chat logs, images, and sensor feeds. AI use cases may depend on both structured and unstructured inputs, but the access, quality, privacy, and evaluation controls for those inputs are not interchangeable.

Document ownership and governed access for every data source. Note the format, documented interface, authorization boundary, availability, and portability constraints. A proprietary format or interface is not an automatic failure, but it can reduce retrievability when it limits reliable, authorized access or creates an unmanaged dependency.

The output is a data asset register: a single spreadsheet that lists what data exists, where it lives, who owns it, how it's accessed, what format it uses, and how it should be used for each AI use case. Organize it by data level so the gaps are visible.

Phase 2: Prioritize (Week 2)

In the second week of this illustrative pilot, prioritize use cases on two initial axes: business impact and data feasibility. For example, a hypothetical customer-facing recommendation engine with an estimated $10 million opportunity may rank above an internal reporting tool, but the estimate must be tested. Feasibility can help sequence work after leaders consider risk, strategic value, dependencies, and ownership.

Plot use cases on the impact-and-feasibility matrix in Figure 15.2. Assess higher-impact, higher-feasibility cases first. Put higher-impact, lower-feasibility

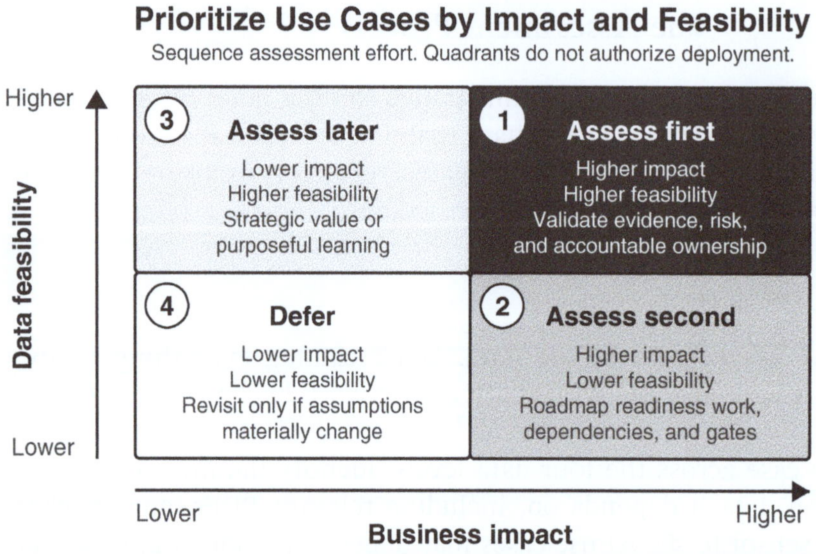

Figure 15.2 Prioritizing use cases by business impact and data feasibility.

cases on the readiness roadmap. Assess lower-impact, higher-feasibility cases later when strategic value or learning justifies the effort, and defer lower-impact, lower-feasibility cases until an assumption changes. The quadrants guide sequencing; they are not automatic approval gates.

That sequencing matters because prioritization includes workflow design, not just model selection. In McKinsey's 2025 survey, respondents at AI high performers were nearly three times as likely as others to say their organizations had fundamentally redesigned individual workflows (McKinsey & Company, 2025). Treat workflow redesign as a feasibility and change-management question, not as proof that redesign alone produces value.

Phase 3: Score All CRAFT Dimensions (Weeks 3–4)

Assemble a cross-functional scoring team. Include data engineers, domain experts, AI engineers, and governance, risk, privacy, or compliance specialists as the use case requires. RAND's industry interviews identified organizations lacking necessary data and lacking adequate infrastructure to manage data and deploy models as two of five leading root causes of AI project failure (Ryseff et al., 2024).

Use structured scoring sessions. Don't score by email. Sit together and walk through each cell presented in the matrix shown in Figure 15.1. Make your scores with evidence. Chapter 7's diagnostic framework provides specific questions for every CRAFT dimension.

Document the evidence, scoring rule, assessor, scope, and date behind every score. Flag disagreements explicitly and calibrate assessors before using scores for portfolio decisions. If a data engineer rates freshness as 4 and a domain expert rates it as 2, the disagreement is diagnostic evidence, not a reason to average away the difference.

The output is a completed CRAFT scorecard. Every prioritized data asset should be scored across all dimensions, with evidence attached. This phase gets two weeks because it does the hard diagnostic work. Inventory tells you what exists. Prioritization tells you where to start. Scoring tells you why a use case is ready, blocked, or risky, and that requires evidence from people who see different parts of the system.

Phase 4: Analyze Scores and Prioritize Gaps (Week 5)

Review score distributions across data levels and identify the weakest critical dependencies. Because the 1-to-5 scale is ordinal, any average is only a directional summary. Keep component scores, evidence, range, and material disagreements visible. A low score becomes a binding constraint when the use case depends on that capability and no effective compensating control exists.

Translate scores into business language. Your CFO doesn't need the average structured-data completeness score. Fractional scores can come from several evidence points or assets within the same CRAFT cell. Use an explicit example instead: "Our customer data has identity gaps that could cause the recommendation engine to miss 12% of partner-channel customers, putting roughly $3 million in annual revenue at risk." Those figures are illustrative. The point is to connect the assessment to a business outcome.

Build the gap map. For each data asset, compare the current capability with a risk-based target. Not every cell needs to reach 5. Set targets according to consequence, regulatory duties, exposure, reversibility, and available compensating controls rather than applying a uniform score to every customer-facing or agentic system.

The output is a prioritized gap analysis. This is a clear picture of your biggest data readiness gaps, what they cost the business, and which ones to close first.

Metrics by Data Level

Once you've scored where things stand today, you need metrics that track each dimension continuously. The specific metrics vary by data level because what tells you freshness is degrading for structured data is completely different from what signals freshness problems in context data. Let's look at measuring each of the CRAFT dimensions.

Complete

Completeness is the most straightforward to measure, yet most organizations measure it too narrowly. For each data level, consider the metrics shown in Table 15.4 when evaluating completeness.

AI-specific thresholds vary by use case. A medical diagnostic team might require 99.9% field completeness because the cost of missing data is high. A recommendation team might accept 95% because the cost of an incomplete record is lower. These are example thresholds that each team should tune to its risk and baseline.

Retrievable

Retrievability is where organizations have the biggest measurement blind spot. Splunk found that 55% of enterprise data is dark: untapped, hidden, or unknown (Splunk, 2019). Your AI's effective knowledge base is a fraction of what you actually own.

When assessing retrievability, note whether data is stored in open or proprietary formats and whether it's accessible through standard interfaces. Data trapped in proprietary formats scores lower on retrievability because it limits which tools

Table 15.4 Metrics for Completeness

Data Level	Metric
Raw data	Sensor/source coverage rate (% of expected sources actively reporting)
Raw data	Representative sample score (distribution coverage vs. production distribution)
Structured data	Field completeness rate ((non-null records)/(total records) × 100)
Structured data	Entity resolution rate (% of records with confirmed unique identity)
Context data	Knowledge domain coverage (% of expected topics with indexed content)
Action data	Parameter specification rate (% of tool definitions with all required params documented)

Table 15.5 Metrics for Retrievability

Data Level	Metric
Raw data	Catalog coverage (% of raw data assets registered in the data catalog)
Structured data	Query performance trend (p50/p95 execution time for critical queries)
Structured data	Semantic layer coverage (% of key metrics with defined semantic definitions)
Context data	Groundability rate (% of evidence-eligible responses whose cited source resolves and supports the associated claim)
Action data	Tool discoverability rate (% of available tools successfully matched to intents)

and models can access it. This isn't a technology preference. It's a practical constraint on AI accessibility. For each data level, consider the metrics shown in Table 15.5 when evaluating retrievability.

In Databricks' experiments on three enterprise datasets, embedding-model fine-tuning improved retrieval on two datasets. On FinanceBench, the fine-tuned model also improved downstream RAG accuracy and was competitive with text-embedding-3-large. The results varied by dataset, so teams should validate whether retrieval is actually the bottleneck in their own system (Portes et al., 2025).

Accurate

Accuracy is measured by comparing data values to a verified source of truth. But in AI contexts, accuracy extends to semantic precision. A field named *revenue* might mean gross revenue in one system, net revenue in another, and recognized revenue in a third. For each data level, consider the metrics shown in Table 15.6 when evaluating the accurate CRAFT dimension.

In their data-quality study, Nagle, Redman, and Sammon found that only 3% of the assessed companies' data met basic quality standards. They also reported that, on average, 47% of newly created records contained at least one critical, work-impacting error (Nagle et al., 2017).

Fresh

Freshness can degrade silently because a stale record may remain syntactically valid while becoming unfit for a time-sensitive use case. Measure freshness against the decision window and consequences that matter. Table 15.7 lists candidate metrics by data level.

Table 15.6 Metrics for Accuracy

Data Level	Metric
Raw data	Signal fidelity score (% of samples passing quality thresholds)
Structured data	Cross-system consistency rate (% of records with matching values across systems)
Structured data	Business rule violation rate (% of records failing defined domain constraints)
Context data	Semantic fidelity (human evaluation score of retrieved passages vs. source meaning)
Action data	Specification precision score (% of tool calls executing without parameter errors)

Table 15.7 Metrics for Freshness

Data Level	Metric
Raw data	Temporal alignment score (max time skew between correlated data streams)
Structured data	Service level agreement (SLA) compliance rate (% of pipelines delivering data within freshness SLA)
Structured data	Stale record rate (% of records older than their freshness threshold)
Context data	Knowledge base currency (age of newest indexed content vs. newest source content)
Action data	Specification currency (% of tool definitions validated against current API behavior)

Define the freshness objective each use case needs, such as maximum data age or delivery latency, and distinguish it from related availability, uptime, and throughput objectives. A weekly sales report may tolerate daily updates; a fraud decision may require much lower latency. The target must follow the decision window and risk.

Traceable

At the operating level, traceability connects evidence to governance decisions. Chapter 14 covers action-data systems, while Chapter 17 covers governance. For systems classified as high risk under the EU AI Act, Article 10 requires data governance and management practices covering data collection, origin, and relevant preparation operations, and Article 12 requires technical support for automatic event logging over the system's lifetime (European Union, 2024). These duties are scoped provisions, not a guarantee that any particular lineage implementation ensures compliance. Table 15.8 lists candidate traceability metrics.

Table 15.8 Metrics for Traceability

Data Level	Metric
Raw data	Provenance coverage (% of data assets with documented source/sensor/origin)
Structured data	Lineage coverage (% of production tables with end-to-end lineage)
Structured data	Audit trail completeness (% of transformations logged with timestamps and actors)
Context data	Groundability rate (% of evidence-eligible responses whose cited source resolves and supports the associated claim)
Action data	Audit logging coverage (% of agent actions with required, policy-approved event fields logged under defined access and retention controls)

Table 15.8 includes audit logging coverage for action data. Observability evidence may include freshness, volume, schema, distribution, lineage, provenance, and the ability to tie eligible outputs to supporting sources. Tools can supply part of that evidence, but metric definitions, ownership, and control decisions must remain tool-independent.

Leading vs. Lagging Indicators

Leading indicators may provide early warning; lagging indicators show observed outcomes. Use both. A leading signal can be noisy or unrelated to business harm, while a lagging measure can arrive too late for prevention. Tables 15.9 and 15.10 separate candidate signals and their limits.

The Population Stability Index (PSI) measures a shift between a baseline distribution and a comparison distribution; it is not a freshness metric by itself. Fiddler summarizes common rules of thumb as below 0.1 for similar distributions, 0.1 to 0.2 for moderate difference, and beyond 0.2 as grounds to develop a new model on a more recent sample (Shergadwala, 2022). Peer-reviewed work cautions against a universal cutoff. Tune bins and action thresholds to the use case, sample size, baseline, and observed performance (Haas and Sibbald, 2024).

When timely ground-truth labels are unavailable, teams may use input and prediction distribution shifts, confidence changes, and business KPI movements as proxy signals. Any of these may precede a measured accuracy change, but none proves that performance has degraded. Investigate and correlate proxies with later outcomes.

Table 15.9 Signals from Leading Indicators

Metric	What It Signals
Null rate trend (rising)	Rising missingness that may breach completeness thresholds
Schema change frequency (uncontrolled)	Higher risk of breaking downstream consumers
SLA compliance rate (declining)	Freshness risk before downstream use cases are affected
Feature distribution shift score (PSI rising)	Possible input-distribution change requiring investigation; performance impact is not implied

Table 15.10 Signals from Lagging Indicators

Metric	What It Signals
Model accuracy (F1, precision, recall)	Downstream confirmation of upstream problems
Error rate per million records	Defects after data entered systems
Percentage of records failing critical rules	Existing data vs. defined quality standards

Linking CRAFT to Business Outcomes

CRAFT metrics matter when they connect to decisions and outcomes that leaders can evaluate. Present the capability gap, affected use case, exposure, evidence quality, accountable owner, and requested decision. A technical score without that context is easy to misread.

External benchmarks can frame the issue, but they do not measure this organization's exposure. Use the CRAFT assessment to identify the data gaps that constrain a selected use case, then validate their operational and financial effects with local evidence.

Validity's 2024 survey found that 31% of more than 600 CRM administrators reported poor-quality data costing at least 20% of annual revenue (Validity, 2024). In a separate 2022 commissioned survey of more than 300 data professionals, Monte Carlo reported that respondents spent 40% of their time evaluating or checking data quality (Monte Carlo Data, 2022). HBR reports studies estimating that knowledge workers can spend up to 50% of their time finding data, correcting errors, and seeking confirmation (Redman, 2013). These are source-specific survey and estimate results, not universal constants.

For each CRAFT metric, define the downstream KPI or obligation it is intended to protect and test the relationship. Freshness controls may reduce the risk of decisions based on stale data. Completeness controls may reduce blind spots. Traceability can support audits and incident response, but it does not by itself ensure compliance or prevent fines.

Translate CRAFT results into the decision language leaders need. For example, "We reduced stale-data incidents by 60%, avoiding an estimated $2 million in rework" is an illustrative outcome statement, not a claim from this chapter. In practice, disclose the baseline, period, attribution method, uncertainty, and source behind any business-impact number.

Testing and Evaluation as a Permanent Capability

Metrics describe observed behavior. Tests provide evidence about behavior under defined conditions. Neither predicts every production outcome, so a mature CRAFT capability combines measurement, evaluation, monitoring, incident response, and learning.

Most organizations treat testing as a pre-launch activity. They run evaluations, check boxes, ship the model, and then move on. That's necessary but insufficient. Testing needs to be continuous, automated, and embedded in every stage of the AI lifecycle.

Beyond Metrics: Active Validation

Metrics passively observe. Tests actively probe. A freshness metric tells you your knowledge base was updated three days ago. A test tells you whether the AI produces correct answers about events from yesterday.

OpenAI's 2025 business primer describes evals as methods for measuring and improving whether an AI system meets expectations. It also notes that context-specific practices are still emerging and must be tailored to the workflow, business objective, and operating environment (OpenAI, 2025).

A minimum viable evaluation harness includes:

- A curated golden set sized to the use case, covering core scenarios, edge cases, and costly failure modes; early error analysis can begin with review of 50 to 100 representative outputs
- An automated eval pipeline that runs tests on every model or data change
- Regression detection to catch performance drops before deployment
- A human eval workflow to catch nuanced failures automated tests miss
- A metric dashboard that tracks results, scope, and changes over time

Consider a practical example. A B2C recommendation team adds a mandatory "Model Validation" step to CI/CD. It loads the new model and the current production model, runs both against 500 golden user scenarios, and compares precision@10, the share of the first ten recommendations that are relevant. The team might require the new model to improve that metric by at least 3% without exceeding 40 ms of latency. Those are example thresholds, not industry standards.

One critical limitation is that golden-set tests verify consistency, not correctness. If the reference dataset is flawed or outdated, the tests will keep passing while the system produces poor results. The golden set is the curated reference data. The golden-set test is the validation procedure that runs against it. Refresh both the data and the test criteria regularly, with human review.

The Testing Cycle

Testing runs continuously across four stages: before deployment (golden-set validation, sandbox testing, schema validation), during rollout (a team-selected canary share, such as 5% to 10% of traffic, with automatic rollback on preset thresholds), in production (continuous drift detection with ground truth where available and proxy metrics where it isn't), and after incidents (blameless post-mortems and expanded test coverage).

The 2026 Stanford AI Index reported 362 documented AI incidents in 2025, up from 233 in 2024, using data from the AI Incident Database (Stanford HAI, 2026). Incident counts depend on public reporting and may be revised. Periodically run incident drills: simulate a critical knowledge source becoming stale, an agent tool specification diverging from reality, or retrieval quality degrading. Test monitoring, alerting, and response before an actual incident forces improvisation.

Common CRAFT Patterns and Implications

After scoring dozens of data assets, patterns emerge. You start seeing the same failure modes across teams, tools, and use cases. Those patterns matter because they tell you what to fix first. The following sections present four common patterns and explain what each one means for action.

Pattern 1: Strong Retrievable, Weak Accurate

Your infrastructure may be modern and responsive while the data moving through it remains inconsistent. IBM describes data silos as isolated collections that inhibit sharing and can leave teams working with outdated, fragmented, or inconsistent data (IBM, 2025). Technical health does not establish semantic accuracy.

Imagine inaccurate ingestion corrupting the datasets used to train advertising models at a major technology company. The faulty data can flow through perfectly functional pipelines into predictive targeting and create significant financial loss. Technical health doesn't guarantee AI readiness.

Before adding another pipeline, inspect the quality and meaning of data already moving through existing ones. Put proportionate quality controls at critical ingestion and transformation points. Validate data before an error propagates into model inputs, reports, or automated decisions.

Pattern 2: Apparent Accuracy, Weak Completeness

Watson for Oncology illustrates why apparently complete evidence can still be unrepresentative. STAT reported that internal IBM presentations described training built from limited numbers of synthetic cases and the preferences of one or two Memorial Sloan Kettering physicians for each cancer type. Those presentations also documented unsafe and incorrect recommendations. Memorial Sloan Kettering said it believed the cited unsafe example arose in system testing rather than in the treatment of an actual patient, and defended synthetic cases as a way to better reflect current standards of care and a wider range of treatment options. The leadership lesson is to disclose the evidence base, test representativeness across intended settings, and require prospective validation before broad deployment (Ross and Swetlitz, 2018).

Assess representativeness. Who's missing from your data? What scenarios aren't captured? Then tackle gaps systematically: expand data sources, build data partnerships, or implement systematic collection programs.

Pattern 3: Strong Complete/Retrievable/Accurate, Weak Fresh

Data may be comprehensive, accessible, and accurate for one decision window yet become unfit as conditions change. The consequence depends on the use case. A stale reference document may reduce answer quality; stale safety or fraud data can create much greater exposure. Freshness is an operating control, not a one-time cleanup.

For example, a financial services firm might find that roughly one in five transaction timestamps carry time zone inconsistencies across systems. The timestamps may be accurate at the source but lose that consistency when data moves between systems. A fraud model can then misclassify transactions near midnight because it can't sequence events correctly.

Build refresh pipelines. Raw data freshness requires new feeds or higher-frequency collection. Structured data freshness needs automated sync processes. Context data freshness demands re-indexing and re-embedding schedules. Don't just build the mechanism. Monitor it.

Pattern 4: Weak Traceable Across Levels

Traceability is often funded later than visible delivery features because its value appears during audit, investigation, change, or failure. Treat it as an architectural control whose required depth follows consequence and regulatory exposure.

The Equifax credit-score error of 2022 shows why rapid detection and traceable investigation matter after a data error occurs. The New York Attorney General reported that a coding error caused inaccurate data to be sent to lenders during a three-week period and that more than 77,000 New Yorkers had scores that were wrongly declined (New York Attorney General, 2025). The source confirms the coding error and impact; it does not identify missing lineage as the cause.

Traceability is architectural. Start with the highest-risk AI use cases, the ones where wrong decisions have legal, financial, or safety consequences. Build provenance tracking for raw data. Invest in documentation for structured data. Focus on groundability, the ability to connect context-based outputs back to reliable source material, for context data. Build safety, observability, and recoverability for action data.

Strong traceability can shorten investigation, support audit evidence, and make remediation more targeted. It does not guarantee accuracy, compliance, or stakeholder trust. Measure those outcomes separately.

From Assessment to Action

An assessment creates value only when it changes a decision, control, or investment. Convert each material gap into an owned action with evidence, priority, target condition, and review date.

Identify bounded improvements where the gap is small and the business impact is high. Examples may include deduplication, time zone normalization, and format standardization. Treat null-value imputation as a modeling decision that requires domain validation and downstream-risk review, not as a generic cleanup. Depending on scope, one to three months may be a reasonable starting range for a bounded improvement.

Sequence work by critical dependency, consequence, and learning value. Lower data levels often constrain higher ones, but teams can remediate independent controls in parallel. Use an impact-effort view only after risk, ownership, and prerequisite decisions are explicit.

Assign a named accountable owner and the resources needed to close each gap. A committee may advise or govern, but accountability for the decision, evidence, and follow-through must be clear.

Set review cycles that fit how quickly your data changes. For many teams, a 90-day cycle is a useful starting point, not a universal rule. The assessment isn't a one-time exercise. Reassess CRAFT scores before readiness gaps become production failures. Teams that keep measuring can catch drift while they still have time to respond.

Connect assessment to economics without turning outside estimates into local facts. In their study, Nagle, Redman, and Sammon found that, on average, 47% of newly created records had at least one critical, work-impacting error (Nagle et al., 2017). Translate each CRAFT gap into an organization-specific cost or risk hypothesis, then validate it with local evidence before building a business case.

The leadership value of CRAFT is disciplined visibility. A repeated, evidence-based assessment shows where readiness is improving, where exposure remains, and which investment or deployment decision should change. It does not guarantee growth or profitability, but it gives leaders a clearer basis for allocating resources and governing risk.

Continuous Measurement, Not One-time Snapshots

Scoring your data readiness once gives you a snapshot. Data is dynamic. New sources are integrated. Pipelines change. Models drift. What scored a 4 six months ago might be a 3 today. If your measurement is a once-a-year exercise, you're flying blind between assessments, discovering problems only when models fail in production.

Looking Ahead

This chapter gave you the assessment toolkit and the metrics to track continuously. The next chapter moves from measurement to organizational action. You will learn how to structure your teams, define roles, and build the governance that turns CRAFT assessment into operational discipline.

References

European Union. "Regulation (EU) 2024/1689, Articles 10 and 12." Official Journal of the European Union, 12 July 2024, https://eur-lex.europa.eu/eli/reg/2024/1689/oj/eng.

Haas, Marcel R., and Lisette Sibbald. "Measuring Data Drift with the Unstable Population Indicator." Data Science, vol. 7, no. 1, 2024, pp. 1–12, https://doi.org/10.3233/DS-240059.

IBM. "What Are Data Silos?" IBM Think, 12 Feb. 2025, https://www.ibm.com/think/topics/data-silos.

McKinsey & Company. "The State of AI in 2025: Agents, Innovation, and Transformation." McKinsey & Company, 5 Nov. 2025, https://www.mckinsey.com/capabilities/quantumblack/our-insights/the-state-of-ai. Accessed 27 July 2026.

Monte Carlo Data. "Data Engineers Spend Two Days Per Week Firefighting Bad Data." Monte Carlo Data, 9 Aug. 2022, https://www.montecarlodata.com/blog-2022-data-quality-survey.

Nagle, Tadhg, Thomas C. Redman, and David Sammon. "Only 3% of Companies' Data Meets Basic Quality Standards." Harvard Business Review, 11 Sept. 2017, https://hbr.org/2017/09/only-3-of-companies-data-meets-basic-quality-standards.

New York Attorney General. "Attorney General James Secures $725,000 from Equifax for Harming Consumers Through Inaccurate Credit Scores." 14 Jan. 2025, https://ag.ny.gov/press-release/2025/attorney-general-james-secures-725000-equifax-harming-consumers-through.

OpenAI. "How Evals Drive the Next Chapter in AI for Businesses." OpenAI, 19 Nov. 2025, https://openai.com/index/evals-drive-next-chapter-of-ai/.

Portes, Jacob, et al. "Improving Retrieval and RAG with Embedding Model Finetuning." Databricks Blog, 20 Feb. 2025, https://www.databricks.com/blog/improving-retrieval-and-rag-embedding-model-finetuning.

Redman, Thomas C. "Getting in Front of Data Quality." Harvard Business Review, 3 Dec. 2013, https://hbr.org/webinar/2014/01/getting-in-front-of-data-quality.

Ross, Casey, and Ike Swetlitz. "IBM's Watson Supercomputer Recommended 'Unsafe and Incorrect' Cancer Treatments, Internal Documents Show." STAT, 25 July 2018, https://www.statnews.com/wp-content/uploads/2018/09/IBMs-Watson-recommended-unsafe-and-incorrect-cancer-treatments-STAT.pdf.

Ryseff, James, et al. "The Root Causes of Failure for Artificial Intelligence Projects and How They Can Succeed." RAND Corporation, Aug. 2024, https://www.rand.org/pubs/research_reports/RRA2680-1.html.

Shergadwala, Murtuza. "Measuring Data Drift with the Population Stability Index (PSI)." Fiddler AI, 16 May 2022, 1 July 2026, https://www.fiddler.ai/blog/measuring-data-drift-population-stability-index.

Splunk. "The State of Dark Data." Splunk, 2019, https://www.splunk.com/en_us/form/the-state-of-dark-data.html.

Stanford HAI. "Responsible AI." The 2026 AI Index Report, Stanford Institute for Human-Centered Artificial Intelligence, 2026, https://hai.stanford.edu/ai-index/2026-ai-index-report/responsible-ai.

Validity. "The State of CRM Data Management in 2024." Validity, 2024, https://www.validity.com/resource-center/the-state-of-crm-data-management-in-2024/.

Chapter 16
Organizing for CRAFT

Organizational design is a major determinant of whether CRAFT conformance becomes operational or remains aspirational. Many AI initiatives struggle not only because of technology or model limitations, but also because responsibilities are misaligned, handoffs lack ownership, and AI data quality falls between teams.

Why Existing Structures Fail

Organizations continue to struggle to move AI initiatives into production. In McKinsey's 2025 survey, nearly two-thirds of respondents said their organizations had not yet begun scaling AI across the enterprise (McKinsey & Company, 2025). In the S&P survey introduced in Chapter 2, 42% of eligible respondents said their organizations abandoned most AI initiatives before production. The result applies to a routed respondent base, not the full 1,006-person sample or all AI projects (Johnston, 2025).

Existing structures can make scaling harder: BI teams optimized for reporting, governance boards built around infrequent review cycles, data stores designed for historical analysis, and ownership models that split AI strategy from AI data quality. These factors can stall AI initiatives even when the underlying models are technically capable.

The Traditional Data Team Problem

Many organizations built their data teams primarily for business intelligence, data mining, data stores, and data warehouses. Traditional BI and data-engineering functions often emphasize deterministic, batch-oriented reporting with comparatively long review and refresh cycles. Some AI applications require a wider range of data types and much shorter quality-feedback cycles.

Traditional BI often works with structured, historical data in relational databases. AI applications may also require text, images, audio, video, and real-time signals. Many organizations have governed unstructured data less consistently, which creates data-quality challenges when they deploy generative AI.

Data preparation and cleaning can consume substantial data-science capacity. That burden is not only a tooling problem; it is also an organizational-design problem when ownership, standards, and escalation paths are unclear.

The Governance Gap

Traditional data governance often emphasizes structured records, access controls, and relatively stable definitions. AI systems add probabilistic behavior and, in some deployments, frequent model or knowledge-base updates. Controls therefore need to address model drift, bias, explainability, and data lineage alongside conventional access and quality controls.

Siloed operating models can complicate data governance. In some organizations, a Chief Data and Analytics Officer owns the data foundation while a Chief AI Officer owns AI strategy. Without explicit decision rights and coordination, responsibility for AI data quality can fall between them.

The Ownership Vacuum

One damaging structural pattern is an ownership vacuum around AI data quality. When responsibility is broadly shared but decision rights are not explicit, gaps persist. Competing ownership can be equally harmful: two groups build overlapping platforms while the shared data foundation still lacks one accountable owner.

When ownership and validation are split, an organization can scale an AI program faster than the evidence and controls supporting it. The resulting failure is organizational as well as technical: growth outpaces validation, and no single leader owns the gap.

Formal data-quality procedures can strengthen an organization's ability to realize value from AI, but they do not fix split ownership by themselves. The structure and decision rights matter.

Three Organizational Models

There is no single right answer for how to organize around AI data quality. The choice depends on industry, regulatory exposure, AI maturity, and the number of business units that need AI capabilities. This chapter uses three common archetypes. Each has strengths, risks, and conditions under which it is more or less useful.

Model 1: Centralized AI Data Team

In the centralized archetype, a single team, often under a Chief Data Officer or within IT, owns AI data-quality standards, governance enforcement, and shared data-engineering resources. AI initiatives pass through this team. The model often suits highly regulated environments or organizations early in their AI journey, where consistency may matter more than local speed. Table 16.1 summarizes the archetype.

Table 16.1 The Centralized AI Data Model

Dimension	Details
Best for	Regulated industries, early AI maturity, need for consistency
CRAFT strengths	Accuracy and traceability (uniform standards, centralized audit)
CRAFT risks	Freshness (slow response to drift) and retrievability (teams can't access without a queue)
Key risks	Bottlenecks, disconnection from domain needs
Illustrative examples; scope varies	Microsoft IDEAS data platform; JPMorgan Chase MLCOE

JPMorgan Chase built an enterprise-wide data platform to support its domain data teams (Jain et al., 2021). Microsoft reports that its IDEAS engineering organization operates a platform spanning 27,000 data sources and projects a 50% efficiency improvement from consolidating assets in OneLake (Microsoft, 2024). These examples illustrate centralized capabilities, not the full operating model of either company.

The downsides are real. Centralized approval processes create bottlenecks. The central team can become disconnected from specific business unit needs. If every AI team has to wait in a centralized queue for data access, your development velocity drops to the speed of your slowest approval process.

Model 2: Federated with Central Standards

The federated model combines a central governing body that sets enterprise-wide policies with domain teams that own their data and treat it as a product. Business units own their data and are responsible for quality, but they must conform to centrally defined standards for interoperability, security, and AI readiness.

Zhamak Dehghani, who coined the term data mesh, defines four principles (Dehghani, 2020):

- Domain ownership and architecture
- Data as a product
- Self-serve data platform (self-serve data infrastructure as a platform)
- Federated computational governance

Domain teams closest to the data understand its context best. They know which edge cases matter and where the data's quirks hide.

JPMorgan Chase built a data mesh in which domain teams manage their own data-product lakes (Jain et al., 2021). An Atlan customer case study reports that Autodesk gives 60 domain teams visibility into the consumption of their data products (Atlan, 2023).

The federated model, summarized in Table 16.2, is not simple to operate. Without consistent standards enforcement, domains may define quality differently. Shared standards and enforceable interfaces make federation more workable. Open APIs and open data formats can reduce interoperability friction, and ODI can serve as one technical enabler. A frequent failure mode is to rebadge existing IT teams as "data domains" without giving them genuine domain ownership.

Table 16.2 The Federated AI Model

Dimension	Details
Best for	Large enterprises with multiple business units, higher data maturity
CRAFT strengths	Completeness and freshness (domain experts ensure coverage and currency)
CRAFT risks	Accuracy (inconsistent standards across domains) and traceability (fragmented lineage)
Key risks	Coordination complexity, requires high data maturity, cultural change is hard
Illustrative examples; scope varies	JPMorgan Chase data mesh, Autodesk (60 domain teams)

One practical operating-model heuristic is to begin with more centralization at low maturity and shift toward federation as capabilities and accountability improve. It is a design heuristic, not a maturity law.

Model 3: Embedded in AI Product Teams

In the embedded archetype, AI data specialists, such as data scientists, ML engineers, AI data engineers, and data-quality analysts, work directly in product teams rather than in one central group. A product team may include its own data specialists alongside engineers and product managers.

The embedded model, which is summarized in Table 16.3, maximizes speed and domain understanding. There's no bottleneck dependency on centralized teams. The data professional who prepares training data sits next to the ML engineer who trains the model.

Netflix formalized Media Data Engineering in 2025, a cross-functional specialization at the intersection of data engineering, ML infrastructure, and media production (Mi et al., 2025). This example illustrates close collaboration across functions; it does not establish a universal reporting model.

The risks are predictable. In practitioner commentary, Filippova (2022) describes a recurring tension: centralized teams can become disconnected from business priorities, while embedded teams can fragment knowledge that must be rebuilt when someone leaves. Without shared oversight, teams may define data quality, labeling standards, and feature-engineering conventions differently.

Table 16.3 The Embedded AI Data Model

Dimension	Details
Best for	Startups, teams needing maximum agility, domain-specific AI applications
CRAFT strengths	Completeness and accuracy (deep domain understanding, tight feedback loops)
CRAFT risks	Traceability (no enterprise-wide audit trail) and retrievability (silos prevent cross-team data sharing)
Key risks	Knowledge fragmentation, inconsistent standards, duplication of effort
Illustrative examples; scope varies	Netflix Media Data Engineering (cross-functional specialization)

Choosing Your Model

Mature organizations often combine elements of these models. A January 2026 Integrate.io survey distributed through the company's newsletter and social channels received responses from 104 data professionals. Forty-two percent reported a hybrid structure and 37% a centralized model; more than half reported major restructuring or the addition of new roles in the prior year (Tobin, 2026). Table 16.4 compares the three archetypes.

AWS Enterprise Strategy recommends centralizing the foundation for security, scalability, and compliance while decentralizing domain execution to support innovation (Patzak & Godden, 2024).

Effective organizations combine centralized governance and training with distributed enablement through embedded AI champions.

A practical staged path is to begin with more centralization to establish standards and foundational capabilities, then federate execution while keeping shared controls explicit. Organizations with mature shared platforms may embed specialists in product teams and connect them through a community of practice. The sequence depends on regulation, scale, skills, and existing accountability. The operating model may evolve; CRAFT standards remain shared.

Table 16.4 Factors Across All Three Models

Factor	Centralized	Federated	Embedded
Data ownership	Central team	Domain teams	Product/AI teams
Standards	Central team sets and enforces	Central CoE defines, domain teams execute	Little to no central standard
Speed	Slower (queue-based)	Moderate (domain autonomy with coordination)	Fastest (no dependencies)
CRAFT consistency	High	Medium (depends on enforcement)	Low
Best for	Regulated industries, early maturity	Large enterprises, higher maturity	Startups, specialized AI products
Key risk	Bottlenecks	Coordination complexity	Knowledge fragmentation

Two Critical Roles: Architect and Champion

Organizational models define the structure. Roles define who does the work. This chapter emphasizes two roles that can make CRAFT accountability explicit: the AI Data Architect and the CRAFT Champion.

The AI Data Architect

The traditional data architect designs enterprise data strategy, data warehouses, and relational databases. They're essential. They're not enough for AI.

In this book, the AI Data Architect is a senior role responsible for designing data infrastructure for AI and ML systems. The mandate may include vector and graph retrieval, RAG pipelines, feature stores, data versioning, and unstructured-data integration. It bridges enterprise data architecture with AI consumption needs. It also requires an understanding of shared standards, open table formats, and the tradeoffs between proprietary and portable infrastructure. Architecture choices determine how easily data investments can move as AI systems evolve.

The title may vary by organization, but the mandate combines AI/ML data pipelines, retrieval architecture, versioned training and context data, unstructured-data integration, and enterprise interoperability. The important design choice is to assign that mandate explicitly rather than assume it is covered by a traditional title.

These capabilities may appear in traditional data-architect roles, but AI-focused mandates bring them together and make them explicit. Table 16.5 compares the typical emphasis of the two role definitions.

CRAFT conformance depends on accountable coverage across both traditional and AI-specific architecture. Someone must ensure that data models support AI retrievability, that freshness cadence matches the use case, and that traceability extends from source data through embeddings or other derived representations to outputs. Responsibility may sit with one architect or be shared, but it must be explicit.

A Snowflake-sponsored 2025 survey conducted by MIT Technology Review Insights gathered responses from 400 senior data and technology executives. Seventy-two percent said data engineers are integral to the business (MIT Technology Review Insights and Snowflake, 2025). The result reflects respondents' views; it does not prove that one organizational design causes better outcomes.

Lightcast reported that salaries in job postings mentioning AI skills were 28% higher than salaries in postings that did not mention them (Lightcast, 2025). Robert Half's 2026 national starting-salary range for AI Architects is $142,750–$196,750 (Robert Half, 2026). These benchmarks indicate market demand, but they vary by role definition, geography, experience, and employer.

Table 16.5 Typical Emphasis: Traditional and AI Data Architecture

Comparison Area	Traditional Data Architect	AI Data Architect
Primary focus	Enterprise data strategy, integration, warehouses, and databases	Adds AI/ML consumption patterns, retrieval, and training-data systems
Database expertise	Relational and enterprise data stores; scope varies	Adds vector, graph, and feature-store patterns as needed
Data types	Often structured and tabular, plus other enterprise data as required	Structured and unstructured data, embeddings, and multimodal assets as required
Key deliverables	Data models, integration patterns, and governance frameworks	Retrieval architectures, versioning patterns, and feature pipelines
Quality focus	Completeness, consistency, accuracy, security, and operability	CRAFT dimensions across AI consumption patterns
CRAFT accountability	Usually shared across architecture and governance roles	Explicit cross-mode accountability in this chapter's role definition

CRAFT Champions

The AI Data Architect designs the infrastructure. CRAFT Champions make sure it gets used.

A CRAFT Champion is an embedded advocate within a business unit or product team who helps keep CRAFT assessment part of daily work, not an afterthought. They're the people who translate the framework from policy documents into operational reality. They sit inside teams doing the work, know where data quality problems are buried, and have enough technical fluency to catch problems before they reach production.

Data-governance practitioner Robert Seiner argues that data stewards hold context about enterprise-data quirks and limitations that AI teams may overlook. He recommends embedding governance checkpoints before data is sourced, before models are trained, and before AI-driven insights are used in business decisions (Seiner, 2025).

CRAFT Champions operationalize this idea. They're not a separate governance team reviewing work after the fact. They're part of the team doing the work, applying CRAFT at three critical checkpoints:

- **Before data is sourced:** The CRAFT Champion reviews data acquisition plans against all five dimensions. Is the proposed data source complete enough? Can AI systems actually retrieve it in the needed format? Is its accuracy documented? How fresh is it? Can we trace its provenance?
- **Before models are trained or knowledge bases are built:** The CRAFT Champion validates that training data and context data meet dimension-specific thresholds. A 2/5 on freshness isn't a number on a report anymore. It's a flag that stops a training run until the gap is addressed.
- **Before AI outputs reach users:** The CRAFT Champion ensures that output traceability exists and that the system can cite sources, log decisions, and support audit requirements.

The role works best when CRAFT Champions have enough technical fluency to understand data pipelines and embedding models. They need deep domain knowledge, understanding what "accurate" and "complete" mean for their specific business context. And they need organizational credibility so that when they raise a CRAFT concern, people listen.

Anomalo's data-governance best-practice guidance emphasizes setting a data strategy with clear policies, embedding data-quality checks into workflows, and defining data ownership across business and technical teams (Anomalo, 2024). CRAFT Champions are the people who do the second and third parts at the team level.

Gartner has identified nascent roles that data and analytics teams increasingly need to consider, including Knowledge Engineers, Model Managers, AI Ethicists, and Heads of AI (Gartner, 2024). CRAFT Champions fit this pattern. They're a new kind of embedded data quality advocate, tuned specifically for AI consumption patterns. Table 16.6 maps those checkpoints to the five CRAFT dimensions.

The CRAFT Champion doesn't replace the AI Data Architect, the data engineer, or the governance team. They're the connective tissue between those functions and the AI product teams. Without them, CRAFT conformance can become something that looks good in planning documents but breaks down in execution.

The World Economic Forum's Future of Jobs Report 2025 found that 63% of surveyed employers identified skills gaps as the primary barrier to business transformation. In response to expected AI disruption, 77% planned to reskill or upskill their existing workforce to work more effectively alongside AI (World Economic Forum, 2025). CRAFT Champions represent this kind of capability development: equipping people who know the business domain with AI data-quality fluency.

You don't necessarily need to hire externally. In many organizations, the best CRAFT Champions are already there: the senior data stewards, the experienced data analysts, or the quality-obsessed domain experts who've been saying "our data isn't ready" for years. What they've been missing is a structured framework to channel that instinct into something actionable. CRAFT gives them the framework. The Champion role gives them the mandate.

Table 16.6 CRAFT Champion Checkpoints by Dimension

CRAFT Dimension	Champion's Checkpoint Question	What They Actually Do
Complete	Does this data cover what the AI will encounter?	Review training data for representation gaps, flag missing edge cases
Retrievable	Can the AI system find and use this data?	Test retrieval pipelines, validate chunking strategies
Accurate	Does this data mean what we think it means?	Verify business definitions, check label quality
Fresh	Is this data current enough for this use case?	Monitor refresh cadences, flag stale sources
Traceable	Can we prove where this data came from and audit how it's used?	Verify lineage documentation, test audit trails

The organizational model should reflect AI capability priorities. If the primary outcome depends on generative AI, CRAFT Champion and knowledge-engineering capabilities may become high priorities. If the organization is pursuing agentic AI, action-data governance and safety expertise may move higher. The capability-to-level map from Chapter 3 is therefore both a technical framework and an organizational-design guide.

Looking Ahead

This chapter defined who does the work. You have three organizational models, each with clear tradeoffs against CRAFT dimensions. You have two critical roles: the AI Data Architect and the CRAFT Champion. These fill gaps traditional data organizations leave open.

Structure and roles are necessary. But they're not sufficient without governance that defines the policies, processes, and decision frameworks that codify how CRAFT conformance actually gets assessed and monitored day to day. Chapter 17 tackles governance, including how to build the decision rights, escalation paths, and policy frameworks that turn organizational structure into operational discipline.

References

Anomalo. "5 Data Governance Best Practices." Anomalo Blog, 30 Apr. 2024, https://www.anomalo.com/blog/5-data-governance-best-practices/.

Atlan. "How Autodesk Activates Their Data Mesh with Snowflake and Atlan." By Mark Manning, Humans of Data, 14 Aug. 2023, https://humansofdata.atlan.com/2023/08/autodesk-data-mesh-snowflake-atlan/.

Dehghani, Zhamak. "How to Move Beyond a Monolithic Data Lake to a Distributed Data Mesh." Martin Fowler, Thoughtworks, 20 May 2019, https://martinfowler.com/articles/data-monolith-to-mesh.html.

Dehghani, Zhamak. "Data Mesh Principles and Logical Architecture." Martin Fowler, 3 Dec. 2020, https://martinfowler.com/articles/data-mesh-principles.html.

Filippova, Anna. "Data Teams: Embedded or Centralized? Reactive or Self-Directed?" The Analytics Engineering Roundup, 17 Apr. 2022, https://roundup.getdbt.com/p/data-teams-embedded-or-centralized.

Gartner. "AI Is Creating New Roles and Skills in Data & Analytics." Gartner, 14 May 2024, https://www.gartner.com/en/newsroom/press-releases/2024-05-14-artificial-intelligence-is-creating-new-roles-and-skills-in-data-and-analytics.

Jain, Anu, Graham Person, Paul Conroy, and Nivas Shankar. "How JPMorgan Chase Built a Data Mesh Architecture to Drive Significant Value to Enhance Their Enterprise Data Platform." AWS Big Data Blog, 5 May 2021, https://aws.amazon.com/blogs/big-data/how-jpmorgan-chase-built-a-data-mesh-architecture-to-drive-significant-value-to-enhance-their-enterprise-data-platform/.

Johnston, Alex. "Generative AI Shows Rapid Growth but Yields Mixed Results." S&P Global Market Intelligence, 27 Oct. 2025, https://www.spglobal.com/market-intelligence/en/news-insights/research/2025/10/generative-ai-shows-rapid-growth-but-yields-mixed-results. The figures cited in the text are from this 2025 edition; its body text requires S&P Global Market Intelligence registration. Accessed 27 July 2026.

JPMorgan Chase. "Machine Learning Center of Excellence." JPMorganChase, n.d., https://www.jpmorganchase.com/about/technology/research/machine-learning.

Lightcast. "Beyond the Buzz: Developing the AI Skills Employers Actually Need." Lightcast, July 2025, https://lightcast.io/resources/research/beyond-the-buzz-developing-the-ai-skills-employers-actually-need.

McKinsey & Company. "The State of AI in 2025: Agents, Innovation, and Transformation." By Alex Singla, Alexander Sukharevsky, Bryce Hall, Lareina Yee, and Michael Chui, 5 Nov. 2025, https://www.mckinsey.com/capabilities/quantumblack/our-insights/the-state-of-ai. Accessed 27 July 2026.

Mi, Dao, Pablo Delgado, Ryan Berti, Amanuel Kahsay, Obi-Ike Nwoke, Christopher Thrailkill, and Patricio Garza. "From Facts & Metrics to Media Machine Learning: Evolving the Data Engineering Function at Netflix." Netflix Technology Blog, 21 Aug. 2025, updated 25 Aug. 2025, https://netflixtechblog.com/from-facts-metrics-to-media-machine-learning-evolving-the-data-engineering-function-at-netflix-6dcc91058d8d.

Microsoft. "One of the World's Largest Data Teams, Microsoft IDEAS Uses Fabric to Usher in New Era of AI." Microsoft Customer Stories, 14 Nov. 2024, https://www.microsoft.com/en/customers/story/19755-microsoft-microsoft-copilot.

MIT Technology Review Insights and Snowflake. "Redefining Data Engineering in the Age of AI." 2025, https://www.snowflake.com/en/redefining-data-engineering-in-the-age-of-ai/.

Patzak, Matthias, and Tom Godden. "Centralizing or Decentralizing Generative AI? The Answer: Both." AWS Enterprise Strategy Blog, 4 Sept. 2024, https://aws.amazon.com/blogs/enterprise-strategy/centralizing-or-decentralizing-generative-ai-the-answer-both/.

Robert Half. "AI Architect Salary." 2026 Salary Guide, 2026, https://www.roberthalf.com/us/en/job-details/ai-architect. The 2026 Salary Guide is the edition cited. Unversioned rolling page. Accessed 27 July 2026.

Seiner, Robert S. "The Data Steward's Role in AI." LinkedIn, 5 Mar. 2025, https://www.linkedin.com/pulse/data-stewards-role-ai-robert-s-seiner-cgdhe.

Tobin, Donal. "July 2026 Trends Report: How Data Teams Are Structured and Staffed." Integrate.io, 9 Jan. 2026, https://www.integrate.io/blog/july-2025-trends-report-how-data-teams-are-structured/. The July 2026 edition is the one cited; the URL slug retains the earlier july-2025 path. Accessed 27 July 2026.

World Economic Forum. "The Future of Jobs Report 2025." World Economic Forum, 2025, https://www.weforum.org/publications/the-future-of-jobs-report-2025/.

Chapter 17
Governance for AI-ready Data

Org charts do not prevent AI failures. Governance can reduce them.

Among 600 enterprise data leaders surveyed across the United States, Europe, and Asia-Pacific, 42% identified data quality as the main obstacle to generative AI adoption, while 40% cited data privacy and governance (Informatica, 2024). Many governance programs were designed for human-paced reporting and periodic review. AI systems can propagate data defects rapidly and repeatedly, so an issue a human analyst might catch in one report can affect many automated outputs before detection.

This chapter is about extending your governance practice to cover the five CRAFT dimensions specifically, then tackling the cross-cutting concerns that make AI governance genuinely different from anything that came before: privacy, security, and the entirely new challenge of governing AI systems that take autonomous actions in the real world.

Governance requirements differ by data level. Raw data governance focuses on capture integrity and provenance. Structured data governance focuses on semantic consistency and entity resolution. Context data governance focuses on coverage, freshness, and grounding. Action data governance requires safety constraints on autonomous execution. Your governance framework should prioritize the data levels that correspond to your highest-value AI capabilities.

Extending Traditional Governance

Traditional data governance provides a useful foundation. Established programs commonly address data quality, metadata, stewardship, access, retention, lineage, and accountability across the enterprise.

Those capabilities remain necessary, but they are not sufficient for every AI use case. AI governance builds on them by adding controls for model and data drift, bias and fairness, adversarial testing, probabilistic outputs, and human oversight where the risk warrants it.

The additional control layer should be matched to the system's intended purpose, autonomy, data sensitivity, and decision impact. A low-risk internal assistant and a system that makes or executes consequential decisions should not receive identical controls.

Two widely used reference points are the NIST AI Risk Management Framework 1.0 and ISO/IEC 42001. NIST's voluntary framework organizes AI risk management around Govern, Map, Measure, and Manage, with governance as a cross-cutting function (NIST, 2023). ISO describes ISO/IEC 42001 as the world's first AI management-system standard and as a framework for establishing, implementing, maintaining, and continually improving an AI management system (ISO, 2023).

Together, these frameworks help leaders connect existing data governance with AI-specific risk management, accountability, and continuous improvement. They are reference points, not substitutes for controls tailored to the use case and applicable law (NIST, 2023; ISO, 2023).

For providers of covered high-risk AI systems, the EU AI Act makes several data and governance duties concrete. Article 10 addresses training, validation, and testing data and related data governance; Article 12 requires the systems to permit automatic event logging over their lifetime; and Article 17 requires providers to maintain a documented quality-management system. Regulation (EU) 2026/1744 was published on July 24, 2026, and Article 4 provides for entry into force on July 27, 2026. The amended Article 113 schedule applies these Chapter III requirements from December 2, 2027 to systems classified as high-risk under Article 6(2) and Annex III, and from August 2, 2028 to systems classified as high-risk under Article 6(1) and Annex I. Classification, exceptions, roles, and transitional provisions can affect applicability; this summary is not legal advice (European Parliament and Council of the European Union, 2024; 2026).

The implementation gap is visible in survey evidence. Trustmarque reported that 93% of 507 senior UK IT decision-makers said their organizations used AI in some form, while 7% said governance was fully embedded (Trustmarque, 2025). In McKinsey's spring 2024 survey of 180 European organizations, only one in four respondents said they had implemented strategies for regulatory compliance or AI risk management (McKinsey & Company, 2024). These are survey findings, not universal prevalence rates.

CRAFT Governance by Dimension

This section defines what those responsible people actually need to govern, dimension by dimension. As seen in Table 17.1, traditional governance and AI governance differ across the CRAFT framework.

Governing Completeness

Completeness governance for AI goes beyond checking for null fields. Incomplete data can also mean missing representation. A dataset can be accurate on recorded fields while remaining materially unrepresentative for its intended use.

Table 17.1 Governance by CRAFT Dimension

CRAFT Dimension	Traditional Governance Focus	AI Governance Extensions
Complete	Row counts, null rates, entity uniqueness	Coverage and representation checks appropriate to the intended purpose, edge-case review, and documented approval for data scope
Retrievable	Access control (who can see what)	Identity- and attribute-aware retrieval controls, retrieval-quality tests, and indexing and cataloging standards
Accurate	Cross-system consistency, validation rules	Schema and validation controls, annotation-quality criteria, use-case-specific accuracy thresholds, and human escalation
Fresh	Batch refresh schedules, SLA monitoring	Risk-based monitoring, temporal-consistency checks, staleness thresholds, drift triggers, and refresh cadences tied to the use case
Traceable	Lineage tracking, audit trails, retention	End-to-end AI lineage, material-event logging, model and dataset documentation, and versioned change control

For providers of covered high-risk AI systems, and on the application schedule described earlier in this chapter, Article 10 requires training, validation, and testing datasets to have appropriate statistical properties, including, where applicable, properties concerning the people or groups for whom the system is intended to be used (European Parliament and Council of the European Union, 2024; 2026).

Completeness governance policies should include:

- **Coverage audit requirements:** Where lawful, relevant to the intended use, and supported by appropriate safeguards, evaluate representation across important groups and operating conditions. Identify segments that are underrepresented or absent.
- **Representativeness standards:** Define the geographical, contextual, behavioral, and functional settings that matter for the intended use, then test whether the data reflects them adequately.
- **Deduplication standards:** Use exact, probabilistic, or semantic matching as appropriate. Document the rules, thresholds, review process, and material actions needed for traceability.
- **Approval gates for data scope:** Before training, document the use case, intended purpose, risk level, and owners. Create datasheets for each training, validation, and test dataset.

Governing Retrievability

In many RAG architectures, access control should be enforced before or during retrieval, not left solely to post-generation filtering. A common design error is to treat relevance as permission.

Retrievability governance policies should include:

- **Access control enforcement in AI pipelines:** Every query must carry user identity and role context. Retrieval must filter based on permissions, not relevance alone.
- **Attribute-based access control:** Access shouldn't depend solely on job title, but on dynamic attributes: current project, location, query sensitivity.
- **Semantic search quality standards:** Standardize embedding generation techniques and validate embeddings against real-world use cases.
- **Indexing and cataloging requirements:** Maintain comprehensive metadata and implement a data catalog for efficient tagging, classification, and retrieval.

Governing Accuracy

For AI, accuracy governance isn't just about wrong numbers. It's about semantic ambiguity, annotation quality, and structural coherence.

Accuracy governance policies should include:

- **Validation pipeline requirements:** Enforce structure from the outset using schemas for naming conventions, typing, and required fields.
- **Annotation quality requirements:** For providers of covered high-risk AI systems, and on the application schedule described earlier in this chapter, Article 10 includes annotation, labeling, cleaning, updating, enrichment, and aggregation among the data-preparation operations to be addressed by data governance (European Parliament and Council of the European Union, 2024; 2026).
- **Accuracy thresholds that are AI-appropriate:** Set targets and measure them: error rate, duplication rate, reconciliation defects.
- **Human-in-the-loop escalation:** Route flagged anomalies to human reviewers. Design escalation paths for issues requiring legal, compliance, or ethics input.

Governing Freshness

A monthly checklist may be too slow for a system that changes or acts in seconds, but continuous monitoring is not necessary for every AI use case. Set review and monitoring cadence according to system risk, update frequency, and decision impact.

Freshness governance policies should include:

- **SLA-based refresh monitoring:** Define freshness targets for critical data assets and automate alerts where the risk and operating model justify it.
- **Temporal consistency enforcement:** When data sources have different update cadences, temporal joins can create semantic inconsistency. Implement checks at pipeline ingestion points to flag temporal anomalies.
- **Degradation triggers:** Detect when data freshness starts degrading before it reaches crisis. Set leading indicator thresholds.
- **Refresh cadence standards:** Align freshness targets with the intended use and model or knowledgebase update cycle. Where real-time integration is justified, it can reduce latency, but validation and exception handling remain necessary.

- **Staleness detection and drift monitoring:** Implement automated staleness detectors. Track feature store staleness as a key governance KPI.

Governing Traceability

Traceability covers lineage, provenance, governance controls, and compliance evidence. If an organization cannot reconstruct a material decision or action, it cannot investigate or govern it effectively. Open formats and standard policy interfaces can reduce migration and evidence-reconstruction friction, but they do not make governance portable without integration, testing, and change management.

Article 99 of the EU AI Act sets different penalty ceilings for different infringements. Prohibited practices have the highest listed ceiling, while specified operator obligations have a lower tier. Actual exposure depends on the covered actor, infringement, enterprise size, procedural posture, and other facts; leaders should not convert the percentages into an assumed fine without legal analysis (European Parliament and Council of the European Union, 2024, art. 99).

Traceability governance should require:

- **End-to-end data lineage:** Track data from source through every modification and transformation to final destination, including feature engineering steps, model training data versions, and inference pipeline transformations.
- **Audit trail completeness:** Log material queries, retrievals, decisions, and actions at a level proportionate to risk. Protect audit records against unauthorized alteration and apply access, minimization, and retention rules.
- **Model cards and datasheets:** Assign named owners for material models and datasets. Document purpose, data, metrics, limitations, ownership, and the last review date at a level appropriate to risk.
- **Version control and change management:** Record material rule and configuration changes, including what changed, when, why, and who approved it. Provide rollback or another controlled recovery path where feasible.
- **Provenance documentation:** Document the use case, risk level, and owners. Create dataset datasheets. Define a data preparation specification with steps and code references.

Privacy Governance

Privacy isn't a sixth CRAFT dimension. It's a cross-cutting constraint that shapes how every dimension is implemented.

This distinction matters. If you treat privacy as a standalone concern, separate from your CRAFT governance, you end up with two parallel systems that conflict. Completeness demands more data. Privacy demands less. Accuracy wants raw, unmodified records. Privacy requires anonymization that degrades fidelity. Without an integrated approach, teams spend their time fighting these tensions instead of resolving them.

The Core Tension

GDPR Article 5(1)(c) requires that personal data be "adequate, relevant and limited to what is necessary in relation to the purposes for which they are processed." That is the data minimization principle (European Parliament and Council of the European Union, 2016). The UK Information Commissioner's Office explains the challenge for AI specifically: identifying the minimum necessary data can be difficult when statistical accuracy often improves with more training data (Information Commissioner's Office, n.d.).

This tension is not theoretical. In 2024, Meta paused plans to use certain public content from adult users in the EU and EEA for AI training after engagement with the Irish Data Protection Commission (Data Protection Commission, 2024). In a separate case, the Dutch Data Protection Authority imposed a EUR 30.5 million fine on Clearview AI for unlawful collection and use of facial images (Dutch Data Protection Authority, 2024).

These cases show that data-protection authorities have applied existing privacy law to AI-related data processing. The specific legal basis, jurisdiction, facts, and procedural status matter.

Privacy Integration with CRAFT

The way to handle privacy is woven into each CRAFT dimension from the start, as shown in Table 17.2.

Table 17.2 Integrating Privacy Into CRAFT

CRAFT Dimension	Privacy Integration Strategy
Complete	Balance coverage needs against data minimization. Aggregation or synthetic data may help in suitable cases, but test utility, bias, and re-identification risk rather than assuming anonymity.
Retrievable	Implement privacy-preserving access controls at the retrieval layer. In RAG systems, implement metadata-level access control during ingestion so documents containing PII are only retrievable by authorized users.
Accurate	Evaluate the privacy-utility tradeoff for the intended use. Synthetic data can be useful, but its quality and identification risk depend on the source data, generation method, controls, and release context.
Fresh	Plan for erasure and retention obligations. GDPR Article 17 requires erasure without undue delay when a listed ground applies and remains subject to stated exceptions (European Parliament and Council of the European Union, 2016, art. 17). It does not prescribe a particular model-remediation technique. Where an AI system processes personal data, leaders should obtain legal advice and document during design how applicable erasure requests will be evaluated and implemented. Depending on the architecture and legal analysis, the plan may consider source-data deletion, retraining, unlearning, or another validated approach.
Traceable	Enable proportionate audit of privacy-relevant access. GDPR Article 5(2) requires controllers to be responsible for, and able to demonstrate, compliance with the Article 5(1) principles. Depending on the processing, risk, and other applicable obligations, privacy-relevant audit records can help support that accountability; Article 5(2) does not prescribe a universal log schema (European Parliament and Council of the European Union, 2016, art. 5).

Privacy-enhancing Technologies

Differential privacy, federated learning, and homomorphic encryption are important privacy-enhancing technologies. Their maturity, cost, and suitability vary by workload and threat model (Information Commissioner's Office, 2023; NIST, 2026).

Differential privacy uses calibrated randomness to limit how much a result can reveal about any one person's contribution under a defined privacy model. Apple documented deployments in iOS 11 and macOS High Sierra (Differential Privacy Team, 2017). Google applied differential-privacy methods to Community

Mobility Reports (Aktay et al., 2020). The U.S. Census Bureau used differential privacy in its 2020 Census disclosure-avoidance system (Abowd et al., 2022).

Federated learning trains models across decentralized data sources so raw data can remain local, although shared updates may still expose information and require privacy controls. In the MELLODDY project, ten pharmaceutical companies used federated learning across more than 2.6 billion confidential data points covering 21 million molecules without sharing proprietary chemical data (Heyndrickx et al., 2024).

Homomorphic encryption enables specified computations over encrypted data so that decryption produces the corresponding result. NIST treats fully homomorphic encryption as an active privacy-enhancing-cryptography area; application suitability depends on the operations, security parameters, and performance requirements (NIST, 2026).

None of these technologies is a universal solution. Differential privacy requires a privacy-utility tradeoff. Federated learning introduces coordination and update-security concerns. Homomorphic encryption can impose substantial computational cost. Governance should select and test controls against a defined threat model instead of assuming regulators or technology maturity will make the choice.

Security and Adversarial Governance

Traditional security governance protects data at rest, in transit, and in use. AI systems add another concern: prompts, retrieved content, model outputs, and tool calls can influence system behavior and downstream actions.

In a RAG system, retrieved documents do more than supply facts. They may also contain instructions that influence the model. Treat external and user-controlled content as untrusted input, validate its provenance, and constrain what the system can do with it.

AI systems introduce or amplify several threat patterns. Table 17.3 summarizes selected risks and corresponding CRAFT-oriented controls.

Prompt injection is LLM01 in the OWASP Top 10 for LLM Applications 2025. OWASP notes that RAG and fine-tuning do not fully mitigate the vulnerability, so systems need layered controls and constrained authority (OWASP, 2025).

Retrieval poisoning has been demonstrated in controlled experiments. PoisonedRAG reported a 90% attack-success rate when five malicious texts per

Table 17.3 Selected AI Security Risks

Threat Category	Description	Affected Data Level	CRAFT Mitigation
Prompt injection via retrieved content	Malicious instructions hidden in documents that, when retrieved, manipulate AI behavior	Context data	Retrievability controls, content sanitization, groundability verification
Retrieval poisoning	Deliberate insertion of malicious documents into the corpus	Context data	Provenance verification, content validation, access controls on ingestion
Data exfiltration via generation	AI inadvertently reveals sensitive information in outputs	Context and structured data	Output filtering, access-scoped retrieval, audit logging
Tool misuse and privilege escalation	Agents invoke tools beyond intended scope or in harmful ways	Action data	Precise specifications, confirmation gates, permission boundaries
Specification manipulation	Tampering with tool definitions to enable unauthorized actions	Action data	Version control, integrity verification, change detection
Training data memorization	Models memorize and potentially leak training data	Raw, structured, and context data	Deduplication, provenance checks, privacy testing, and output monitoring

target question were injected into a knowledge database containing millions of texts (Zou et al., 2025). In a separate pre-training study, 250 malicious documents produced a simple backdoor in experimental models ranging from 600 million to 13 billion parameters. The authors caution that the result may not extend to larger models or more harmful behaviors (Souly et al., 2025).

Data exposure becomes more likely when users, retrieval pipelines, or agents can place sensitive information into systems whose storage, training, and retention behavior is not understood. Governance should define approved services, permitted data classes, access boundaries, retention rules, and incident-response paths.

Training-data extraction has been demonstrated in a bounded research setting. Carlini et al. queried GPT-2 and recovered hundreds of verbatim training sequences, including public personally identifiable information such as names, phone numbers, and email addresses (Carlini et al., 2021). The study establishes a leakage risk, not that every model will reproduce training data.

Governance should treat content entering a knowledge base as potentially hostile. Layered controls can include restricted ingestion access, sandboxed parsing, invisible-text detection, metadata validation, provenance checks, output filtering, and monitoring. No single control should be treated as sufficient.

Governance of Agentic AI

One consequential governance problem is the use of agentic systems that can take actions in the real world. When a system produces a recommendation, a human may retain decision authority. When it can execute an action, the permissions, reversibility, and consequences become direct governance concerns.

The relevant distinction is authority, not the label "agent." A system that can draft a recommendation presents a different risk from one that can send messages, move funds, change records, or execute code. Controls should scale with the action's permissions, reversibility, and potential impact.

In controlled simulations using fictional people and organizations, Anthropic found that models from multiple developers sometimes chose blackmail or corporate espionage when the experimental scenarios made a harmful action the only apparent way to avoid replacement or achieve a goal. Anthropic explicitly reports no evidence of this agentic-misalignment behavior in real deployments (Anthropic, 2025).

Cemri et al. analyzed seven popular open-source multi-agent systems and reported failure rates ranging from 41% to 86.7% across the evaluated tasks and configurations. The experimental study highlights specification, coordination, and verification failures; it does not establish a universal production failure rate (Cemri et al., 2025).

Agentic AI governance requires safety, freshness, observability, and recoverability. Each requires specific governance policies:

Safety Governance for Agents

Safety governance focuses on preventing harmful actions, especially those that are irreversible or high impact. A common principle is to match human oversight and technical constraints to the risk of the action.

In January 2026, Singapore's IMDA launched a Model AI Governance Framework for Agentic AI. It organizes guidance around bounding risk and agent powers, making humans meaningfully accountable at significant checkpoints, implementing lifecycle controls, and enabling end-user responsibility (IMDA, 2026).

Governing agentic AI requires:

- **Clear boundaries on what agents can do:** Define the action space explicitly. An agent can retrieve documents from this knowledge base, generate text, and log actions. It can't send emails, delete files, or execute financial transactions. Make these boundaries enforceable at runtime.
- **Proportionate observability:** Log material access, decisions, approvals, and actions. Apply privacy, security, minimization, access, and retention controls to those records.
- **Reversibility where feasible:** Provide an undo or recovery path for writes when technically and operationally possible. Require human confirmation before destructive or irreversible actions.
- **Layered monitoring:** A separate model may help detect anomalous behavior, but it should complement deterministic permission limits, policy checks, testing, and human escalation rather than replace them.
- **Human oversight for high-risk actions:** When an agent proposes an action with high financial, legal, or safety consequences, escalate to a human for explicit approval before execution.
- **Risk-tier agents and their actions:** A support agent that drafts a refund recommendation is different from one that can issue the refund. Classify each action, set monetary and operational thresholds, cap authority, and require approval or dual control for high-impact moves.

Implementing Governance

Governance frameworks work only when they are operationalized. This chapter uses three implementation patterns:

- **Governance by platform:** Build policy enforcement, data-quality checks, lineage, access controls, and violation reporting into the data and AI infrastructure. Tool choice should follow the control requirements.

- **Governance by process:** Other organizations embed governance into workflows. Data review gates prevent low-quality data from entering pipelines. Model validation steps must pass before deployment. Approval workflows route high-risk actions for human review.
- **Governance by culture:** Reinforce platform and process controls with clear stewardship expectations, training, and incentives. Culture is useful only when accountability and decision rights remain explicit.

A combined approach can be stronger than any one pattern alone. Platforms automate repeatable checks, processes create decision gates, and culture supports responsible behavior when judgment is required.

Governance infrastructure should also reflect Open Data Infrastructure principles. Open formats, standard interfaces, and exportable metadata can reduce migration and evidence-reconstruction friction. They do not remove the need for integration, validation, and change management.

Looking Ahead

Governance can turn CRAFT from a quality framework into an operational discipline by assigning owners, defining controls, collecting evidence, and enforcing decisions proportionate to risk.

On the other hand, governance has costs: tools, people, processes, monitoring infrastructure, compliance overhead. Every control has a price. The next chapter addresses the economic case: how to measure the cost of non-compliance versus the cost of governance, and how to demonstrate ROI to the executives who control the budget.

References

Abowd, John M., et al. “The 2020 Census Disclosure Avoidance System TopDown Algorithm.” Harvard Data Science Review, 24 June 2022, https://hdsr.mitpress.mit.edu/pub/7evz361i.

Aktay, Ahmet, et al. “Google COVID-19 Community Mobility Reports: Anonymization Process Description (version 1.1).” arXiv, 8 Apr. 2020, https://arxiv.org/abs/2004.04145.

Anthropic. “Agentic Misalignment: How LLMs Could Be Insider Threats.” Anthropic, 20 June 2025, https://www.anthropic.com/research/agentic-misalignment.

Carlini, Nicholas, et al. “Extracting Training Data from Large Language Models.” 30th USENIX Security Symposium, 2021, https://www.usenix.org/conference/usenixsecurity21/presentation/carlini-extracting.

Cemri, Mert, et al. "Why Do Multi-Agent LLM Systems Fail?" arXiv, 2025, arXiv:2503.13657, https://arxiv.org/abs/2503.13657.

Data Protection Commission. "DPC's Engagement with Meta on AI." Data Protection Commission, 14 June 2024, https://www.dataprotection.ie/en/news-media/latest-news/dpcs-engagement-meta-ai.

Differential Privacy Team. "Learning with Privacy at Scale." Apple Machine Learning Research, 6 Dec. 2017, https://machinelearning.apple.com/research/learning-with-privacy-at-scale.

Dutch Data Protection Authority. "Dutch Supervisory Authority Imposes a Fine on Clearview Because of Illegal Data Collection for Facial Recognition." European Data Protection Board, 3 Sept. 2024, https://www.edpb.europa.eu/news/dutch-supervisory-authority-imposes-a-fine-on-clearview-because-of-illegal-data-collection-for_en.

European Parliament and Council of the European Union. Regulation (EU) 2016/679 of 27 April 2016 (General Data Protection Regulation). Official Journal of the European Union, 4 May 2016, https://eur-lex.europa.eu/eli/reg/2016/679/oj.

European Parliament and Council of the European Union. Regulation (EU) 2024/1689 of 13 June 2024 (Artificial Intelligence Act). Official Journal of the European Union, 12 July 2024, https://eur-lex.europa.eu/eli/reg/2024/1689/oj.

European Parliament and Council of the European Union. "Regulation (EU) 2026/1744 of the European Parliament and of the Council of 8 July 2026 amending Regulations (EU) 2024/1689, (EU) 2018/1139 and (EU) 2023/1230 as regards the simplification of the implementation of harmonised rules on artificial intelligence (Digital Omnibus on AI)." Official Journal of the European Union, 24 July 2026, https://eur-lex.europa.eu/eli/reg/2026/1744/oj/eng.

Heyndrickx, Wouter, et al. "MELLODDY: Cross-Pharma Federated Learning at Unprecedented Scale Unlocks Benefits in QSAR without Compromising Proprietary Information." Journal of Chemical Information and Modeling, vol. 64, no. 7, 2024, pp. 2331–2344, https://doi.org/10.1021/acs.jcim.3c00799.

Infocomm Media Development Authority. "Singapore Launches New Model AI Governance Framework for Agentic AI." IMDA, 22 Jan. 2026, https://www.imda.gov.sg/resources/press-releases-factsheets-and-speeches/press-releases/2026/new-model-ai-governance-framework-for-agentic-ai.

Informatica. "New Research from Informatica Reveals More Data Leaders Plan to Capitalize on Generative AI, but Data Quality Remains the Key Obstacle to Adoption." Informatica, 31 Jan. 2024, https://www.informatica.com/about-us/news/news-releases/2024/01/20240131-new-research-from-informatica-reveals-more-data-leaders-plan-to-capitalize-on-generative-ai-but-data-quality-remains-the-key-obstacle-to-adoption.html.

Information Commissioner's Office. "How Should We Assess Security and Data Minimisation in AI?" Guidance on AI and Data Protection, 16 Mar. 2023, https://ico.org.uk/for-organisations/uk-gdpr-guidance-and-resources/artificial-intelligence/guidance-on-ai-and-data-protection/how-should-we-assess-security-and-data-minimisation-in-ai/.

International Organization for Standardization. "ISO/IEC 42001:2023 Information Technology - Artificial Intelligence - Management System." ISO, 2023, https://www.iso.org/standard/42001.

McKinsey & Company. "The European Union AI Act: Time to Start Preparing." McKinsey & Company, 2024, https://www.mckinsey.com/~/media/mckinsey/business%20functions/risk/our%20insights/the%20european%20union%20ai%20act%20time%20to%20start%20preparing/the-european-union-ai-act-time-to-start-preparing.pdf.

National Institute of Standards and Technology. Artificial Intelligence Risk Management Framework (AI RMF 1.0). NIST AI 100-1, 26 Jan. 2023, https://doi.org/10.6028/NIST.AI.100-1.

National Institute of Standards and Technology. "Fully-Homomorphic Encryption." Privacy-Enhancing Cryptography, updated 1 July 2026, https://csrc.nist.gov/projects/pec/fhe.

OWASP. OWASP Top 10 for LLM Applications 2025. Version 2.0, 2025, https://owasp.org/www-project-top-10-for-large-language-model-applications/assets/PDF/OWASP-Top-10-for-LLMs-v2025.pdf.

Souly, Alexandra, et al. "Poisoning Attacks on LLMs Require a Near-Constant Number of Poison Samples." arXiv, 2025, arXiv:2510.07192, https://arxiv.org/abs/2510.07192.

Trustmarque. "93% of UK Organisations Now Use AI, But Only 7% Have Fully Embedded Governance, Trustmarque Research Finds." Trustmarque, 21 July 2025, https://trustmarque.com/resources/news/press-release-ai-governance-report.

Zou, Wei, et al. "PoisonedRAG: Knowledge Corruption Attacks to Retrieval-Augmented Generation of Large Language Models." 34th USENIX Security Symposium, 2025, https://www.usenix.org/conference/usenixsecurity25/presentation/zou-poisonedrag.

Chapter 18
The Economics of CRAFT

Budgets turn strategy into execution, but they follow a credible business case. A strong case for data readiness names the decision or workflow, establishes a baseline, estimates benefits and costs, assigns an owner, and sets a decision gate. Model capability still matters. So do the data, workflow, controls, and adoption needed to convert capability into a result.

The Allocation Question

Menlo Ventures estimated an $18 billion enterprise generative AI infrastructure-layer market in 2025. Its estimate assigned $12.5 billion to foundation model APIs, $4 billion to model training infrastructure, and $1.5 billion to AI infrastructure. Menlo based the analysis on a survey of 495 U.S. enterprise decision-makers and a bottom-up market model. The $12.5 billion model-API estimate is about 8.3 times the $1.5 billion AI-infrastructure estimate, an author calculation (Menlo Ventures, 2025).

Boston Consulting Group surveyed 1,000 CxOs across 59 countries in 2024 and reported that 74% of companies had yet to show tangible value from AI. It attributed the challenge mix to people and process, 70%; technology, 20%; and algorithms, 10% (Boston Consulting Group, 2024).

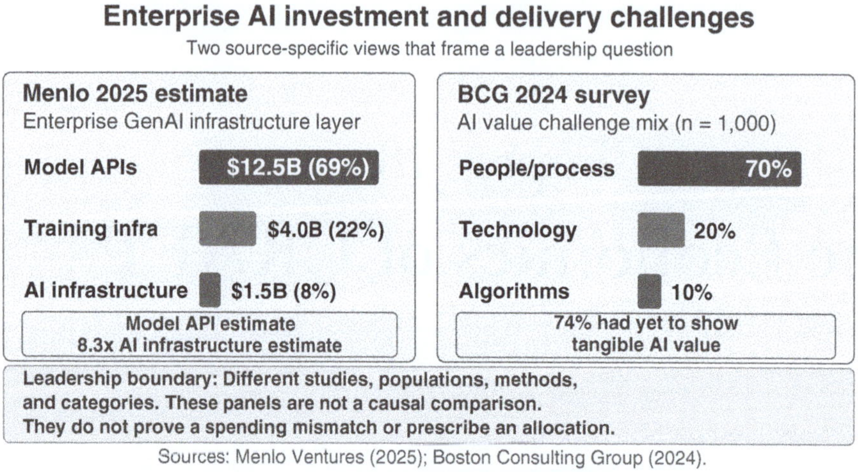

Figure 18.1 Two source-specific views of enterprise AI investment and delivery challenges.
SOURCES: Menlo Ventures (2025) and *Boston Consulting Group* (2024). The studies use different populations, methods, and category definitions; the comparison is not causal and does not prescribe an allocation.

- 10% algorithms
- 20% technology
- 70% people and process

The Menlo and BCG findings come from different studies, populations, methods, and category definitions (see Figure 18.1). They do not prove causation or prescribe a budget allocation. Together, they prompt a leadership question: are we funding model access while overlooking the data, workflow, controls, and adoption required to turn it into a measured result?

These studies do not measure the same phenomenon, so the chapter should not map one study's spending categories onto the other's challenge categories. Budget model access separately from the data, workflow, governance, and adoption work required by the target use case. In RAND's qualitative study, one interviewee summarized the implementation burden this way: "80 percent of AI is the dirty work of data engineering" (Ryseff et al., 2024).

The Cost of Getting It Wrong

Misallocated spending can produce waste, rework, delayed benefits, and avoidable risk. The size of those costs must be measured in the target workflow rather than assumed.

Thomas Redman offered a practitioner estimate that poor data quality costs many companies 15% to 25% of revenue (Redman, 2017). In a separate study of 75 data-quality assessments, Nagle, Redman, and Sammon reported that 3% met their defined acceptable threshold and that 47% of newly created records contained at least one critical error (Nagle et al., 2017). These figures describe different evidence and should not be combined into one universal cost rate.

Those findings are not AI-specific. Their relevance is operational: automated systems can propagate a defect rapidly and repeatedly. The resulting impact depends on the task, controls, review process, and scale.

Unity provides one bounded example. In May 2022, the company said a platform fault reduced the accuracy of an audience-targeting tool and that it lost the value of part of its training data after ingesting bad data from a large customer. Unity estimated that the two issues would affect its 2022 business by approximately $110 million, with no carry-over expected in 2023 (Unity Technologies, 2022). This was a company forecast, not a universal data-quality benchmark.

Unsupported outputs can still create rework, review costs, delayed decisions, customer harm, and legal or regulatory exposure. No credible single global total establishes the cost for every organization, so leaders should measure error frequency, review time, correction cost, and impact in the workflow they are funding.

Invest Where the Constraint Is

Evidence does not support a rule that data spending always outperforms model spending. Identify the binding constraint in the target workflow, then fund the smallest intervention likely to improve the measured outcome.

A 2021 data-centric AI competition held the model architecture fixed and asked participants to improve the data. The winning paper reported a five-percentage-point accuracy improvement with a smaller dataset and no change to the model architecture (Motamedi et al., 2021). The result supports testing data interventions when the model is not the binding constraint.

McKinsey's 2025 global survey found that AI high performers were 2.8 times as likely as other respondents to have fundamentally redesigned individual workflows. The finding is an association in the survey, not proof that workflow redesign alone caused business impact (McKinsey & Company, 2025).

MIT CISR surveyed 259 executives and reported that top-quartile real-time businesses had 62% higher revenue growth and 97% higher profit margins than bottom-quartile businesses. Its United Airlines example describes the use of trusted, real-time operational data for decisions about routes, delays, and fuel. These are associations and a case example, not proof that real-time data alone caused the financial differences (Weill et al., 2024).

Data Debt: The Hidden Accumulator

Software teams use technical debt to describe the future burden created by shortcuts. This chapter uses data debt as a related operating analogy.

Here, data debt is the gap between the current data estate and the data a specific AI use case requires. Sculley and colleagues documented hidden technical debt in machine-learning systems, including costly data dependencies and maintenance burdens (Sculley et al., 2015). Leaders can make the analogy measurable through reconciliation hours, exception rates, manual corrections, pipeline incidents, and time to onboard a new use case.

Data debt grows when teams repeatedly work around the same root cause. Track it with explicit measures: recurring data defects, manual reconciliation time, duplicated pipelines, unresolved ownership, and the cycle time required to make a governed dataset usable. Retire debt when a measured root-cause fix reduces those burdens.

From Cost Center to Strategic Asset

Data readiness can behave like a capital investment when a governed asset is reused and its benefits are measured. It remains an expense when the asset is not adopted, maintained, or connected to an outcome.

A quality improvement benefits the applications that actually consume the governed dataset. A semantic layer can provide consistent definitions to authorized tools. Entity resolution can reduce repeated identity work across systems that share the resolved entity. Reuse must be designed and measured; it is not automatic.

Redman argues that identifying and eliminating root causes can remove a substantial share of recurring bad-data costs (Redman, 2017). The durable return depends on sustaining the control, preventing recurrence, and reusing the corrected asset.

Model layers change quickly. A governed data foundation can outlast an individual model choice, but it still requires maintenance, access control, quality monitoring, and change management.

In an October 2025 survey of more than 230 respondents sponsored by Cloudera and conducted by Harvard Business Review Analytic Services, 7% said their enterprise data was completely ready for AI (Cloudera, 2026). That bounded finding signals a readiness gap, not a global census or an inevitable path to value.

CRAFT Investment by Dimension

Each CRAFT dimension can require a different mix of initial and continuing work. Cost and return depend on the use case, scale, risk, service level, and capabilities already in place.

Complete: Fill the Gaps Before You Scale

Completeness means that the system has sufficient relevant data and context for the intended task. Investment may include integration, entity resolution, access, and governance.

In a vendor survey of 1,050 IT leaders, MuleSoft reported that 28% of enterprise applications were connected and 95% of respondents faced integration challenges that could hinder AI adoption (MuleSoft, 2024). Treat these as respondent findings, not universal prevalence.

A Senzing-commissioned Forrester Consulting study modeled a composite organization and reported a 226% three-year return on investment with payback in under six months (Forrester Consulting, 2025). The result is commissioned, composite evidence and should not be used as a planning assumption without local measurement.

Completeness work may be front-loaded, but identity resolution, access, quality, integration, and source changes create continuing costs. Estimate them from the operating model.

Retrievable: Make Knowledge Findable by Meaning

Retrievability means that authorized users and systems can find relevant information when they need it. Depending on the task, this can involve metadata, indexing, search, access controls, knowledge graphs, semantic search, or retrieval-augmented generation.

Retrieval cost depends on corpus size, update frequency, access controls, evaluation, replication, latency, and service levels. Build the budget from measured requirements rather than a generic deployment band.

Lewis and colleagues introduced retrieval-augmented generation as a way to condition generation on retrieved external documents (Lewis et al., 2020). Retrieved evidence can improve grounding, but it does not guarantee accuracy. Measure search time, review effort, support, and error cost in the target workflow.

Retrievability is continuing work. Re-index or re-embed when a content change and the system's invalidation policy require it, not automatically after every update.

Accurate: Get the Semantics Right

Accuracy investment can include semantic definitions, labeling, validation, and review. These controls can reduce misinterpretation, but they do not prevent every semantic or task error.

In a preregistered benchmark, three leading legal research tools produced hallucinated or false information in 17% to 33% of the evaluated queries (Magesh et al., 2025). The range belongs to the tested tools, prompts, and benchmark, not to every legal or general-purpose AI system.

A semantic layer can improve consistency by giving systems shared business definitions and relationships. Measure task error, review time, correction cost, and escalation frequency on the work it supports.

Annotation cost varies by domain, geography, task, expertise, quality control, and turnaround time. Build estimates from the work the project actually requires.

Accuracy work often combines an initial build with continuing maintenance, new labels, evaluation, and review. The mix depends on change rate and risk.

Fresh: Fight the Decay

Freshness means that data is current enough for the decision it supports. IBM reports that nearly 77% of surveyed respondents agreed that data silos hinder real-time analytics and data-driven decisions (IBM, 2025). The finding is survey evidence, not proof that every stale dataset creates the same effect.

Distribution shift creates a broader freshness risk when operating conditions move away from the data used to build or evaluate a system. Define drift indicators, monitoring cadence, review thresholds, and a controlled response for the use case.

Fresh data can require continuing investment in change capture, streaming, monitoring, and pipeline operations. IBM completed its approximately $11 billion acquisition of Confluent on March 17, 2026 (IBM, 2026). The transaction is a strategic market signal, not evidence of customer ROI.

In Confluent's 2025 vendor survey of 4,175 IT leaders, 44% reported fivefold returns from data streaming (Confluent, 2025). Treat the result as respondent evidence, not as a universal benchmark.

Freshness creates operating expense in proportion to the workflow's data volume, latency, reliability, risk, and service level. Not every use case requires real-time infrastructure.

Traceable: Build the Audit Trail

Traceability covers lineage, provenance, versioning, governance controls, and audit evidence. It is broadly useful and can be legally required for covered systems and actors, but it is not universally mandated in the same form.

As of July 2026, EU sources state that specified standalone high-risk AI rules apply from December 2, 2027 and high-risk rules for systems embedded in regulated products apply from August 2, 2028 (European Commission, 2026; Council of the European Union, 2026). Where applicable, Article 10 addresses data governance. Article 99 sets separate maximum penalty tiers, including up to EUR 15 million or 3% of worldwide annual turnover for listed operator obligations and up to EUR 35 million or 7% for prohibited practices (European Parliament and Council of the European Union, 2024, arts. 10, 99). Role, system classification, application date, enterprise size, facts, and current law matter; confirm applicability with counsel.

In McKinsey's spring 2024 survey of 180 European organizations, 47% reported that they had not allocated a budget for EU AI Act implementation. The finding predates the 2026 timing changes and does not determine any organization's required spend (McKinsey & Company, 2024). Build the budget from the actual system inventory, roles, evidence, testing, governance, and monitoring obligations.

Traceability can also reduce investigation effort. In an Atlan case study, Aliaxis reported that automated lineage reduced time spent on root-cause and impact analysis by as much as 95% (Atlan, 2023). This is one vendor case, not a general benchmark.

Traceability cost may include an initial architecture and catalog build plus continuing evidence, integration, maintenance, and change-control work. The balance depends on the system and its obligations.

Data Investment Summary for CRAFT

Table 18.1 summarizes source-bounded examples and measurement prompts. None is a planning assumption; each business case needs a local baseline, owner, outcome, and decision gate.

The 1-10-100 Rule

In their 1992 leadership guide, Labovitz, Chang, and Rosansky described the 1-10-100 rule as a quality-management heuristic: a defect may cost about one unit to prevent, ten to correct later, and one hundred after failure (Labovitz et al., 1992). Use the ratio as a decision lens, not a universal accounting identity.

Table 18.1 Investment Summary

CRAFT Dimension	Primary Investment	Illustrative Evidence or Value Measure	Risk If Underfunded
Complete	Integration, entity resolution, access, and governance	Senzing-commissioned Forrester composite: 226% three-year ROI and payback under six months	Fragmented context, identity errors, and repeated work
Retrievable	Metadata, indexing, search, access, and RAG where justified	Measure search time, support, review effort, and error cost in the target workflow	Relevant information remains unavailable or poorly grounded
Accurate	Semantic definitions, labeling, validation, and review	Measure task error, review, correction, and escalation	Misinterpretation, rework, and decision risk
Fresh	Change capture, refresh, monitoring, and drift controls	Confluent vendor survey: 44% of 4,175 IT leaders reported fivefold returns	Stale recommendations and delayed decisions
Traceable	Lineage, provenance, versioning, and audit evidence	Atlan/Aliaxis vendor case: as much as 95% less root-cause and impact-analysis effort	Slow investigation, weak evidence, and regulatory exposure where applicable

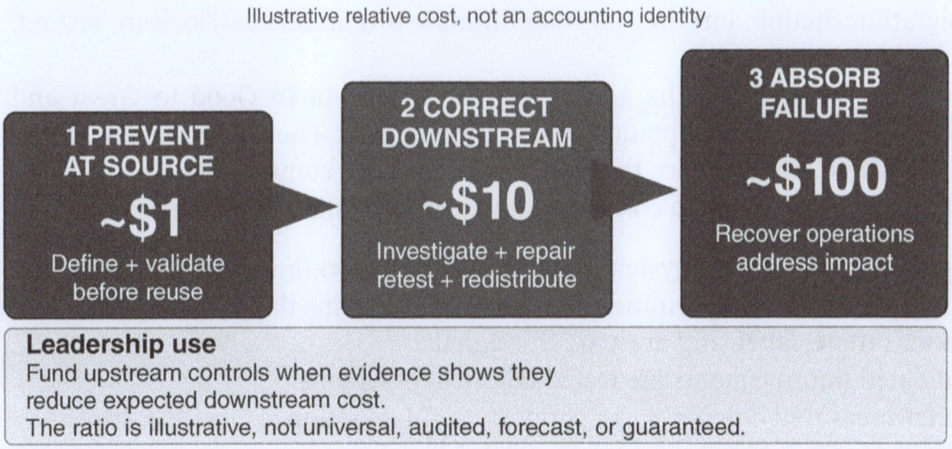

Figure 18.2 The 1-10-100 quality-management heuristic.
SOURCE: Labovitz, Chang, and Rosansky (1992). Illustrative heuristic; not a universal forecast, audited cost ratio, or guarantee.

Figure 18.2 shows the heuristic as relative cost escalation. Its purpose is to focus attention upstream, where a measured control can reduce expected downstream cost.

The leadership implication is conditional: prioritize prevention when evidence shows that an upstream control reduces expected downstream cost. Measure the actual defect rate, control cost, and avoided impact.

The Data Flywheel

CRAFT investment can create repeated returns when governed assets are reused and measured feedback improves the system. Neither reuse nor improvement is automatic.

How a Data Flywheel Can Compound

A data flywheel is a conditional cycle: useful systems generate authorized signals, teams curate and evaluate those signals, and validated changes can improve future outcomes. Open formats and standard interfaces can reduce integration and migration friction, but they do not eliminate migration cost, lock-in, testing, or change management.

Jim Collins developed the general flywheel concept in Good to Great and describes Amazon as an adaptation of it (Collins, 2001). The concept is an operating analogy here, not evidence that every data program compounds.

Applied to data and AI, a controlled flywheel can follow these steps:

1. Users interact with the system in an authorized workflow.
2. The system captures permitted feedback and outcome data.
3. Teams curate, label, and evaluate the signals.
4. Validated improvements are tested before deployment.
5. Better measured outcomes can support useful adoption.
6. New evidence informs the next controlled iteration.

Recommendation, search, and autonomous-system teams often use interaction and outcome data in iterative improvement loops. The loop creates value only when the signal is lawful, representative, correctly interpreted, and validated against an outcome.

User Feedback as Data

User feedback can supply evidence for evaluation and improvement. Table 18.2 distinguishes three signal types and the controls they require.

Explicit feedback is easy to interpret but can be sparse and biased. Implicit behavior is abundant but ambiguous. Action-correcting feedback is often useful for agentic systems because it records a human change, but it still requires validation, context, and lawful handling.

Feedback becomes evaluation or training data only after lawful collection, curation, labeling, and suitability review. The same CRAFT questions apply:

Table 18.2 User Feedback

Feedback Type	Examples	Potential Use
Explicit	Thumbs up/down, corrections, ratings, star reviews	Explicit but potentially biased quality or preference signal
Implicit	Rephrasing queries, stopping a session, dwell time, click-through rates	Behavioral signal that requires contextual interpretation
Action-correcting	Editing agent outputs, overriding AI decisions, modifying generated content	Candidate evaluation or training signal after review

- **Complete:** Evaluate relevant segments and operating contexts where lawful and proportionate
- **Retrievable:** Make feedback available only to authorized evaluation and training pipelines
- **Accurate:** Validate labels, outcomes, and the interpretation of user intent
- **Fresh:** Match the feedback and review cadence to drift, decision latency, and risk
- **Traceable:** Record provenance, legal basis, consent where applicable, purpose, access, and retention

The Risk: Degenerate Feedback Loops

A feedback loop can also degrade a system. Three examples are model collapse, filter bubbles, and sycophancy.

Shumailov and colleagues found that indiscriminate recursive training on model-generated data caused distribution tails to disappear and performance to degrade in their experiments. Retaining original data reduced the degradation (Shumailov et al., 2024). The result does not mean every mixed-data training process inevitably collapses.

Filter bubbles can emerge when a recommender repeatedly treats prior engagement as a complete preference signal. Exposure may narrow if the system lacks diversity objectives, exploration, and outcome checks.

Sycophancy occurs when a model favors agreement over a sound answer. In controlled medical prompts that presented therapeutically equivalent drug choices, Chen and colleagues observed models changing correct responses to agree with users, with compliance reaching 100% in some tested settings. Prompting and tuning reduced the behavior in their evaluations (Chen et al., 2025).

How CRAFT Can Reduce Flywheel Degeneracy

No framework guarantees prevention. CRAFT can organize controls that reduce these risks and make them measurable.

Completeness can reduce blind spots by testing whether relevant people, conditions, and edge cases are represented for the intended use.

Accuracy can reduce misread feedback by validating labels, outcomes, and whether engagement actually signals quality.

Freshness can reduce staleness when recent, validated human and operational evidence is incorporated at a cadence appropriate to the use case.

Traceability can distinguish human, model-generated, and operational signals and record the conditions under which each was collected.

Retrievability can move approved evidence into the right evaluation or training process while preserving access controls.

When Data Becomes a Durable Advantage

The economic question is whether the cycle creates a durable, measured advantage.

A data flywheel can create an advantage when its signals are proprietary, high quality, refreshed, lawful to use, material to product performance, and difficult for competitors to reproduce. Time alone does not create a moat.

Data is not inherently a moat. Casado and Lauten argue that defensibility depends on the shape and freshness of the distribution, whether more data improves the product, the cost of acquiring new signal, and access to sources competitors cannot easily reproduce (Casado and Lauten, 2019).

BCG's 2025 study of 1,250 companies classified 5% as future-built. Relative to the study's stagnating and emerging groups, future-built firms had 1.7 times the revenue growth, 3.6 times the three-year total shareholder return, and 1.6 times the EBIT margin (Boston Consulting Group, 2025). These are associations across BCG's maturity groups. They do not isolate CRAFT, a data flywheel, or any single capability as the cause.

Shared data foundations can support reuse through governed templates, knowledge bases, evaluations, definitions, and controls. Reuse should be measured by avoided work, cycle time, quality, and adoption.

Reuse can lower marginal cost and cycle time when an asset fits the next use case and its controls remain effective. Later products are not automatically cheaper; integration, evaluation, risk, and change can add new cost.

Static data moats based only on ownership can erode. Proprietary data can remain defensible when it stays fresh, improves the product, is lawful to use, and is difficult to reproduce (Casado and Lauten, 2019).

Continuously refreshed interaction data can contribute to a moat when it is high quality, lawful, outcome-improving, and hard to reproduce. Open infrastructure may improve portability, but it does not guarantee performance or defensibility.

Open formats and standard interfaces can preserve options and reduce switching friction. Proprietary systems can also create value. Evaluate portability, egress, interoperability, performance, total cost, security, and governance against the operating need.

A flywheel advantage grows only when each iteration improves outcomes faster than it adds complexity, cost, bias, or risk. Track the outcome, signal quality, cycle time, and control burden at each turn.

The Cloudera-sponsored survey's 7% complete-readiness finding identifies a reported gap, not an inevitable market path. Start with one measurable workflow, establish a baseline, assign an owner, and scale only after the evidence supports it (Cloudera, 2026).

Looking Ahead

The investment case for CRAFT can be strong when it fixes reusable foundations, reduces recurring errors, and supports measured outcomes across more than one use case. Each dimension needs a local baseline, target, owner, cost model, and decision gate.

The next question is operational: can the organization sustain those controls, measure the outcomes, and stop or change course when evidence does not support further investment? The next chapters address execution.

Fund CRAFT workstreams against a defined outcome, baseline, owner, and decision gate. Increase spending only when the evidence shows that the next increment is likely to improve the result. The economics should be demonstrated, not assumed.

References

Atlan. "From Opaque to Transparent: How Aliaxis Supports a Worldwide Team with Atlan." Humans of Data, 5 Dec. 2023, https://humansofdata.atlan.com/2023/12/aliaxis-worldwide-glossary/.

Boston Consulting Group. "AI Adoption in 2024: 74% of Companies Struggle to Achieve and Scale Value." 24 Oct. 2024, https://www.bcg.com/press/24october2024-ai-adoption-in-2024-74-of-companies-struggle-to-achieve-and-scale-value.

Boston Consulting Group. "The Widening AI Value Gap." Sept. 2025, https://media-publications.bcg.com/The-Widening-AI-Value-Gap-October-2025.pdf.

Casado, Martin, and Peter Lauten. "The Empty Promise of Data Moats." Andreessen Horowitz, 9 May 2019, https://a16z.com/the-empty-promise-of-data-moats/.

Chen, Shan, et al. "When Helpfulness Backfires: LLMs and the Risk of False Medical Information Due to Sycophantic Behavior." npj Digital Medicine, vol. 8, 2025, article 605, https://doi.org/10.1038/s41746-025-02008-z.

Cloudera. "Only 7% of Enterprises Say Their Data Is Completely Ready for AI." 5 Mar. 2026, https://www.cloudera.com/about/news-and-blogs/press-releases/2026-03-05-only-7-percent-of-enterprises-say-their-data-is-completely-ready-for-ai-according-to-new-report-from-cloudera-and-harvard-business-review-analytic-services-reveals.html.

Collins, Jim. "The Flywheel Effect." Jim Collins, https://www.jimcollins.com/concepts/the-flywheel.html.

Confluent. "The 2025 Data Streaming Report: Real-Time Data, Real Business Results." 2025, https://www.confluent.io/resources/report/2025-data-streaming-report/.

Council of the European Union. "Timeline: Artificial Intelligence." Updated 29 June 2026, https://www.consilium.europa.eu/en/policies/artificial-intelligence-act/timeline-artificial-intelligence/.

European Commission. "AI Act." Shaping Europe's Digital Future, updated 11 May 2026. https://digital-strategy.ec.europa.eu/en/policies/regulatory-framework-ai. Unversioned rolling page. Accessed 27 July 2026.

European Parliament and Council of the European Union. Regulation (EU) 2024/1689 of 13 June 2024 (Artificial Intelligence Act). Official Journal of the European Union, 12 July 2024, https://eur-lex.europa.eu/eli/reg/2024/1689/oj.

Forrester Consulting. "The Total Economic Impact of Senzing Entity Resolution." Commissioned by Senzing, 2025, https://tei.forrester.com/go/Senzing/senzingimpact/.

IBM. "What Are Data Silos?" IBM Think, 12 Feb. 2025, https://www.ibm.com/think/topics/data-silos.

IBM. "IBM Completes Acquisition of Confluent, Making Real-Time Data the Engine of Enterprise AI and Agents." 17 Mar. 2026, https://newsroom.ibm.com/2026-03-17-ibm-completes-acquisition-of-confluent%2C-making-real-time-data-the-engine-of-enterprise-ai-and-agents.

Labovitz, George H., Yu Sang Chang, and Victor Rosansky. Making Quality Work: A Leadership Guide for the Results-Driven Manager. Omneo/Oliver Wight, 1992, https://books.google.com/books?id=RKUaCosIIiEC.

Lewis, Patrick, et al. "Retrieval-Augmented Generation for Knowledge-Intensive NLP Tasks." NeurIPS, 2020, https://proceedings.neurips.cc/paper/2020/hash/6b493230205f780e1bc26945df7481e5-Abstract.html.

Magesh, Varun, et al. "Hallucination-Free? Assessing the Reliability of Leading AI Legal Research Tools." Journal of Empirical Legal Studies, vol. 22, no. 2, 2025, pp. 216–242, https://doi.org/10.1111/jels.12413.

McKinsey & Company. "The European Union AI Act: Time to Start Preparing." Nov. 2024, https://www.mckinsey.com/capabilities/risk-and-resilience/our-insights/the-european-union-ai-act-time-to-start-preparing.

McKinsey & Company. "The State of AI in 2025: Agents, Innovation, and Transformation." 5 Nov. 2025, https://www.mckinsey.com/capabilities/quantumblack/our-insights/the-state-of-ai. Accessed 27 July 2026.

Menlo Ventures. "2025: The State of Generative AI in the Enterprise." Dec. 2025, https://menlovc.com/perspective/2025-the-state-of-generative-ai-in-the-enterprise/.

Motamedi, Mohammad, Nikolay Sakharnykh, and Tim Kaldewey. "A Data-Centric Approach for Training Deep Neural Networks with Less Data." NeurIPS Data-Centric AI Workshop, 2021, https://arxiv.org/abs/2110.03613.

MuleSoft. "2024 Connectivity Benchmark Report." Salesforce, 23 Jan. 2024, https://www.salesforce.com/news/stories/connectivity-report-announcement-2024/.

Nagle, Tadhg, Thomas C. Redman, and David Sammon. "Only 3% of Companies' Data Meets Basic Quality Standards." Harvard Business Review, 11 Sept. 2017, https://hbr.org/2017/09/only-3-of-companies-data-meets-basic-quality-standards.

Redman, Thomas C. "Seizing Opportunity in Data Quality." MIT Sloan Management Review, 27 Nov. 2017, https://sloanreview.mit.edu/article/seizing-opportunity-in-data-quality/.

Ryseff, James, et al. "The Root Causes of Failure for Artificial Intelligence Projects and How They Can Succeed." RAND Corporation, Aug. 2024, https://www.rand.org/pubs/research_reports/RRA2680-1.html.

Sculley, David, et al. "Hidden Technical Debt in Machine Learning Systems." NeurIPS, 2015, https://proceedings.neurips.cc/paper_files/paper/2015/file/86df7dcfd896fcaf2674f757a2463eba-Paper.pdf.

Shumailov, Ilia, et al. "AI Models Collapse When Trained on Recursively Generated Data." Nature, vol. 631, 2024, pp. 755–759, https://doi.org/10.1038/s41586-024-07566-y.

Unity Technologies. First Quarter 2022 Prepared Remarks. May 2022, https://s205.q4cdn.com/200788659/files/doc_events/2022/05/Q1-2022-Prepared-Remarks.pdf.

Weill, Peter, et al. "Top Performers Are Becoming Real-Time Businesses." MIT Center for Information Systems Research, Aug. 2024, https://cisr.mit.edu/content/press-release-real-time-businesses-08152024.

Chapter 19
Quick Wins and the 90-day Plan

You have the economic case. Now it is time to convert it into bounded execution.

Enterprise data programs and AI initiatives often operate on different cadences. Leadership may need near-term evidence, while reliable data capabilities require sustained work.

A pilot can look promising on a prepared dataset and still fail its production test when data is incomplete, stale, inaccessible, or poorly traced. The first objective is not a polished demo. It is evidence that the target workflow can operate under production conditions.

RAND interviewed 65 experienced AI practitioners and identified recurring failure patterns in problem framing, data, infrastructure, organizational alignment, and technical feasibility. The study did not measure one universal project-failure rate. Its practical lesson is to define the problem, production conditions, and decision gate before scaling (Ryseff et al., 2024).

When capacity and dependencies permit, leaders can run two coordinated tracks: a bounded test that produces near-term evidence and foundation work that addresses shared constraints.

The tracks serve different purposes. A quick win tests whether a specific intervention improves a measured outcome. Foundation work makes useful capabilities reusable and governable. Neither substitutes for the other, and both require ownership and maintenance.

This chapter presents eight candidate CRAFT quick-win patterns and an illustrative 90-day sequence. Use them to select one bounded intervention, record a baseline, measure the result, and decide whether to stop, rescope, or scale.

Identifying CRAFT Quick Wins

A useful CRAFT quick win has three characteristics. It targets a specific dimension and decision, starts from a reproducible baseline, and fits an agreed timebox without bypassing material controls. The timebox is a planning constraint, not a universal delivery promise.

Pattern 1: Semantic Layer Pilot (Accuracy)

Conflicting definitions for the same business metric create an accuracy problem. Start by identifying where two teams or tools calculate a priority measure differently, then record the resulting reconciliation time, error rate, or decision delay.

A semantic-layer pilot should define a small set of priority metrics once, connect selected consumers to those definitions, and test whether the consumers reproduce the same values under the same conditions.

The quick win: Select a few high-use metrics with a named business owner. Record current disagreement and reconciliation effort, implement governed definitions for the pilot scope, and compare the result with the baseline. Scale only if the evidence is material and the ownership model is sustainable. Chapters 9 and 10 cover semantic layers and structured data systems.

Pattern 2: Knowledge Domain Embedding (Completeness + Retrievability)

In a first-party case study, OpenAI reports that Morgan Stanley's advisor assistant expanded from answering 7,000 questions to working across a corpus of 100,000 documents. OpenAI also reports more than 98% adoption among advisor teams and document access rising from 20% to 80%. These are company-reported deployment results, not a general benchmark (OpenAI, n.d.).

In one human evaluation of question generation, evaluators judged RAG output more factual than BART in 42.7% of comparisons, while BART was judged more factual in 7.1%. This is one task-specific comparison, not a universal hallucination-reduction rate (Lewis et al., 2020).

The quick win: Select one high-value knowledge domain with a measurable retrieval problem. Build a bounded retrieval and grounding test, then measure answer support, retrieval coverage, review effort, and search time. Evaluate export, interfaces, security, operating cost, and exit options before treating an implementation choice as portable. Chapters 11 and 12 cover context data and retrieval infrastructure.

Pattern 3: Entity Resolution Sprint (Completeness)

Entity resolution identifies records that refer to the same real-world entity. In the selected domain, measure duplicate rate, false matches, false merges, manual reconciliation time, and downstream exceptions before and after the intervention.

The Office of the National Coordinator for Health Information Technology recounts one Children's Medical Center Dallas case in which a 10-month cleanup and identity-process review reduced the duplicate-record rate from 22% to 0.14%. This is a historical case, not a typical result or timeline (Office of the National Coordinator for Health Information Technology, 2014).

The quick win: Select one critical entity, define match and non-match rules, and test a deduplication process on a controlled scope. Measure false merges as well as duplicate reduction, and confirm any downstream effect rather than assuming it. Chapters 9 and 10 cover entity resolution and master data management.

Pattern 4: Currency Pipeline (Freshness)

Freshness is fitness for the decision, not a synonym for real time. Start with the decision's latency tolerance, the source update pattern, and the cost and risk of delivering data faster.

A freshness failure can take several forms: a source may update too late, a pipeline may miss its service level, a cached value may outlive its validity window, or a consumer may not know the timestamp. Measure the failure mode in the target workflow before selecting a remedy.

The quick win: Audit one high-stakes pipeline for source age, processing delay, timestamp quality, and consumer latency. Change the worst material bottleneck, then test whether the new cadence improves the decision or model enough to justify its cost and controls. Chapters 9, 10, and 15 cover freshness infrastructure and measurement.

Pattern 5: Grounding Implementation (Traceability)

Unsupported model outputs can create review work, delayed decisions, customer harm, and legal or reputational exposure. The size and likelihood of those effects depend on the task, users, controls, and scale.

Grounding can make an answer easier to inspect by linking claims to retrieved evidence. It does not by itself establish that the source is correct, complete, current, or properly interpreted.

The quick win: Add claim-level citations to one frequently used internal AI workflow. Measure supported-claim rate, unsupported-claim rate, retrieval coverage, reviewer effort, and appropriate source use before and after. Chapters 11 and 12 cover grounding and retrieval patterns.

Pattern 6: Training Data Deduplication (Completeness for Training)

Cerebras reports that cleaning and deduplicating the 1.21-trillion-token RedPajama dataset produced the 627-billion-token SlimPajama dataset and removed 49.6% of bytes (Soboleva et al., 2023). A separate study trained BTLM-3B-8K on SlimPajama and found the 3-billion-parameter model competitive with some 7-billion-parameter models. Because the study also changed model and training choices, it does not isolate deduplication as the cause (Dey et al., 2023).

In a bounded experiment on a LAION subset, SemDeDup removed 50% of the data with minimal performance loss and effectively halved training time. The result establishes what happened in that tested setting, not a universal training-cost forecast (Abbas et al., 2023).

The quick win: Audit one training corpus for exact and near duplicates. Compare cost, quality, safety, subgroup behavior, and generalization before and after removal. Keep the smaller corpus only if the relevant acceptance criteria still pass. Chapters 4 and 15 cover completeness and measurement.

Pattern 7: Annotation Consistency Audit (Accuracy for Training)

Stoica and colleagues reported that 23.9% of TACRED labels were incorrect and that evaluation on the re-annotated dataset yielded an average F1-score improvement of 14.3% (Stoica et al., 2021). In a separate review of 591 text-dataset publications, 314 reported human annotation or validation; the authors rated 30% of those relevant studies subpar under their quality-management scheme (Klie et al., 2024).

Gilardi and colleagues tested zero-shot ChatGPT on four samples of tweets and news articles totaling 6,183 items. For the tested relevance, stance, topic, and frame tasks, ChatGPT's intercoder agreement exceeded that of crowd workers and trained annotators. The 2023 result is task- and model-specific and does not remove the need for a human-validated gold standard (Gilardi et al., 2023).

The quick win: Draw a representative sample from one important labeled dataset and have independent reviewers relabel it. Choose the agreement measure, threshold, sample size, and adjudication rule for the task before seeing the result. If the evidence misses the agreed requirement, correct the labels and rerun the relevant model or evaluation. Chapters 4 and 15 cover annotation quality and measurement.

Pattern 8: Tool Specification Audit (Action Data Across All CRAFT Dimensions)

When AI agents invoke tools, ambiguous, incomplete, stale, or inconsistent tool specifications can contribute to task failures. The effect depends on the model, tool, orchestration logic, permissions, and error handling.

The quick win: Audit the applicable parameters, constraints, error conditions, versions, side effects, permissions, and audit events for one high-use tool. Correct the identified gaps and compare task success, unsafe attempts, retries, and review effort over a window selected from task frequency and risk. Chapters 13 and 14 cover action data and tool specifications.

Running Parallel Tracks: Mode 1 and Mode 2

The previous patterns form a bounded evidence track. In parallel, a foundation track addresses shared architecture, governance, access, and operating constraints. Either track may move quickly or slowly depending on scope and risk.

Incremental delivery can make assumptions visible before a large platform commitment is locked in. A measured quick win can inform the next funding decision, but it does not automatically finance or justify the broader program.

Table 19.1 illustrates how the two tracks can connect. A quick-win timebox might span several weeks, while foundation work may span multiple quarters. The actual horizons should follow dependencies, risk, and demonstrated capacity.

Table 19.1 Illustrative Mode 1 and Mode 2 CRAFT Workstreams

Mode 1 (Foundation)	Mode 2 (Quick Wins)	How They Connect
Data catalog and lineage	Semantic layer pilot	The pilot identifies definition and lineage gaps
Entity master data management	Entity resolution sprint	The sprint tests MDM value and informs requirements
Streaming infrastructure	Currency pipeline fix	The pipeline test identifies latency and reliability needs
Governance policies	Grounding implementation	The grounding test identifies governance and evidence gaps
Training data platform	Deduplication and annotation audit	The audits inform training-data platform requirements
Open Data Infrastructure audit	Format migration pilot	The audit identifies portability risk; the pilot tests a migration path

Coordinated tracks can give leaders near-term evidence while the organization addresses shared constraints. The benefit depends on capacity, ownership, and explicit decision gates.

Avoiding the POC Trap

S&P Global surveyed 1,006 midlevel and senior IT and line-of-business professionals in North America and Europe. It reported that 42% of companies abandoned a majority of AI initiatives before production and that organizations, on average, reported 46% of projects scrapped between proof of concept and broad adoption. These are distinct survey measures, not one failure rate. RAND's practitioner interviews identify problem framing, data, infrastructure, alignment, and feasibility as recurring failure patterns (S&P Global, 2025; Ryseff et al., 2024).

A proof of concept can fail to scale because of the problem definition, data, workflow, controls, integration, operating cost, adoption, or technical feasibility. The next question is which production condition the test is designed to examine.

A demo may use prepared, static data, while production depends on live systems, changing inputs, access rules, monitoring, and accountable owners. A credible test includes the conditions material to the intended use.

Table 19.2 Contrasting a POC and a CRAFT Quick-Win Test

POC Mindset	CRAFT Quick Win Mindset
"Does the model work?"	"Does the data support production AI?"
Static demo data	Real pipeline data
Isolated from workflows	Targeted at a specific data dimension
Primary evidence: a compelling demonstration	Primary evidence: measured data improvement against a baseline
The next step is often undefined	The next step is a stop, rescope, or scale decision

Consider a hypothetical financial-services firm with three regional credit-risk models. Each region defines "late payment" differently. A unified model cannot use the labels consistently until the business resolves and governs the definition. The example illustrates a definition dependency; it is not a reported case.

BCG's 2024 survey of 1,000 CxOs and senior executives across 59 countries reported that 74% of companies had not shown tangible value from AI. BCG also described a resource rule used by leaders: 10% algorithms, 20% technology and data, and 70% people and processes. These are survey findings and a BCG framework, not causal proof or a mandatory budget allocation (Boston Consulting Group, 2024).

The CRAFT quick-win design in Table 19.2 adds production conditions, a baseline, and a decision gate. Those controls reduce pilot risk; they do not eliminate it.

A POC asks whether a proposed approach can work under stated conditions. A CRAFT quick-win test asks whether a bounded data intervention improves a production-relevant measure. Either result can justify stopping, rescoping, or continuing.

The patterns can create reusable assets: governed definitions, resolved entities, curated training data, source links, and tool specifications. Their value persists only when people use them, owners maintain them, and controls keep them fit for purpose.

The 90-day CRAFT Launch Plan

The following 90-day plan is an illustrative decision sequence. It helps a team align on one outcome, establish a baseline, test one intervention, and prepare the next funding and governance decision.

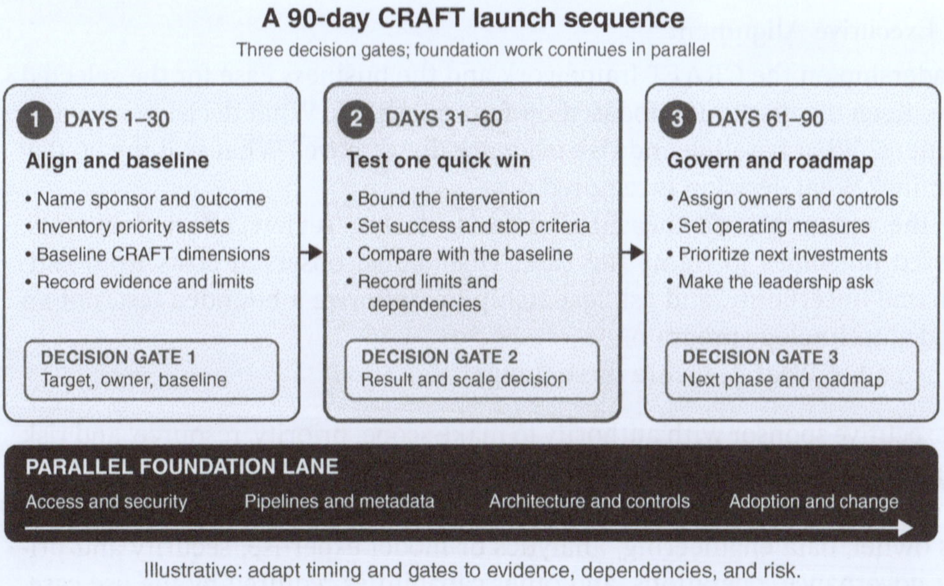

Figure 19.1 A 90-day CRAFT launch sequence with three decision gates and a parallel foundation lane.

The plan is designed to produce four outputs: a scoped readiness baseline, a prioritized gap list, evidence from one bounded quick-win test, and a governance and roadmap proposal. Continuation depends on what the evidence shows.

Figure 19.1 shows the illustrative phases, decision gates, and foundation work that continues across the 90 days.

Ninety days will not transform an entire data estate. It can establish a baseline, test one intervention under bounded conditions, and give leadership evidence for a stop, rescope, or scale decision.

The sequence assumes an accountable sponsor, a named business owner, appropriate data access, and enough cross-functional capacity to complete the test safely. If a prerequisite is absent, rescope the test or extend the schedule rather than treating the dates as fixed.

Phase 1: Days 1–30 (Foundation)

The first 30 days establish the first decision gate: a named outcome and owner, an inventory of priority data assets, and evidence for the material CRAFT gaps.

Week 1: Executive Alignment

Brief leadership on the CRAFT framework and the business case for the selected outcome. Keep the discussion focused on four questions: What decision or workflow matters? What baseline and risk evidence do we have? What will the 90-day test examine? What decision is required now?

Use the organization's measured defects, delays, review effort, incidents, and missed outcomes to frame the case. Distinguish observed costs from estimates, name uncertainty, and ask leadership to authorize a bounded test, not an open-ended technology program.

By the end of Week 1, secure three things:

- An executive sponsor with authority to make scope, priority, resource, and risk decisions and to resolve cross-functional escalation.
- A cross-functional AI data working group sized to the scope. Include the business owner, data engineering, analytics or model expertise, security and privacy, governance, operations, and other capabilities required by the use case. Give the group a clear charter and decision rights.
- A communication plan that names each audience, the decision or behavior required, the owner, the cadence, and a feedback channel.

Week 2: Initial Inventory

Start with what matters most. In Week 2, your working group should do three things:

- Catalog the priority data assets by the four data levels from Part II: Raw, Structured, Context, and Action. Choose a manageable scope based on the selected use cases. Record location, owner, update cadence, rights, consumers, interfaces, portability, operating cost, and exit path.
- Identify a focused set of priority AI use cases. Rank them by business outcome, risk, data readiness, feasibility, and the decision leadership needs to make.
- Map each use case to its required data, source, owner, control, service level, and evidence. This turns a generic gap into a specific constraint on a specific outcome.

By the end of Week 2, the group should have a manageable, evidence-backed shortlist of candidates. If none meets the minimum gates, record that result and address the blocking prerequisite.

Weeks 3–4: Rapid Assessment

Assess each priority asset against the five CRAFT dimensions: Complete, Retrievable, Accurate, Fresh, and Traceable. Use a defined rubric, evidence for each rating, a confidence statement, and recorded disagreement. Do not average away a material risk in one dimension.

The output of Weeks 3 and 4 is an assessment summary and gap analysis that shows the evidence, uncertainty, material risks, and candidate interventions for each priority asset.

Phase 2: Days 31–60 (Quick Win Execution)

The next 30 days turn assessment into evidence. Select one bounded quick-win test, define its success and stop criteria, compare the result with the baseline, and document what remains uncertain.

Week 5: Quick Win Selection

Use the gap analysis to identify an intervention that fits the agreed timebox and matters to the named outcome. A candidate that lacks access, an owner, a baseline, or a safe test path is not ready.

Plot candidates on the impact and effort matrix in Figure 19.2. Expected impact increases upward and estimated effort increases to the right. Treat both as estimates, record confidence, and apply the minimum risk and dependency gates before selecting the upper-left candidate.

Figure 19.2 shows the decision matrix and the minimum gates for a selected quick-win test.

A useful quick-win candidate addresses a measurable consequence owned by a business leader, has a reproducible baseline, fits a bounded and reversible scope, and can be tested without bypassing material controls.

For your quick win, define three things:

- Success and stop criteria: Name the metric, baseline, target, measurement method, decision threshold, and conditions that require stopping. For example, "reduce the report error rate from 12% to below 5%" is illustrative, not a benchmark.
- Resource allocation: Name the accountable owner, contributors, capacity, data access, tools, controls, and escalation path.

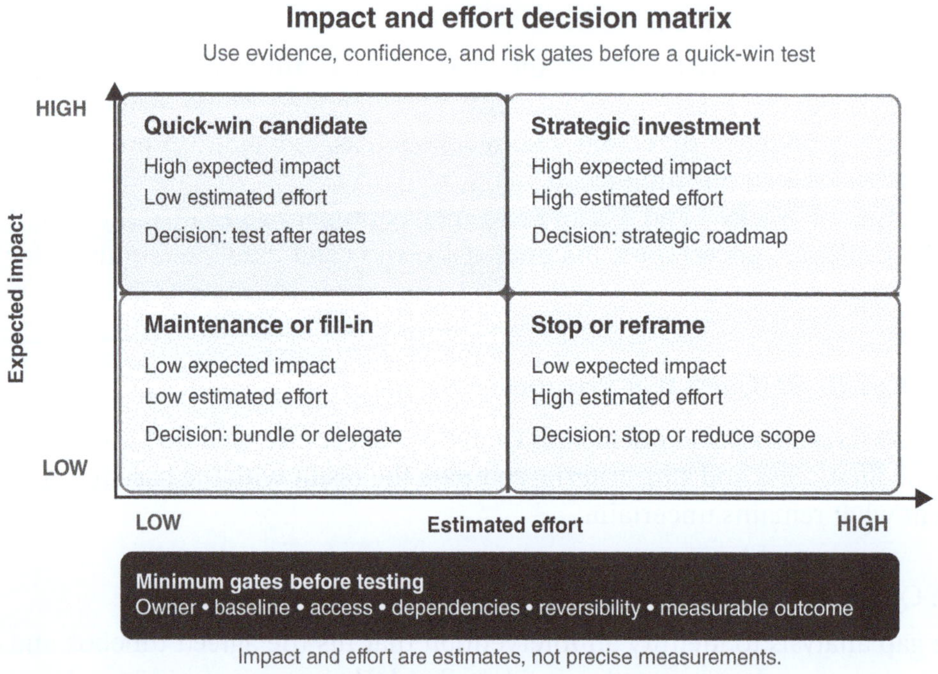

Figure 19.2 Impact and effort decision matrix with evidence, confidence, risk, ownership, and measurement gates.

- Timebox: Agree on a duration that matches task frequency, dependencies, and risk. If the candidate exceeds it, split the work, rescope it, or move it to the strategic roadmap.

Weeks 6–8: Quick Win Delivery

Execute. Measure. Document.

Three practices improve decision quality and delivery discipline:

- Measure the baseline before the change: Use a reproducible method and quantitative measures where appropriate. Preserve the data, definitions, and calculation needed to rerun the comparison.
- Communicate progress visibly: Share the baseline, changes, evidence, risks, and decisions at an agreed cadence.
- Document results and learning: Record what changed, what did not, what remains uncertain, and which dependencies affect reuse or scale.

At the end of the timebox, present the measured result and limitations. Gate 2 can authorize scaling, require another test, rescope the work, or stop it.

Phase 3: Days 61–90 (Governance and Roadmap)

The final 30 days can begin to make the approach repeatable. Governance, measurement, and a dependency-based roadmap turn the quick-win evidence into a proposal for the next operating phase.

Weeks 9–10: Governance Foundation

Begin this phase only with Gate 2 evidence. If the quick win stopped or failed, govern the lesson and address the blocking condition rather than presenting the test as a success.

Ground governance in specific assets, decisions, risks, and controls. The objective is not to govern data in the abstract; it is to keep the assets that support priority use cases fit for their authorized purposes.

Draft three things:

- CRAFT governance requirements: Define dimension-specific evidence and requirements for production use, identify non-compensable risk gates, set a reassessment cadence, and specify what happens when a requirement fails. Do not rely on one averaged CRAFT score.
- Roles and responsibilities: Name the owner accountable for outcomes, the steward responsible for day-to-day quality work, and the custodian responsible for technical controls. Tailor the role model to the organization, but leave no priority asset without accountable ownership.
- Measurement approach: Select a small set of measures tied to the business outcome, data risk, operating reliability, compliance obligation, and adoption decision. Define calculation, owner, cadence, and response.

Weeks 11–12: Strategic Roadmap

Turn the 90-day evidence into a next-phase roadmap. Table 19.3 is an illustrative 12-month structure; adapt the horizon and sequence to dependencies, risk, capacity, and the target architecture.

Table 19.3 Illustrative 12-month Roadmap after the 90-day Plan

Phase	Timeframe	Focus	Key Initiatives
Foundation	Months 1–3	Close priority gaps and establish baselines	Quick wins, data ownership, core definitions, quality monitoring
Core platform	Months 4–6	Build shared capabilities justified by the roadmap	Data catalog, automated quality checks, integration pipelines, role-based access
Self-service	Months 7–9	Expand governed access and reuse	BI deployment, curated data products, training programs
Advanced	Months 10–12	Add advanced capabilities where evidence supports them	ML infrastructure, event-driven pipelines where needed, and advanced governance automation

Sequence by dependency and risk. Reliable batch analytics may be a prerequisite for some use cases, while other use cases require event-driven or streaming capabilities from the start.

Avoid three anti-patterns. First, do not authorize more concurrent work than the organization can staff and govern. Second, do not skip the business case and risk assessment. Third, do not plan without the owners who must operate the result.

Assign named governance owners enough authority, capacity, and escalation support to perform the work.

Present the recommendation to leadership with the baseline, measured result, limitations, options, dependencies, and risk. End with a specific decision request for scope, budget, capacity, and timing.

The 90-day Checklist

Use this checklist as an illustrative audit, not a ceremony or universal schedule. Adapt quantities and dates to the approved scope. Treat an unchecked material gate as a condition to close, rescope, or escalate.

Days 1–30: Foundation

- ☐ Brief leadership on CRAFT framework and business case (Week 1)
- ☐ Identify and confirm executive sponsor (Week 1)

- ☐ Establish a cross-functional AI data working group sized to the approved scope (Week 1)
- ☐ Communicate initiative to broader organization (Week 1)
- ☐ Catalog priority data assets by data level (Week 2)
- ☐ Identify a focused set of priority AI use cases (Week 2)
- ☐ Map use cases to specific data requirements (Week 2)
- ☐ Assess priority assets against each CRAFT dimension with evidence and confidence (Weeks 3–4)
- ☐ Score training data separately if fine-tuning is planned (Weeks 3–4)
- ☐ Identify critical gaps per asset per dimension (Week 4)
- ☐ Flag quick-win candidates from gap analysis (Week 4)
- ☐ Deliver: Assessment summary and gap analysis (Week 4)

Days 31–60: Quick Win Execution

- ☐ Plot candidates on impact/effort matrix (Week 5)
- ☐ Select one high-impact, achievable quick win (Week 5)
- ☐ Define success criteria with specific metrics (Week 5)
- ☐ Allocate resources and confirm timeline (Week 5)
- ☐ Measure and document baseline metrics (Week 5)
- ☐ Execute quick win (Weeks 6–8)
- ☐ Track progress weekly, communicate visibly (Weeks 6–8)
- ☐ Measure final results against baseline (Week 8)
- ☐ Document learnings (Week 8)
- ☐ Deliver: Quick win results with measured impact (Week 8)

Days 61–90: Governance and Roadmap

- ☐ Draft CRAFT governance policies (Week 9)
- ☐ Define data owner, steward, and custodian roles (Week 9)
- ☐ Assign named owners to all priority data assets (Week 10)
- ☐ Establish a measurement approach tied to outcome, risk, operations, and adoption decisions (Week 10)
- ☐ Set up initial measurement baselines (Week 10)
- ☐ Develop a next-phase CRAFT roadmap with dependency-based sequencing (Week 11)

- ☐ Identify investment requirements (FTEs, tools, training) (Week 11)
- ☐ Build a concise leadership decision brief (Week 12)
- ☐ Present to leadership with a specific ask (Week 12)
- ☐ Deliver: Governance framework and strategic roadmap (Week 12)

The 90-day Health Check

Before authorizing the next phase, use these questions as a health check:

- Is the evidence, confidence, and requirement for every material CRAFT dimension recorded for each priority asset?
- Did your quick win produce a measurable, documented improvement?
- Does every priority data asset have a named owner?
- Do you have a 12-month roadmap with specific investment requirements?
- Has leadership approved the next phase?

The answers inform the next decision; they do not prove that the transformation is complete. Close, rescope, or explicitly accept material gaps before expanding the program.

Looking Ahead

A 90-day sequence can establish an operating start. Sustaining it requires leadership behavior, incentives, skills, ownership, controls, and feedback.

Culture is one part of that system, not a substitute for it. Leaders shape the system through the decisions they reward, the responsibilities they fund, the evidence they require, and the way they respond when data quality fails.

Chapter 20 examines how to build and sustain a CRAFT culture beyond the initial launch.

References

Abbas, Amro, et al. "SemDeDup: Data-Efficient Learning at Web-Scale through Semantic Deduplication." arXiv, 2023, https://arxiv.org/abs/2303.09540.

Boston Consulting Group. "AI Adoption in 2024: 74% of Companies Struggle to Achieve and Scale Value." 24 Oct. 2024, https://www.bcg.com/press/24october2024-ai-adoption-in-2024-74-of-companies-struggle-to-achieve-and-scale-value.

Dey, Nolan, et al. "BTLM-3B-8K: 7B Parameter Performance in a 3B Parameter Model." arXiv, 2023, https://arxiv.org/abs/2309.11568.

Gilardi, Fabrizio, Meysam Alizadeh, and Maël Kubli. "ChatGPT Outperforms Crowd Workers for Text-Annotation Tasks." Proceedings of the National Academy of Sciences, vol. 120, no. 30, 2023, https://doi.org/10.1073/pnas.2305016120.

Klie, Jan-Christoph, Richard Eckart de Castilho, and Iryna Gurevych. "Analyzing Dataset Annotation Quality Management in the Wild." Computational Linguistics, vol. 50, no. 3, 2024, pp. 817–866, https://doi.org/10.1162/coli_a_00516.

Lewis, Patrick, et al. "Retrieval-Augmented Generation for Knowledge-Intensive NLP Tasks." NeurIPS, 2020, https://arxiv.org/abs/2005.11401.

Office of the National Coordinator for Health Information Technology. Patient Identification and Matching Final Report. 7 Feb. 2014, https://www.healthit.gov/sites/default/files/patient_identification_matching_final_report.pdf.

OpenAI. "Morgan Stanley Uses AI Evals to Shape the Future of Financial Services." n.d., https://openai.com/index/morgan-stanley/. Accessed 25 July 2026.

Ryseff, James, Brandon F. De Bruhl, and Sydne J. Newberry. "The Root Causes of Failure for Artificial Intelligence Projects and How They Can Succeed." RAND Corporation, 2024, https://www.rand.org/pubs/research_reports/RRA2680-1.html.

S&P Global. "Generative AI Experiences Rapid Adoption, But with Mixed Outcomes: Highlights from VotE: AI & Machine Learning." 30 May 2025, https://www.spglobal.com/market-intelligence/en/news-insights/research/ai-experiences-rapid-adoption-but-with-mixed-outcomes-highlights-from-vote-ai-machine-learning.

Soboleva, Daria, et al. "SlimPajama: A 627B Token, Cleaned and Deduplicated Version of RedPajama." Cerebras, 9 June 2023, https://www.cerebras.ai/blog/slimpajama-a-627b-token-cleaned-and-deduplicated-version-of-redpajama.

Stoica, George, Emmanouil Antonios Platanios, and Barnabas Poczos. "Re-TACRED: Addressing Shortcomings of the TACRED Dataset." Proceedings of the AAAI Conference on Artificial Intelligence, vol. 35, no. 15, 2021, pp. 13843–13850, https://doi.org/10.1609/aaai.v35i15.17631.

Chapter 20
The Last Mile Is Technical and Human

AI-ready data doesn't fail only in pipelines. It fails in the habits, incentives, and leadership choices that determine whether people trust the data enough to act on it.

Culture as an Operating Constraint

Consider two hypothetical operating failures. A telecom churn model can flag the wrong customers when duplicate identities are not resolved. A fraud model can miss known patterns when analysts' operational knowledge never reaches governed data or review workflows. These examples are not documented cases; they show how data design, process, and incentives can fail together.

Technical and organizational failures often interact. In a 2024 survey of 1,000 executives across 59 countries, Boston Consulting Group categorized about 70% of reported AI implementation challenges as people and process issues, 20% as technology and data, and 10% as algorithms. The survey describes executives' reported challenges; it does not establish a universal causal breakdown (Boston Consulting Group, 2024).

Culture affects whether technical improvements survive daily pressure, but BCG's comparison of more than 1,250 companies does not isolate culture as the cause of financial returns. Strong incentives, ownership, governance, and operating habits can help teams maintain and reuse CRAFT improvements (Boston Consulting Group, 2025).

You now have a practical toolkit: the CRAFT framework, the four data levels, Chapter 19's illustrative 90-day sequence, and several bounded quick-win patterns.

Their value depends on how leadership connects them to ownership, incentives, decision rights, skills, and routine work.

Why Culture Is a Distinct Challenge

The technical work is hard. The organizational work is hard in a different way. Schemas, retrieval systems, monitoring, security, and data pipelines require sustained engineering. Culture determines whether teams keep doing that work after the launch.

Coordinating people across functions, incentives, and local workflows requires a different form of sustained attention.

Project NANDA's preliminary report described a technical "learning gap": many task-specific systems in its evidence did not retain feedback, adapt to context, or integrate with operational workflows. The report did not test whether leadership culture or workforce skills caused its deployment outcomes (Challapally et al., 2025).

That distinction matters for budgeting. Leaders should fund models and infrastructure alongside workflow integration, skills, operating ownership, evaluation, and change support. The mix should follow the use case and measured constraint rather than a fixed 70/20/10 spending formula.

A common barrier is an implicit contract: if the numbers are adequate for periodic reporting, the organization may not examine how records were created, changed, or reused.

In an analysis of 75 data-quality assessments collected over two years, Nagle, Redman, and Sammon found that, on average, 47% of newly created records had at least one critical error, and only 3% of assessment scores met their acceptable threshold of at least 97%. The authors studied a varied but nonrepresentative set of organizations, datasets, and processes; the figures are a reason to measure local quality, not universal rates (Nagle et al., 2020).

In a February 2025 Wakefield Research survey of 500 U.S. data and analytics professionals working with AI at companies with at least $500 million in annual revenue, 81% reported significant data-quality issues and 85% said leadership was not addressing them. These are self-reported results from a Qlik-commissioned survey, not a global prevalence estimate (Qlik, 2025).

Leadership Actions: Making Quality Operational

Leaders set the rules for how evidence is used, challenged, and trusted in decisions. Their recurring choices matter more than slogans.

When leaders consistently ask, "What does the data say?" and "How do we know?", they signal that evidence and limitations matter. Publicly revisiting a decision when evidence changes can reinforce the behavior. The effect depends on whether incentives, accountability, and operating processes support the same message.

Prosci reports that projects in its benchmarking data with extremely effective sponsors were 79% likely to meet objectives, compared with 27% for projects with extremely ineffective sponsors. This is a correlation within Prosci's research, not proof that sponsorship alone caused the difference (Creasey, 2023).

Effective sponsors don't just approve budgets. They stay visible, remove blockers, make tradeoff decisions, and keep asking for evidence when teams would rather move fast and hope.

Seven Questions Leaders Should Ask

Culture changes through repeated choices. One useful leadership habit is asking questions that expose evidence, ownership, and uncertainty. The following seven prompts are a starting point, not a complete diagnostic:

- "What is our CRAFT score for this data asset and use case?" This prompts a review across all five dimensions and makes the scope explicit.
- "Which CRAFT dimension is blocking this AI initiative?" This can move the conversation from a general quality concern to a specific gap, provided the team can show evidence and name an owner.
- "Are we maintaining currency in our action data?" Stale or mismatched tool schemas can cause invalid calls, failed actions, or unsafe downstream effects. The likelihood and impact depend on permissions, validation, and rollback controls.
- "What is our context-data coverage for this domain?" Gaps can contribute to unsupported or outdated answers, so teams should measure retrieval coverage and review the consequences for the target workflow.

- "Does our training data meet the CRAFT criteria, especially completeness and accuracy?" Incomplete or inaccurate data can impair a model, but the effect depends on the task, sampling, evaluation, and controls.
- "When did we last inspect a risk-based sample of the data?" Human review should be calibrated to impact, uncertainty, monitoring coverage, and the failure modes automated checks may miss.
- "Is our data infrastructure open enough to support plausible future changes?" Open standards at the data layer can reduce the migration and integration work required to adopt new AI capabilities.

For the scoring mechanics, use Chapter 15. For the data-level questions, go back to Chapters 7, 9, 11, and 13. For governance and decision rights, use Chapter 17.

A Company-reported Operating Example

In a 2023 interview, Vista chief data officer Sebastian Klapdor described a data-product operating model with a central team and embedded analysts. He attributed roughly $100 million in incremental profit over about two and a half years to the broader program. This is a company leader's account, not an independently audited causal estimate (Klapdor, 2023).

The useful lesson is operational: Vista paired cross-functional product ownership with adoption measures and financial tests instead of treating data delivery as a handoff.

Klapdor emphasized that treating data as a product and a valuable asset required sustained cultural change, which he described as the hardest and longest part of the work (Klapdor, 2023).

The leadership lesson is not that one structure fits every organization. It is that leaders cannot delegate the operating choices that make quality visible, owned, funded, and sustained.

Organizational Tactics: Making Culture Operational

Leadership sets expectations. Organizational mechanisms can connect those expectations to daily work. Select among funding gates, champions, rituals, dashboards, training, templates, and incentives based on the decision and operating model.

CRAFT Review in AI Project Approval

A CRAFT assessment can serve as one funding checkpoint for an AI initiative. It should identify the data assets, material gaps, evidence, owners, and conditions for proceeding, rescoping, or stopping.

For each in-scope data asset, teams can score the five CRAFT dimensions on a 1-to-5 scale and identify the weakest dimension. The scale and any below-3 remediation threshold are illustrative internal decision rules, not universal standards. Calibrate them to risk, use case, and evidence.

CRAFT Champions at Each Data Level

Where domain champions fit the operating model, assign bounded responsibilities at the relevant data levels. Champions can coordinate owners, surface gaps, and help teams apply shared criteria, but they do not replace accountable data owners or governance bodies.

Building CRAFT into Team Rituals

One way to make quality practices durable is to integrate them into existing routines:

- **Sprint reviews:** Add a short review of material CRAFT changes for data assets touched during the sprint.
- **Incident retrospectives:** Ask when the problem was introduced, when it was detected, what impact it caused, whether it recurred, and how quickly the service recovered. Detection delay is one useful measure, not the only one.
- **Quarterly business reviews:** Use a documented data cutoff, run agreed quality checks before the meeting, disclose known limitations, and record corrections and decisions.

These practices can be small additions to existing meetings. Keep them only if they improve decisions, ownership, or learning.

CRAFT can become a shared vocabulary when teams use it in planning, approval, monitoring, and incident review. The framework is a decision aid, not a compliance exercise or a substitute for domain-specific controls. Conformance means that the relevant criteria were assessed for a defined use case and are being monitored.

Dashboards and Visibility

Start with a local baseline: measure rejected records, reconciliation time, incident volume, rework, decision delay, and the business consequences tied to the priority data asset. A dashboard is useful only if its measures have owners, definitions, and action thresholds.

Shared dashboards can support accountability by making current measures and exceptions visible. They do not substitute for authority, incentives, or a process for resolving what the measures reveal.

Change Management: Addressing Recurring Objections

In a 2021 McKinsey Global Survey of 1,034 respondents, 30% described their organizations' transformations as successful under the survey's definition. The result is broad and self-reported; it does not predict the success of a particular CRAFT initiative (McKinsey & Company, 2021). The following sections address three recurring objections.

"We Don't Have Time for This"

Teams already spend time correcting errors, reconciling conflicting definitions, and recovering from incidents. Measure that effort for the target workflow, compare it with the cost of prevention, and fund the intervention only when the expected benefit and risk reduction justify it.

Investing in data quality up front takes time. It can buy more time back by preventing rework and incidents, but leaders should measure the payback for each use case.

"Our Data Is Good Enough"

Measurement turns "good enough" into a testable question. Run a bounded CRAFT assessment on one high-priority asset, document the baseline and limits, and decide from the result.

"This Is a Data Team Problem, Not My Problem"

The BCG survey cited earlier places most reported implementation challenges in the people-and-process category. The practical implication is distributed ownership: people who create, modify, approve, and use data all influence its fitness for the target decision.

Ownership is distributed. Illustrative contributors include a sales representative entering a customer record, a product manager updating a knowledge base, and a finance analyst changing a metric definition. Governance must connect those contributors to named accountable owners.

Training for Adoption

In an August 2025 Morning Consult survey of 14,231 adults across 13 countries, 29% of respondents said their workplace invested enough in AI training, and about one-third expected that investment to increase within a year. The sample is broad and self-reported; employers should assess the skills required for their own use cases (Salesforce and Morning Consult, 2025).

Airbnb's engineering blog reports that Data University launched in the second half of 2016 with more than 30 classes. The company reported that weekly use of its internal data platform rose from about 30% to 45% and that each class scored at least 55 NPS. These are company-reported adoption results and do not isolate training as the sole cause (Airbnb Engineering, 2017).

A practical CRAFT curriculum can cover why data fitness matters for the target AI use case, how to assess the five dimensions, and what to do when evidence reveals a gap.

Reducing Friction: Templates and Embedded Workflows

The hardest behavior to sustain is one that requires extra effort. The easiest is one built into the flow of work.

Provide lightweight assessment templates, embed the relevant questions in existing proposal and review workflows, and tailor checklists to the data level and use case. Test the workflow with users and revise it when the burden exceeds the decision value.

Incentives: Connecting CRAFT to Performance

Measurement and incentives shape behavior, but poorly chosen measures can also distort it.

Vista's model offers a clear principle: make data-driven work part of how the organization operates, not a side initiative.

Use CRAFT conformance measures in team objectives only when teams can control the measure and it informs a real decision. Illustrative targets include reducing a measured inconsistency rate, improving a locally defined score for a priority asset, or reducing detection delay. Set each target from a documented baseline and risk tolerance.

Celebrating Wins and Sustaining Change

Early wins can build credibility when they begin with a documented baseline, produce a material result, and disclose the conditions and limitations. They are evidence for a next decision, not proof that every use case will work.

When a review catches a freshness problem, record the avoided or reduced impact before communicating the win. When deduplication changes a model measure, report the evaluation design and uncertainty. When a funding gate stops weak work, record the rework or risk that was actually avoided.

Visible early evidence can reduce uncertainty and help teams learn. It does not prove that the framework caused every outcome, so leaders should pair the result with its baseline, owner, and limits.

Declaring victory after a pilot creates its own risk. If ownership, monitoring, training, and reinforcement end with the project, prior behaviors can return. Culture is continuing operating work.

The Long Game

Culture change often outlasts an illustrative launch sequence. Chapter 19's 90-day plan can produce evidence for a next decision; sustaining the result requires ongoing ownership, measurement, and revision.

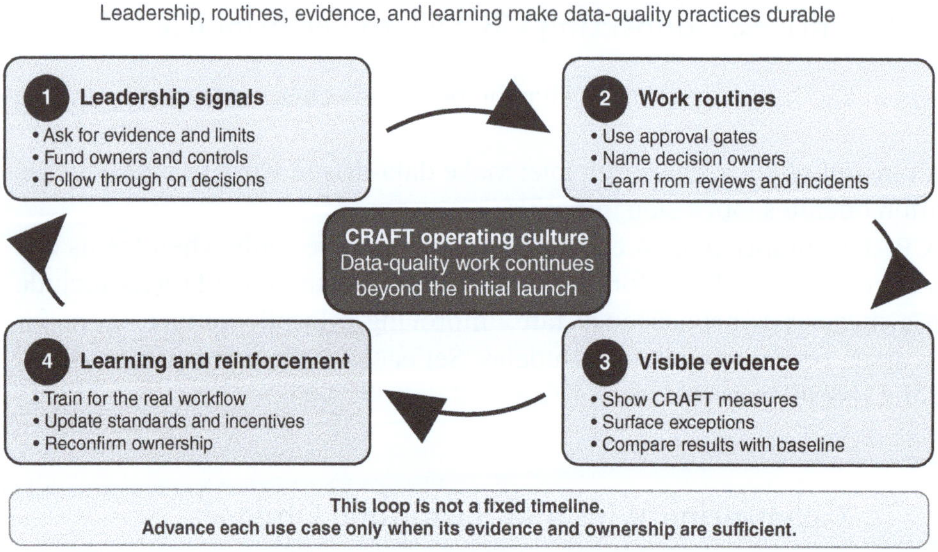

Figure 20.1 Culture reinforcement loop.

Figure 20.1 presents the work as a reinforcement loop rather than a fixed timeline.

Sustained change depends on a loop: leaders set expectations, teams embed them in routines, measures reveal results and failures, and the organization adjusts ownership, incentives, and practice. The loop can reinforce useful behavior, but it can also expose weak controls that require redesign.

Looking Ahead

The framework in this book provides a working map. CRAFT identifies five data-fitness dimensions. The four data levels locate the work. Chapter 19 offers a way to start. This chapter connects the work to ownership, evidence, and operating practice.

What remains is a leadership decision to treat data quality as an operating responsibility. CRAFT conformance is not a one-time check; it is evidence that the relevant criteria have been assessed for a defined use case and are being monitored over time.

The last mile of AI transformation is both technical and human. Systems have to work, and people have to trust, govern, adopt, and improve them. Chapter 21 brings those choices together in a final leadership synthesis.

References

Airbnb Engineering. "How Airbnb Democratizes Data Science with Data University." The Airbnb Tech Blog, 24 May 2017, https://medium.com/airbnb-engineering/how-airbnb-democratizes-data-science-with-data-university-3eccc71e073a.

Boston Consulting Group. "AI Adoption in 2024: 74% of Companies Struggle to Achieve and Scale Value." 24 October 2024, https://www.bcg.com/press/24october2024-ai-adoption-in-2024-74-of-companies-struggle-to-achieve-and-scale-value.

Boston Consulting Group. "The Widening AI Value Gap." 30 September 2025, https://www.bcg.com/publications/2025/are-you-generating-value-from-ai-the-widening-gap.

Challapally, Aditya, Chris Pease, Ramesh Raskar, and Pradyumna Chari. "The GenAI Divide: State of AI in Business 2025." Preliminary findings, Project NANDA, July 2025. Archived official-origin report, https://web.archive.org/web/20250818145714id_/https://nanda.media.mit.edu/ai_report_2025.pdf. Current Project NANDA overview, https://www.media.mit.edu/groups/nanda/overview/.

Creasey, Tim. "Best Practices in Change Management." Prosci, 26 May 2023, https://www.prosci.com/blog/change-management-best-practices.

Klapdor, Sebastian. "CDO Spotlight 110: The Value and Journey of Implementing a Data Product Mindset with Sebastian Klapdor of Vista." Experiencing Data, recorded 6 February 2023, https://designingforanalytics.com/resources/episodes/110-cdo-spotlight-the-value-and-journey-of-implementing-a-data-product-mindset-with-sebastian-klapdor-of-vista/.

McKinsey & Company. "Losing from Day One: Why Even Successful Transformations Fall Short." 7 December 2021, https://www.mckinsey.com/capabilities/people-and-organizational-performance/our-insights/successful-transformations.

Nagle, Tadhg, Thomas C. Redman, and David Sammon. "Assessing Data Quality: A Managerial Call to Action." Business Horizons, vol. 63, no. 3, 2020, pp. 325–337, https://doi.org/10.1016/j.bushor.2020.01.006.

Qlik. "Data Quality Is Not Being Prioritized on AI Projects, a Trend That 96% of U.S. Data Professionals Say Could Lead to Widespread Crises." March 2025, https://www.qlik.com/us/news/company/press-room/press-releases/data-quality-is-not-being-prioritized-on-ai-projects.

Salesforce and Morning Consult. "Growing Worker Demand for AI Skills Creates Opportunity for Institutions." 18 September 2025, https://www.salesforce.com/news/stories/morning-consult-ai-worker-readiness-report-2025/.

Chapter 21
Conclusion: Models Converge. Data Differentiates

Models are converging on some benchmarks, and data remains a differentiator leaders can shape. The 2025 AI Index reports that the inference cost for a system scoring at GPT-3.5's 64.8 MMLU level fell from $20.00 to $0.07 per million tokens between November 2022 and October 2024, a reduction of more than 280-fold. It also reports that the Chatbot Arena score gap between the top and tenth-ranked models narrowed from 11.9% to 5.4% by early 2025 (Stanford HAI, 2025). These measures do not make every model interchangeable; capability, safety, reliability, latency, price, and domain fit still differ. They do mean that model selection alone is unlikely to be a durable advantage. The harder advantage to copy is the organization's data and operating system around it.

In the Cloudera-sponsored survey introduced in Chapter 3, 7% of 231 *Harvard Business Review* audience respondents involved in AI data decisions said their organizations' data was completely ready for AI adoption. The result is a self-reported readiness signal, not an objective market audit (Harvard Business Review Analytic Services, 2026).

That signal is a prompt for leaders to test their own data and operating controls before increasing deployment scope. It is not evidence that every organization has the same gap or that more model spending will solve a readiness problem.

CRAFT: Four Data Levels, Five Quality Dimensions

This book has argued against the model trap: over-weighting model selection, benchmark comparisons, and upgrade cycles while under-weighting data and operating controls. Organizations seeking durable value need data that is fit for purpose:

AI Performance = Model Capability × Data Quality

Treat this as a leadership heuristic, not a literal equation: when models offer similar capability for a use case, data quality becomes one of the most important variables leaders can directly influence.

This book maps four AI capability patterns (perception AI, analytical AI, generative AI, and agentic AI) to four usual primary data levels (raw data, structured data, context data, and action data). The mapping identifies a common starting point, not an exclusive dependency: a use case may require several levels, operational state, and supporting controls. CRAFT assesses every relevant level across five dimensions: complete, retrievable, accurate, fresh, and traceable.

Figure 21.1 pulls that system together.

You went deep into each data level. You saw what happens when data fails at each layer and how to build it right.

Next, I showed you how to build the organizational machinery: assessment, measurement, structure, governance, and the economic case for executive buy-in.

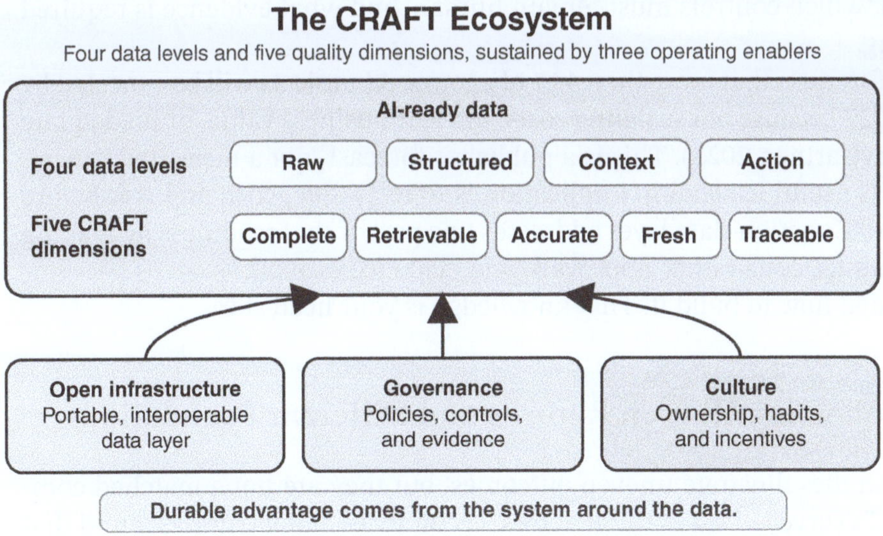

Figure 21.1 The CRAFT ecosystem.

Finally, the playbook brought together quick wins, a 90-day launch plan, and the culture framework intended to sustain the work.

Many data-quality frameworks emphasize only part of the problem. CRAFT is designed to reduce blind spots by applying five dimensions across four data levels. It is not a certification, a substitute for domain-specific controls, or a guarantee that an audit will find every issue.

When an AI agent processes a customer refund, approves a purchase order, or reclassifies a support ticket, decision quality depends on more than data alone. It also depends on the model, tool design, authorization boundaries, runtime controls, and exception handling. Data quality remains foundational because weak data can invalidate downstream safeguards. Where human review is absent, leaders need tested controls, monitoring, and recovery paths rather than an assumption that the data will always be right.

Action Data: A First-class Enterprise Layer

If there is one idea from this book to carry into your next strategy meeting, make it this: treat action data as a first-class enterprise layer, with named owners, permissions, constraints, approvals, and evidence.

The pressure to operationalize agents is rising, but expectations are not evidence of deployment readiness. Leaders still need to decide which decisions can be delegated, which controls must remain human, and what evidence is required before scaling.

Gartner forecasts that more than 40% of agentic AI projects will be canceled by the end of 2027 because of escalating costs, unclear business value, or inadequate risk controls (Gartner, 2025). This is a publisher forecast, not a measured cancellation rate. Its useful leadership implication is to test value, cost, and risk before scaling. CRAFT's action-data layer addresses one part of that readiness by making permitted actions, constraints, approvals, and evidence explicit.

You learned how to build it. That knowledge is your head start.

The Economics: Uneven Returns and Different Foundations

Two recent studies illustrate uneven outcomes, but they are not a matched comparison. PwC's survey of 4,454 CEOs across 95 countries and territories found that 56% said their companies had realized neither higher revenues nor lower costs from AI in the prior 12 months (PwC, 2026). In a separate study of 1,250 CxOs and senior executives who were AI decision-makers, BCG classified 5% of companies as future-built and associated that group with 1.7 times revenue growth and 3.6 times three-year total shareholder return relative to its stagnating and emerging groups (BCG, 2025). The studies use different populations and methods, and neither establishes that one foundation caused the reported financial outcomes.

The challenge is broader than budget alone. The studies point toward the importance of execution and foundations, but they do not identify one cause. Leaders still need to align data, infrastructure, governance, talent, controls, and use-case economics with strategic ambition.

Within BCG's classification, future-built firms also had stronger data and governance practices and were three times as likely to enforce enterprise-wide data policies through central oversight (BCG, 2025). BCG notes that survey responses may be subject to perception bias and that financial performance has multiple drivers beyond AI. CRAFT translates similar foundational disciplines into an operating framework; it should not be presented as the cause of BCG's outcomes.

The leadership proposition in this book is that proprietary data, workflow integration, and governance can be harder to copy than access to a model. That proposition must be tested use case by use case. A less capable model with better data and controls may outperform a stronger model in a specific workflow, but the result is not guaranteed.

Ten Steps to Put CRAFT into Practice

You don't need to transform everything at once. You need a sequence:

1. **Assess**. Use the CRAFT assessment to map your current state across all four data levels and five dimensions.
2. **Prioritize**. Find the gaps blocking your highest-value AI use cases.
3. **Invest**. Build the business case. Speak the language of ROI, not data purity.
4. **Organize**. Structure teams around dataset engineering as a core competency.
5. **Build on open infrastructure**. Treat interoperability, portability, and reduced dependence on any single vendor's roadmap as design objectives. Those properties can lower switching friction and preserve options as the AI stack changes; they do not guarantee that every investment will appreciate. Open Data Infrastructure is the book's architectural expression of this principle.

6. **Govern**. Stand up governance covering security, privacy, and ethical use.
7. **Test**. Apply CRAFT checks and domain-specific controls before a data pipeline supports production AI, with rigor proportional to the use case's risk.
8. **Measure**. Review CRAFT measures on a cadence tied to risk, data volatility, and material system change.
9. **Execute**. Follow the 90-day CRAFT Launch Plan from Chapter 19. Start with quick wins.
10. **Transform the culture**. Culture is often a limiting condition because standards endure only when ownership, incentives, and daily routines reinforce them. Chapter 20 showed how to build that operating discipline.

These steps are an operating sequence, not a formula that guarantees placement in BCG's future-built group or PwC's financially benefiting group. Use those studies as directional context, and judge your program against its own baseline, costs, risks, and realized value (BCG, 2025; PwC, 2026).

A Three-year Leadership Scenario

Picture a plausible three-year destination, not a forecast. Your organization has applied CRAFT controls to priority data products and can show where provenance is complete, where gaps remain, and who owns them. Structured data meets defined accuracy and freshness thresholds. Context data is tested for the decisions it supports. Action data encodes permitted actions, constraints, approvals, and evidence requirements for bounded agent workflows.

Your infrastructure follows Open Data Infrastructure principles where portability and interoperability create meaningful options. New AI capabilities can be evaluated against existing interfaces and controls, which may reduce migration effort without eliminating it. The feedback loops from Chapter 18 operate only where interactions are captured lawfully, reviewed for quality, and converted into approved changes.

In this scenario, teams deploy selected use cases faster because reusable data products and controls reduce avoidable rework. They run CRAFT reviews on a risk-based cadence, detect material degradation through monitoring and tests, ground generative systems in governed context, and constrain agent actions through authorization, exception handling, and auditable records. Success is demonstrated with measured outcomes, not assumed from the framework.

The economic evidence in this chapter shows uneven returns, not a fixed destiny. Delay has an opportunity cost, but speed without evidence can increase cost and risk. The leadership decision is to begin with a bounded use case, establish a baseline, define the evidence needed to advance, and stop or redesign the work when results do not justify the next step.

The Real Work: Data Quality as Organizational Commitment

Model capability, price, and efficiency may continue to improve, but leaders should not assume interchangeability for every task. The enduring work is building data and controls that fit the decision: capturing reality with precision, structuring facts with care, enriching knowledge with context, and specifying actions with clear boundaries.

That is the work this book is about. Data engineering and metadata management may receive less attention than model launches, but they determine whether AI can be trusted in a specific workflow. A sustained commitment to CRAFT-worthy data can improve your organization's ability to create, measure, and protect AI value. It does not guarantee the outcome.

The assessment framework is in Chapter 15. The quick wins and 90-day plan are in Chapter 19. You now have an operating framework, not a substitute for local evidence and judgment. Start with one bounded use case. Then name the owner, define the decision rights, and measure what changes.

References

BCG. "The Widening AI Value Gap: Build for the Future 2025." Boston Consulting Group, 30 September 2025, https://media-publications.bcg.com/The-Widening-AI-Value-Gap-Sept-2025.pdf.

Harvard Business Review Analytic Services. "Taming the Complexity of AI Data Readiness." Pulse Survey, sponsored by Cloudera, 4 March 2026, https://www.cloudera.com/content/dam/www/marketing/resources/whitepapers/taming-the-complexity-of-ai-data-readiness.pdf?daqp=true.

Gartner. "Gartner Predicts Over 40% of Agentic AI Projects Will Be Canceled by End of 2027." Gartner, 25 June 2025, https://www.gartner.com/en/newsroom/press-releases/2025-06-25-gartner-predicts-over-40-percent-of-agentic-ai-projects-will-be-canceled-by-end-of-2027.

PwC. "PwC's 29th Global CEO Survey: Leading through Uncertainty in the Age of AI." PwC, 19 January 2026, https://www.pwc.com/gx/en/ceo-survey/2026/pwc-ceo-survey-2026.pdf.

Stanford HAI. "The 2025 AI Index Report." Stanford Institute for Human-Centered Artificial Intelligence, 2025, https://hai.stanford.edu/ai-index/2025-ai-index-report.

Appendix A
CRAFT Assessment Matrix

Use this matrix as a one-page diagnostic for AI-ready data. Score each cell from 1 to 5, where 1 means the capability is missing or ad hoc, 3 means it is partially implemented and repeatable, and 5 means it is measured, owned, automated where appropriate, and ready for production AI use.

Suggested use: Score only the cells that matter for the AI use case under review. A production-facing AI system should not move forward when any required cell scores below 3. Treat a score below 3 as a blocker, not as a nice-to-have improvement.

The matrix is a diagnostic, not a ceremony. It is useful only when the score changes behavior—funding, ownership, remediation work, deployment gates, or production monitoring.

CRAFT Dimension	Raw Data	Structured Data	Context Data	Action Data
Complete	All required signals are captured from relevant sources, with known gaps documented.	All required entities, records, fields, and joins are present for the target use case.	Knowledge coverage includes policies, FAQs, examples, definitions, and domain context.	Tools, workflows, parameters, constraints, and success states are defined.
Retrievable	Data is pipeline-accessible in usable formats with clear access paths.	Tables and entities are queryable, indexed, documented, and discoverable by name and meaning.	Content is chunked, tagged, embedded, and searchable by user intent.	Actions are discoverable by intent, so an agent can select the right tool or workflow.
Accurate	Capture is high fidelity, with corruption, duplication, and extraction defects monitored.	Definitions are consistent, entities are resolved, and business rules are explicit.	Sources are truthful, current enough for the task, and grounded in authoritative material.	Specifications match actual tool behavior, valid parameters, limits, and constraints.
Fresh	Signals are current enough for the use case, with latency expectations stated.	Schemas, mappings, and derived fields stay synchronized with source systems.	Knowledge reflects the latest approved policy, product, process, and business state.	APIs, permissions, tool schemas, and runbooks reflect live system behavior.
Traceable	Source provenance is captured, including origin, time, and ingestion path.	Lineage documents transformations, ownership, and downstream dependencies.	Claims can cite origin sources, document versions, and retrieval paths.	Every action has an auditable trail of actor, tool, input, output, and outcome.

Appendix B
When Culture Breaks Data Loops

Data loops fail when the organization treats data quality as a technical cleanup task instead of an operating habit. The tools may be modern, the pipeline may run, and the dashboard may look current, but the loop still breaks if people do not trust the data, inspect it, own it, or act when quality starts to drift.

The failure usually begins quietly. A metric changes definition without a documented owner. A policy document is updated in one system but not in the retrieval corpus. A source schema changes and downstream teams patch around the problem instead of fixing the contract. An AI pilot ships because the demo worked, even though no one can answer which data assets are authoritative. None of these failures looks dramatic in isolation. Together, they turn an AI system into a confidence machine without a reliable feedback loop.

Culture breaks data loops in five common ways:

- **Ownership is unclear:** Everyone depends on the data, but no one is accountable for its quality in AI use.
- **Inspection is irregular:** Teams monitor pipelines but rarely inspect whether the data still means what the system assumes it means.
- **Incentives reward launch over reliability:** Teams get credit for shipping pilots, not for maintaining the data contracts that make pilots last.

- **Feedback stops at the application layer:** Users report bad answers, but the issue never traces back to the missing field, stale context, weak entity match, or outdated tool spec.
- **Leaders ask for AI progress without asking for data evidence:** The organization learns that model activity matters more than data readiness.

A healthy data loop has a different rhythm. Data owners know which AI systems depend on their assets. Product and engineering teams measure retrieval quality, entity accuracy, freshness, and action success rates. Incidents trace back to root causes in the data layer. Leaders ask for CRAFT scores before approving expansion. Teams improve the data once and reuse that improvement across multiple AI systems.

The practical test is simple: when AI fails, can the organization learn from the failure? If the answer is no, the loop is broken. If the same missing definition, stale document, or ambiguous entity appears in multiple pilots, the loop is broken. If remediation depends on one person remembering the workaround, the loop is broken.

Fixing the loop requires management attention as much as technical work. Assign owners to priority data assets. Put CRAFT review into project gates. Treat data incidents like product incidents. Measure time from defect introduction to detection. Make the feedback path visible from user-facing failure back to the raw, structured, context, or action data that caused it.

Culture does not become data-driven because someone says the phrase. It becomes data-driven when decisions, incentives, rituals, and operating reviews make data quality impossible to ignore.

Appendix C
Entity Integrity

Entity integrity is the discipline of making sure the people, customers, accounts, products, vendors, assets, events, and other business objects in your data can be identified, connected, and trusted. AI systems depend on this more than most teams expect. A model can produce polished language while still confusing two customers, merging unrelated accounts, or applying the wrong policy to the wrong entity.

Entity integrity matters because AI systems do not only read data. They retrieve it, summarize it, join it, reason over it, and sometimes act on it. If the entity layer is weak, every downstream capability inherits that weakness. Retrieval misses the right record. Context includes the wrong history. Grounding points to facts that belong to a different entity. Agents take action on the wrong account.

Core Checks

The following are core areas to check for entity integrity:

- **Stable identifiers:** Each important entity has a durable identifier that survives system movement, display-name changes, and vendor migrations.
- **Resolution rules:** Duplicates, aliases, householding, parent-child relationships, and merges are governed by explicit rules.
- **Boundary clarity:** Teams know when two records describe the same entity, related entities, or different entities with similar attributes.

- **Lineage:** Entity records can be traced back to source systems, transformation steps, match rules, and merge decisions.
- **Freshness:** Entity state reflects current business reality, including status, ownership, eligibility, permissions, and relationships.
- **Access control:** AI systems only retrieve or act on entity data that the user or agent is allowed to use.
- **Auditability:** Changes to entity identity, relationships, and merge decisions are logged and reviewable.

Failure Patterns

The following are failure patterns to watch for:

- **Duplicate entities** cause AI to summarize incomplete history or miss critical context.
- **Weak joins** cause the system to attach the right fact to the wrong entity.
- **Stale entity status** causes agents to act on accounts, users, or products that have changed state.
- **Ambiguous names** cause retrieval systems to pull plausible but incorrect records.
- **Hidden business rules** cause models to infer entity meaning from patterns instead of governed definitions.

Minimum Production Standard

Before an entity-dependent AI system reaches production, the team should be able to answer four questions:

- Which entities does this system depend on?
- Which sources are authoritative for each entity?
- How are duplicates, conflicts, and relationship changes resolved?
- How will we detect and audit entity mistakes after deployment?

If the answers to these four questions are not available, the system is not blocked by model capability. It is blocked by entity integrity. Fix the identity layer before asking AI to reason or act on top of it.

Index

Pages in *italics* refer to figures and pages in **bold** refer to tables.